I0729693

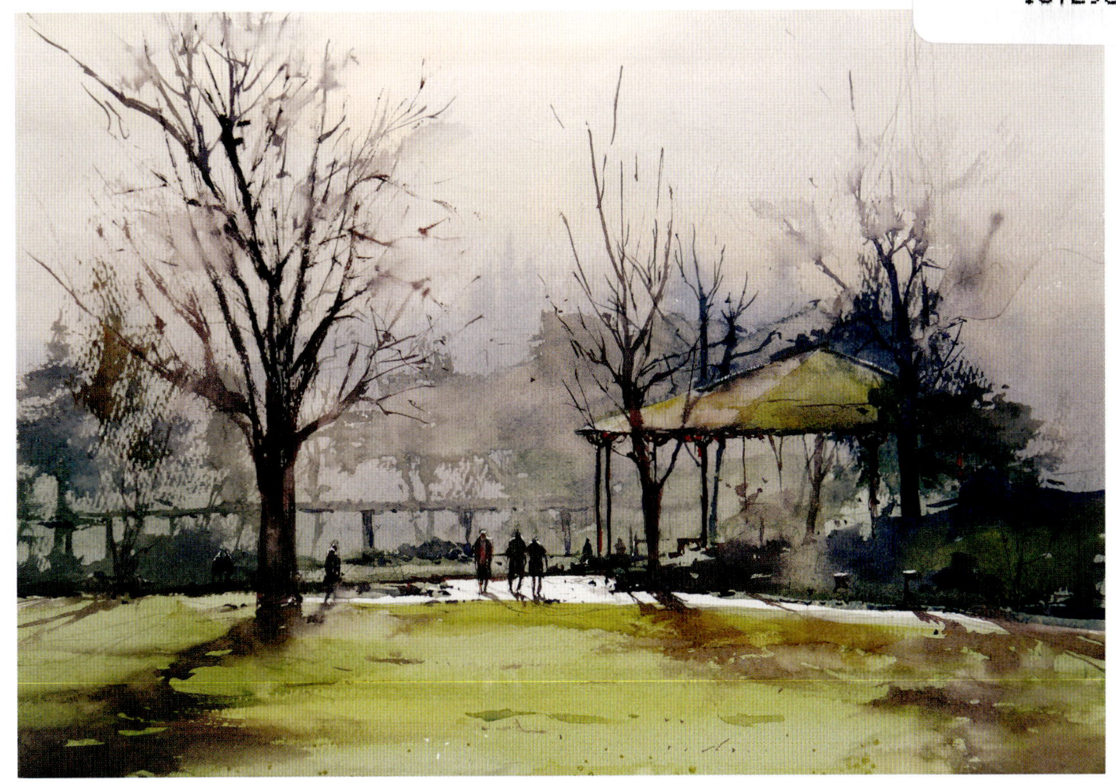

PLEIN AIR PAINTING

WITH WATERCOLOURS

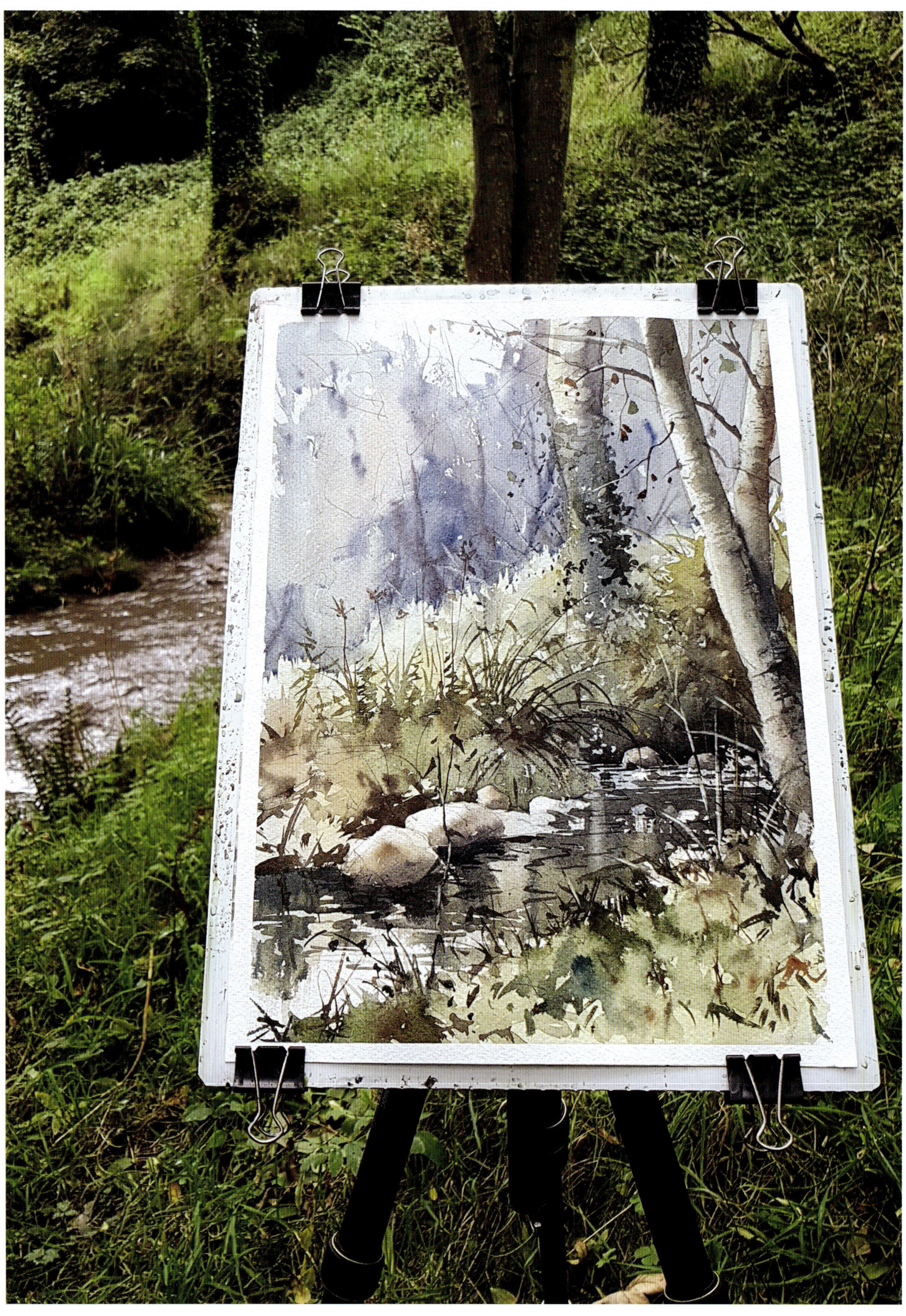

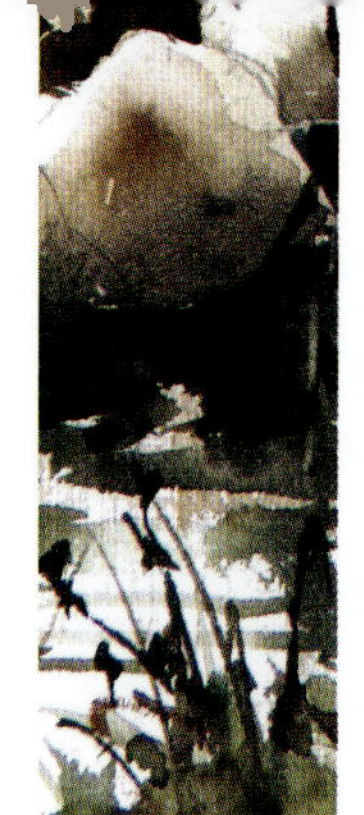

Grahame Booth

PLEIN AIR PAINTING

WITH WATERCOLOURS

A practical and inspirational
guide to painting outdoors

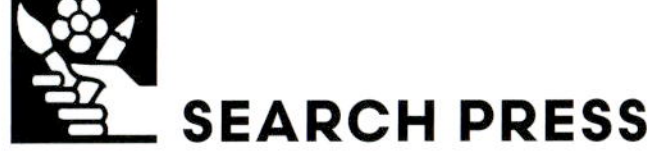

Page 1:
WINTER IN THE PARK
38 x 28cm (15 x 11in), Millford CP 300gsm (140lb)

Page 2:
FOREST FLOW
38 x 28cm (15 x 11in), Millford CP 300gsm (140lb)
(see also page 11)

Below:
BURANO
38 x 28cm (15 x 11in), Bockingford CP 425gsm (200lb)

Opposite:
STRANGFORD LOUGH FROM SCRABO HILL
51 x 38cm (20 x 15in), Millford CP 300gsm (140lb)

Dedication

To my grandchildren who are at the age where art is just fun. My eldest grandchild Scout fills sketchbooks with wonderful drawings that would have been beyond me at her age, and she has just had a solo exhibition at her local library, beating me by some 40 years! May all children continue to be excited by art and may the fun never stop.

Acknowledgements

It is always a delight to see a finished book and also a reminder of the many other people who are part of it. Thanks to all at Search Press for creating this opportunity for me to pass on my plein air adventures and especially to my editor, Becky Robbins. This is our fourth book together and her infectious enthusiasm always lifts my spirits when the inevitable doubt creeps in.

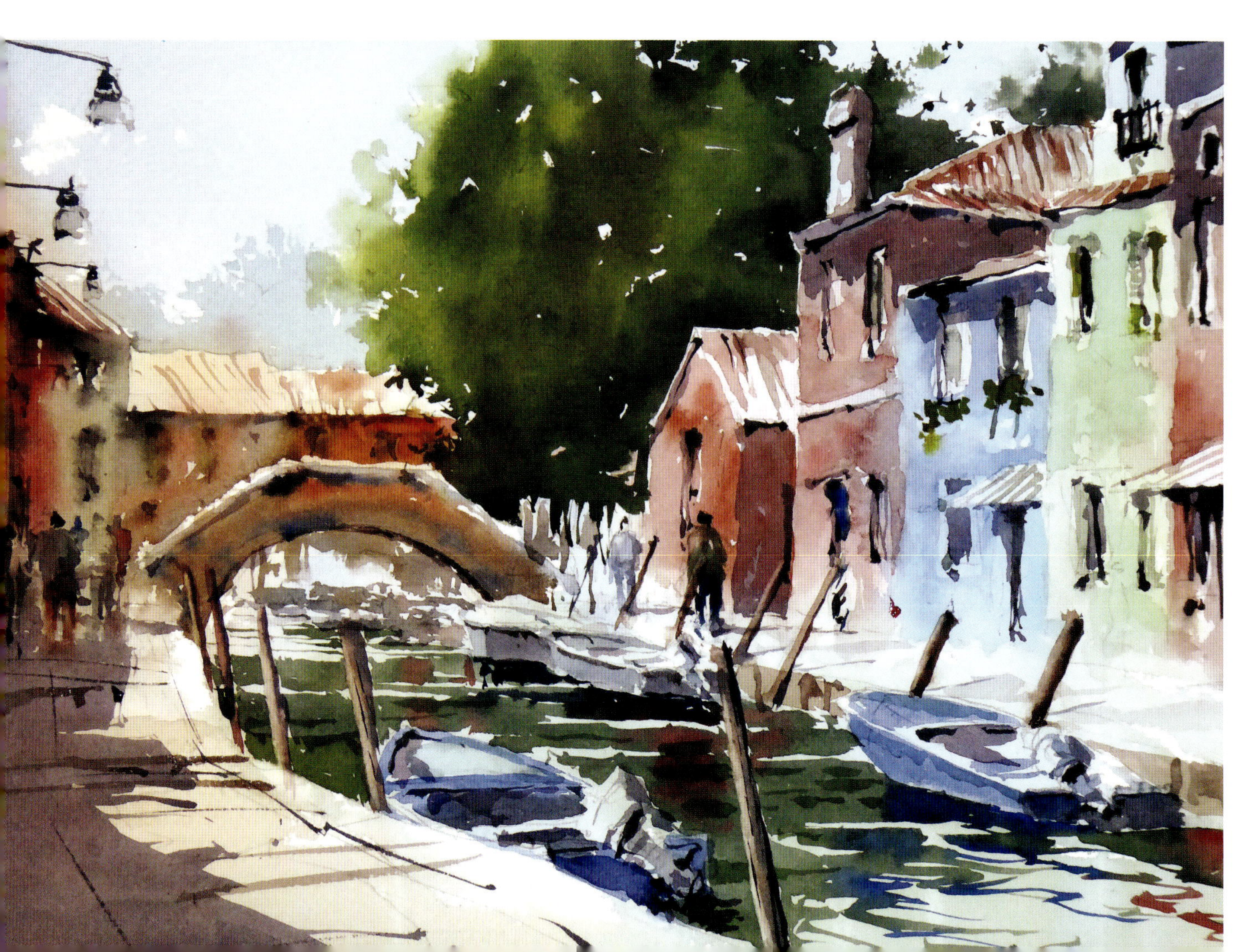

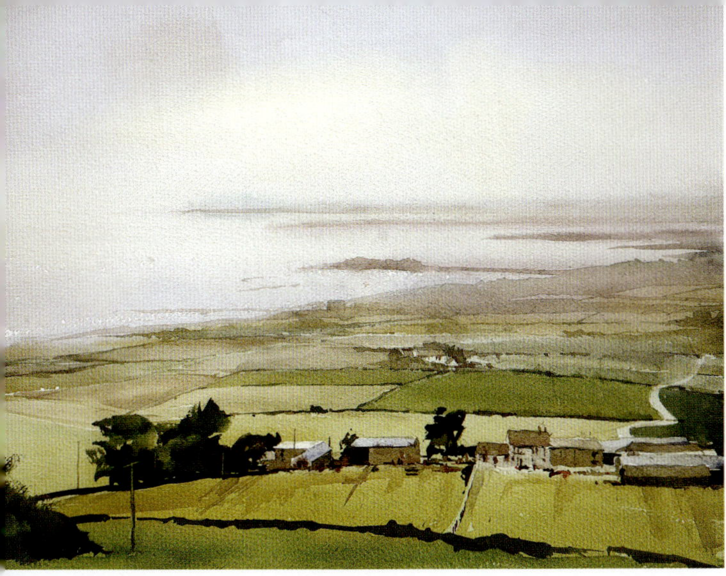

CONTENTS

INTRODUCTION

EN PLEIN AIR

adverb 'in the open air', chiefly referring to painting

S O WHAT IS ALL THE fuss about plein air painting? After all, sitting at home in a nice warm studio (if you're lucky) with a cup of coffee to hand is surely much more pleasant than fighting with the elements. So why do it? Well, there is one big difference between plein air and studio painting. In a studio you may be working from your imagination, a photograph or a sketch, but the important point is that you don't have the actual subject in front of you, merely a representation of it.

It is the difference between listening to a CD and being at a concert; watching a travel programme and actually visiting. With plein air you don't just see your subject, you feel it and you are literally part of it. Being there confers several major advantages that I will expand upon in the pages to come. I'll pass on information and learning that I have accumulated over many, many years, indeed everything that you might need to embark on or continue with the great adventure of painting outdoors.

I was quite a late starter at painting. One day, when I was in my early 30s, my mother-in-law needed a lift to her watercolour class. I obliged (always do what your mother-in-law asks), intending to sit at the back of the hall and read a book while the class was on. Well, the book didn't get opened and I was completely hooked by the demonstration. That looked easy, I thought, and almost 40 years later I'm still trying to work out where the easy part is! I joined the class and a few years later, when the tutor retired, he asked if I would like to take over the class… and that in turn started my teaching career.

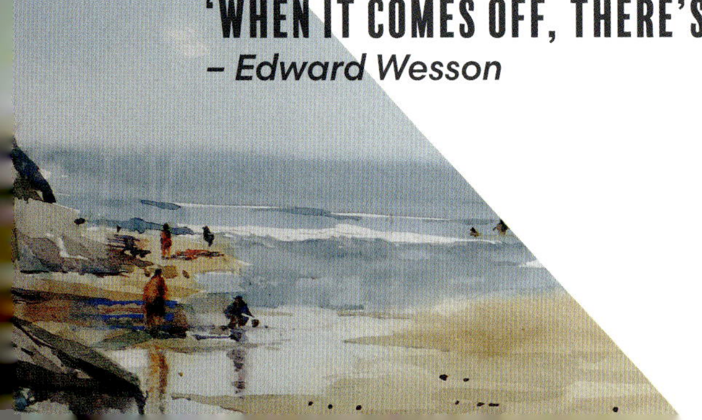

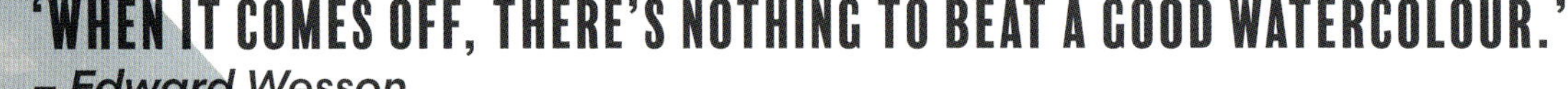

'WHEN IT COMES OFF, THERE'S NOTHING TO BEAT A GOOD WATERCOLOUR.'
– Edward Wesson

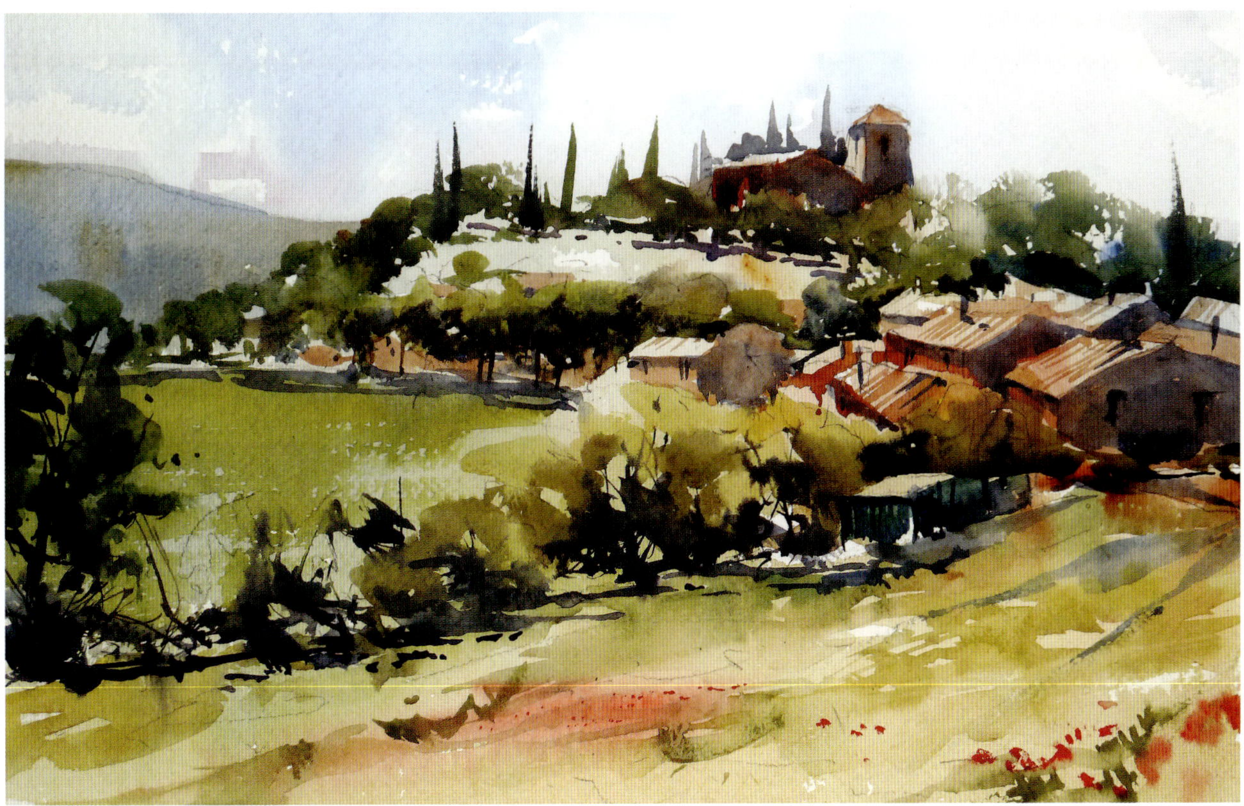

TOURTOUR, PROVENCE
38 x 28cm (15 x 11in), Bockingford CP
425gsm (200lb)

In hot countries it is essential to take cover from the sun, and this often dictates your painting location. Happily, this was below some trees, with a perfect view of this beautiful Provençal village.

I was very fortunate in that my tutor, James Watson, just happened to be one of Ireland's finest watercolour painters: a wonderful artist and teacher whose influence remains with me to this day. James was an unassuming painter – he would never refer to himself as an artist ('I'm just a painter'), but he had very strong views on the subject that he was never afraid to air. Sadly he died before the internet really took off and it is rare today to find any of his paintings online. The relevance to this book is that he also ran plein air painting workshops during the summer months. Right back when I could barely paint at all I probably painted as much outside as in, which gave me both a love for outdoor painting and an appreciation of its benefits to painting in general. In those early days I was painting with a group, and even today my local art club has a plein air group, meeting every week throughout the year. Painting with a group definitely gives a gentler introduction to plein air painting.

Just as important as the painting, one of the great pleasures of plein air is just the fact of being outside. The ability to hear birdsong or the flow of a river or the wind rustling the leaves is not only pleasurable but I firmly believe it also adds to our understanding of our subject. And the coffee tastes much better outside as well. Every painting in this book was painted en plein air at a different location around the world. All of the projects were painted within a short drive of my home on the outskirts of Belfast in Northern Ireland. Travel can be fun but it is not essential for enjoyable plein air painting. Your garden or local park is just as plein air as anywhere in the world.

PREPARING FOR PLEIN AIR PAINTING

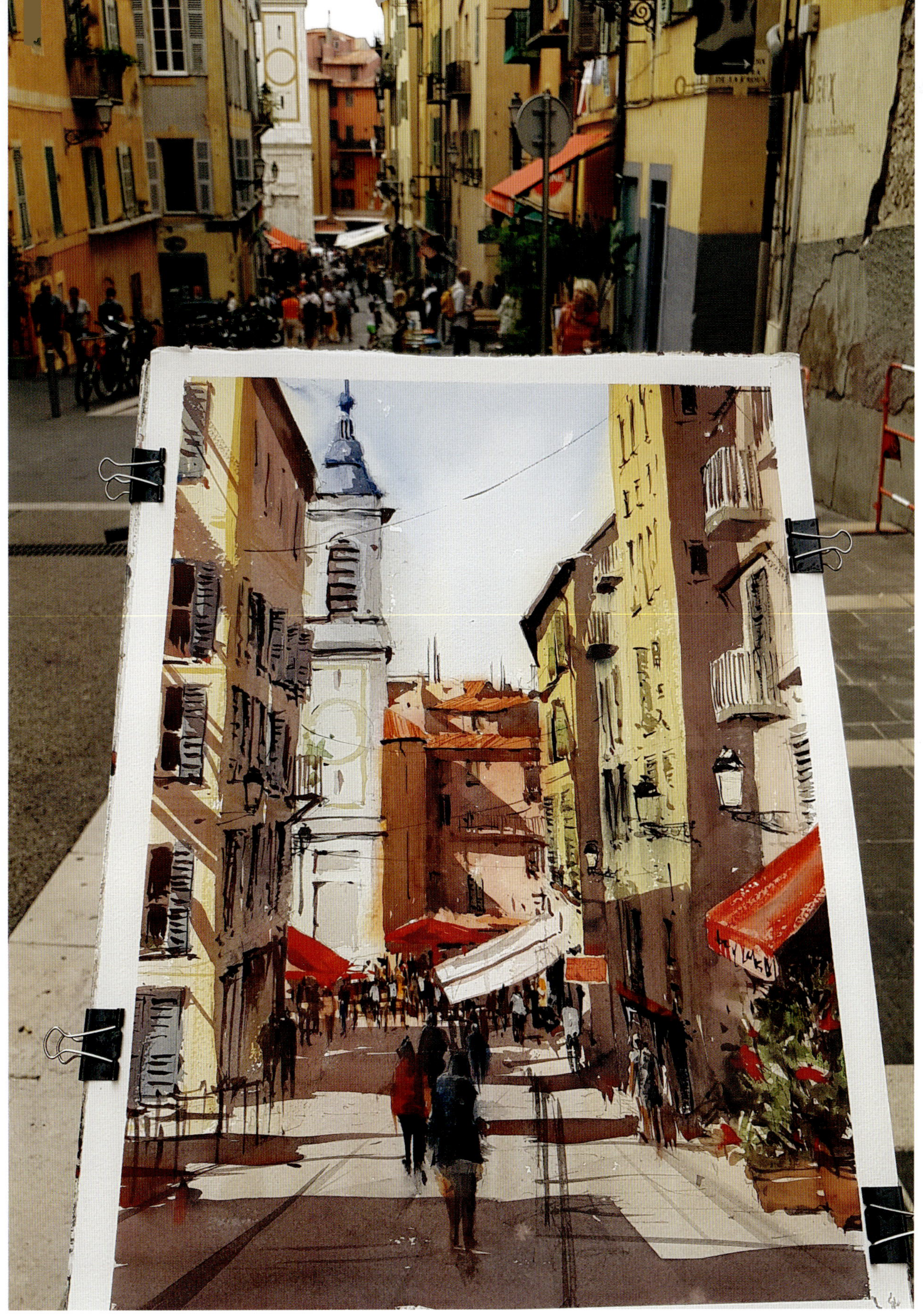

THE CATHEDRAL, NICE

38 x 51cm (15 x 20in), Saunders CP 425gsm (200lb)

You can see just how many people are in the square in front of the cathedral and yet only a few metres away I was left relatively undisturbed, even though I was almost in the middle of the street!

WHY PLEIN AIR?

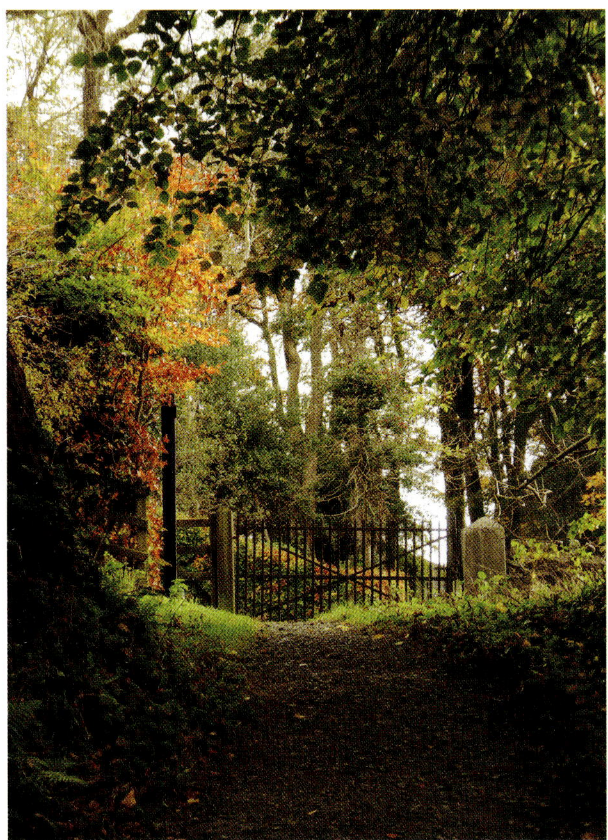

The trees stretch from right in front of me to around 100m (100yd) away. Because the photograph is flat, it is extremely difficult to work out where things are in relation to each other. The trunks of the trees against the sky in the centre are the most distant, but there are leaves that appear to be part of these trees yet are in fact much closer. The mass of leaves at the top right could well be one single group, but, again, they vary in distance from right in front of me to level with the gate. The trees behind the gate are actually across quite a wide road that you can't see in the photograph. Standing there in reality the relative positions of all the trees and leaves are immediately obvious.

WHEN WE PAINT, AT LEAST in a representational way, we are generally trying to create an impression of something that is real. Almost everything that is real has one very important attribute: it has depth. Our paper, on the other hand, is completely flat, and what we are attempting to do when we paint is to create the illusion of three dimensions on our flat two-dimensional paper. It is absolutely vital to be able to understand that third dimension in order to create an illusion of it. We do this by using perspective, both linear and aerial (more about that later).

SEEING DEPTH

'So what is wrong with a photograph?', you may ask. Well, a camera simply flattens that third dimension. The camera is entirely unable to consider how to maintain an illusion of it, save for the natural effect of perspective. This is most easily seen in a photograph of a forest. The photograph (left) shows the forest just as a flat, merging green mass, whereas if we are actually standing there we will see the scene as divided into foreground trees, middle ground trees and background trees. Being there makes the process of creating the illusion of three dimensions so much easier.

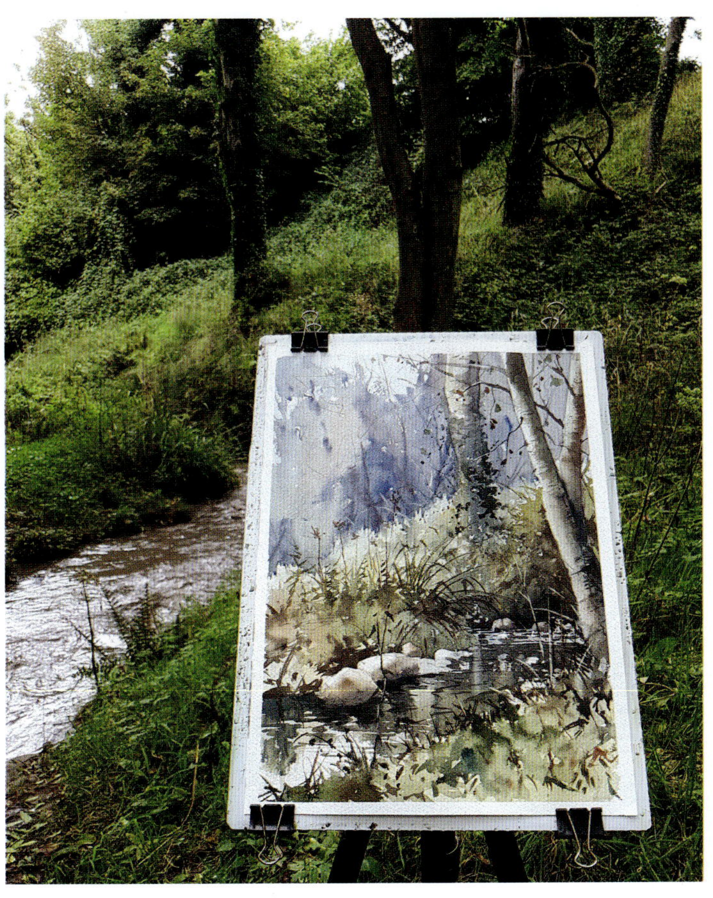

FOREST FLOW
38 x 28cm (15 x 11in), Millford CP 300gsm (140lb)

In reality, the colour and strength of the greens were much the same at the back of this subject as at the front, but in the painting I deliberately made them paler, softer and more blue in order to 'push them back'. I kept my strongest darks and lights for the rocks in the water, my focus. As you can see, the rocks are barely visible in the photograph but to me, on the day, surrounded by the noise of flowing water, they were the obvious focus for the subject. If I had only taken the photograph instead of painting on location I am pretty sure the finished work would never have been completed.

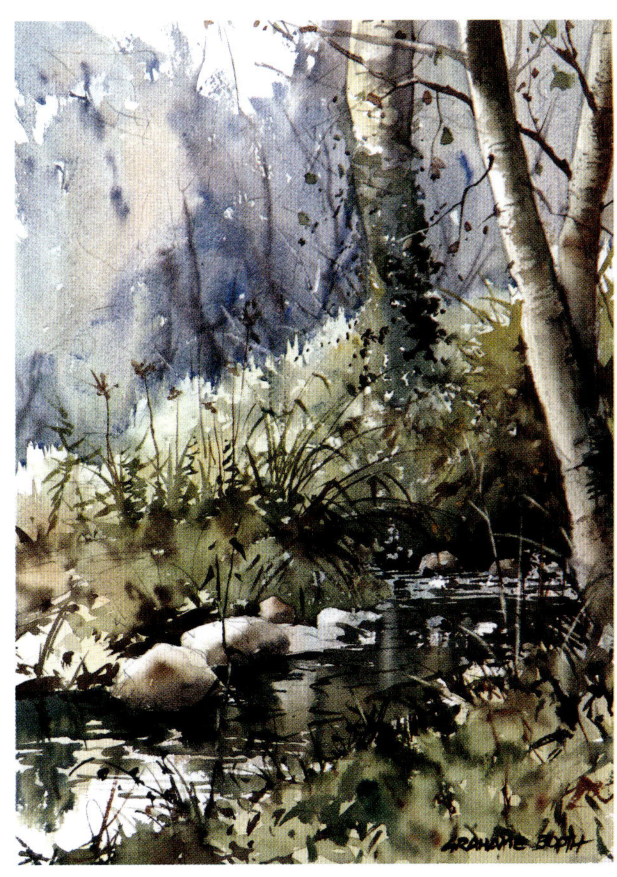

SEEING DETAIL

Another advantage to plein air painting is clarity and detail. When we are standing in front of a subject we will see everything in much greater detail than a photograph can ever produce. As an impressionist painter, I am always trying to create a simpler version of my subjects, but in order to simplify something I must first understand what it is. It is often recommended in a tongue-in-cheek way that taking off your spectacles will automatically simplify the subject, but sadly this is not the case! Simplifying requires us to carefully consider our subject and to concentrate on the parts that are important to us while minimizing the importance of the rest.

When we look at something in reality we can actually only see detail within a very narrow angle of vision and this automatically begins the process of simplification. Try this for yourself. Look at only this word and try to discern the words around it without looking directly at them. It is impossible. When we look at our real subject we will see only the detail that is important to us, the detail that we actually look at. While something similar will work to a certain extent when we look at a photograph, the photograph is really much too small to match what we would see in reality and, of course, we lose that all-important third dimension. You can see what I mean by following the stages to the right: the photograph of the scene (1), the version of the scene that my eyes see (2), and my finished painted version (3).

Photographs are a great resource. 90 per cent of painters use them and I suspect the other 10 per cent are probably telling fibs, but experience of plein air painting makes it so much easier to make allowances for their limitations. If you do use photographs, it is better for them to be as large as possible. When I paint in my studio I use a 102cm (40in) television screen for my source images.

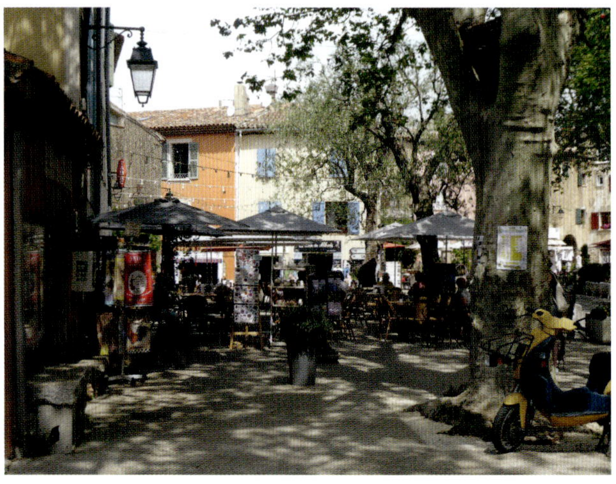

1. This sharp photograph is what the camera sees. Everything is crisp and clear. We can work out depth fairly easily because the shapes overlap each other.

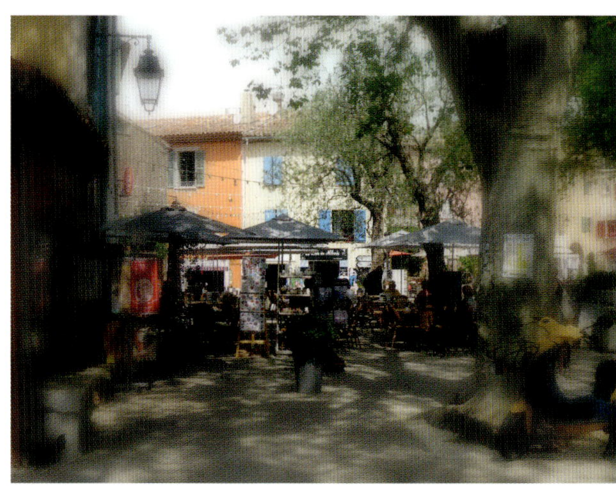

2. In reality, if we focus on the café tables, this is akin to what our eyes see: only the tables are clear. We are aware of everything else but can't see it clearly unless we direct our focus to it.

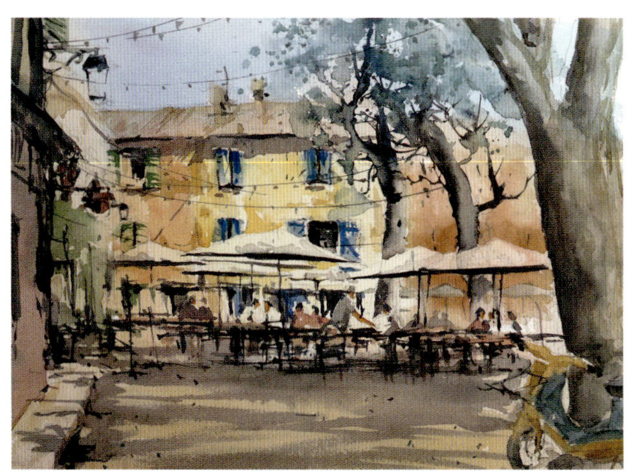

3. In the painting I have concentrated on what I find interesting – the café tables. Everything else is simplified, softened or ignored.

IMPROVING YOUR TECHNIQUE

The ultimate benefit of plein air is that you will almost certainly become a better painter. Speaking for myself, I can safely say that if I look at what I would consider to be my more successful paintings, probably around 70–80 per cent of them have been painted en plein air. Painting outside tends to concentrate the mind, making it much easier to think about the important elements in your subject rather than to start fiddling with unnecessary detail – something that can happen so easily in the comfort of a studio.

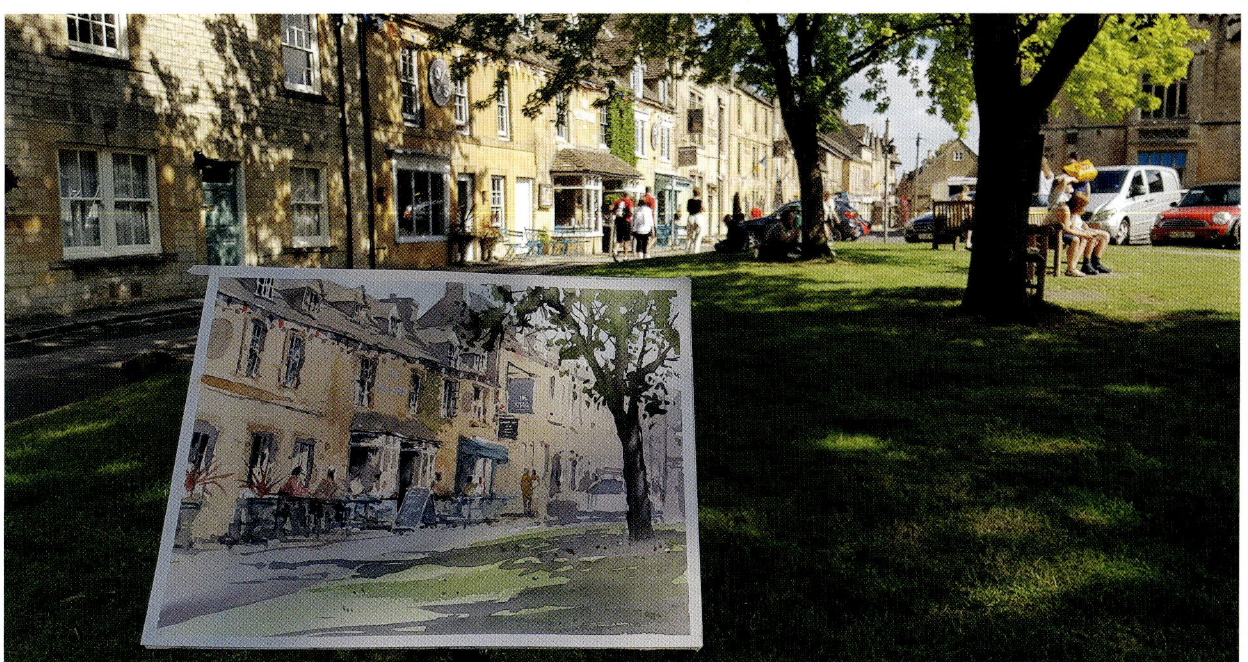

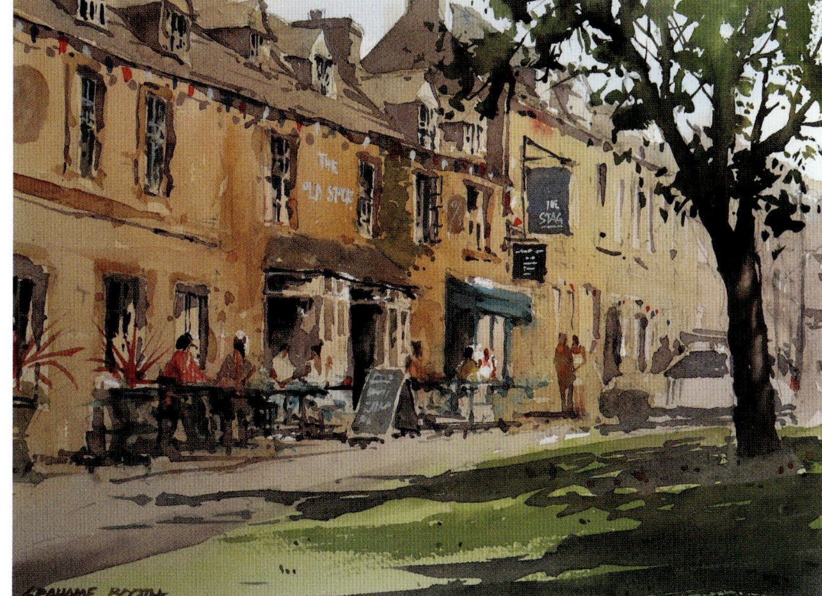

STOW ON THE WOLD, ENGLAND
38 x 28cm (15 x 11in), Millford CP
300gsm (140lb)

My focus was the area in front of the pub. The camera showed the area further up the street just as clearly but in my painting I simplified this considerably to maintain attention on the pub.

WHY USE WATERCOLOUR FOR PLEIN AIR?

I REALLY DON'T THINK THERE CAN be any argument as to why watercolour is the ideal plein air medium. When painting outdoors it is important that we can concentrate on the painting instead of organizing our equipment, and, without doubt, watercolour gives us by far the most compact outdoor painting system. A simple sketching kit will fit in a large coat pocket and even the most comprehensive outdoor watercolour kit can be contained in a backpack. Unlike oils, there are no solvents to worry about and no environmental issues with the disposal of waste. Relatively few colours are needed, unlike pastels or coloured pencils, and although rain can definitely be a problem, a compact system makes shelter easier to find in a hurry.

LOW TIDE, STRANGFORD LOUGH
38 x 51cm (15 x 20in), Saunders Waterford CP 425gsm (200lb)
This is a shallow sea lough that almost drains at each low tide. My compact watercolour kit made it easy to trek the hundred metres or so of muddy foreshore to reach my chosen painting position.

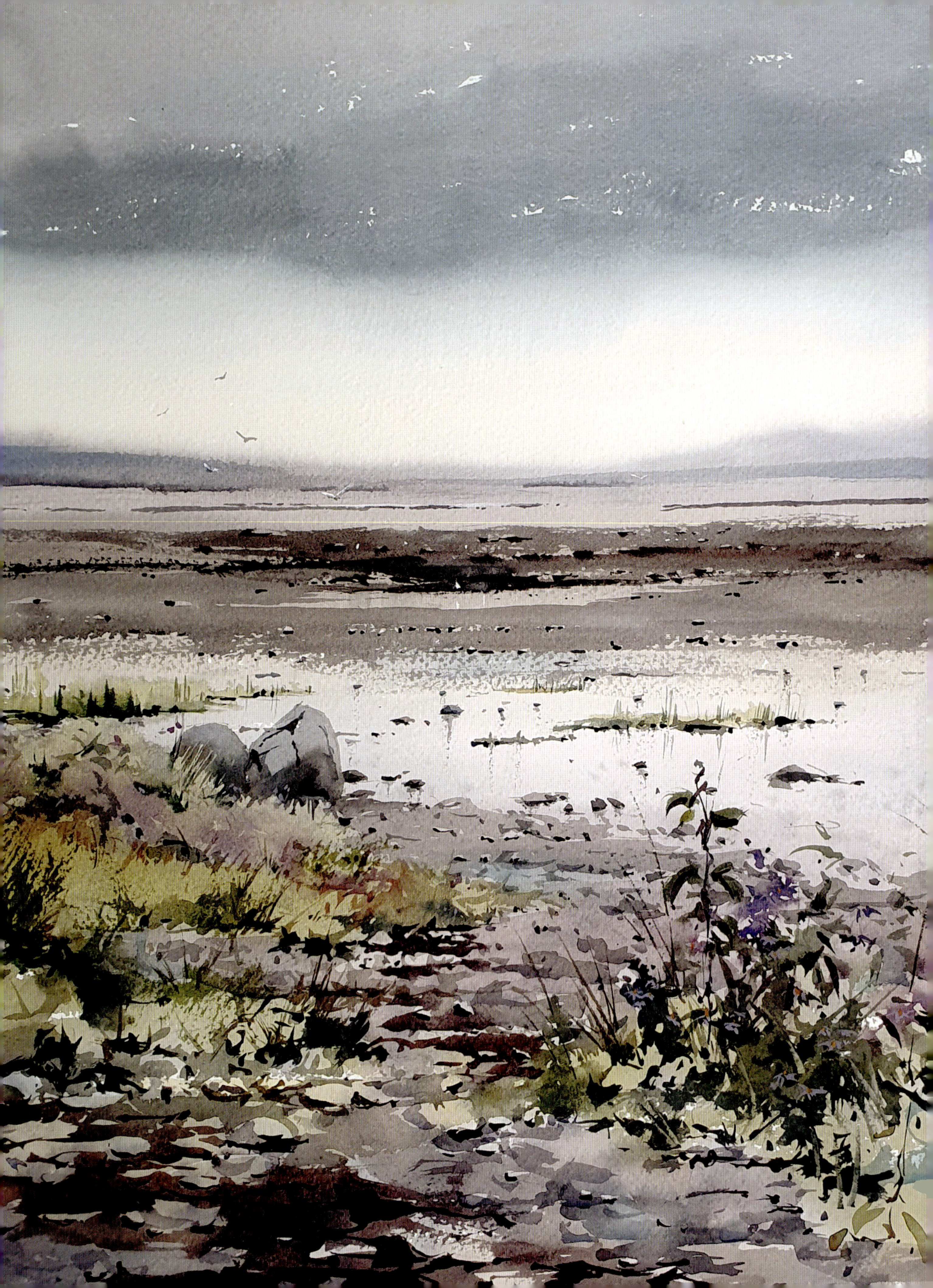

Arguably, one downside to plein air watercolour is that drying is extremely slow in humid conditions, but this can also be a bonus, as it can give you plenty of time to play with wet-in-wet techniques. Wet-in-wet painting is much more problematic in a studio because the paper dries so quickly. It is no coincidence that famous oil painting masters such as Constable and Turner used watercolour extensively for plein air painting. Constable's plein air watercolour sky studies have an immediacy and vibrancy that clearly influenced the creation of his wonderful English landscapes. Winslow Homer was an accomplished painter in oils who eventually became best remembered for the plein air watercolours he painted in his latter years. His fellow American John Singer Sargent, one of the Edwardian world's most sought-after portrait painters in oils, would escape outdoors with his watercolours and, like Homer, is today appreciated as much for those watercolours. I do enjoy a quotation attributed to Sargent when he described painting in watercolour as 'making the best of an emergency'. Obviously I am not the only one!

Plein air painting doesn't have to stop when the rain starts. I often paint in my car if the conditions outside don't really encourage being properly outdoors. Most of the advantages of plein air painting are still there – the major disadvantages are not being able to step back from your painting and being severely restricted in the choice of subjects. I suppose spilling paint over the car upholstery might also be a problem, but, being watercolour, at least it should wash off! Obviously large works are out of the question unless you have a really big car, but quarter sheet is just about doable and for pen and wash sketching, a car is pretty much ideal.

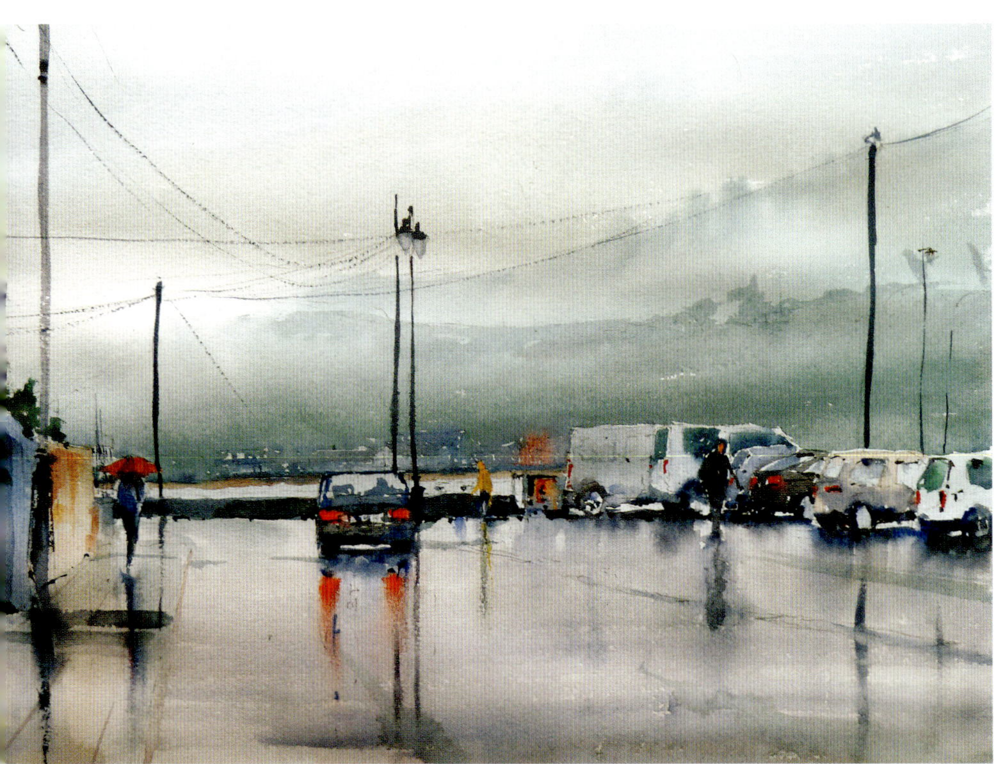

WET DAY, BALLYHACK
38 x 28cm (15 x 11in), Millford CP
300gsm (140lb)

This was painted from my car as the day was every bit as wet as it appears. The high humidity meant that the drying time was greatly extended, giving me plenty of time to create the juicy wet-in-wet passages that are vital to a subject like this.

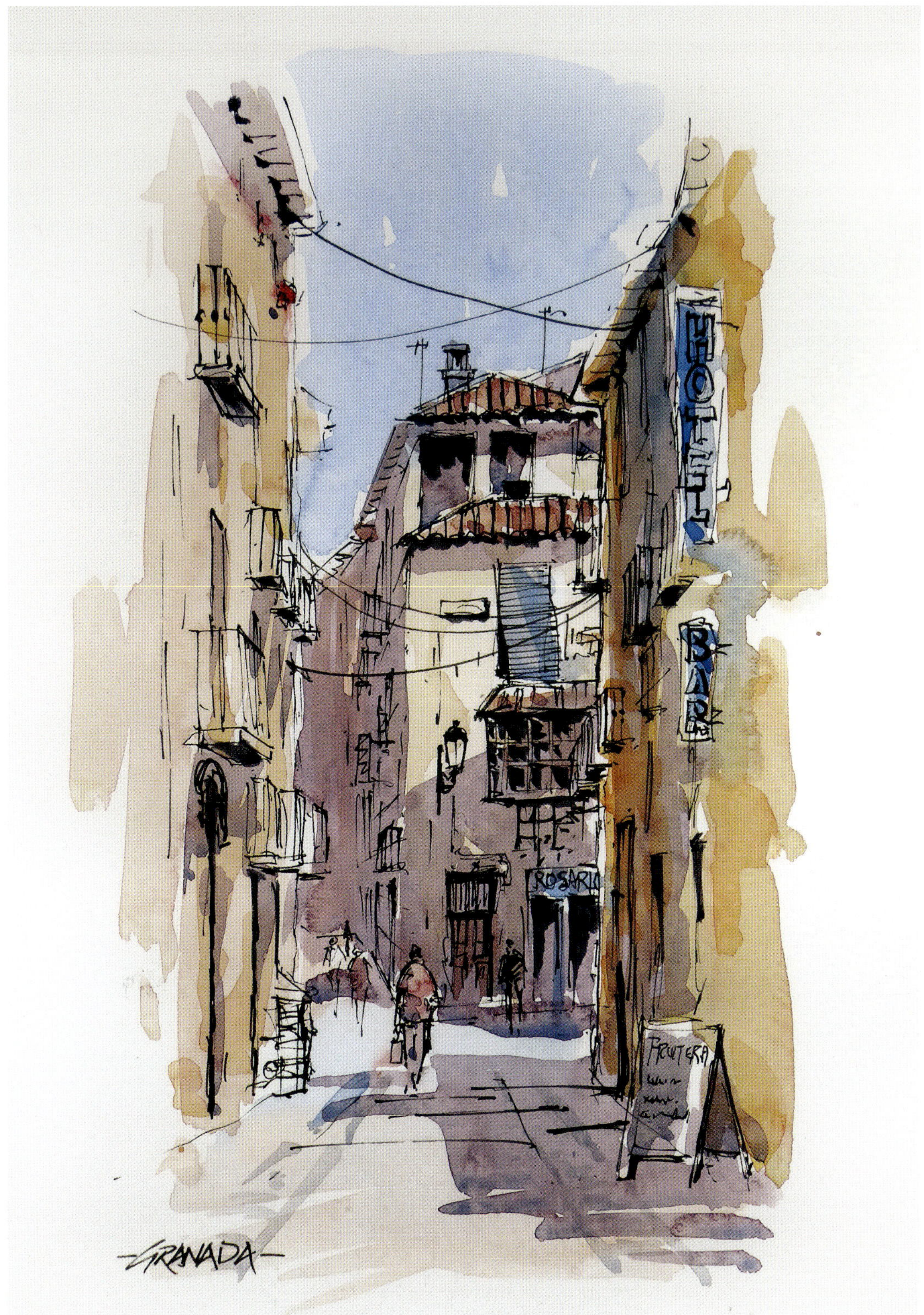

BACK STREET, GRANADA
15 x 21cm (6 x 8¼in), cartridge paper in sketchbook

Watercolour can be applied much more loosely in pen and wash. Because the structure of the painting is created by the black ink, it doesn't really matter too much where the watercolour goes, and indeed if too much care is taken there is a danger of it becoming a coloured-in drawing – not the same thing at all.

EQUIPMENT AND MATERIALS

THE CHOICE OF EQUIPMENT AND MATERIALS for plein air painting is exactly the same as for studio painting but, given the need to carry it all, it makes sense to keep it compact. My studio kit is pretty much exactly the same as I use for plein air, other than using a larger easel in the studio.

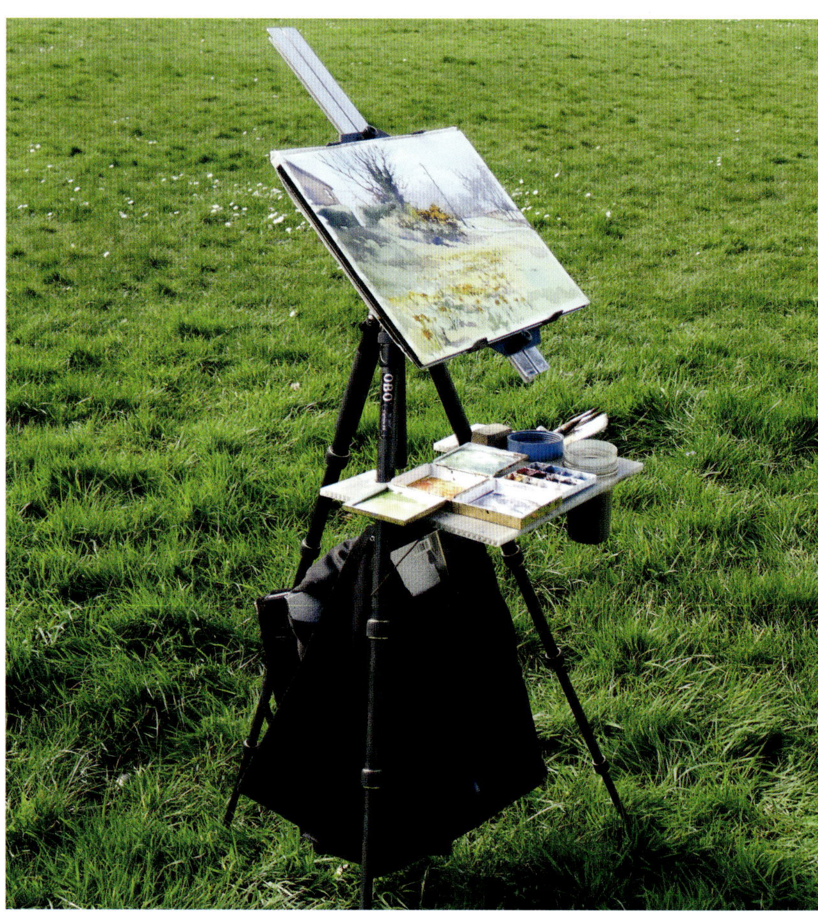

This is my complete outdoor painting kit, although here I am using an adapted board holder to take my block of paper. Everything you see fits in the bag hanging underneath. As well as keeping the bag off the ground, it also adds some weight, preventing the easel from blowing over in windy conditions.

MARK MAKING

Everyone will have their own personal and often extensive range of brushes, but for plein air work I would suggest keeping the numbers to a minimum. As a start, remove any brush you haven't used in the last year. I am an ambassador for Princeton Artist Brush Co. and I use synthetic brushes from their Neptune™ and Aqua Elite™ ranges. In the past, natural hair brushes such as squirrel or sable would always have been recommended, but modern synthetic hair is so good that I now paint only with synthetic hair brushes.

A little suggestion for if the tip of your brush becomes bent: dip the hairs of the brush into a cup of very hot water (80–90°C/176–194°F) for a few seconds and you will be able to reform your perfect point. This works with sable, squirrel and the synthetic brushes I use.

Essential brushes

A: SIZE 10 RIGGER, SYNTHETIC KOLINSKY

Riggers all have long hairs with a fine point and are ideal for painting twigs and boat masts or indeed anything that needs a thin consistent line. The very small ones hold very little paint so go for as large as you can find. Swordliners and reservoir brushes are good alternatives.

B & C: SIZES 8 & 12 ROUND BRUSHES WITH FINE POINTS, SYNTHETIC KOLINSKY

If the point is good enough, these brushes will be sufficient for 95 per cent of your painting. I prefer a long round brush with an extended point.

D: SIZE 6 QUILL, SYNTHETIC KOLINSKY

Substantially larger than the size 12 round but still with a fine point. This is technically a mop – it holds good amounts of paint and has that important needle-like point.

E: SIZE 12 ROUND, SYNTHETIC SQUIRREL

This has much softer hair than the size 12 synthetic Kolinsky. I use this sometimes just for a change. I can offer no reason why – either would do the job!

F: SIZE 8 MOP, SYNTHETIC SQUIRREL

This has very soft hair and is perfect for the first wash where I need to be able to cover the paper quite quickly (only needed for quarter sheet or larger sized paper).

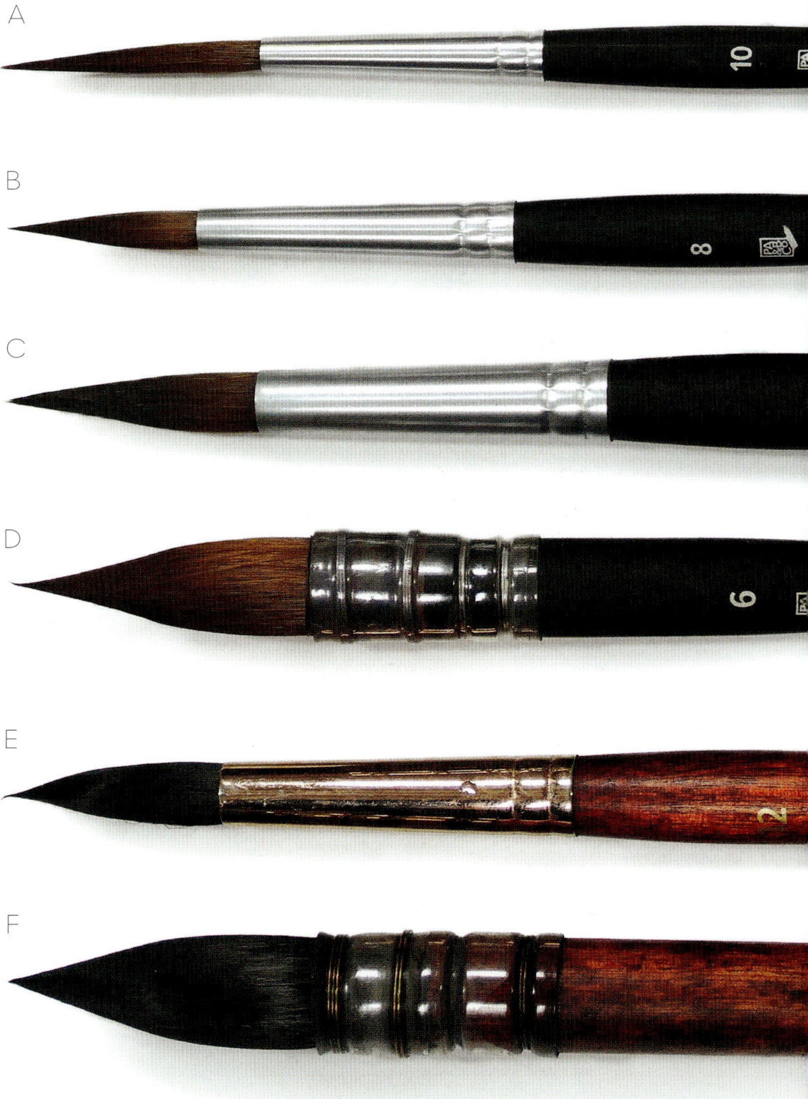

Extra tools

G: SIZE 8 ROUND

This is a very old worn sable brush around a size 8. My father gave it to me about 60 years ago. He used it in the factory where he worked for painting lines on aircraft parts, and the brushes were disposed of at the end of each day. Sable brushes! I would suspect that does not happen in today's workplace. This brush is perfect for softening edges and lifting out. These actions will cause a brush to wear rapidly, so it is best to avoid using your nice new pointed brushes for these actions.

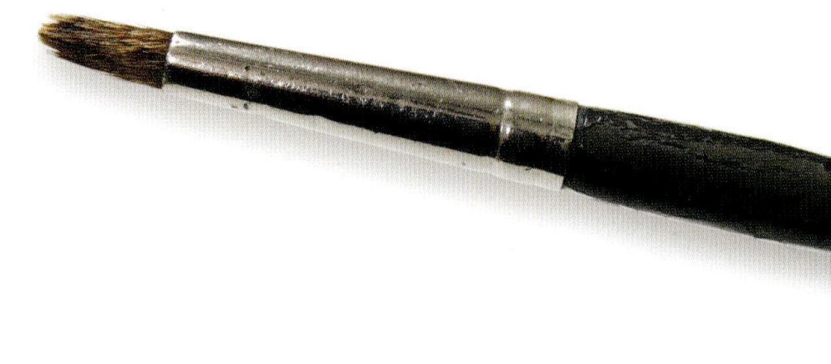

H: TRAVEL BRUSHES

Some of these brushes will also be available as travel brushes, where the brush handle can be reversed to form a cover that protects the brush hairs. Fine points can easily become damaged. Not all brushes are available in travel versions but you can easily make your own. The cover here is part of a little syringe used for dosing children's medicine and it so happens that it is slightly narrower than most size 12 brushes. I just cut the brush down, shaved the end a little and I had a perfect travel brush. Alternatively, if you don't want to cut your brush, the syringe will fit over and protect the hairs on the full length brush.

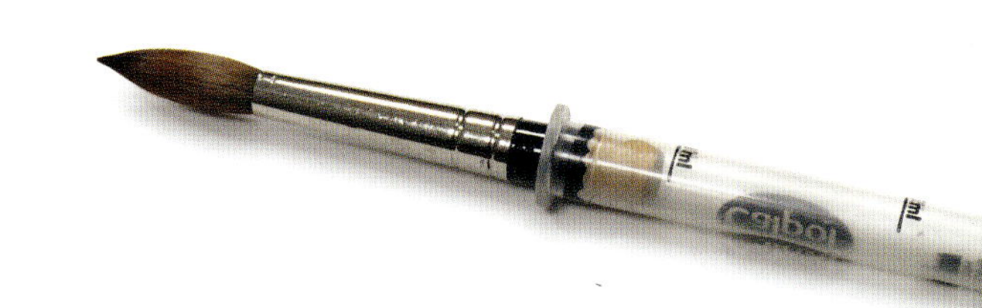

I: RULING PEN

Strictly speaking this is not a brush, but is known as a ruling pen. The little wheel adjusts the gap between the two blades which essentially act as a nib, allowing me to paint lines of consistent width using a watercolour wash. Stroking a brush fills the gap between the blades. The pen is used by framers to make wash lines around a mount but I find it invaluable when painting overhead wires, mooring ropes and rigging lines. They can all be painted with a fine brush but the ruling pen avoids the risk of a sudden thickening of the line, something that can easily happen when using a brush.

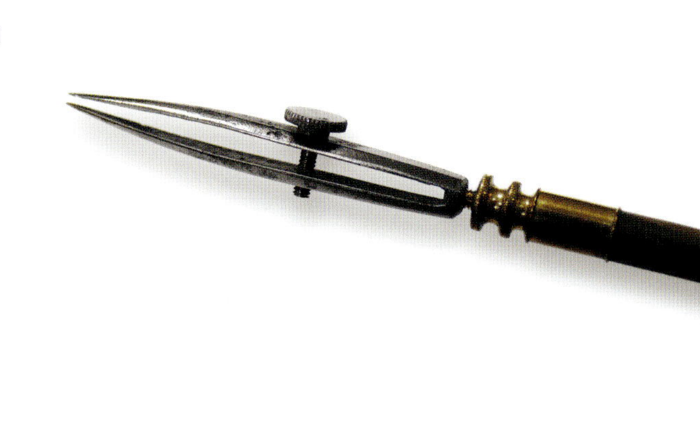

J: CLUTCH PENCILS

I prefer clutch pencils to traditional wooden pencils and I use both 2mm and 0.9mm diameter leads. The 0.9 is useful in that it needs no sharpening, but the 2mm feels a little more substantial. I use the little lead sharpener to give a point to it. The length of string attached to it comes in useful to check my perspective lines (see pages 50–51). I choose 2B or 3B leads – soft enough not to dent the paper but hard enough not to smudge too much.

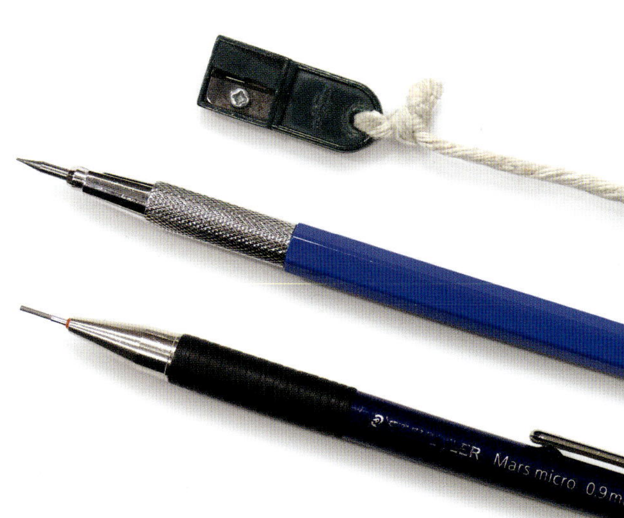

TOOTHBRUSH (NOT SHOWN)

An old toothbrush is very useful for producing very fine splatter to suggest fine sand or gravel. Just dip the brush in your paint mix and run the top of your thumb across the bristles.

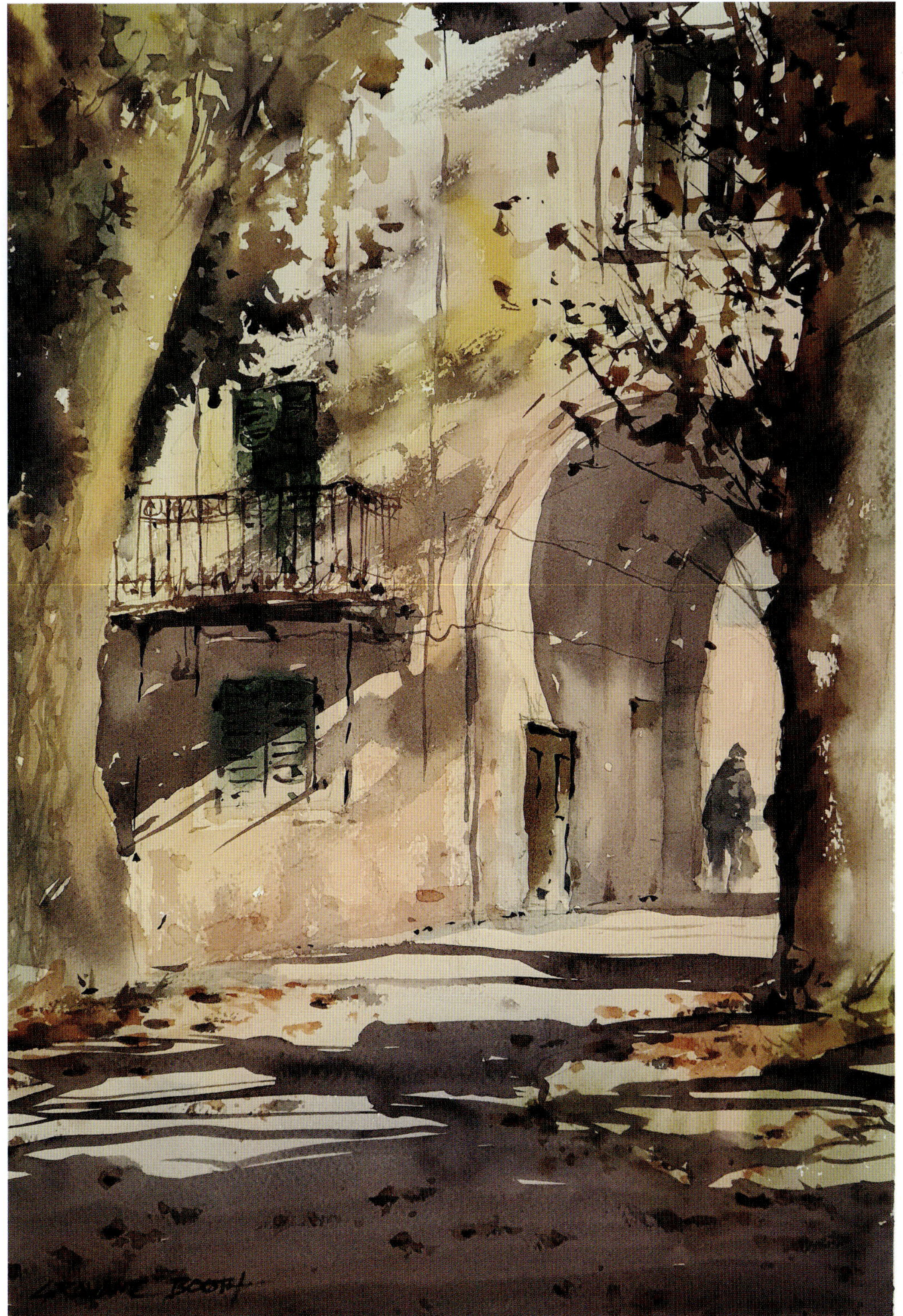

ENTRANCE TO FIVIZZANO, TUSCANY
38 x 51cm (15 x 20in), Millford CP 300gsm (140lb)

In general, the bigger the mark, the bigger the brush, although with a well-pointed large brush such as the size 6 quill I can paint probably 95 per cent of a subject like this. For very fine lines such as the twigs and the electrical cables I used the size 10 rigger. You definitely do not need a huge number of brushes.

THE IMPORTANCE OF PAINT

Over the years I have used paint from all of the recognized watercolour paint manufacturers and although there may be slight differences in consistency or strength, in general all are good.

I use paint from MaimeriBlu, for whom I am a brand ambassador. I prefer to use tubes for both studio and plein air work simply because the paint is soft and more readily available to the brush. The downside of this is that my paintbox must be kept flat at all times to avoid the soft paint flowing everywhere and creating a very annoying mess!

I rarely use pans but my limited experience of them suggests a huge variation in performance even within a range from the same manufacturer. Some pans can be quite soft, almost like soft clay, and they release the paint very well, but others can be extremely hard, requiring serious scrubbing with the brush to release sufficient paint. As well as delaying the painting process, this will definitely cause undue wear to the point of the brush. One major downside of pans is that they can be wasteful, often requiring replacement before the pan is completely empty. Of course you could instead fill the empty pan with tube paint!

Whether you choose tubes or pans I would always recommend using artists' quality paint. Yes, it is more expensive than students' quality, but usually it will be more concentrated and more transparent. Buy as large a tube as you can afford. The smallest tubes are generally 5ml (⅙fl oz) and the largest are up to 37ml (1⅓fl oz), but the largest tube can work out at almost half the cost per ml/fl oz.

Many of the manufacturers of artists' quality watercolour also make a less expensive students' range, but please avoid the sets of watercolour paint you often find in discount stores where you can buy a whole set for the price of a single tube of the good stuff. Without exception, every one of these I have ever tried (we all love a bargain) has been absolutely horrible with dull, gritty, opaque colour and dubious lightfastness.

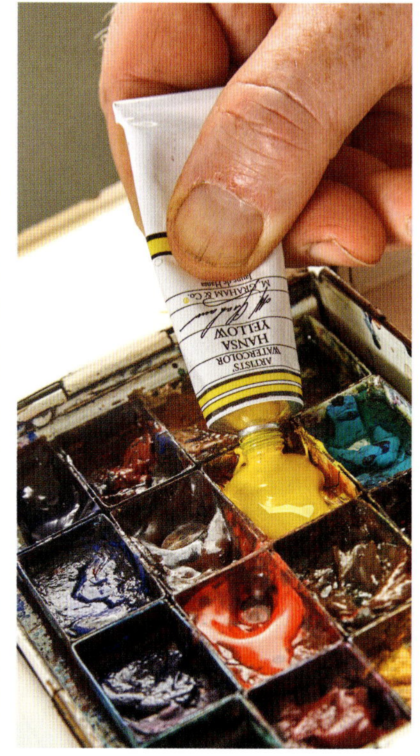

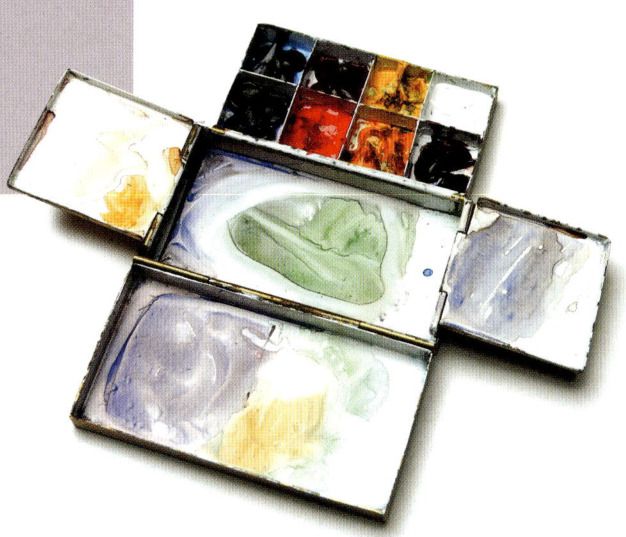

When sketching and using pen and wash it is important to keep equipment to a minimum, ideally with everything you need fitting into a large pocket or small bag. My little sketching palette is only 10 x 5cm (4 x 2in) when closed but opens up to give me two large and two small mixing areas.

WATER

Water is, of course, absolutely essential when painting, indoors or out, but when painting en plein air you will generally need to take it with you. If your painting location is near a lake, river or fountain, you can pick it up locally (note that sea water is not suitable). I carry mine in a 250ml (8¾fl oz) plastic cup with a screw lid, which I also use for holding the water while I am painting – one less piece of kit to carry if I am only painting for a half day.

Don't fall for the often repeated advice that painting with dirty water will make your painting muddy. Your water would have to be extremely murky before there would be any effect at all. Certainly use fresh water as much as possible, but don't panic if your water becomes the colour and consistency of beef consommé!

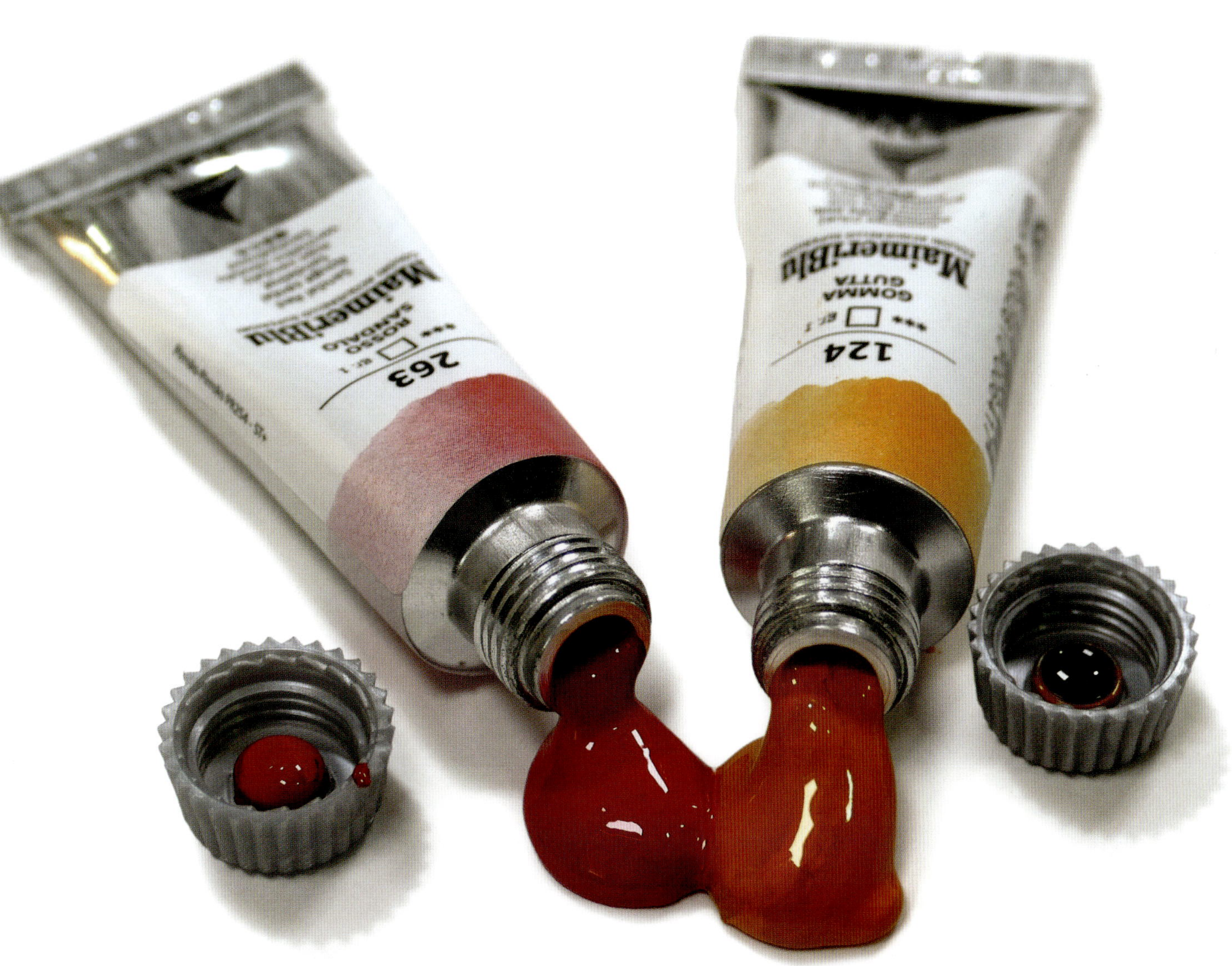

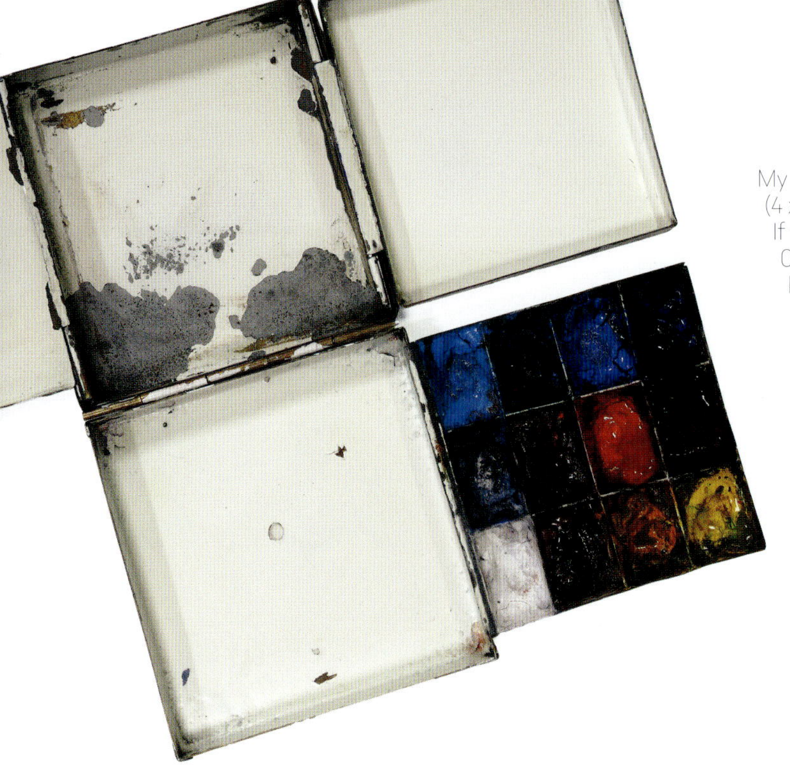

YOUR PALETTE

When painting plein air, a paintbox with a built-in palette is for me the only sensible choice. I use the same home-made brass paintbox for studio and plein air work with a second smaller brass paintbox for sketching and pen and wash. Although I could use pans, I just fill the wells with my tube paint, leaving the box open for a few hours, allowing the paint to dry sufficiently to avoid any mess.

Brass paintboxes are relatively cheap to make if you have the necessary metalworking skills but very expensive to purchase. Although a brass box should last several lifetimes, there are some plastic paintboxes that are well-designed and relatively inexpensive. The important factors when choosing a paintbox is that it should have sufficient deep paint wells for the number of different colours you wish to use, coupled with at least three deep mixing wells in which to create your washes. Using a cheap open plastic palette is false economy. Any remaining paint will dry out and be unusable, the mixing wells tend to be very shallow and they are often rather unwieldy for plein air painting.

Colours are very individual – we all have our favourites – but you certainly don't need a huge number. As with brushes, set aside any colours you haven't used in the last year. I base my colour palette on the twin primary system where I have two versions of each of the three primary colours.

My six basic colours are:
Ultramarine deep: a blue biased towards red that will mix bright purples and dull greens.
Primary blue (cyan): a blue biased towards yellow that will mix dull purples and bright greens.
Sandal red: a red biased towards yellow that will mix bright oranges and dull purples.
Quinacridone magenta: a red biased towards blue that will mix dull oranges and bright purple.
Gamboge: a yellow biased towards red that will mix bright oranges and dull greens.
Primary yellow: a yellow biased towards blue that will mix dull oranges and bright greens.

From these colours I can mix practically anything I require but, because I use so much of it, I also use burnt sienna. (I could mix something similar from quinacridone magenta and primary yellow.) In addition, I will usually have a few extra colours just for fun. It can be good to literally mix things up a little!

Identifying pigment numbers

Pigment numbers will be listed on all quality paints. Use these to compare colours. Different manufacturers will often call the same pigments by different names. For example, pyrrole red, pyrrol red, Winsor red (Winsor & Newton) and sandal red (MaimeriBlu) are all PR254.

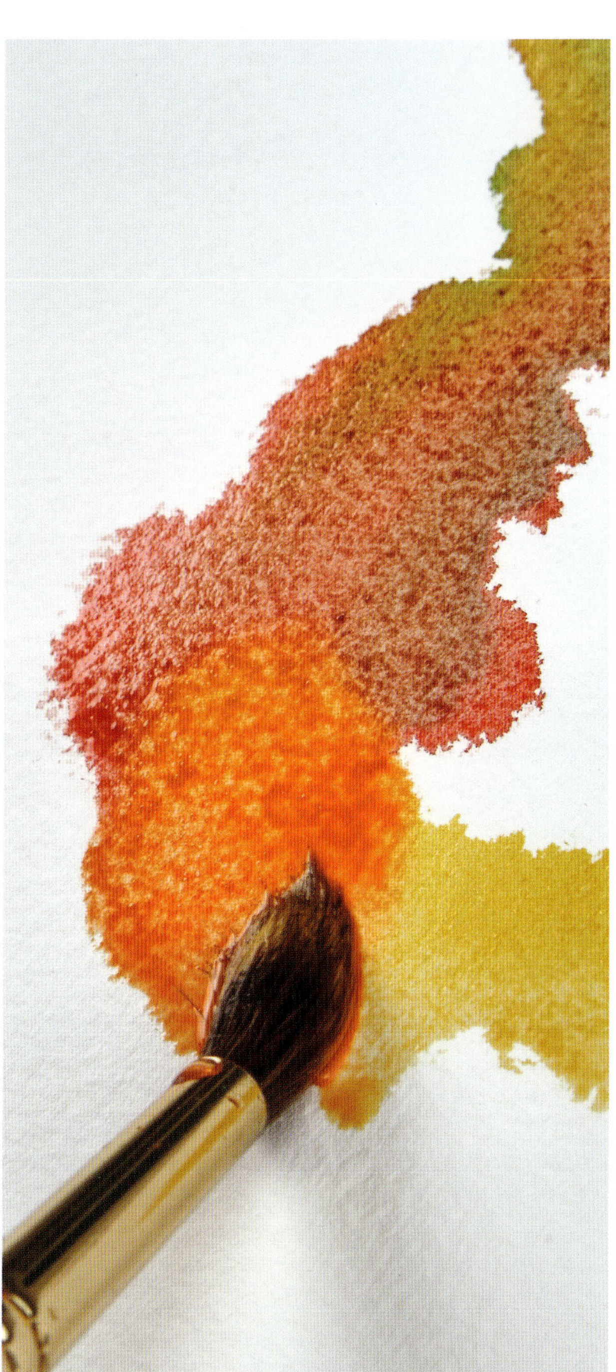

Paint names

Colours from different manufacturers can vary considerably even if they have the same name – I find yellows to be most varied. As such, when I refer to cool or warm shades of colours, this could be any of the following:

Cool yellow
Primary yellow (MaimeriBlu); Winsor yellow (Winsor & Newton); azo yellow; lemon yellow; bismuth yellow; cadmium lemon; aureolin.

Warm yellow
Gamboge (MaimeriBlu); cadmium yellow; Indian yellow; Winsor yellow deep (Winsor & Newton).

Warm red
Sandal red (MaimeriBlu); cadmium red; pyrrole red; Winsor red (Winsor & Newton).

Cool red
Quinacridone magenta is fairly consistent across the ranges. Some painters choose alizarin crimson as their cool red, but there are two major problems with this – it isn't particularly cool and it fades dramatically in light. There is really no reason to use this paint when there are so many lightfast alternatives. However, if you like the colour, most manufacturers also make a permanent lightfast version generally (and perhaps rather predictably) known as permanent alizarin crimson!

Warm blue
Ultramarine (this is fairly consistent across all ranges – the pigment should be listed as PB29).

Cool blue
This too is fairly consistent across all ranges but often has widely different names – phthalo blue (green shade) is the most common and the one that I will use in the text, but primary blue (cyan), Winsor blue, phthalocyanine blue and intense blue all use the same pigment: PB15:3. Paint made with PB 15:0, 15:1 or 15:6 is phthalo blue (red shade), which is not the same and much closer to ultramarine.

THE IMPORTANCE OF PAPER

Paper, probably more than anything else, will have the greatest effect on your painting. I would always recommend using paper only from the major paper mills. I have always used paper from St Cuthberts Mill in Somerset, England, who have been making paper on the same site in the city of Wells since the 1700s. I have been an ambassador for St Cuthberts for many years.

Good watercolour paper is expensive but you can save money by buying the paper in full sheets and then cutting it down to a size you prefer. Good art shops should be willing to cut the paper for you, usually at no additional cost. Having said that, blocks of paper are very suited to plein-air work. A block of paper will be glued all-round with a little gap to insert a knife, which will allow you to remove each sheet. Do not remove the sheet until you have finished your painting and it has dried thoroughly! The paper will tend to cockle while you are painting but will dry perfectly flat, even with comparatively lightweight paper.

Paper comes in three surface textures: rough, cold pressed, CP (also known as NOT) and hot pressed, HP. NOT paper is so called because it isn't hot pressed! Hot pressed has a very smooth surface that can be quite tricky to paint on, so for general landscape work rough or CP/NOT would be more suitable choices. I use HP for pen and wash as the smooth surface is a delight to draw on.

Paper comes in different weights: 300gsm/140lb is a good average weight for sheet sizes up to half sheet, but heavier and lighter papers are available at a relatively higher or lower cost.

Poor-quality paper will frustrate and annoy. Instead, use the back of the unsuccessful paintings piled up in the corner of your studio (yes, we all have them). Modern paper can be painted on either side. Often there can be a difference in texture but both sides will have been treated in the same way at the factory.

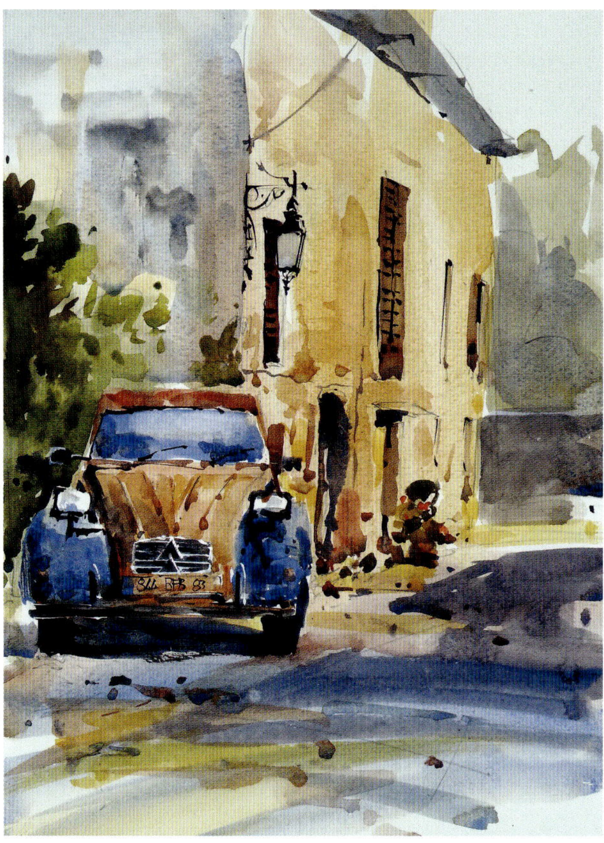

2CV, PROVENCE
28 x 38cm (11 x 15in), Bockingford HP 300gsm (140lb)
Hot pressed paper can be tricky to paint on. The downsides are that cauliflowers will appear as if by magic, and it is difficult to get a smooth wash. However, the upside is that as the paint dries there is less dulling. The dried paint looks almost as if it is still wet. Hot pressed paper does not react well to overworking: it is best for making marks and leaving them alone.

Choosing a sketchbook

I am sure there are as many manufacturers of
sketchbooks as there are of brushes and paints.
I like to use relatively inexpensive cartridge paper,
ideally in a case-bound sketchbook. Case-binding
is where the paper is stitched together in sections,
usually with a hard cover. I choose this simply
because removing any of the paper is awkward
and will probably lead to the book falling apart.
I don't want a sketchbook where the sheets
can be easily removed simply because I might
be tempted to produce 'paintings' rather than
sketches. The whole point of a sketchbook is that it
should be used for ideas, for trying things out – not
for paintings or drawings that could be framed.
Your sketchbook should take away any pressure of
having to 'perform'. With smooth cartridge paper
such a sketchbook is suitable for pen and pencil
drawing and for limited watercolour. Cartridge
paper is not as forgiving as watercolour paper and
washes must be applied simply and very wet, then
left alone, something we should be doing anyway
on watercolour paper. Even with only a little overworking, cartridge paper will quickly be destroyed.

I have several sketchbooks on the go at any one
time. Apart from the one in the car, I will always
put one in my pocket when going for a walk. You
never know when you will see a potential subject.

Sketchbooks are available in many different
sizes and aspects. I prefer A5 (148 x 210mm/
6 x 8¼in) size in both portrait and landscape.
These are small enough to fit in a large pocket,
but, with the portrait shape, I can get a bigger
sheet if I need it by working across the stitched
divide. A spring clip is a very useful
addition when sketching. You can only
hold one side of the sketchbook
as your other hand will be taken
up with your pencil or brush.
The spring clip is a simple way
of stopping the wind lifting the
paper on the other side.

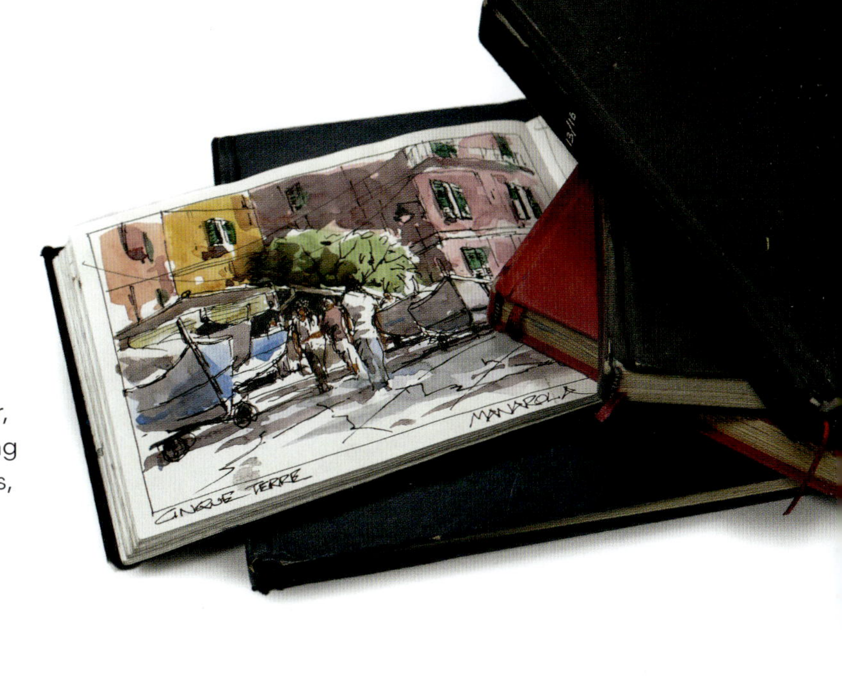

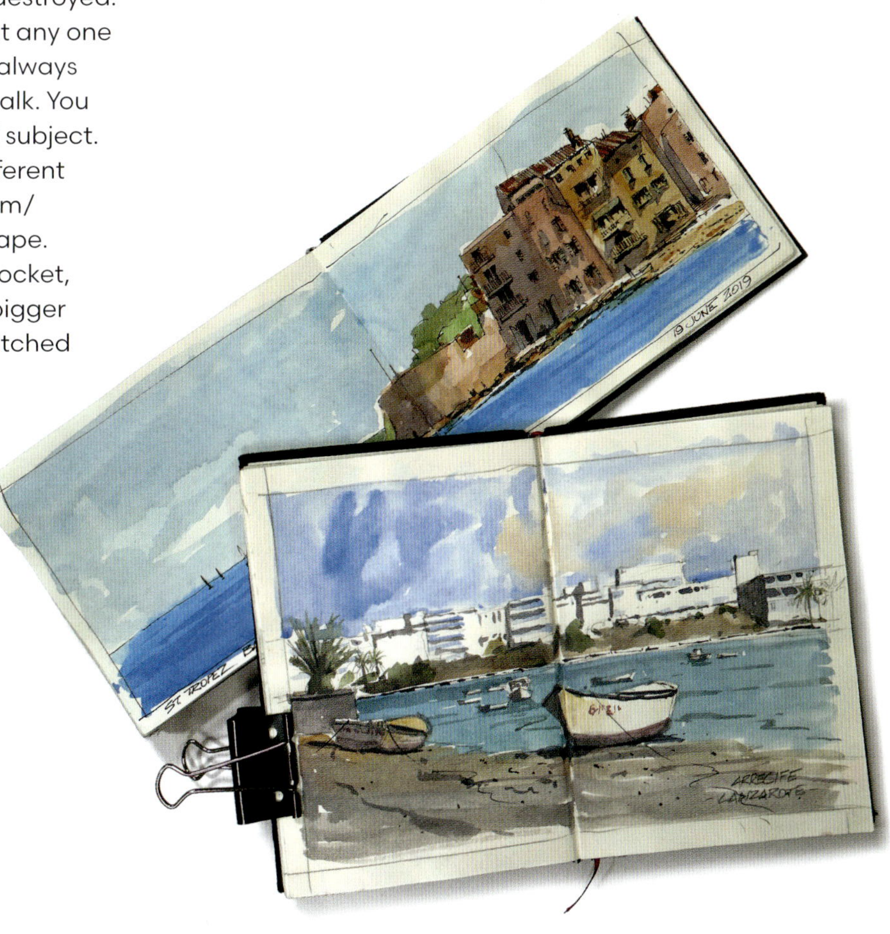

EASELS

I have yet to find a painting easel that is perfect for plein air. Dedicated painting easels can be heavy, cumbersome or expensive and sometimes all three. Lighter versions are available, but these can be time consuming to put together and are often unsteady in even the lightest wind. Camera tripods on the other hand are generally less expensive, more stable, compact when folded and quick to set up. The good news is that converting a tripod to a painting easel is pretty straightforward.

There are two types of camera tripod, one where the easel screws directly to the camera, and another (which I would recommend) that has a separate tripod plate that is designed to fix to the camera with the plate in turn fixing to a special quick connector on the tripod. Here you will find instructions to convert the second of these tripods. You will still be able to use your tripod for a camera but it would be better to purchase a second tripod plate. These can usually be found on auction sites and in camera shops.

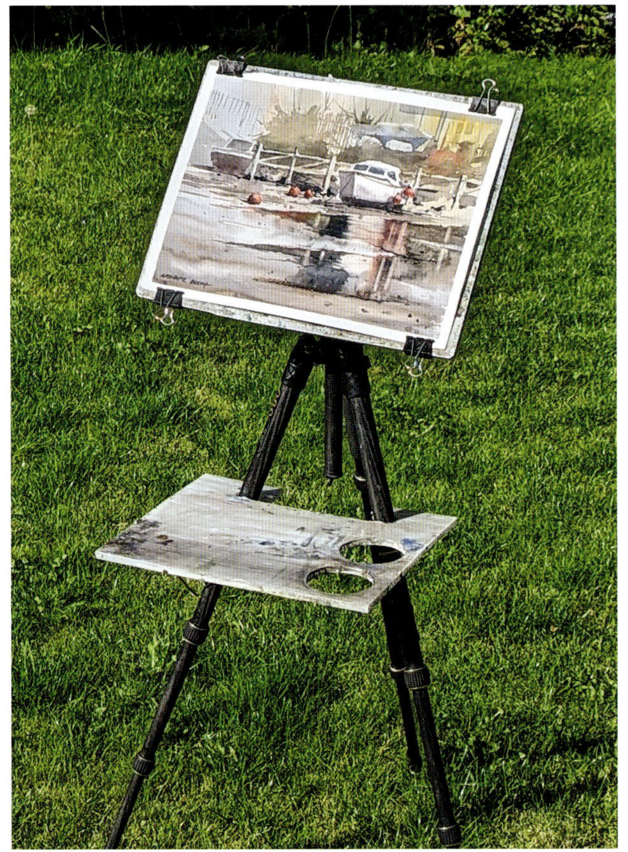

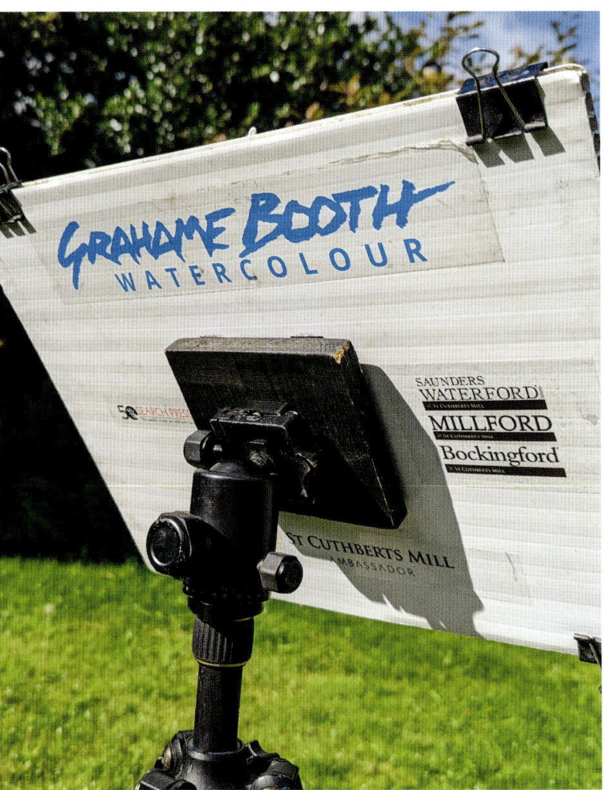

My easel is made from an adapted camera tripod and I use it for everything outside my studio, including demonstrations to art clubs. There is a vast range of adjustment of both height and tilt – much greater than that offered by a dedicated artist's easel.

Adapting a photographic tripod

A tripod plate would usually be screwed to your camera and then slotted into the tripod. Instead I have removed the camera screw and screwed the tripod plate to a block of wood 11.5cm (4½in) square and about 15mm (½in) thick (A). These sizes are not absolute. The size specified may seem quite small but it easily holds my half-sheet lightweight board, even in windy conditions. In very windy conditions the easel can blow over, but I have never had the board blow off the wood block. Actually, if it is that windy, the local coffee shop might be a better bet!

On the other side of the block of wood, I have stuck four 'hooked' strips of hook-and-loop tape, reinforced with staples. The block of wood will now fit to your tripod to take your painting board.

My painting board is made from lightweight corrugated polypropylene sheet 10mm (½in) thick. In the UK this is known by names such as Correx® and Corriboard® and, in the US, Cor-X®. If you have trouble obtaining this material, try your local printer as the same materials are used to print outdoor signs. On this quarter sheet board I stick two 'loop' strips of hook-and-loop tape (three for a half sheet board). This will allow it to fix securely to my wooden block (see below image, opposite).

An optional tray can be made from the same material – I fitted mine around the back of the legs and reinforced it with a wire coat hanger (C). The wire passes through one of the corrugations and the ends of the wire are bent and inserted into a small hole drilled in each of the front legs. Make sure the legs are extended before you drill! The tray is also quarter-sheet size, made to fit in my bag.

Most tripods have a hook at the bottom of the centre pole. As well as keeping my painting bag off the ground, this adds valuable extra stability, preventing all but the strongest gust of wind threatening to blow everything over.

A

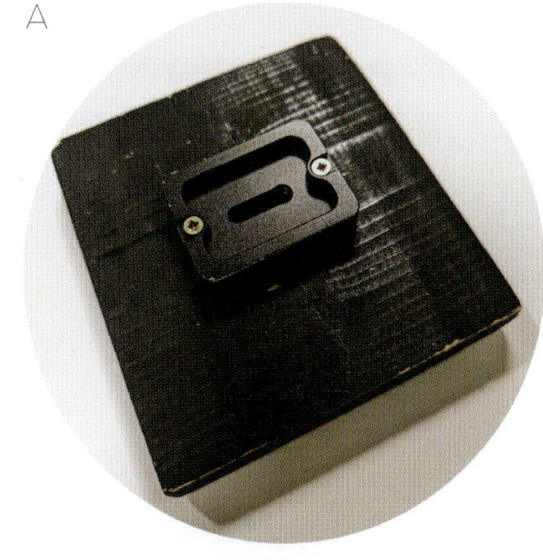

B

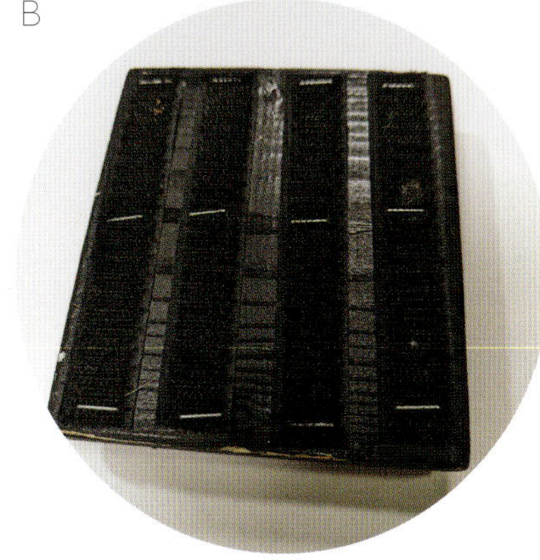

C

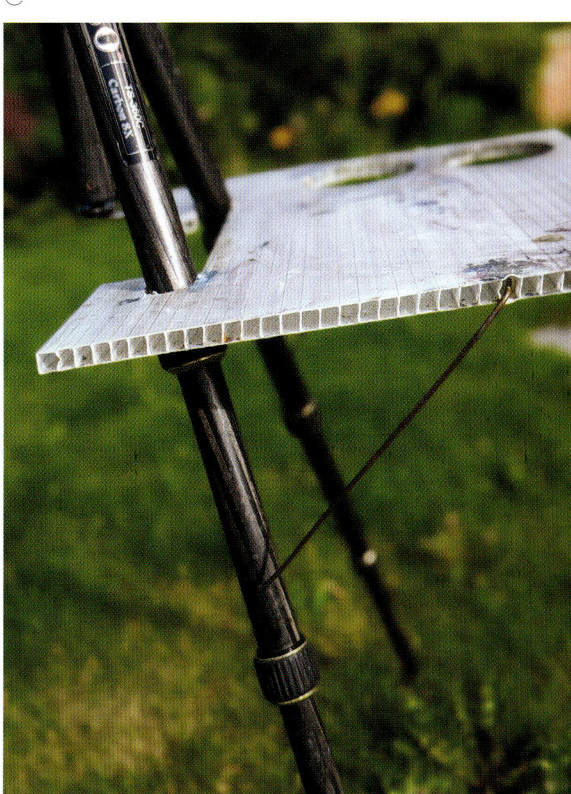

PRACTICAL CONSIDERATIONS

PLEIN AIR PAINTING SHOULD BE FUN and if there is one thing that gets in the way of that, it is poor organization, usually combined with too much equipment. I have seen painters spend more time dealing with poor planning than they spend painting; with watercolour as your medium it is important that everything is well planned and that your tools are conveniently to hand. Searching for a missing brush could spell disaster at a critical time in the painting!

Travelling light

Very often, plein air painting is synonymous with travel. Space won't be an issue if you are travelling by car, although I still believe it is good practice to pack economically. Flying, on the other hand, demands great care in your choice of equipment if you are to avoid hefty baggage charges. If your equipment is travelling in the hold, then you have no restrictions on what you can take, but with carry on baggage a little more thought is needed. Check restrictions before you fly. At the time of going to press, tubes of paint are classed as liquids and so must fit in the clear plastic bag with your toiletries (another reason to use a limited palette).

If you have a metal paintbox, it is a good idea to remove this from your bag when going through security. The scanners often cannot identify a metal paintbox, and, if it stays in your bag, there is a good chance it will be shunted off into the dreaded manual search lane. When travelling by air I always allow the paint in my palette to air dry for a couple of hours beforehand so that the paint will not run when my bag is inevitably laid on its side at some point, and for this reason I always wait until I reach my destination before refilling my paint wells. A tripod or easel is also permitted in hand baggage.

Staying safe

It is important to pick a safe place to paint. Setting up in a busy street could be a problem if you get in the way of pedestrians or traffic, and take care when setting up at the coast – you may not notice the incoming tide (I have ended up with wet feet on more than one occasion!). The countryside can pose risks too. Large farm animals can be threatening even if they are only curious. I recall painting by myself in the US countryside and suddenly remembering that someone had mentioned bears…

Appropriate clothing

Bear in mind that you'll be standing or sitting relatively still, and in cold conditions you can become chilled without realizing it. On one occasion, I was painting in cold weather and suddenly began to shiver uncontrollably. I was so caught up in my painting that I hadn't noticed how cold I was getting, so do take occasional breaks and walk around a little. Rechargeable hand warmers are available, and I have also tried wearing gloves in cold weather, but they just don't feel right to me as I don't feel I have the same control.

In hot conditions we have the opposite problem. I always advise setting up to paint in a shady area. Standing or sitting in the full sun can easily cause overheating and sunburn, and, if the sun is shining on your paper, the glare can make it very difficult to judge tonal differences. I prefer to wear a hat with a brim in all conditions. It really does help to deal with any glare, even in the winter.

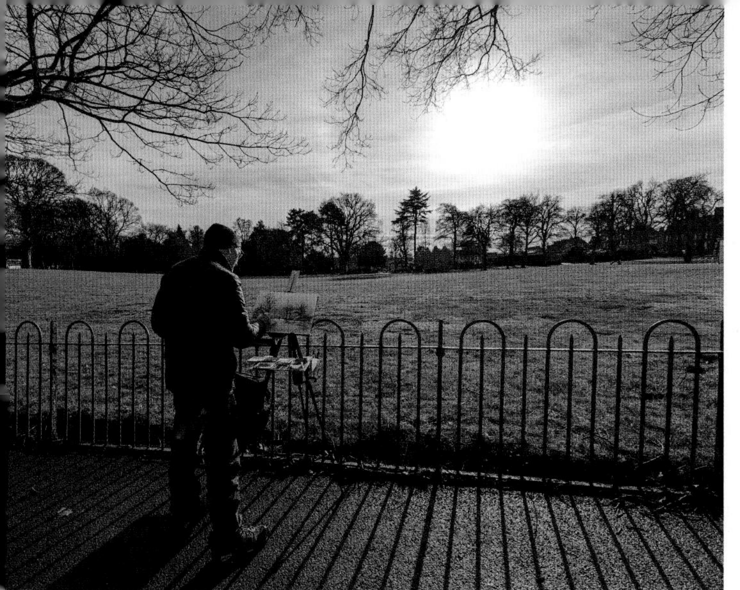

'WATERCOLOUR IS MAKING THE BEST OF AN EMERGENCY.' – *John Singer Sargent*

Onlookers

I have been interrupted by swimmers in their costumes in midwinter and by horse riders passing by (see page 124); my view of a subject has, at various times, been blocked by drivers of cars, coaches, trucks and boats.

The thought of onlookers can be off-putting; some painters don't even try plein air painting because they're worried about comments from passers-by. I can honestly say that in all my years of outdoor painting, even when a beginner, I have only ever received kind words (... sometimes perplexing, but always kind). Many times I have been asked, 'What is it you're painting?' (make of that what you will), and there are always the old chestnuts: 'My brother is a painter and he's very good' and 'It must be a lovely relaxing hobby'. When someone mentions relaxation I know they have never painted!

Take a friend

If passers-by concern you, there are some things you can try. The best option is to paint with a like-minded group. It doesn't have to be anything formal, even a casual get-together with a painting friend or two, but painting with other people definitely reduces the anxiety that can be felt when alone. Start with subjects that are relatively remote, or squeeze yourself against a wall or corner. The middle of a muddy field is unlikely to garner many onlookers. And the best piece of advice I have: put a hat on the ground with a few coins in it! That should keep them away!

Changing light

One of the biggest issues with outdoor painting is the moving sun and this really will dramatically alter your subject. Many times I have walked past a particular subject and barely noticed it, yet when it is perfectly lit by the sun it is completely transformed. The problem of course is that when painting outdoors the light is changing continuously, so before beginning a painting I try to predict how the sun will make it look in around an hour. If I judge that it won't be perfectly lit then, I'll either give it more time if I'm early or come back another time if I'm too late. One thing you can't do is 'follow the sun'. At some point, you have to settle on your sun and shadows and stick to them.

The weather

I always prefer painting in sunny weather simply because the light and shade make it much easier to suggest three dimensions. On the other hand, cloudy conditions do offer a more predictable light and can often be more dramatic.

A stormy sky will always beat a flat blue sky for interest. Rainy days can have very interesting light created from reflections, but you must find somewhere to protect your painting from the rain.

Transporting your work home

Unlike for our oil painting colleagues, transport of finished paintings isn't an issue for us. Usually a completed painting will be dry in minutes, although care will be needed on very humid and damp days, when drying times will be very considerably lengthened in the open air.

PLEIN AIR PAINTING IN PRACTICE

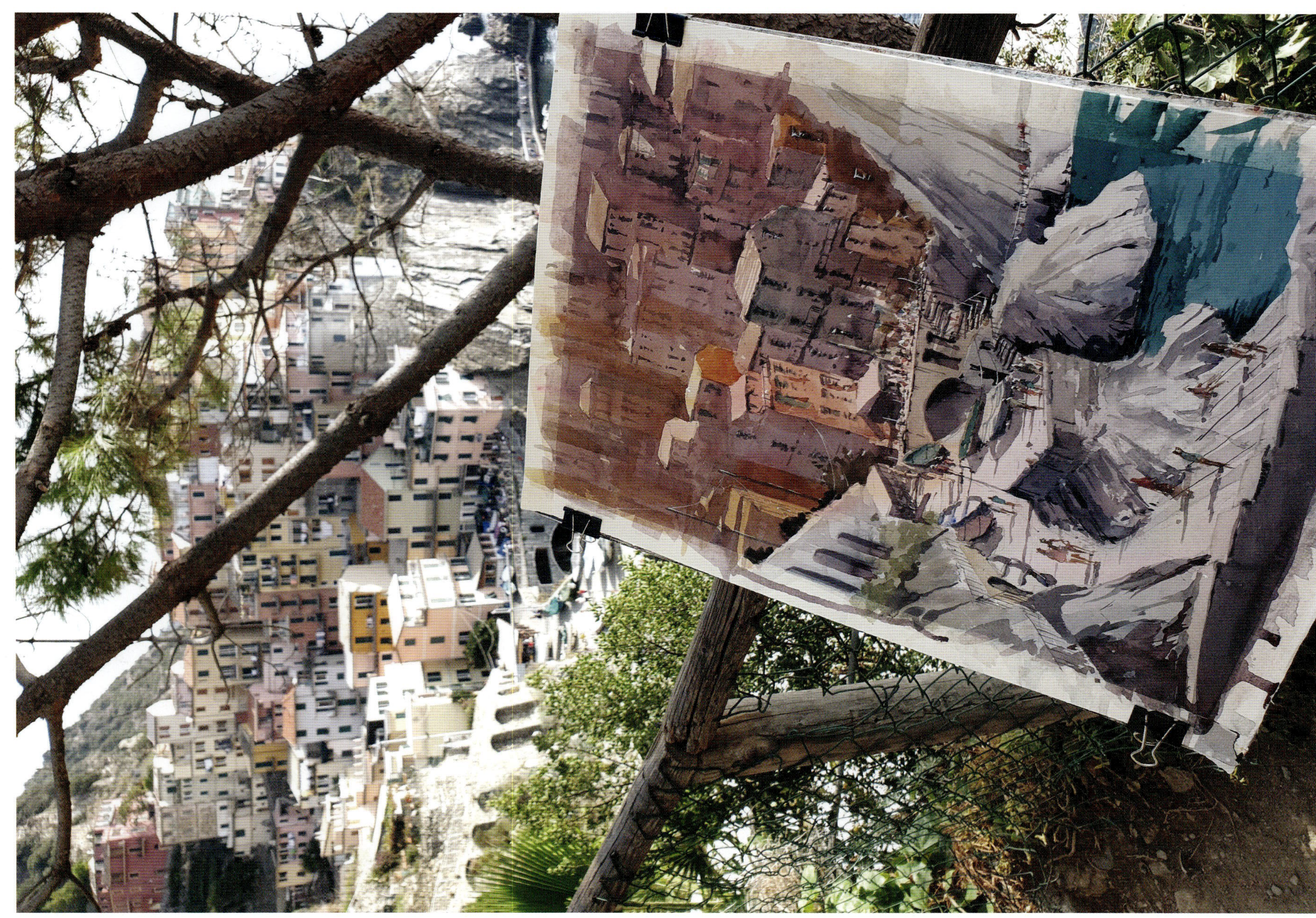

CHOOSING A SUBJECT

PLEIN AIR PAINTING IS VERY different from using a photograph. When you are outside there are no boundaries to what you see. You essentially have 360° of possibilities all around you, so the first job is to narrow down your viewpoint. You will probably have already considered a rough subject, but, before making a final decision, have a good look around. When you start thinking about possibilities you may find more potential with a slightly different viewpoint. This is one of the major advantages of painting outside. With a photograph you're restricted to what is there. I am sure, like me, there will have been times that you have thought, 'If only I had taken that photograph from a slightly different angle…' Outside, you don't have that restriction – so take advantage of it.

This is perhaps 160° of the 360° available to you when painting outdoors. This is why a viewfinder can be so useful (see page 38).

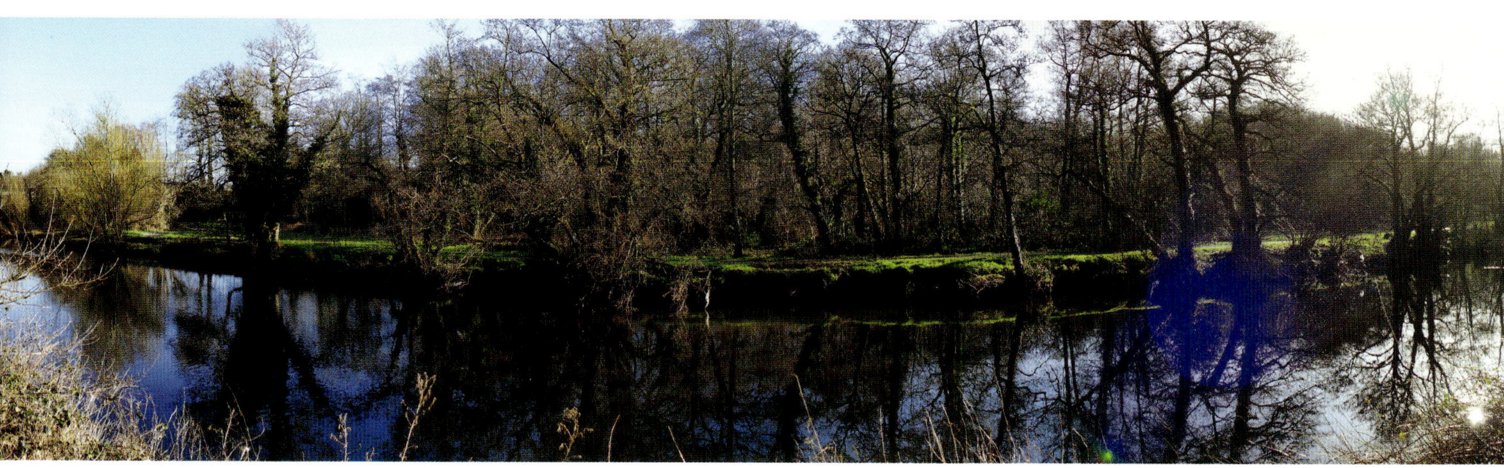

NARROWING DOWN A VIEWPOINT FROM 360°

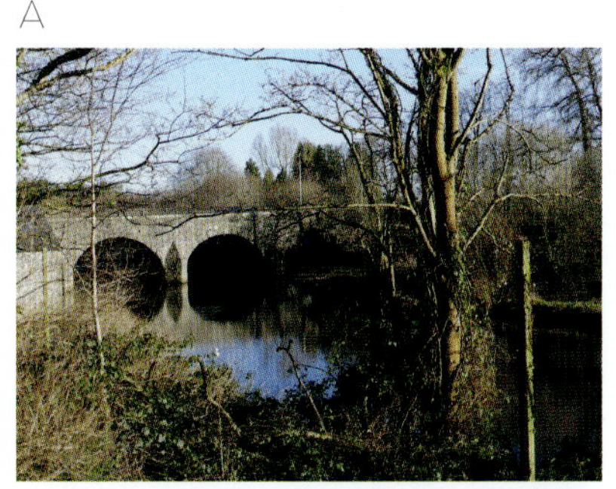

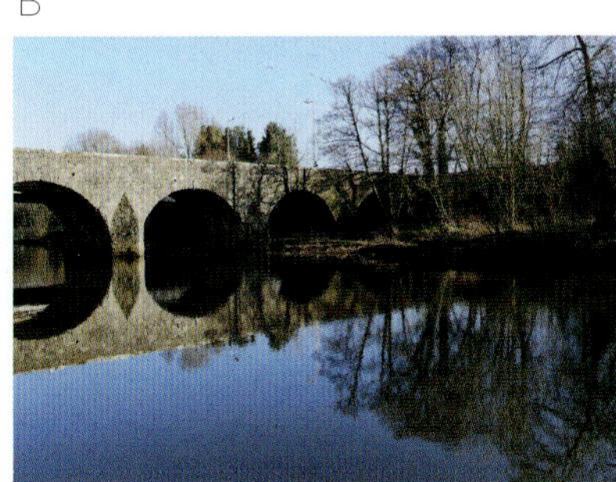

Before I arrived, I thought the bridge would be a good choice for a subject, and although I had a look from several different places (two of them are shown here – A and B) none of them really filled me with enthusiasm on the day.

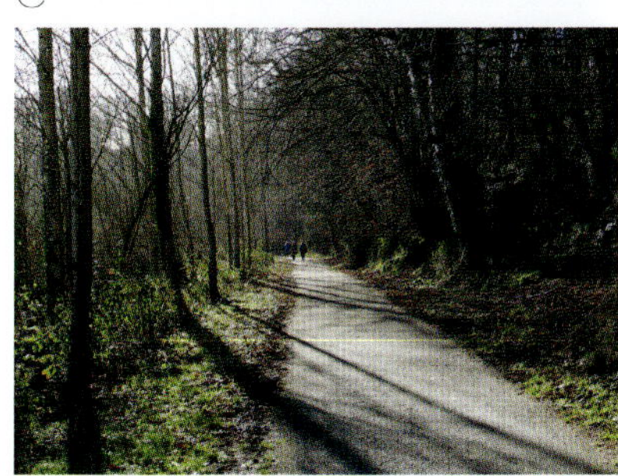

Turning slightly away from the river produced this perfectly presentable subject (C). At the risk of looking as though you are dancing, always take a few steps forward, a few steps back, a couple to either side and turn right round!

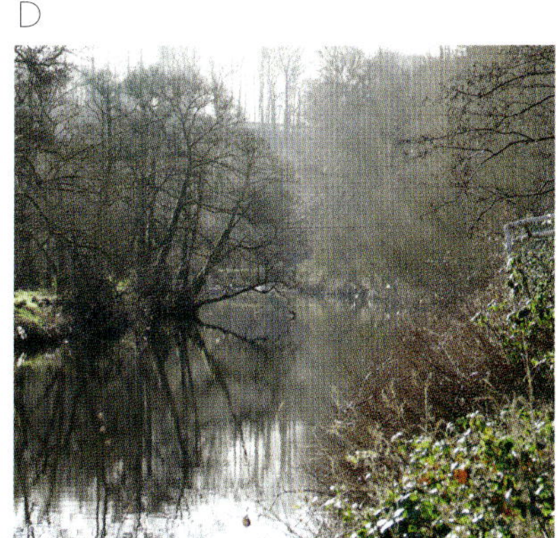

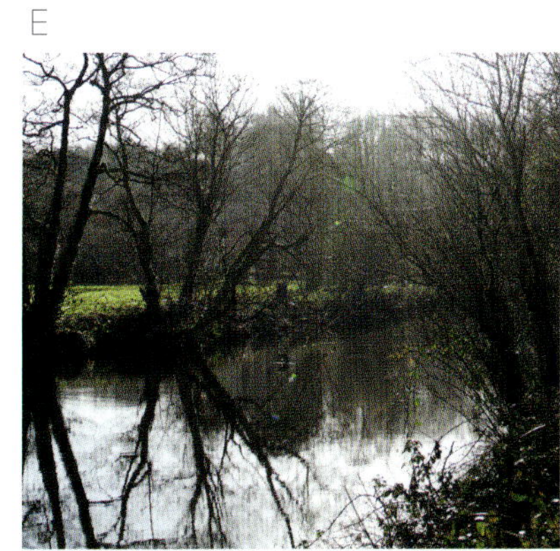

At the other end of my panorama the backlighting of the trees and river looked rather nice. As you can see, the same subject from varying positions looks quite different (D and E) – this perfectly illustrates the problem with photographs, even when plenty are taken.

Fortunately on the day I didn't have to worry about less than perfect photographs and was able to position myself *almost* exactly where I wanted to be... (The *perfect* position would have been slightly too near the soft bank, and river water in January is rather cold!)

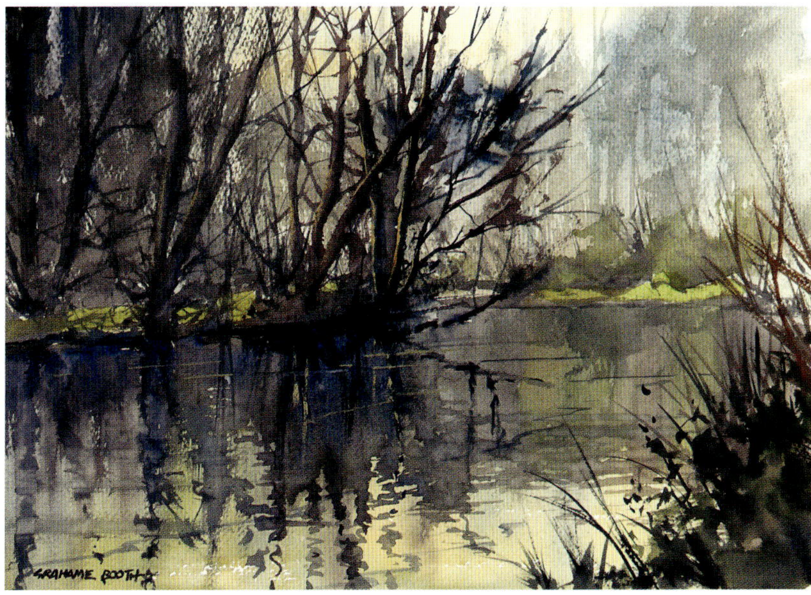

CHANGING PERSPECTIVE

When you have found your potential subject, walk a little to the left or right and have another look. It is remarkable how much this can change things. Likewise, a lower or higher viewpoint will also give you different options. Even more importantly, walk a little closer to or further away from the subject if you can. This does not just change the size of the objects in front of you, it changes the relative sizes between them: it changes the perspective. If you are looking at a building in the distance with a tree halfway, walking towards the tree will gradually make it appear larger in relation to the building.

A

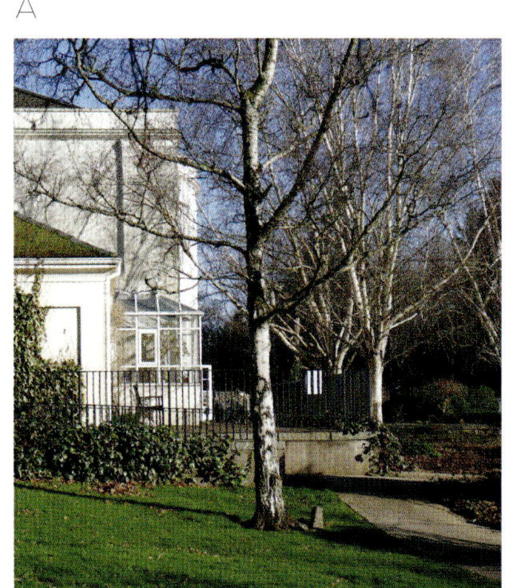

B

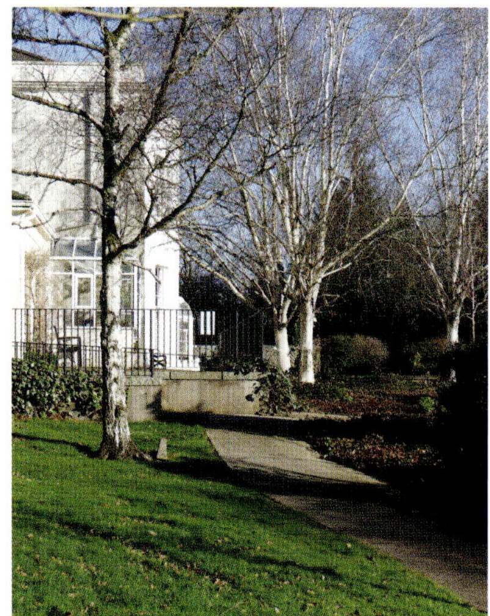

For each of these photographs (A–D) I moved three steps to the right. You can see how the relative positions of the trees, path and house change dramatically. Never stick with the first painting spot you see. Walk around a little and you may just find something even better.

C

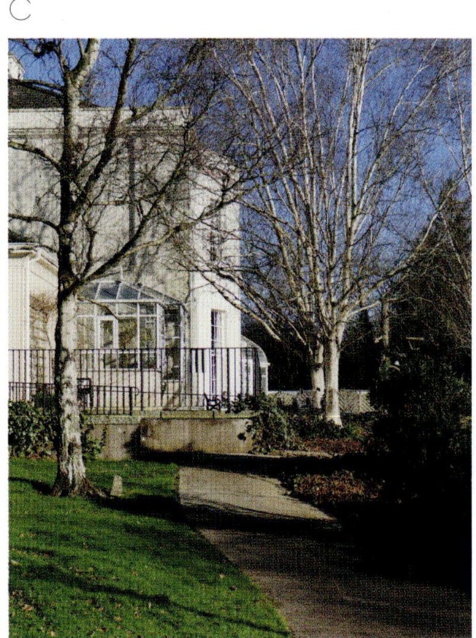

D

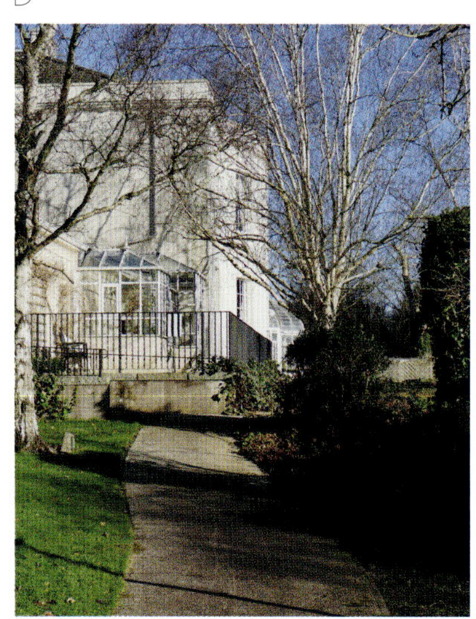

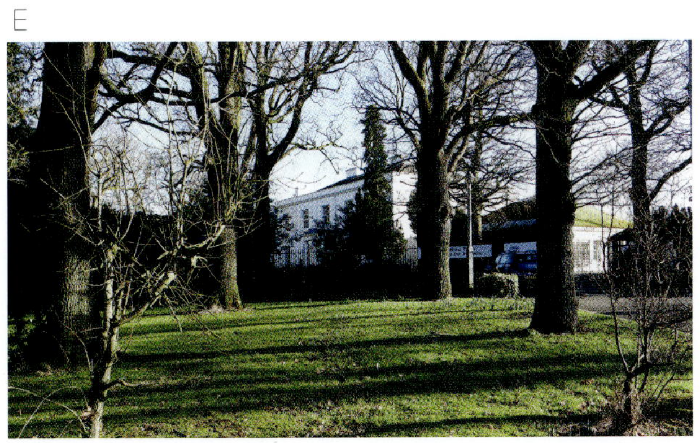

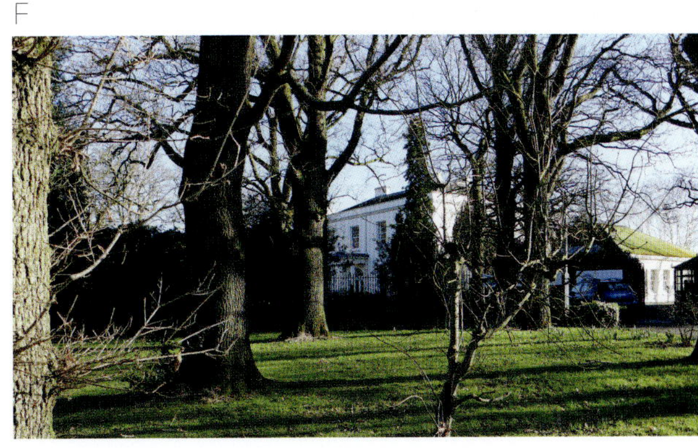

At first glance, photograph E might look like a reasonable viewpoint from which to paint the building and trees, but consider how symmetrical the trees are. They are almost perfectly spaced – something best avoided. Moving just a couple of steps to the side keeps the appearance of the building much the same but dramatically changes the arrangement of the trees, creating much more interest (F).

These four photographs show the effect of moving closer to a subject. Usually when using a camera we tend to just zoom in if we want to get closer, but this is not the same thing as actually moving closer. Moving closer changes the perspective of the elements in the subject. As I get closer to the large tree on the left, from G to J, you can see how the distant trees appear to become smaller and further away in relation to the large tree. In image G, the trees all appear quite flat and it is difficult to pick out the different planes (the major problem with photographs). Notice how in image J there is a much better feeling of depth, even on the flat photograph. As we move closer to the subject the relative distances between the planes increases and becomes more obvious.

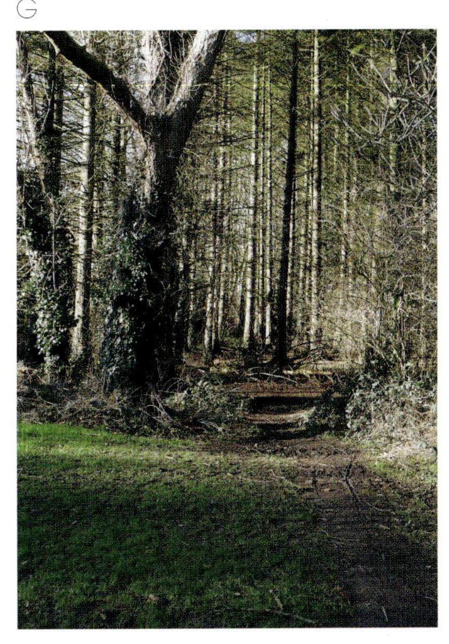

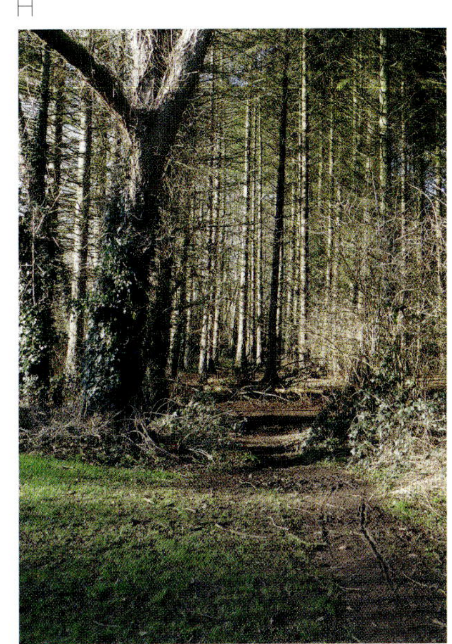

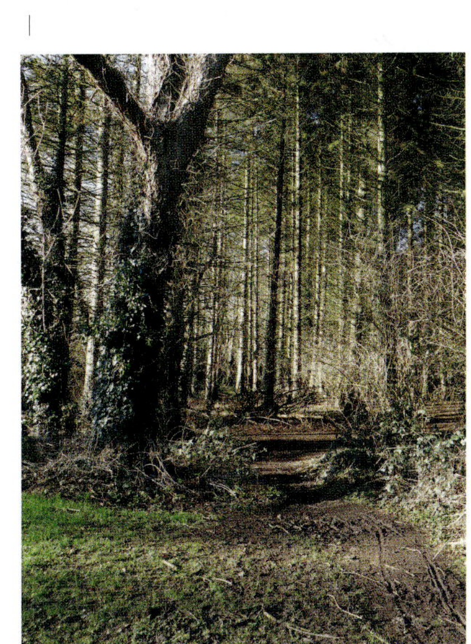

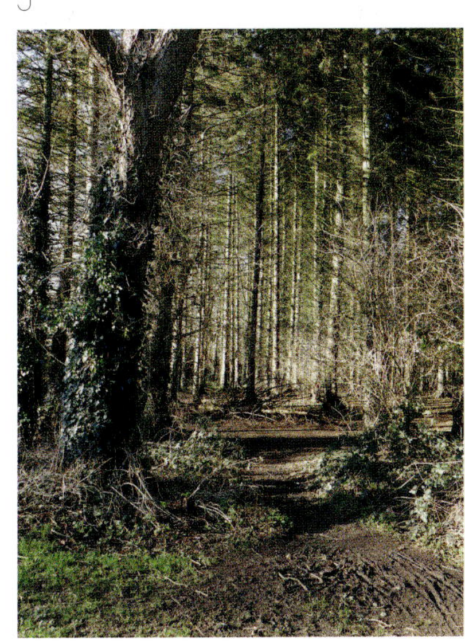

COMPOSITION

Once you decide on your viewing position, you need to create the boundaries to your subject so that they match your paper size – using a **viewfinder** will help with this. You can purchase viewfinders with various aspects from your local art shop but you can easily make one from a piece of cardboard. Simply cut out a window with the same relative aspect (length x width) as the paper you use (see right). Even simpler, you can use your hands. With any of these methods, what the viewfinder does is to create boundaries. By moving the viewfinder around and in and out you will be able to find appropriate boundaries for a painting. This is where composition comes in. What you should be doing is looking to find a pleasing arrangement of shapes. That is composition at its simplest.

An excellent aid for composition is the **rule of thirds**. This states that if you divide your paper into thirds horizontally and vertically, then the rough crossing point of these lines is a good place for the major focus of your painting. You don't need to be entirely accurate, though. Just avoid having anything important at the extreme edges of your paper or halfway vertically or horizontally.

Don't forget about **depth**. Although our paper is flat, the illusion of depth is made much easier if something is leading the eye into the paper. Obvious things are roads, rivers and pathways; in short, something that is obviously getting smaller as it recedes. Less obvious but equally useful could be trees or buildings, becoming smaller as they move into the distance.

Balance is something else to consider. Avoid compositions where everything of interest is in one small part of your paper. Much better to spread the interest around so that there is something to draw the eye beyond the obvious focus.

Remember how our brains see a subject. Although our field of vision is around 120°, we can only actually see strong definition within about 6°, so when you look at the focus of a subject it is only that area that you will see clearly. You will be aware of what is around it but you will not be able to see detail. This is the basis of choosing a focus or a focal area for your painting and giving that part the strongest definition.

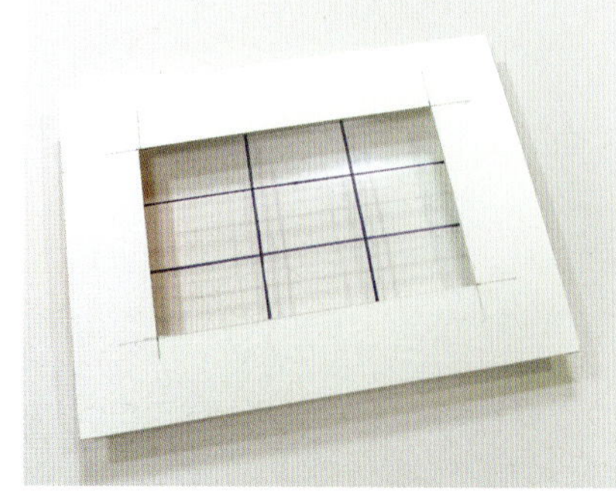

A viewfinder is very easy to make from a piece of mountcard. Up to 15 x 21cm (6 x 8¼in) is perfect. Any larger and you may find your arms are not long enough to enclose your subject! Rule a window with the same aspect as your painting paper (mine is roughly 4:3) and cut it out using a sharp craft knife (take care!). If you wish, you can add a transparent acetate window with rule of thirds lines drawn on it.

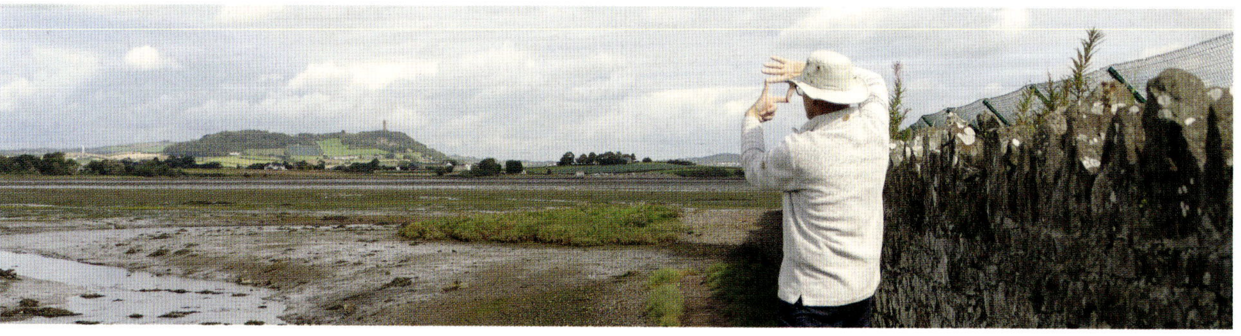

Using your hands works as well as any proprietary viewfinder. They don't take up space and there is no risk of leaving them at home!

TWEAKING YOUR SUBJECT

Once you have chosen your subject, don't be afraid to make changes to it. Paintings are not photographs: if you want an accurate representation of what is in front of you, use a camera. As painters, we should be creating paintings *based on* what is in front of us. You are free to leave things out or put things in and you can move things around to improve the **composition**. Never paint something just because it is there. If I am debating whether or not to include certain elements, the question I ask myself is: if it wasn't there in reality, would it be a good idea for me to add it? If the answer is yes, I keep it, and if the answer is no, I'll leave it out.

Feel free to paint parts of your painting with more or less **detail** than there may be in reality. And you can change **colours and tones**. Use this power wisely. As a representational painter you will want the painting to resemble the subject. Make too many changes and you are venturing into the world of abstraction. On the other hand, it is highly unlikely that anyone will ever be holding your painting up in front of the real subject, so don't be afraid to make changes for the good of the painting.

I hope I am not shattering any illusions here, but the perfect subject does not exist. I don't think I have ever painted a subject without making changes to it. Look instead for a subject that has interesting shapes or interesting colours or interesting tones. Tones are important, probably the most important aspect of your painting. When I choose a subject, I will generally look for interesting areas of light and dark. I really don't mind if it's a pretty cottage or an industrial building. Don't let reality stand in the way of a good painting.

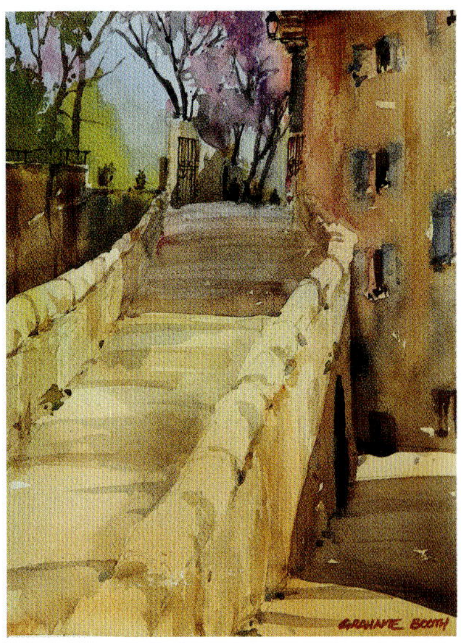

ENTRECASTEAUX, PROVENCE
28 x 38cm (11 x 15in),
Saunders Waterford CP 425gsm (200lb)

Don't be afraid to break the rules if it will help the painting. Here, I thought it might be interesting to keep the bright purples of the Judas trees right at the top, rather than on a third, in order to emphasize the steepness of the street.

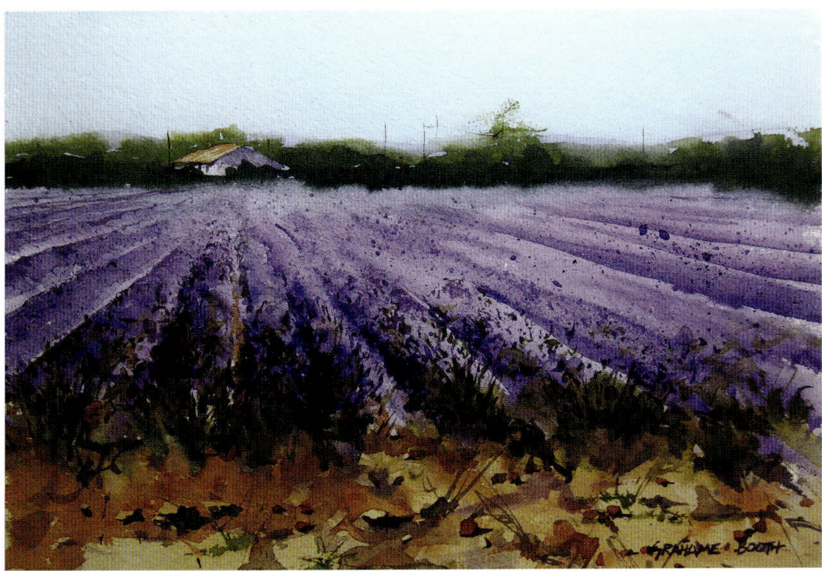

LAVENDER FIELD, PROVENCE
30 x 20cm (12 x 8in),
Saunders Waterford CP 425gsm (200lb)

The perfect subject doesn't exist... but some come close. I assumed one lavender field would be much like another, but if I remember correctly, this was the eleventh or twelfth I visited before everything was right: the angle of the sun and the direction of the lavender, together with the position of the trees and the building at the end of the field.

SKETCHING

THE DICTIONARY DEFINES SKETCHING AS making a 'rough drawing', but I like to stretch that a little to include the following: a preliminary drawing made before painting; drawing as an end in itself; and also quick and relatively simple paintings generally made in a sketchbook. Although applicable to studio work too, of course, your life as a plein air painter will be made very much easier if you have the ability to draw at least a reasonably accurate representation of your subject.

I have no natural ability to draw accurately. In art class at school I was consistently awarded C grades, which basically translated as 'turns up and doesn't cause disruption'! I vaguely remember being annoyed that my drawings didn't look anything like the proper artists' drawings in the class, but at that time science was my thing, so art was quickly dropped. I can state firmly and with complete conviction that drawing is a learnable skill. Some people will always have more of a flair for it than others but everyone can learn to draw accurately. I know that for certain because I am one of them.

If you can write your name or draw a tracing, then you can draw. Basic drawing skills require you to place the outlines of the different elements of your subject on the paper in the right place. With a tracing you don't need to think about where you are placing your lines, but when drawing from life you need to be able to work out where they need to go: you do this by measuring. You can easily measure the relative sizes, positions and proportions of the elements in your subject just by using your pencil. I have lost count of the number of students with an inaccurate drawing to whom I have said, 'Did you measure?', and they always reply, 'Erm... no'. If I don't measure, I will also produce an inaccurate drawing and I'm supposed to be a professional! So how do we go about this?

'I DON'T WANT TO SEE REALITY, I WANT TO SEE A BEAUTIFUL LIE.' *– Edgar Whitney*

SKETCHING DEMO

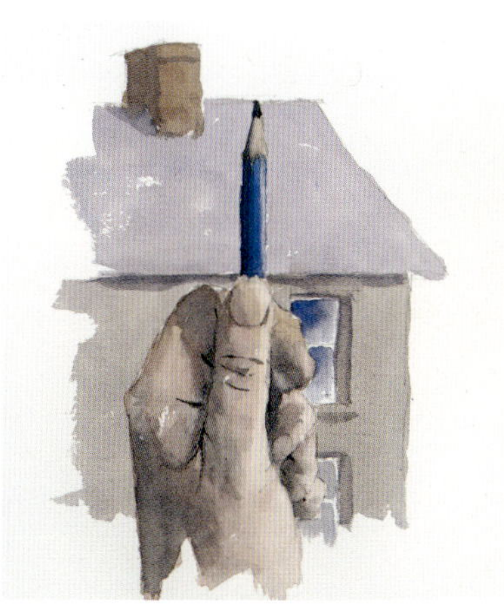

1. The measuring process is very simple. Hold your pencil at arm's length and move your arm so that the tip of your pencil is at one end of the object you wish to measure. Holding the pencil in that position, slide your thumb up or down the pencil so that the top of your thumb is at the other end of the object, in this example, the roof. Keep your thumb fixed and you can move the pencil all around your subject to see how different measurements compare with that first one. Keep your arm outstretched at all times so that your measurements are constant – if you bend your elbow the measurement may vary.

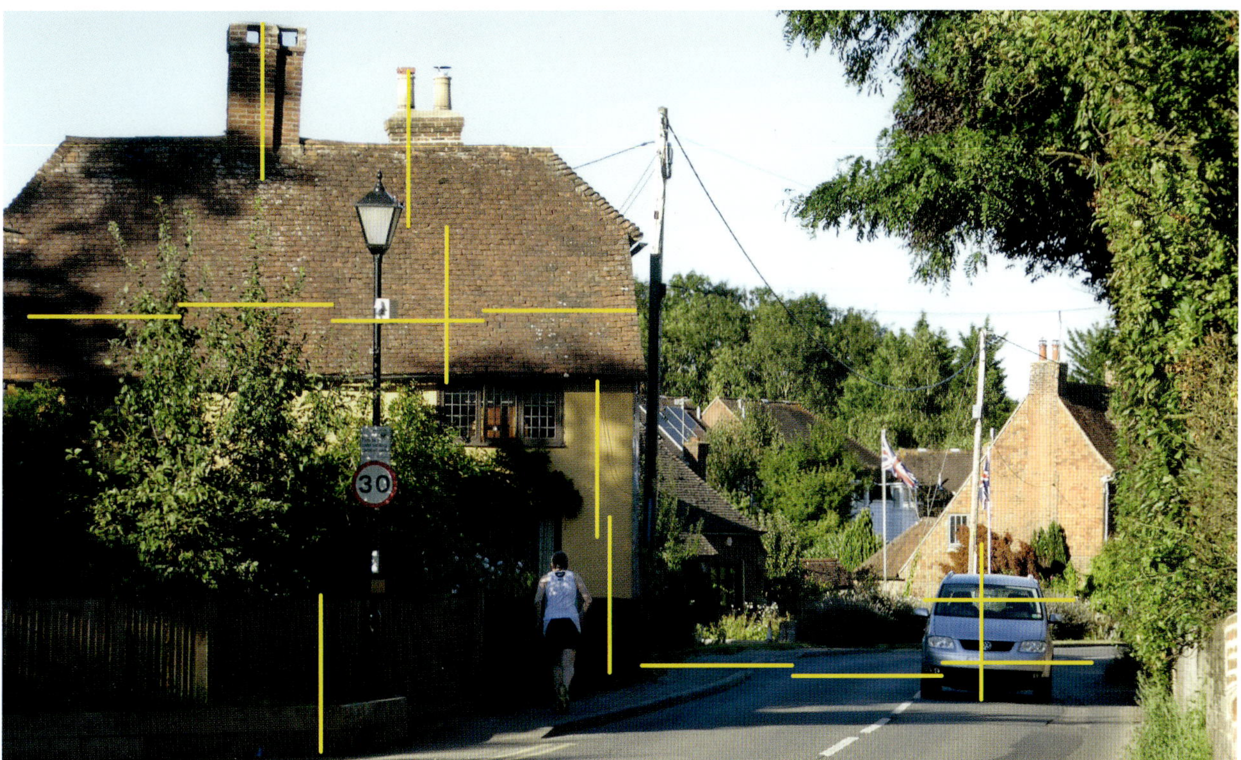

2. In order to draw accurately, we must place the different elements of the subject in the correct place on the paper. Initially it can help if you are using a viewfinder with the thirds drawn on it, as it gives you the relative positions and rough sizes of the different elements in your subject. Choose a dimension in your subject that is neither too long nor too short. I have chosen to use the top of the fence down to the road. I will use this measurement to work out the relative measurements of everything else.

3. Using that single measurement I can see, for example, that the height of the wall of the house is almost 2 'fences' high and the width of the house just over 4 fences. The roof, including the smaller chimney, is 2 fences high and the large chimney alone is almost 1 fence. I can now plot all the measurements on my paper. The more complex the subject, the more measurements you will need. Use the same measurement for everything so that any slight inaccuracies will not be compounded.

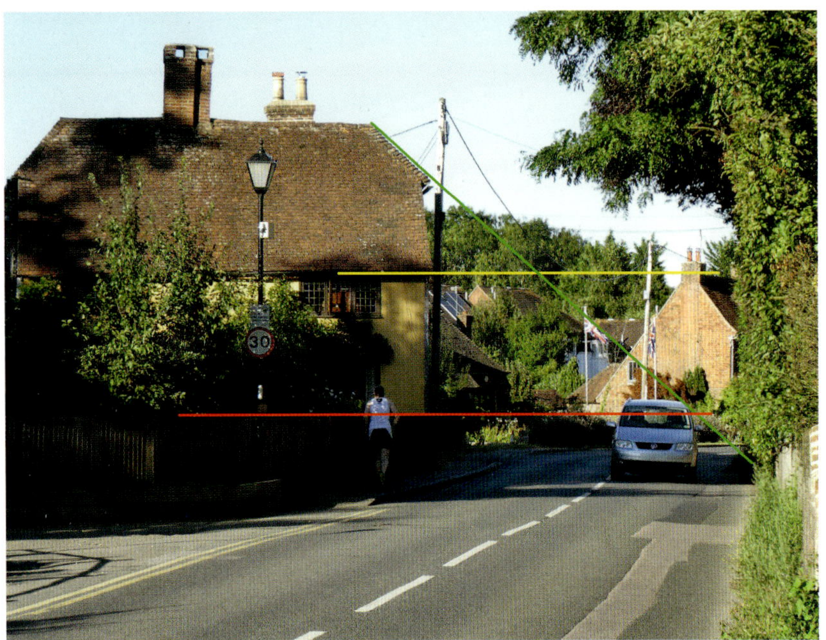

4. As well as measuring the relative sizes of the different elements you will need to know where to place them in relation to each other. This can be done using straight lines or any straight edge when outdoors. A piece of string pulled taut is perfect for this. Using horizontal lines I can see that the roof of the further house is roughly in line with the bottom of the roof of the main house (yellow). I can see that the top of the car is slightly above the fence top (red), and, if I draw a diagonal line (green) from the top right corner of the main roof to the far side of the road directly opposite the house, this gives me the angle of the roof gable, the position of the left side of the more distant house, the positions and sizes of the flagpoles and the position of the top right corner of the car.

To summarize

Using measuring and relative positioning you will be able to draw accurately. Please don't be alarmed if your head is spinning somewhat – mine certainly is – but I must stress that this process is harder to explain than to actually do. Measuring will rapidly become second nature and you will find you no longer need to measure as much... although even with my 40 years' experience I will still find myself measuring something in everything subject I draw.

SKETCHING TIPS

When drawing, begin with the large elements. There is no point starting with details, only to eventually find you have started drawing too large or too small. If you start with just the outline of the large elements, any mistakes will be quickly noticed. Once you have the large elements in place, then just gradually work down in size to complete the drawing.

When drawing on watercolour paper before painting there is no need to get too detailed or to think about shading. For a standalone drawing, however, it's entirely up to you how much detail you use and it will be important to include shading to indicate the lighting on the subject. You won't always have the time to do a complete painting outside, but sketching outside and using your sketch as the basis for a painting in the studio is the next best thing.

When time is short

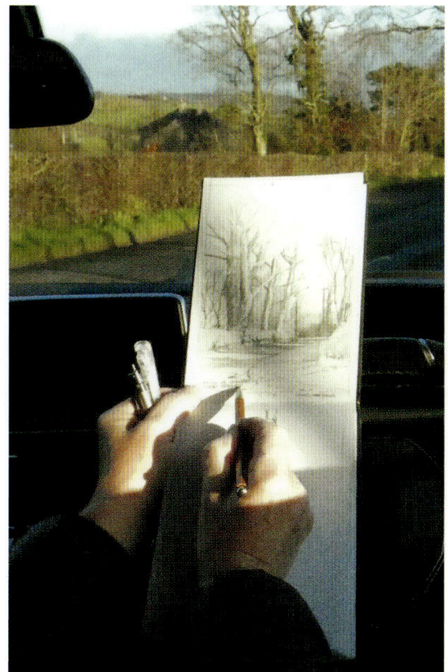

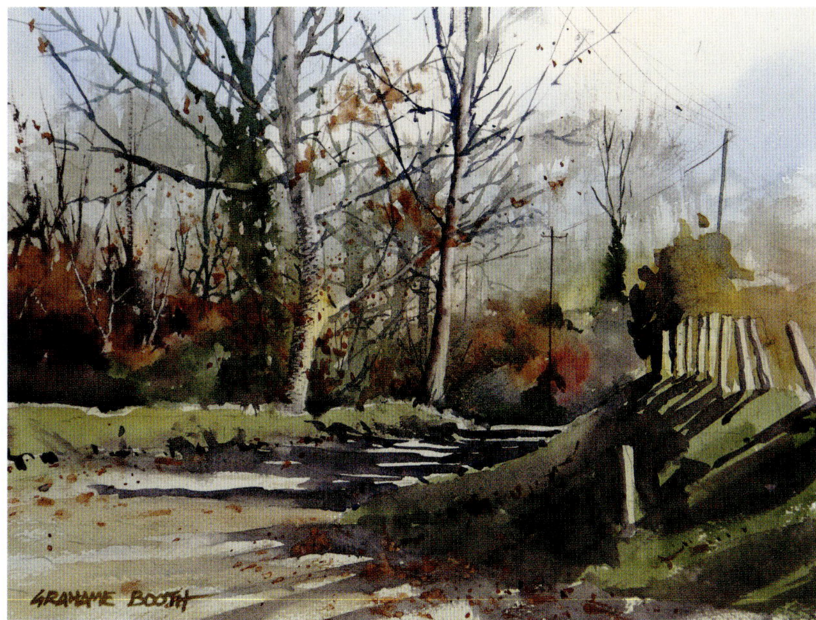

You can sketch from a car in all weathers, and even if you don't have time to do a painting, a plein air sketch is the next best thing (above left). Just as with a painting, the sketch will record your feelings about the subject, something a photograph can never do. Take a photograph by all means, but use it only to get information – maybe to check inaccuracies in your drawing or to be reminded of the rough colours. Using your plein air sketch as the basis for your studio painting will allow you to experience at least some of the plein air benefits. The studio painting (above right) was painted using the pencil sketch as my main resource. I believe I always paint more loosely when using a plein air sketch.

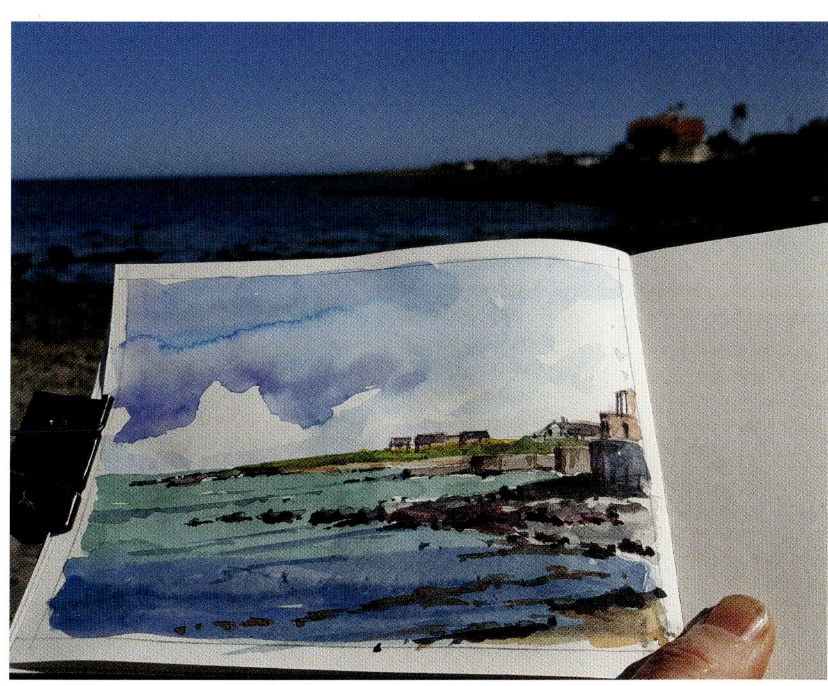

You will not always have time for a full painting session outdoors but cartridge paper in a sketchbook will take simple washes. I spent an enjoyable half hour painting this coastal subject. It is always much more relaxing using a sketchbook, as it avoids the pressure of producing a 'painting'. Painting on cartridge paper is perfectly possible, but too many brushstrokes will result in the paper becoming degraded. Keep it simple and you will be rewarded with very clean, fresh washes.

PEN AND WASH

Pen and wash is a medium that could have been invented for plein air painting and one that has been taken to heart by the worldwide urban sketching movement. As the name suggests, pen and wash consists of a pen drawing followed by watercolour washes. The pen drawing must be completed with waterproof ink so that the subsequent washes do not smudge the lines. Although watercolour is used, the approach is quite different. In traditional watercolour, we show the edge of an object by a change in tonal value, but in pen and wash the edges are shown as lines.

In traditional watercolour, when the sketch is completed the real work is just beginning, but in pen and wash the drawing itself is arguably the most important part, with the washes really just to decorate the line work. That said, pen and wash is a great way to loosen up your approach to watercolour as well as being good drawing practice, so it's important to include it here.

Tools

Disposable pens are extremely convenient to use for pen and wash. Just make sure that the ink is waterproof and fade-proof when dry. This is usually stated on the pen barrel.

Indian ink is a really rich black and a lovely ink to use, but it can only be used with a dip pen and so is not very convenient for plein air. Using Indian ink with a fountain pen will quickly clog it and ruin the pen but there are now inks available for fountain pens that dry waterproof on paper and don't ruin the pen. They are not quite as black as Indian ink and they don't have that lovely slight sheen from the shellac, but many painters prefer the feel of a metal nib on the paper, so, if this is you, consider investigating this option.

Although I always stand when painting, I usually sit when using pen and wash; indeed, often my subjects will be dictated by the presence of a suitable seat. These bollards seemed to meet my requirements for a suitable perch, but hard concrete becomes increasingly uncomfortable after a few minutes (see image A, below)! Very compact flat cushions can be purchased from outdoor activities shops but of course I had forgotten mine. See the finished painting, B.

A

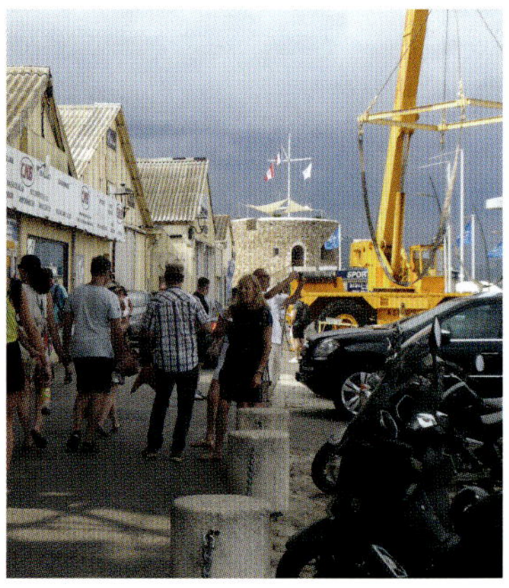

B

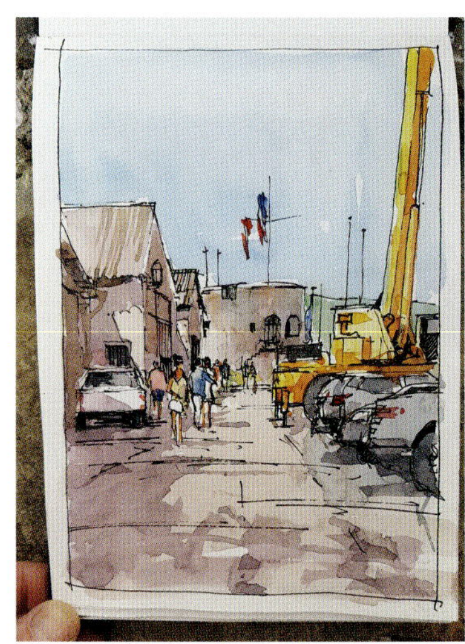

Clockwise from top left, all worked in a
cartridge paper sketchbook:

TAYNTON, COTSWOLDS **15 x 21cm (6 x 8¼in)**;
CARTAGENA, SPAIN **15 x 21cm (6 x 8¼in)**;
ST. TROPEZ HARBOUR **15 x 42cm (6 x 16½in)**.

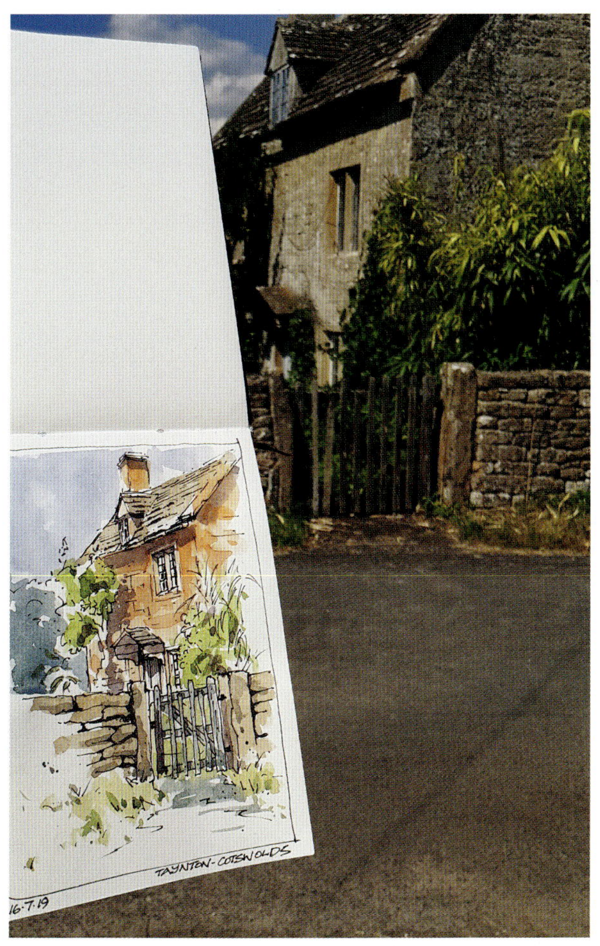

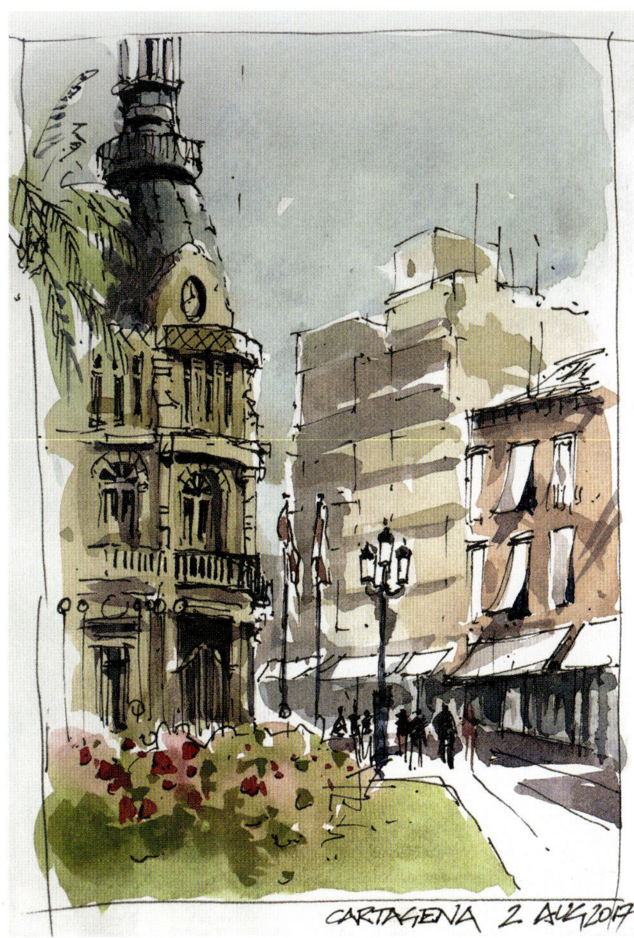

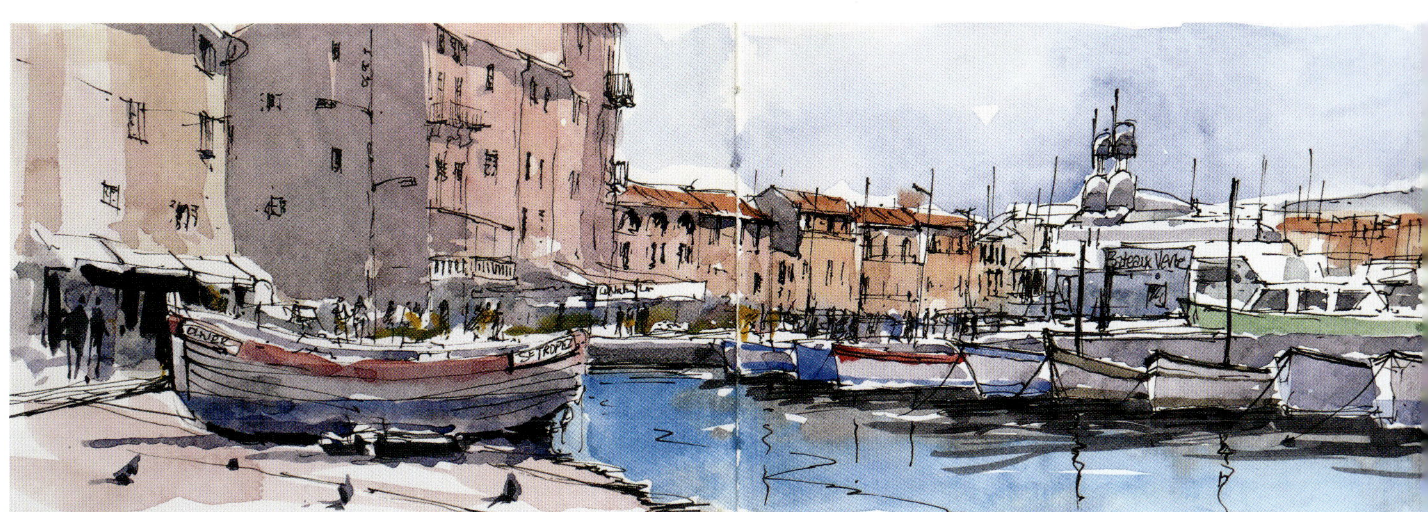

Pen and wash demo

This subject is an old spinning mill, now converted into apartments.
The mill owners were the Andrews family, the best known of whom is
probably Thomas Andrews who preferred shipbuilding to spinning.
Not a good choice: he designed the *Titanic* and perished on its
maiden voyage. Anyway, I digress – on with the demonstration.

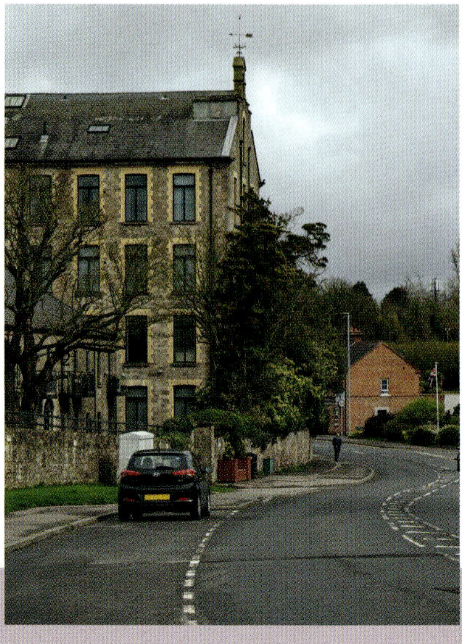

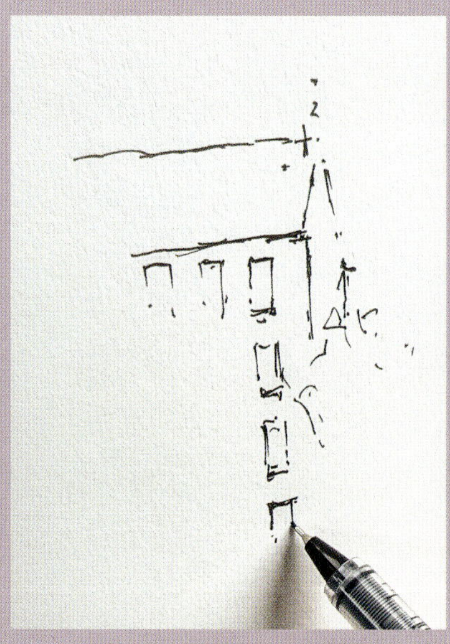

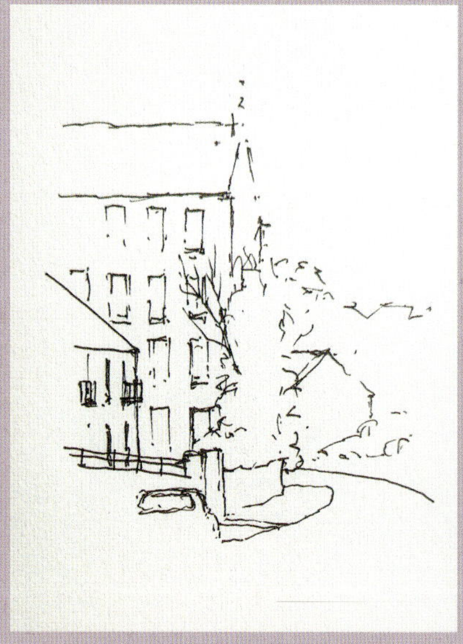

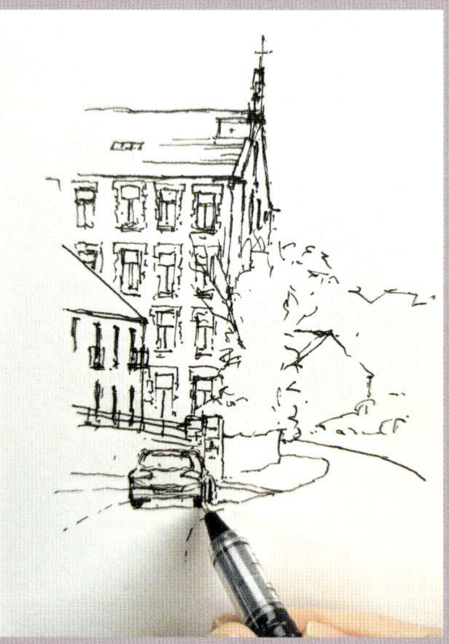

1. I prefer to paint pen and
wash as a vignette: a painting
that stops short of the edges
of the paper. I feel a vignette
adds to the sketchy nature of
the medium. The simplest way
to create a vignette is to begin
the drawing with whatever is in
the centre, then simply to work
outwards a suitable distance
and stop.

2. As with all drawings, I avoid
detail until I am satisfied that
I have got the sizes of the subject
elements correct. I also draw
directly with my pen. Obviously
mistakes will happen but I take
care to avoid anything too
terrible. Many painters prefer
to use a pencil for the drawing
and then to draw over the lines
with their pen, but I feel this can
lead to a stilted result. If you
work this way, I would suggest
drawing with the pen very
quickly to help retain some
of the spontaneity.

3. Once the essential elements
are there I start to add detail.
In a pure watercolour I will
always keep the detail to a
minimum, but in a pen and
wash, as the drawing is the
structure of the painting, there
really can't be too much detail.

'I DON'T PAINT THINGS, I ONLY PAINT THE DIFFERENCE BETWEEN THINGS.'
– Henri Matisse

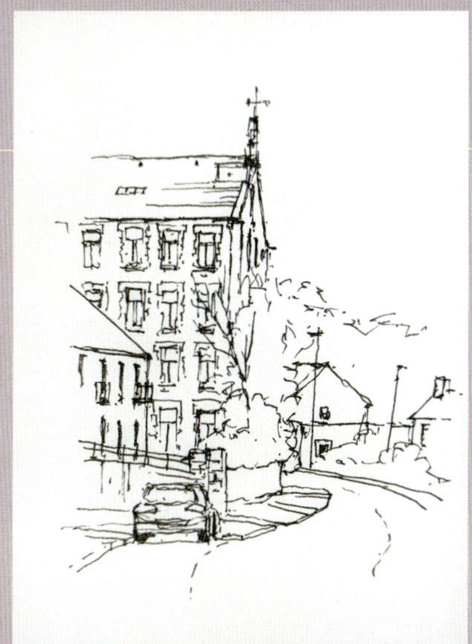

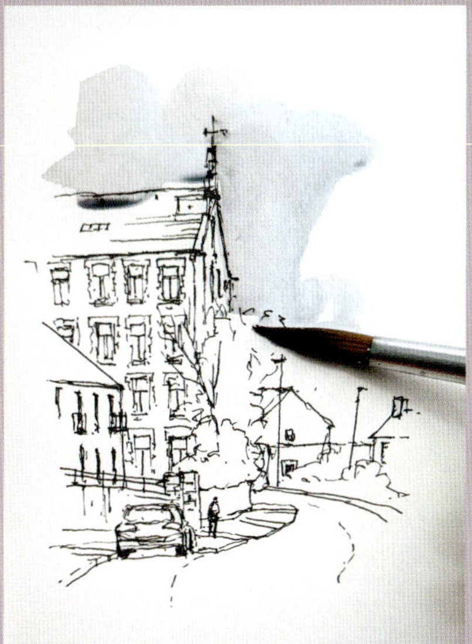

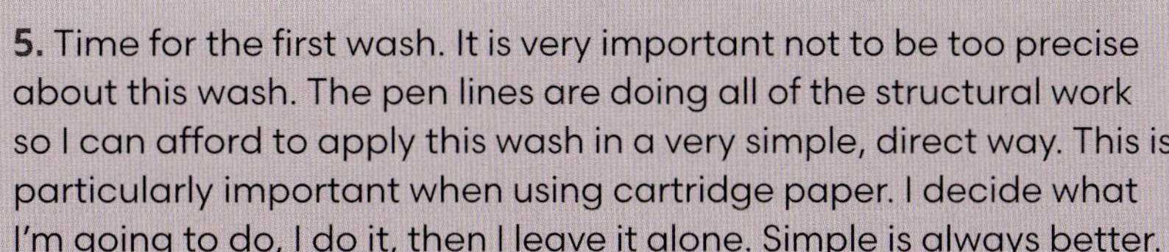

4. I don't use crosshatching or any other indication of shading, preferring to leave this to the paint, but I try to avoid leaving large areas with no pen marks at all. If there really isn't much there I will add a few lines to suggest the directional structure of the object – a few vertical lines for example, to suggest a vertical wall.

5. Time for the first wash. It is very important not to be too precise about this wash. The pen lines are doing all of the structural work so I can afford to apply this wash in a very simple, direct way. This is particularly important when using cartridge paper. I decide what I'm going to do, I do it, then I leave it alone. Simple is always better.

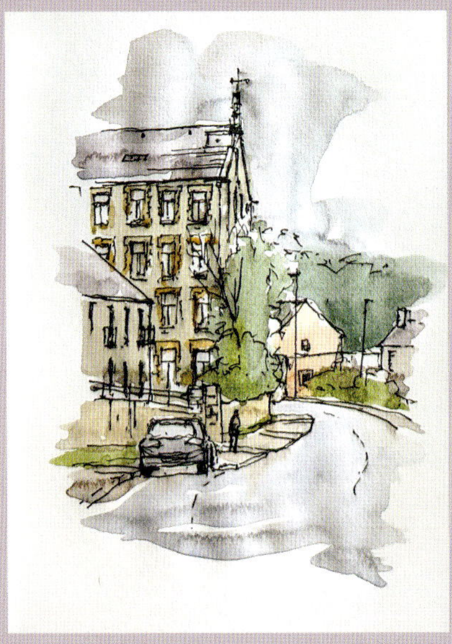

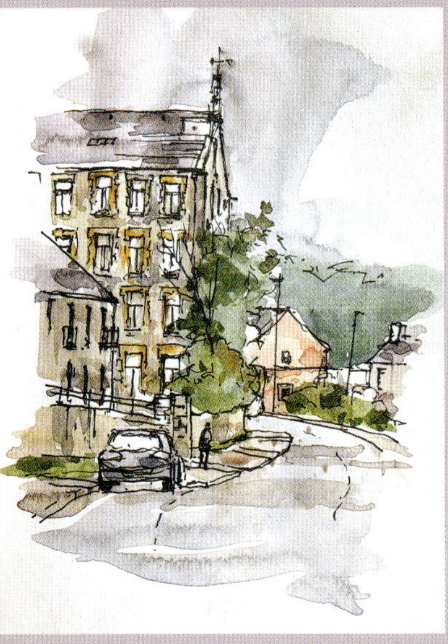

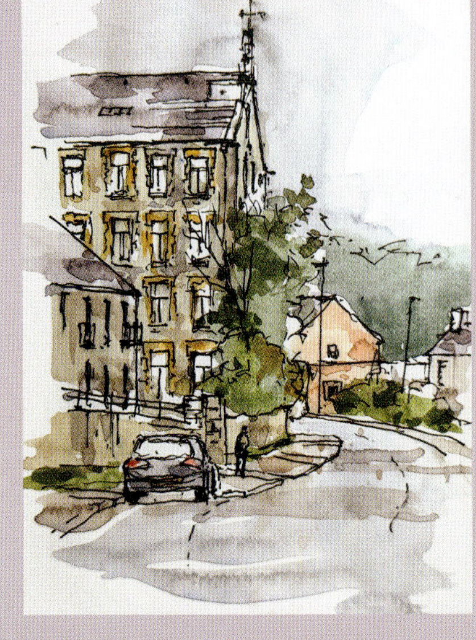

6. I use my little car hairdryer to make sure the first wash is completely dry.

7. The second wash is basically a repeat of the first but covering no more than 50 per cent of that first wash. The idea here is to add some variety to the paint, mainly to help avoid a 'coloured in' look. I do not paint any second wash over the sky or distant landscape as this would tend to pull those elements forward.

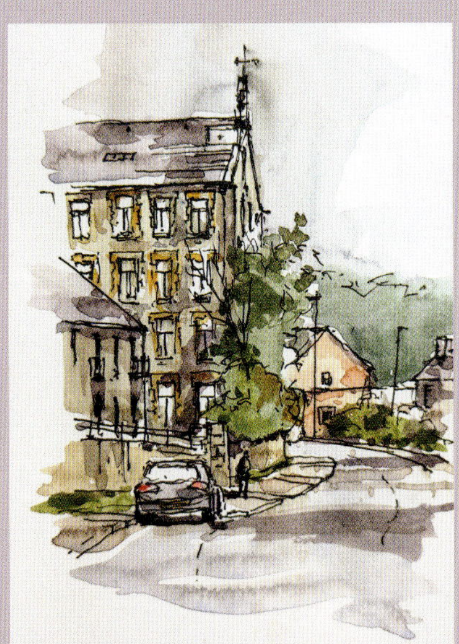

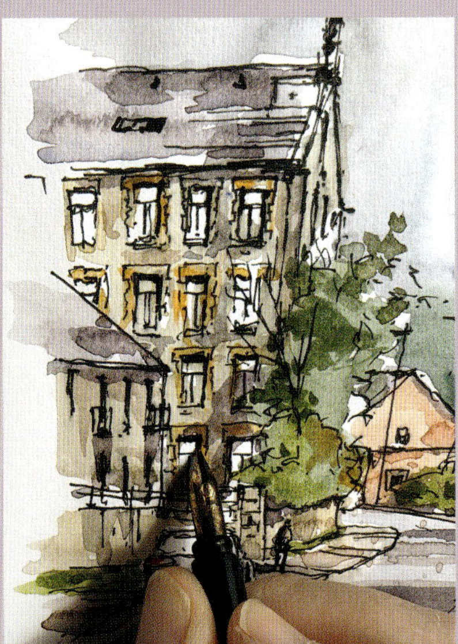

8. Next comes the shadow wash. As this was a mostly cloudy day there were no strong cast shadows, but softer shadows were visible below the eaves, below the car, underneath the balconies and underneath the trees. The shadow wash adds contrast, which adds impact.

9. After all of this painting the pen lines will have become slightly subdued and have maybe even softened slightly depending on the pen or ink. Now is the opportunity to reinforce some of these lines, mainly in the main focus area of the painting. Once again, it is all about contrast. The addition of these rich darks helps to add more contrast and, with that, more impact.

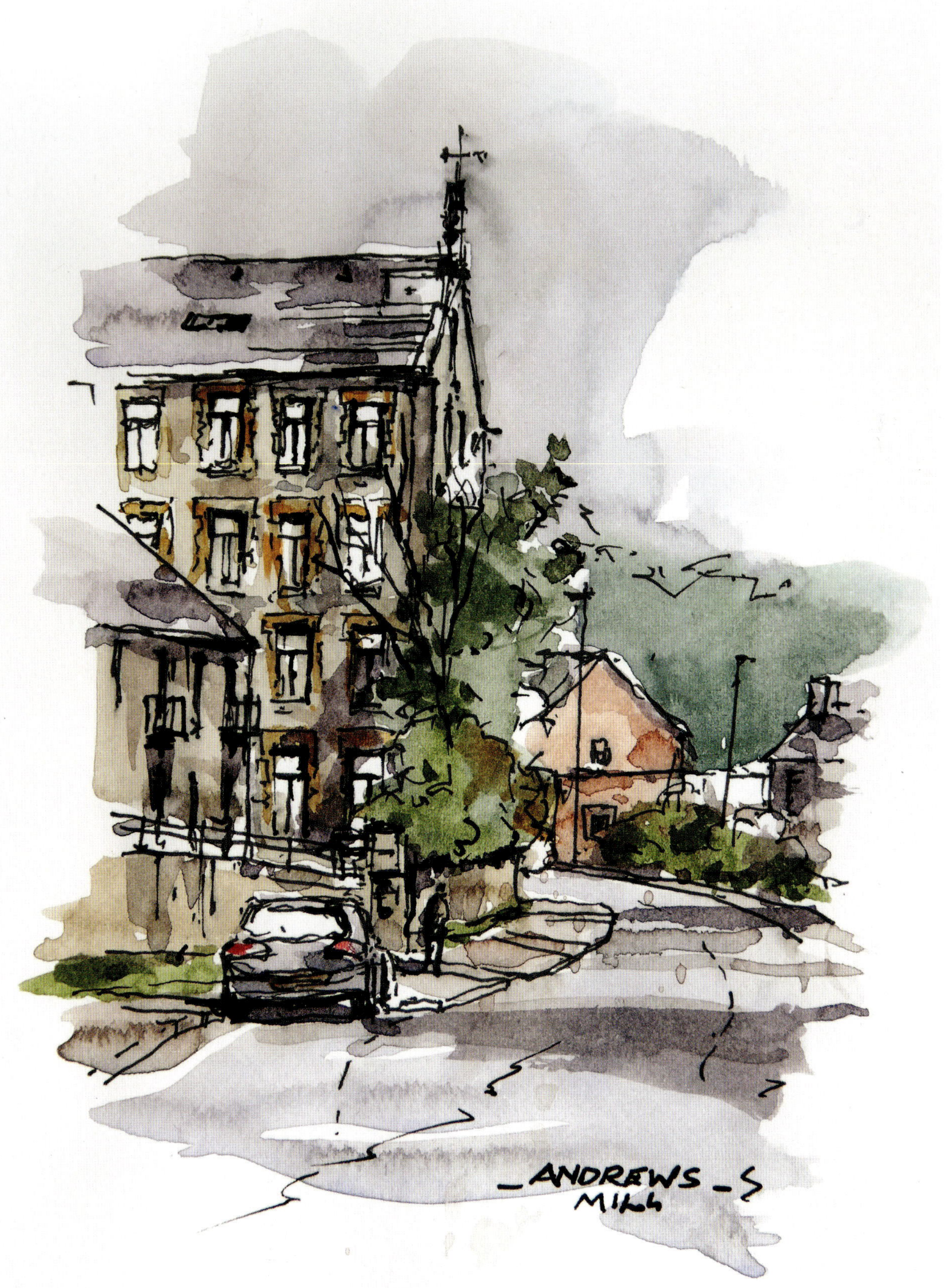
_ANDREWS_S
MILL

PERSPECTIVE

LINEAR PERSPECTIVE

I find perspective fascinating, but I do know from experience that many people struggle with it. We use linear perspective to create the illusion of depth on our flat sheet of paper using the fact that horizontal, parallel, receding lines appear to slope towards eye level and meet at a single point known as the vanishing point (see right). The eye-level line is also the horizon line. In reality, of course, they don't slope. The illusion is created simply because, for example, the height of the far end of a wall will appear to be smaller than the height of the near end. The great thing about this rule is that there are no exceptions and it is very easily shown in practice (see right).

It is important to understand that the rule will only apply to horizontal lines that are parallel and receding, that is, moving away from us. These will be lines such as the top and bottom of a roof, the top and bottom of lines of windows and doors and mortar lines of bricks or blocks. The line at the bottom of a building could be horizontal but we can't be sure. Most streets or roads are likely to slope a little up or down so the line at the bottom of a building will probably not recede to the vanishing point on eye level. If the road is sloping downhill, the line will slope to below the eye-level vanishing point, and, if it is sloping uphill, the line will slope to above.

Bear in mind that verticals are always vertical. A photograph looking up at a tall building will show converging verticals but our brain corrects this in reality. Converging verticals should only be used if you are seeking a dramatic effect where you want to exaggerate the height or depth of something.

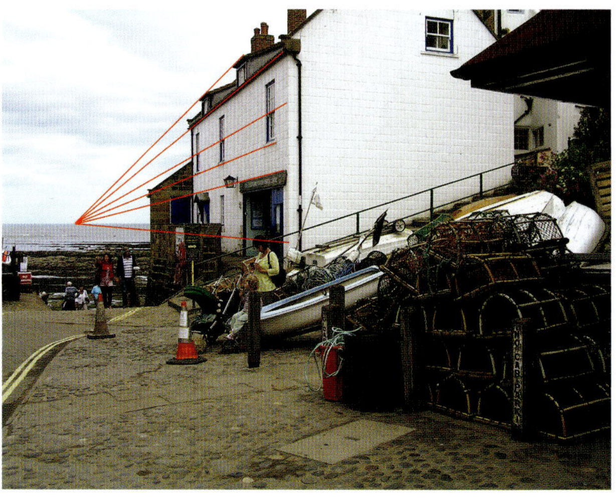

Eye level and the horizon are exactly the same thing

If we continue the horizontal, parallel, receding lines on the white house, you can see clearly that they all meet on the horizon (eye level) at a single point. It is absolutely essential to determine the placement of our eye-level/horizon line on our paper right at the very start. We can place it anywhere, high or low, but the position of this line will determine the perspective of the entire subject. Subjects that include the horizon make life a little easier as we can immediately see where our eye-level line is. A drawing can easily be checked for accuracy by holding a piece of string at the vanishing point and moving the other end up or down to coincide with horizontal lines.

'PAINTING IS EASY WHEN YOU DON'T KNOW HOW BUT VERY DIFFICULT WHEN YOU DO.' *– Edgar Degas*

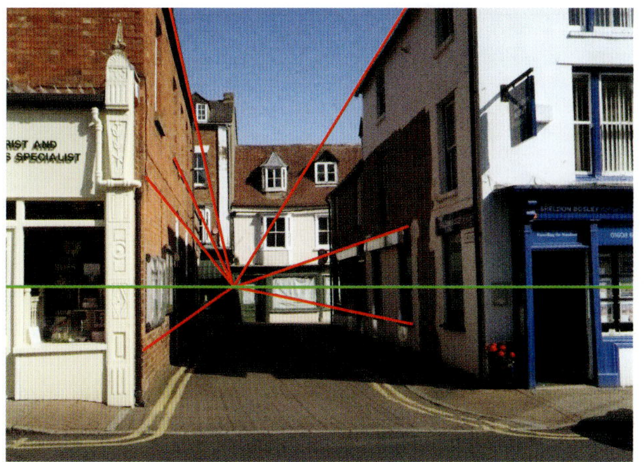

Single-point perspective

If our subject includes, for example, a street where both sides are parallel to each other, then a single vanishing point will allow us to construct every perspective line down the street, irrespective of how long the street may be. The vanishing point in this case will be directly in front of us. Although there is no horizon to see, the vanishing point will determine where it is. This single point will apply no matter how tall the buildings may be. A perfectly straight street of multi-storey buildings with parallel sides will have only one vanishing point.

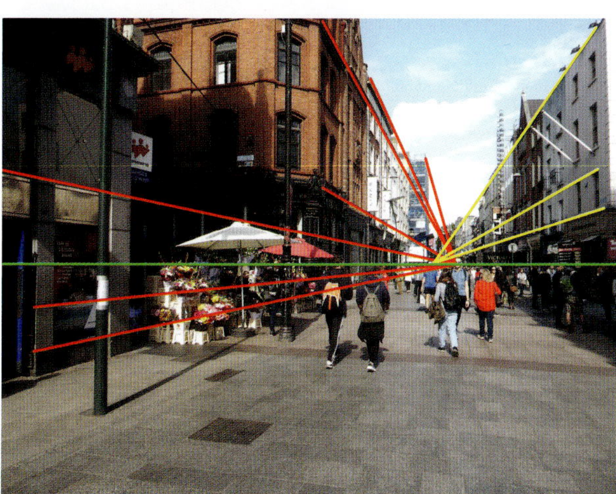

Not all streets are parallel

In this subject you can see how the lines from the left and right sides of the street do meet at single points but not at the same point. This indicates that the sides of the street are not parallel. However, the vanishing points for each side will still be on eye level. Notice too how the eye-level line is roughly in line with other people's eyes, irrespective of how far down the street they are. Obviously people are of different heights and so not all of them will be on the eye-level line but this is a good guide to placing your figures in a subject where figures are standing on flat horizontal ground.

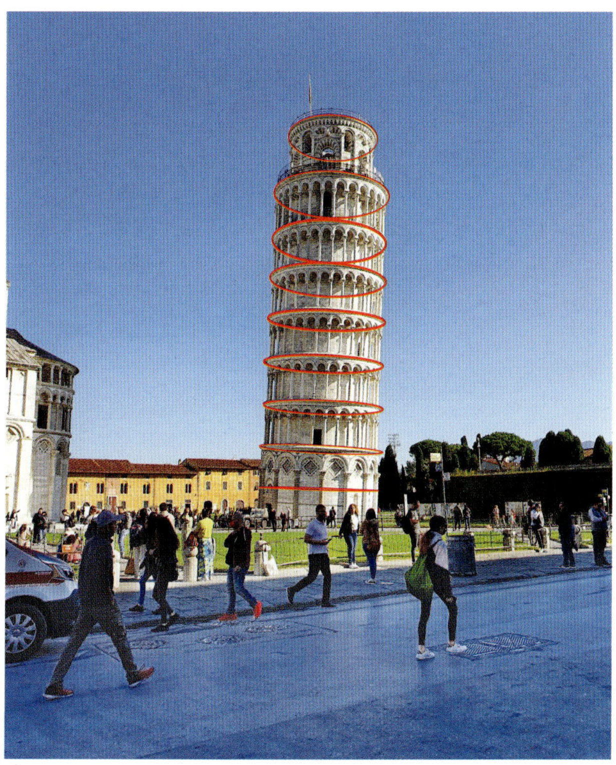

Circles in perspective

Cylindrical buildings do not follow the standard perspective rule. However, slices through a cylindrical building will be circles; if we are viewing these obliquely they will appear as flattened circles, known as ellipses. At eye level the ellipse will be completely flat; in other words, a line, and as we move above or below eye level, the ellipse will gradually become more circular. Although perhaps not as mathematically obvious as linear perspective, understanding this should help with the construction of cylindrical buildings or objects.

AERIAL PERSPECTIVE

Aerial or atmospheric perspective allows us to create the illusion of depth on our paper by mimicking the natural effects of our atmosphere on distant objects. Anything receding into the distance will gradually become cooler and less saturated in colour. Detail will be less apparent, edges will appear softer and there will be no extremes of tone, no pure whites or blacks. In reality, aerial perspective is only really noticeable over quite a great distance but exaggerating the effect over shorter distances in our painting will help to create the illusion of depth.

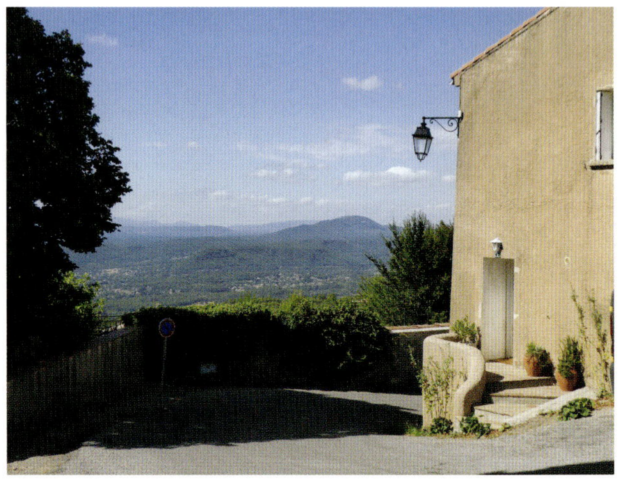

In this photograph of Tourtour, a mountain village in Provence, the effects of aerial perspective can clearly be seen. The effects become stronger with distance, so much so that the most distant mountains, which are many miles away, appear little different to the blue sky.

Exaggerating aerial perspective to create depth in your painting

Here, the trees are only 100m (109yd) or so away and so there is no obvious aerial perspective visible in the photograph (A), but softening and simplifying the trees in the painting (B) allowed the boat to appear much stronger, creating a better sense of depth.

A

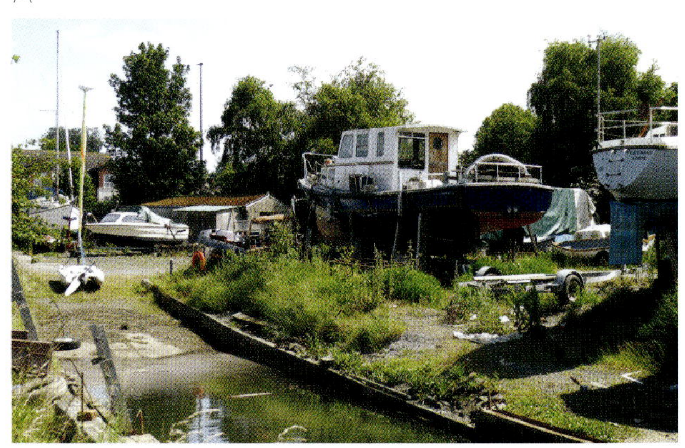

B

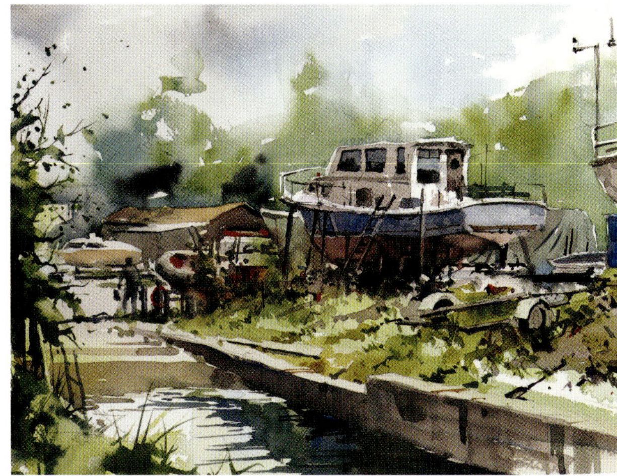

The railing is close but the horizon is far away

There is a common misconception about eye level/horizon that can cause confusion. How can eye level be the same as the horizon when eye level can change but the horizon is clearly fixed?

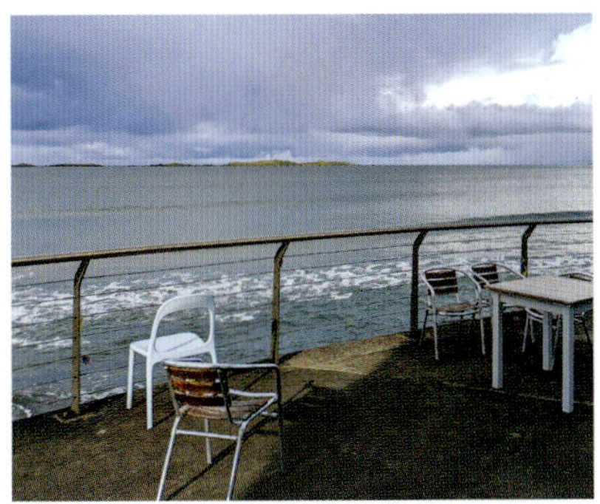

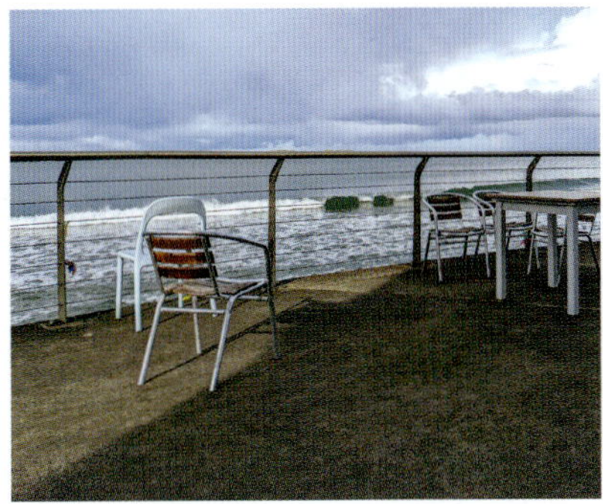

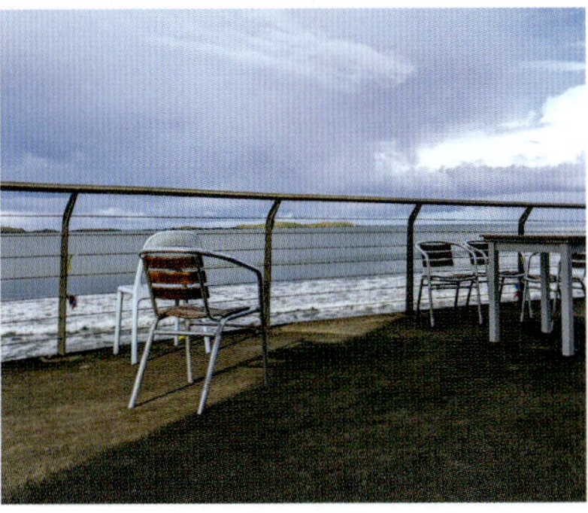

I took this photograph standing up. The camera lens is in front of my eye and so is on my eye level. Notice the position of the horizon. This too is on my eye level.

When I crouch down so that the top of the railing is directly in front of my eyes, notice that the horizon is now also in line with the top of the railing. The horizon seems to have moved with my eyes but actually the railing is now higher, relative to where my eyes were.

When I crouch down further, you can see that the horizon seems to have moved down again along with my eyes, but, as with the previous photograph, the railing is further raised relative to the position of my eyes.

The glass of water trick

If you can't see the horizon, guessing where eye level is can be very hit and miss. You can, of course, work out where the vanishing points are, which will give you the position of the eye-level line, but it is good to know before beginning the drawing exactly where it is. Close one eye and hold a transparent container of water or other liquid in front of you so that you are looking down on the surface (A), lift it slowly (B) until the surface just disappears. That line is your eye level (C). Because the surface of the water in the container is always horizontal, it will disappear exactly at your eye level.

A

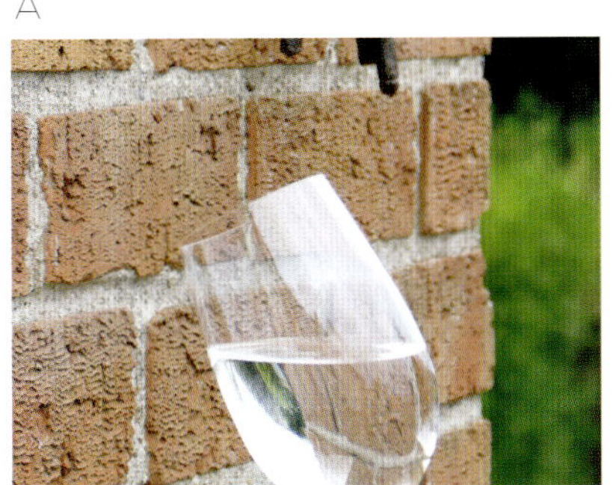

B

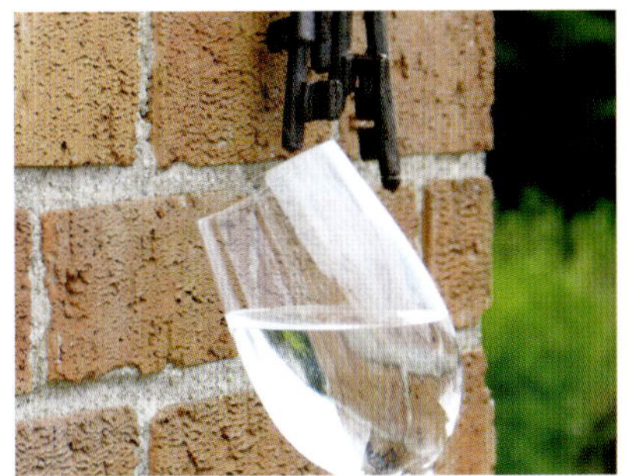

C

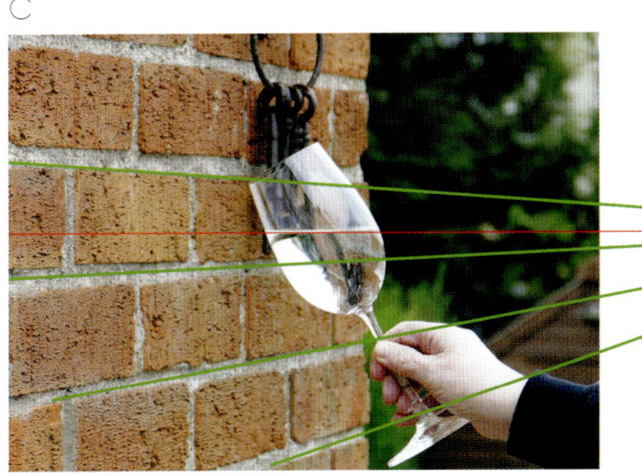

WATERCOLOUR TECHNIQUES

BEFORE WE LOOK AT SOME plein air demonstrations it might be useful to recap on some essential watercolour techniques. Every watercolour painting is created from watercolour washes, and, as well as being able to apply a wash, we must also be able to control the edge of the wash. If we can draw and manage both of these techniques, that will go a long way towards creating a successful watercolour. The techniques appear to be quite simple in execution, but many things can and often do go wrong. As with most things, practice is the key. The more you do it, the better you will become.

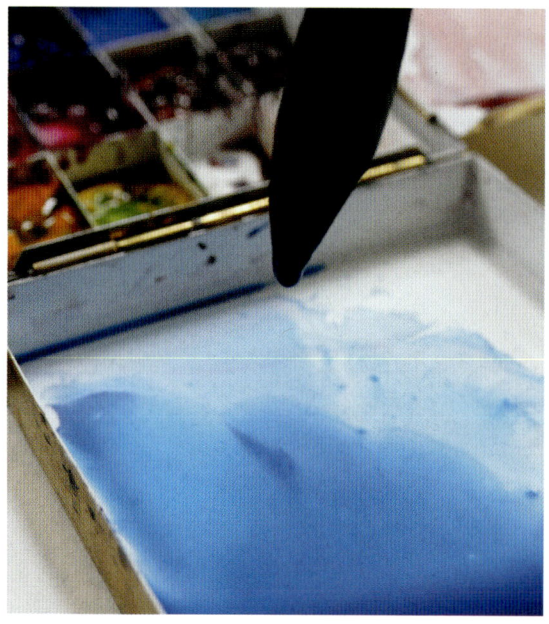

PAINTING TIPS

A full brush is the key to producing a perfect wash. If your brush doesn't drip when you lift it out of the paint mix, then it isn't wet enough!

The strength and colour of the paint can be varied as a wash is painted, but the brush must still be kept full, as with the **flat wash** (see opposite). A wash where the strength is varied is known as a **graduated wash**. Where the colour is varied, it is a **variegated wash**. In effect, washes will almost always be graduated or variegated to some extent. This produces variety – essential for creating interest in your painting.

PAINTING A WASH

The key to a successful wash is keeping your brush fully loaded with paint. Get into a routine of dip, stroke, dip, stroke and you stand a much better chance of painting a flat wash without any indication of brush marks.

A flat wash

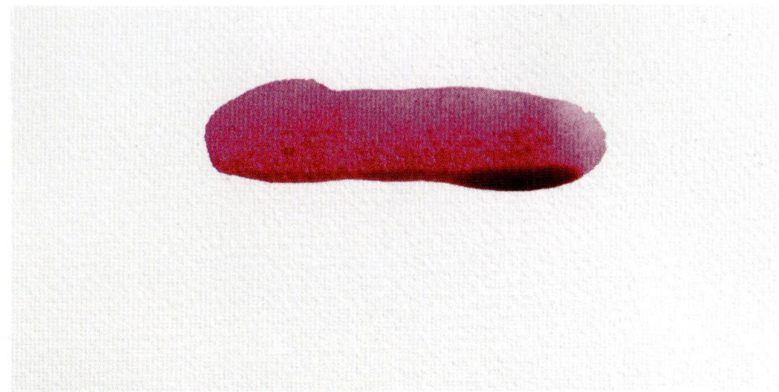

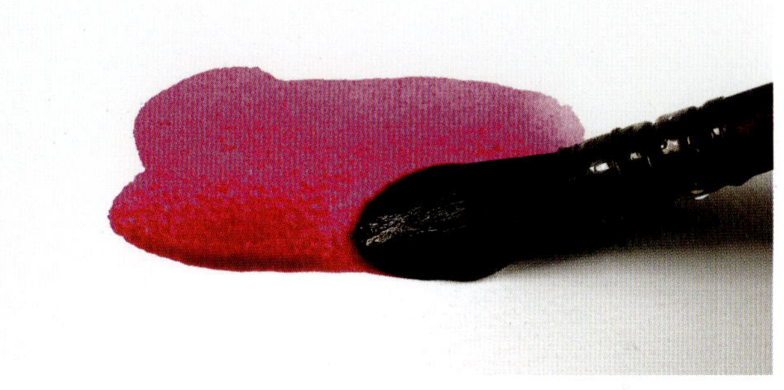

1. Create a simple wet brushstroke. The key is that pool of colour you can see on the bottom edge. It is this that allows the continuation of the stroke to produce a wash. If you don't have that pool, you are unlikely to produce a clean wash.

2. Dip into your paint mix, then paint a second stroke, picking up the lower edge of the first. Once again, there should be that little reservoir of paint on the bottom edge.

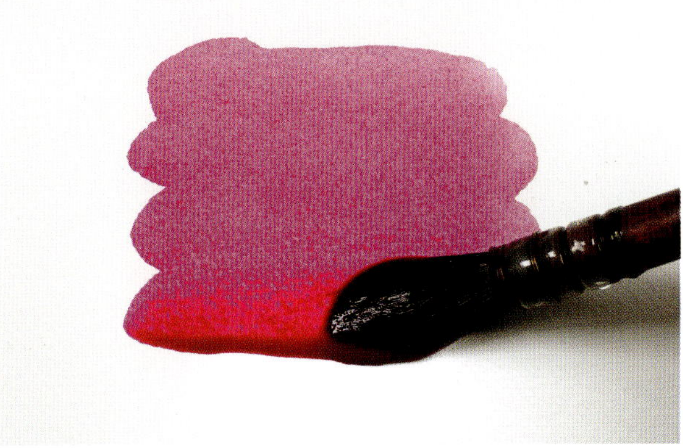

3. Don't press down hard on the brush, as – counterintuitively – this actually allows *less* paint to be released. Keep dipping. It is vital that your brush remains fully charged.

4. Continue the process in exactly the same way until you reach the end of the wash. The worst thing that can happen is to run out of paint, so mix plenty. Trust me, you will have plenty of opportunity to use up any excess during your painting. After your last stroke you should still have that pool of colour on the bottom edge. Use a barely damp brush to suck up the excess.

SALERNES, PROVENCE
38 x 28cm (15 x 11in), Fabriano Artistico CP 300gsm (140lb)

This painting of Salernes in France consists of two washes, one for each building, but each wash varies continuously in both strength and colour. A simple flat wash would not have been very interesting. I also changed the colour of the nearer building slightly to create a greater contrast with the church.

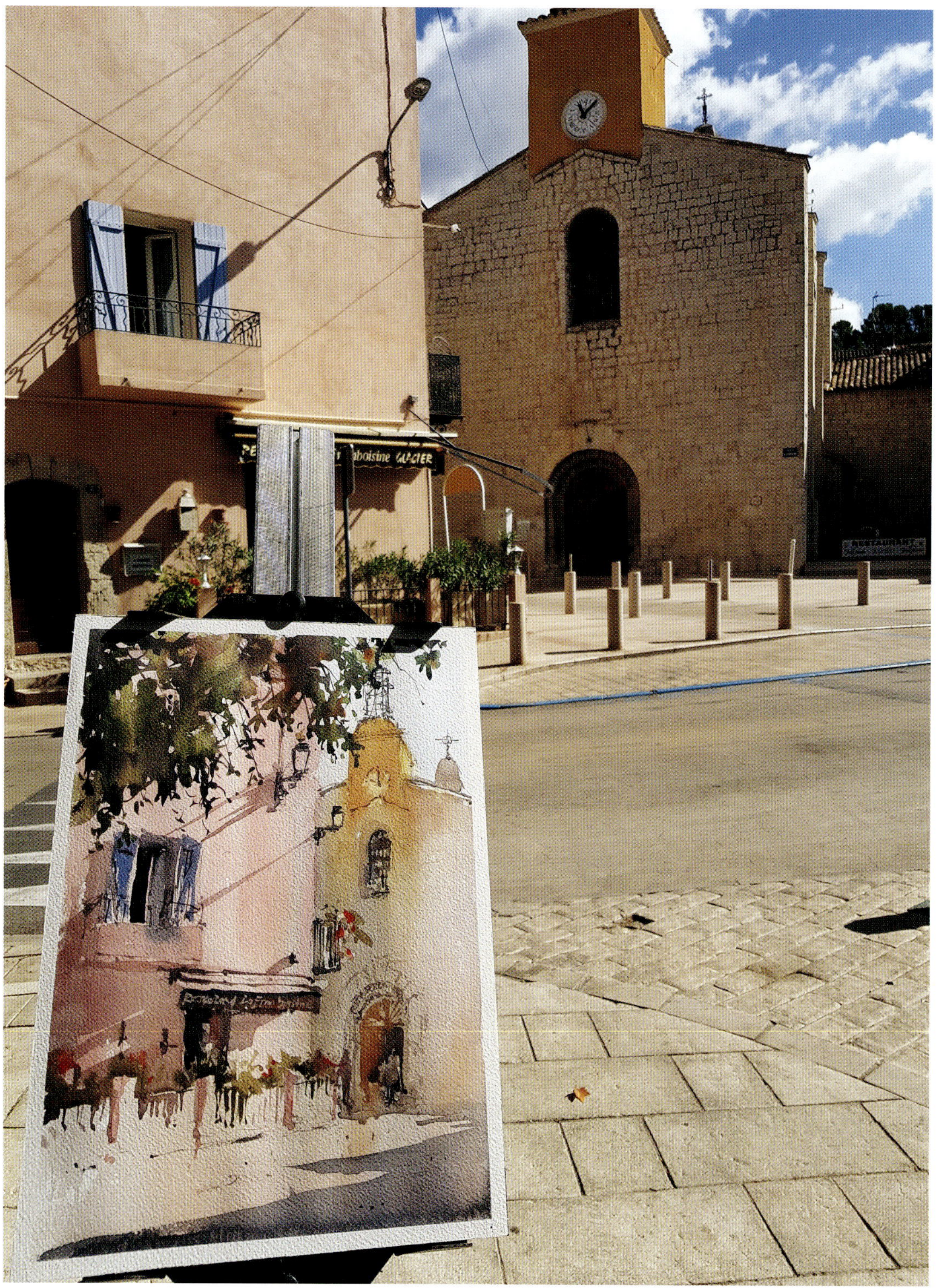

EDGE CONTROL

Edge control is probably one of most poorly understood yet most important techniques in watercolour. Very often, particularly in the early stages of a painting, you will need to create many soft edges. These help to avoid defining things too early. Creating definition too early ties you down, whereas soft edges give you options. The simplest soft edge is where you change to a different colour and allow the first colour to blend with the second, but there will be many more occasions where you will need to soften a wet edge on dry paper, essentially to make it disappear. In this demonstration I want to soften the right-hand edge of the block of wet colour. My softening brush is an old sable with the point worn away. This makes it ideal for softening edges and lifting out paint.

Softening an edge

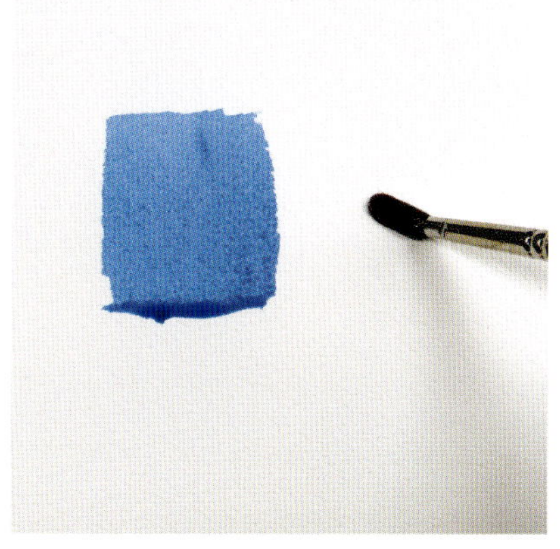

1. Paint in your initial shape, and work while the paint is still wet. Ensure that your brush is quite wet but not dripping. Place the brush on the paper slightly away from the edge of your shape.

2. Keeping the brush on the paper, move it towards the edge. From this point onwards, do not lift the brush from the paper until the process is complete. When the brush contacts the edge, move it up and down as far as you need. The paint on the wet edge will start to move into the wet area you have created. Vary the pressure of the brush on the paper to control the amount of excess water. Remember, do not lift the brush.

3. When the edge is sufficiently soft, move the brush back to where you started, still keeping it in contact with the paper. When you get back to the starting point you can lift the brush. The reason for not lifting it before this is that a little blob of water will be left behind and this would almost certainly cause a cauliflower (runback) on the edge itself. This is why dabbing just the edge you want to soften with your brush will not work.

Cauliflowers

Speaking of cauliflowers, this is a fault or an effect (depending on your opinion) that will happen in almost every painting. Many painters love them and enjoy the uncertainty they provide but others consider them a major problem. Fortunately, it is relatively easy to avoid them. They form when wet and weaker paint meets dryer and stronger paint. Most commonly they form where paint has accumulated at the bottom of a wash. The wash dries but the little pool of paint at the bottom stays wet and tries to push back up into the drying paint, producing the characteristic crinkly edge. To avoid them, just make sure you dry up your excess drips. Plein air painters will be very familiar with cauliflowers, as it is often the appearance of lots of them that tells us it has started to rain!

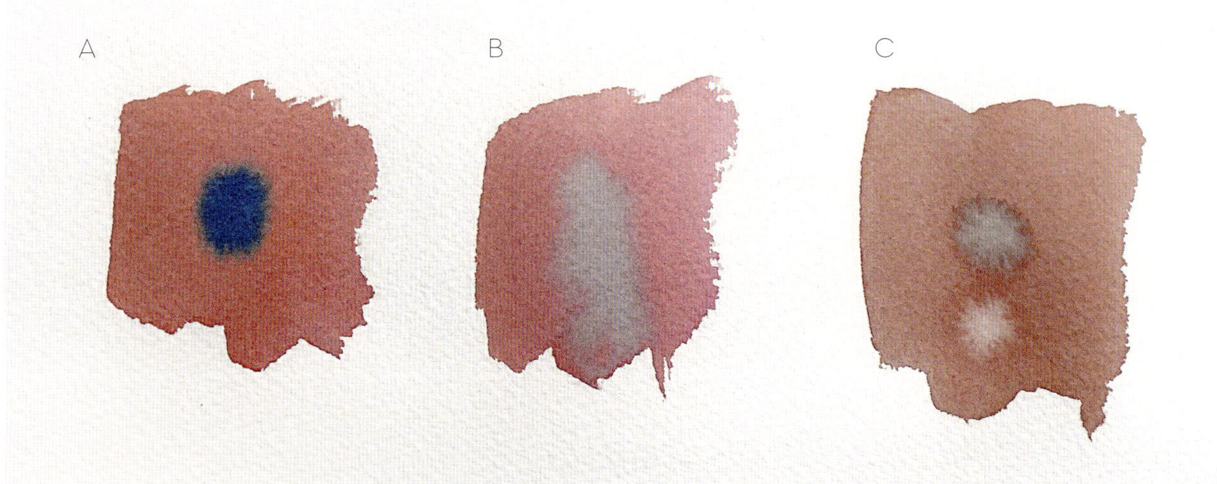

A: A cauliflower will never form when you add strong paint (blue) to weak (pink). Stick to this and your problems should largely be over.

B: If your wash is still very wet and you add weak paint (pale blue) to it, you might be lucky and avoid the dreaded crinkly edge.

C: The danger time for cauliflowers is when your wash has almost but not quite dried. If you are looking obliquely at the surface of the paper against the light, it is when the shine has gone off the wash. You can still add strong paint if you must*, but adding weaker paint (above) or indeed plain water (below) will both result in a cauliflower. At this point, the only way of stopping it is if you immediately add stronger paint, but this is not always practical or desirable. Unless it can be dealt with immediately, I suggest leaving it until the end when it can often be disguised by overlaying it with something else.

*Touching a wash when it has almost dried is almost never a good idea. Play with it while it is very wet, but once it starts to dry, leave it alone until drying is complete.

Dry brush

A slightly different form of edge control is dry brush. As the name suggests, dry-brush marks are created using a dry or almost-dry brush. Take a look through the images in the book and you will see many examples of hard edges, blended edges, soft edges, scrubbed edges and dry brush, sometimes in the same painting!

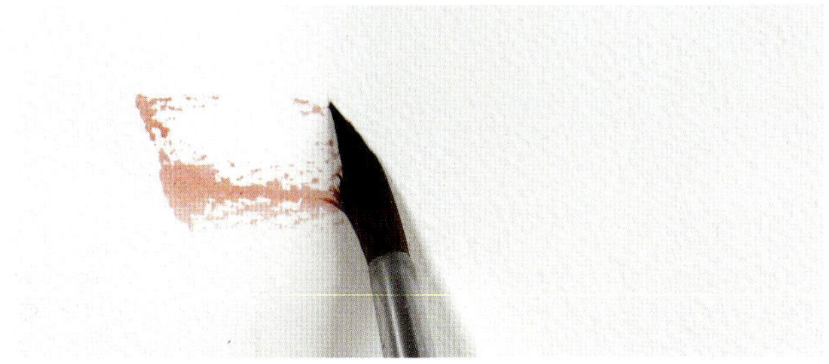

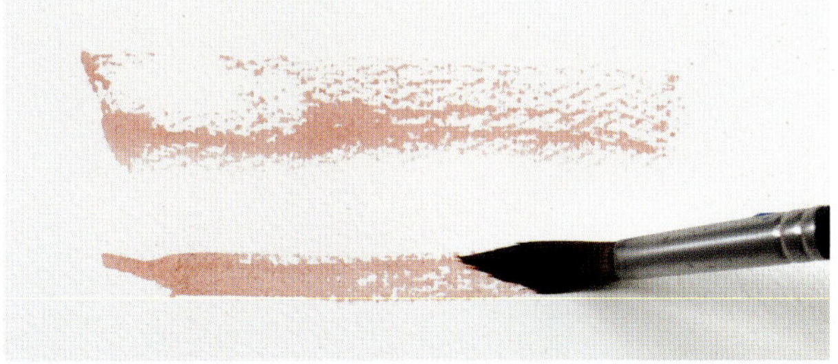

1. To create dry-brush marks, dip your brush into your mix but then stroke the brush on the edge of your palette to remove most of the paint. Stroke the brush onto the paper. Using the side of the brush will create the best effect because a brush is not designed to release paint from the edge.

2. The tip of the brush will also work to a lesser extent. The faster you make the stroke, the greater the effect will be.

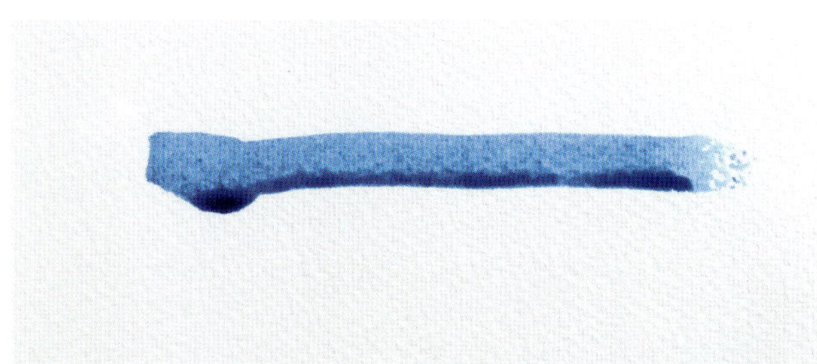

1. A slightly different dry-brush effect can be created on a normal wet edge.

2. Stroke a barely damp brush across the wet edge to produce an effect rather like a cross between full-scale softening and dry brush. If a completely dry brush is used in the same way, there is less softening, giving more of a scrubbed effect.

And now, on with the projects...

SPRING

OR MANY PAINTERS, SPRING WILL mark the beginning of their painting year. Days are longer, temperatures are more conducive to painting outdoors and the landscape is reinvigorated with new life. It is so nice when springtime comes around with its bursts of strong colour chasing the drabness of winter away.

NEWTOWNARDS SAILING CLUB
51 x 38cm (20 x 15in), Millford CP 425gsm (200lb)

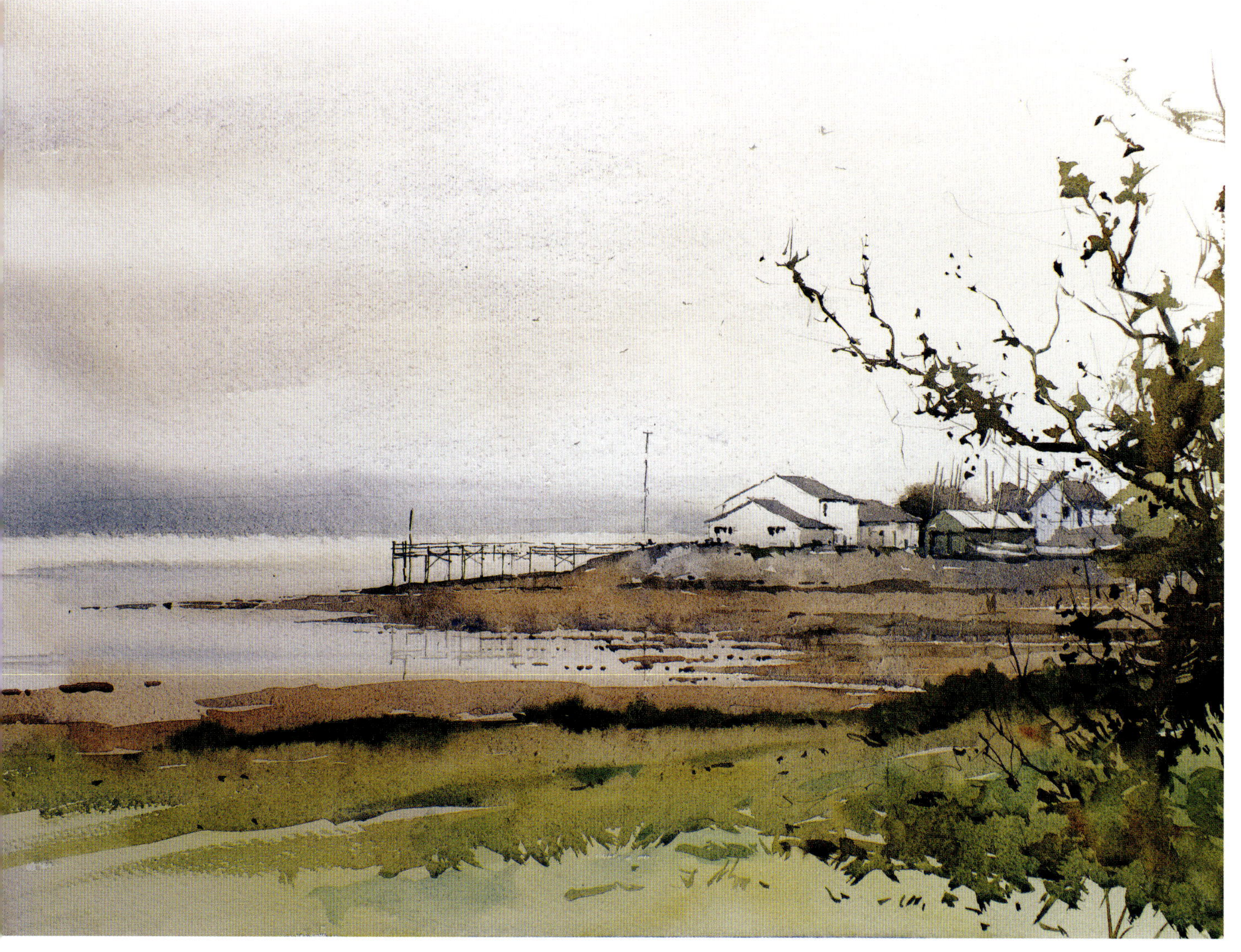

Light conditions

The sun is higher in the sky with cooler light and shorter shadows than in winter.

Potential weather conditions

Probably a little bit of everything, including storms, snow, fog and mist.

Seasonal features

Spring flowers, daffodils, bluebells, bright green new leaves.

DAFFODILS IN ORMEAU PARK
51 x 38cm (20 x 15in), Saunders CP
425gsm (200lb)

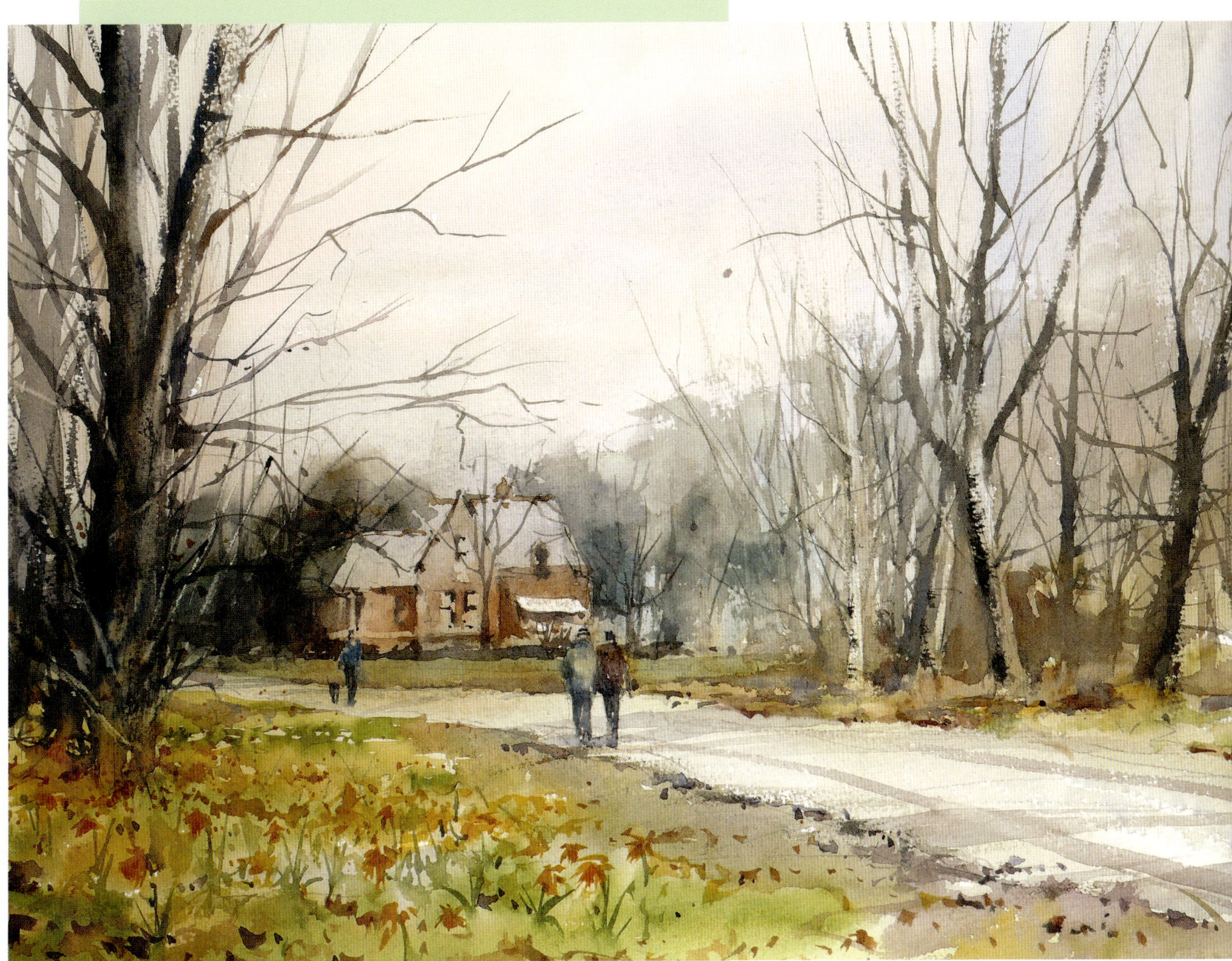

1. SPRING DAFFODILS

Spring daffodils are one of the first colourful flowers to appear, and the trick to painting them convincingly is to suggest many but only paint a few!

YOU WILL NEED

PAINTS

- » **Cobalt blue**
- » **Ultramarine**
- » **Phthalo blue (green shade)**
- » **Warm yellow**
- » **Warm red**
- » **Brown madder**
- » **Burnt sienna**
- » **White gouache**

BRUSHES

- » **Mop or other large soft brush, squirrel or synthetic**
- » **Size 6 pointed mop, sable or synthetic**
- » **Size 12 and 8 round, sable or synthetic**
- » **Size 10 rigger, sable or synthetic**
- » **Old size 8 sable for softening and lifting out**

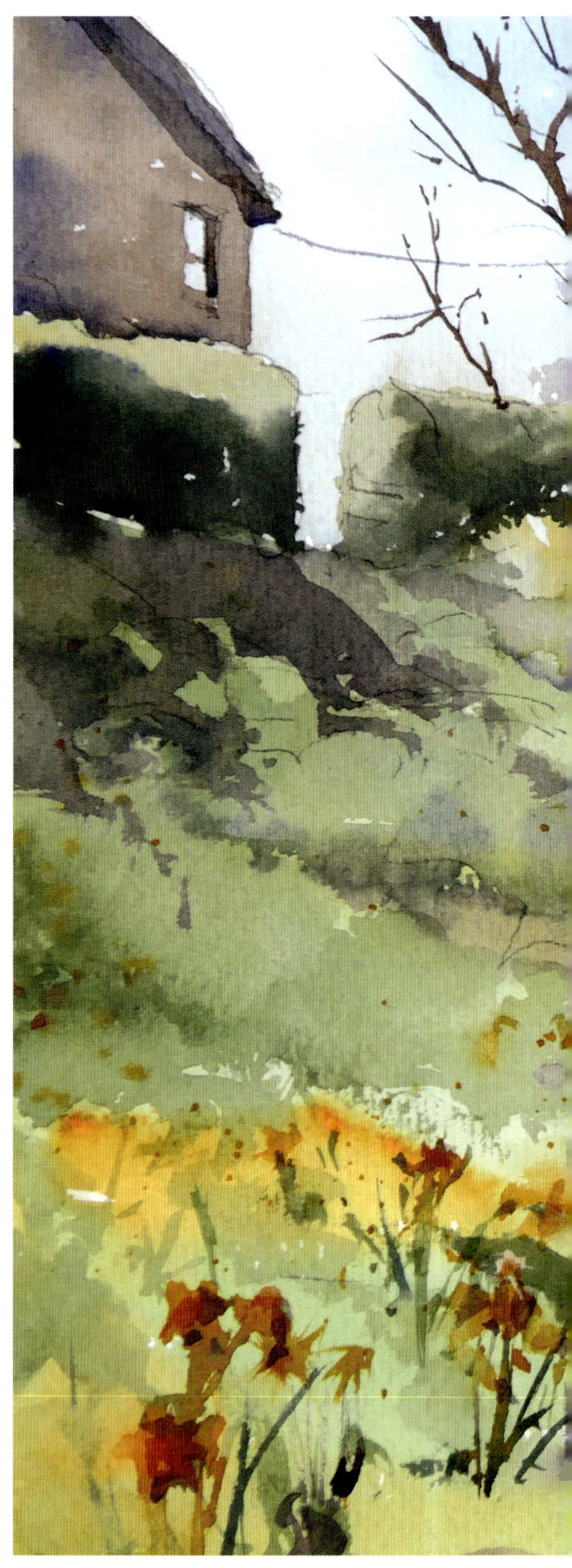

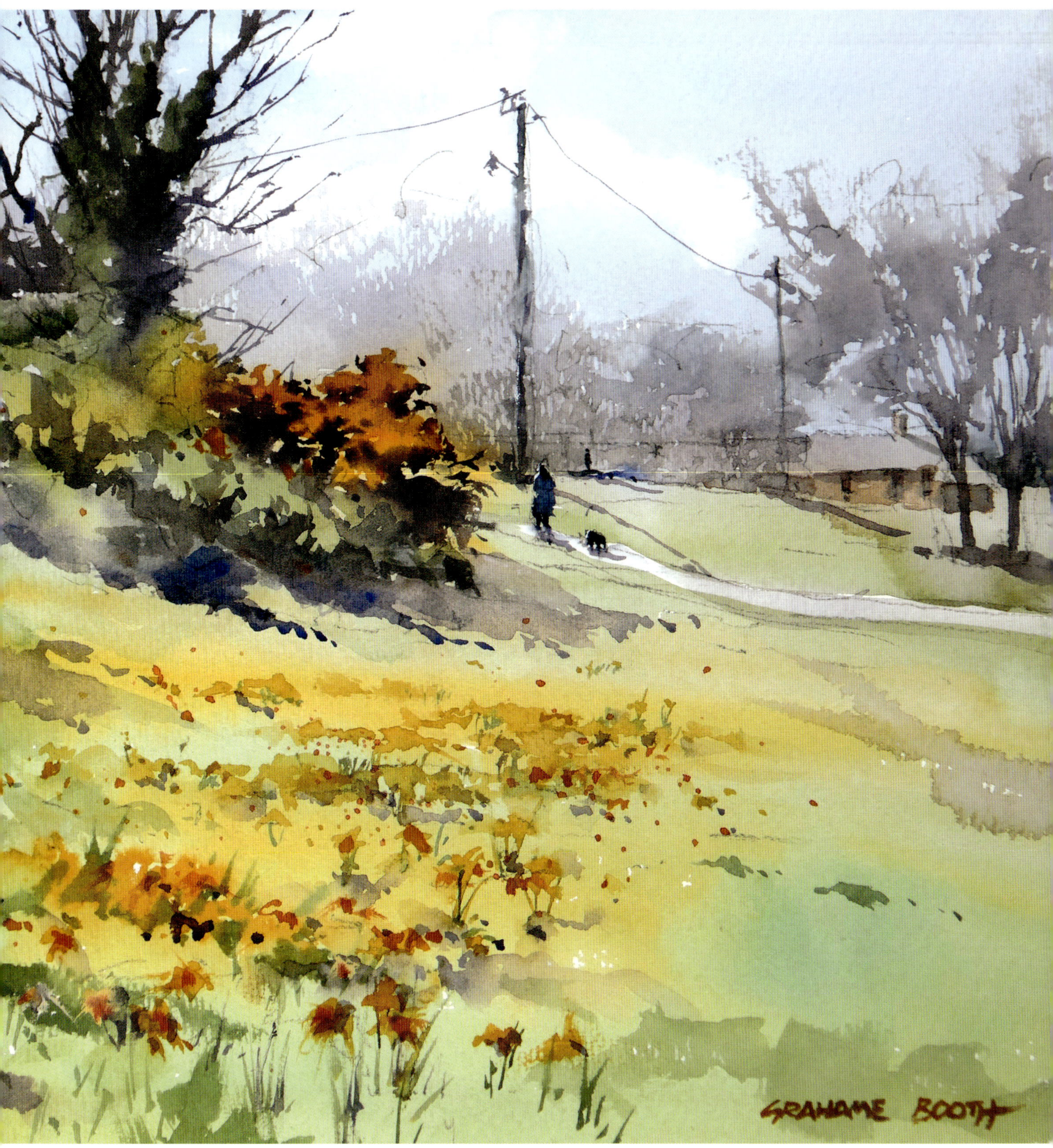

SPRING DAFFODILS
39 x 29cm (15 x 11in),
Saunders Waterford Rough 300gsm (140lb)

1. The initial sketch

As with most landscape drawings, it is important to make sure the different parts relate to each other correctly in size, but you don't want to draw any detail. Drawing in the daffodils, for instance, could lead to very stiff painting. If you refer to the photograph (1A), you can see which parts of the original scene I chose to omit or change in the final sketch (1B).

» There is the gable of a house just out of the photograph to the left and I think I'll move it into the picture. Technically it could be considered too strong a shape in the top left-hand corner, but even so, I think it will help to avoid the main tree from being too isolated.

» The cars are not really adding anything, so I'll leave them out. I want to keep the more distant right side simpler.

» I think I'll change the white daffodils to yellow for two good reasons: white daffodils are much more difficult to paint, and yellow is the colour we expect a daffodil to be. Pragmatism is recommended in watercolour!

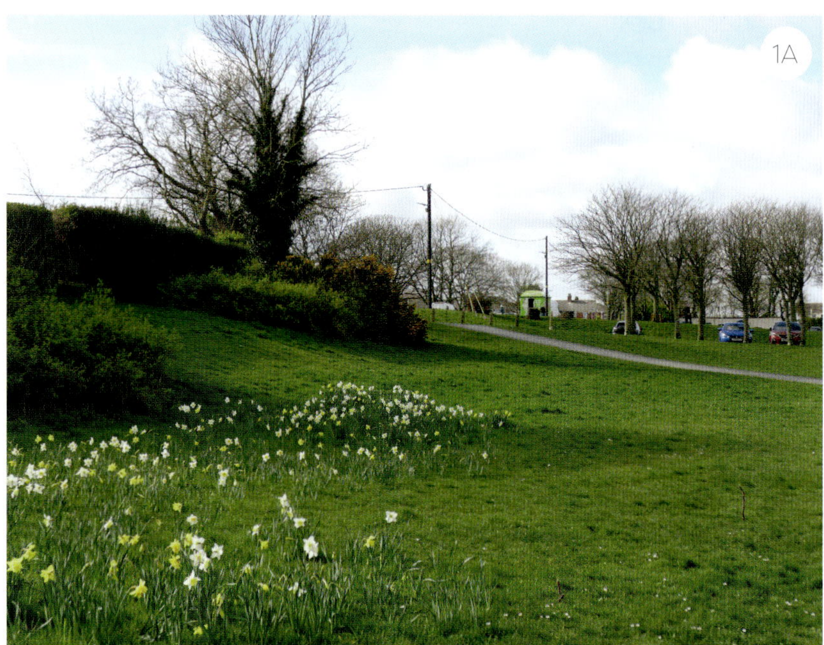

2. The sky wash

Use a soft mop and a wash of cobalt blue for the sky. Keep your brushed loaded with paint to ensure that you create a smooth, even wash.

Lift out the suggestion of a few white clouds by gently dabbing with a paper towel. You don't want any hard edges in the sky as this would likely compete with the main landscape.

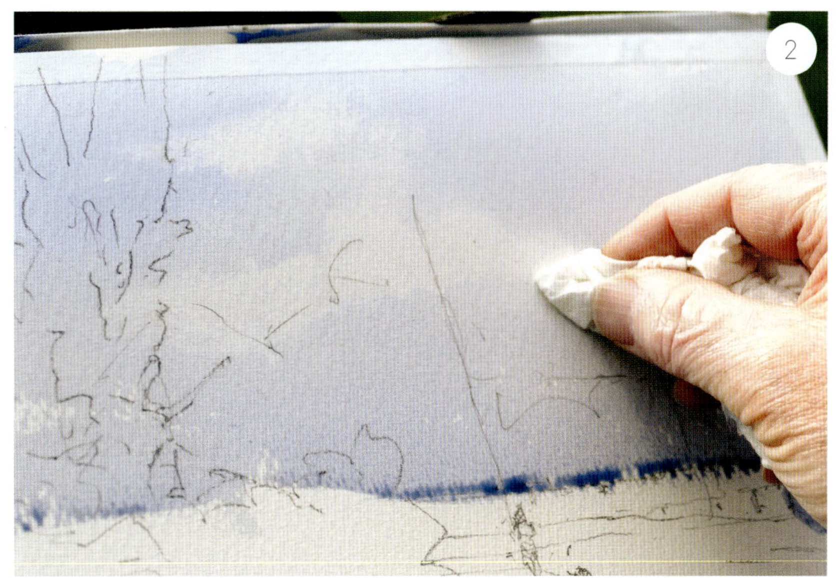

3. The gorse hedge

Continue with the first wash, adding warm yellow to create a dull green at the top of the bank. Use neat warm yellow to suggest the colour of the gorse flowers. Continue on to the next stage without letting the paint dry.

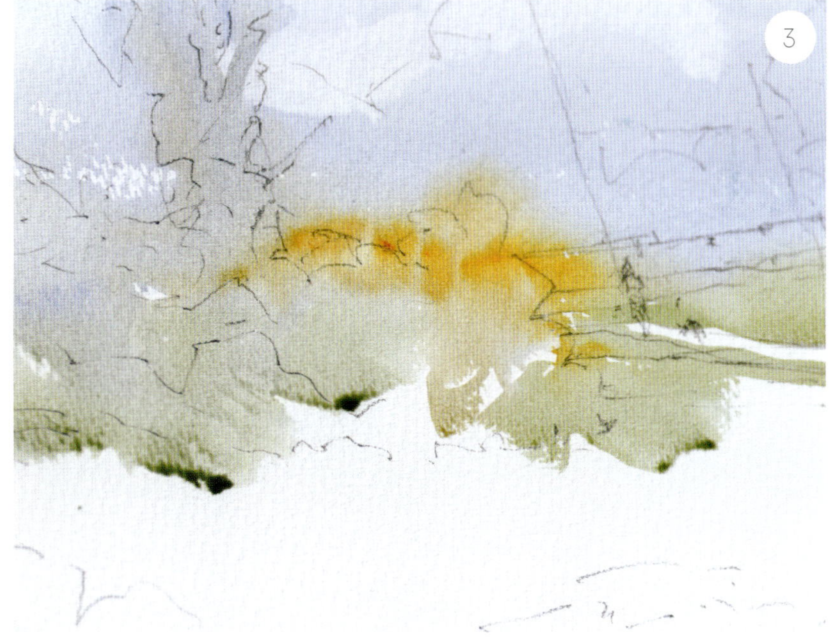

4. The daffodils

You want the daffodils to gradually appear in the grass, so begin by introducing some pure warm yellow into the green (4A). This is intended to start the suggestion of the drifts of flowers. Avoid the temptation to paint actual flowers at this stage.

Continue working in this way, creating irregular bands of green and yellow (4B), keeping your brush well-loaded with paint each time, until the whole of the grassy area is filled; leave a strip of paper unpainted for the path (4C).

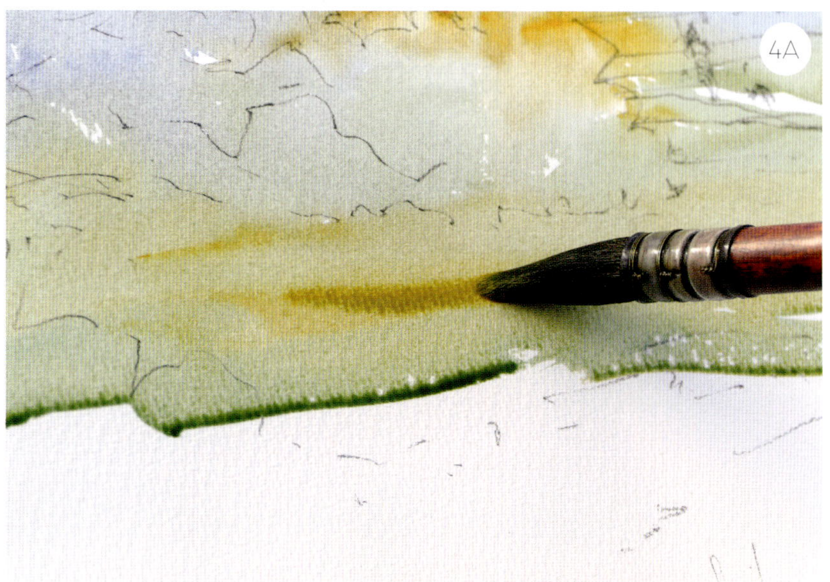

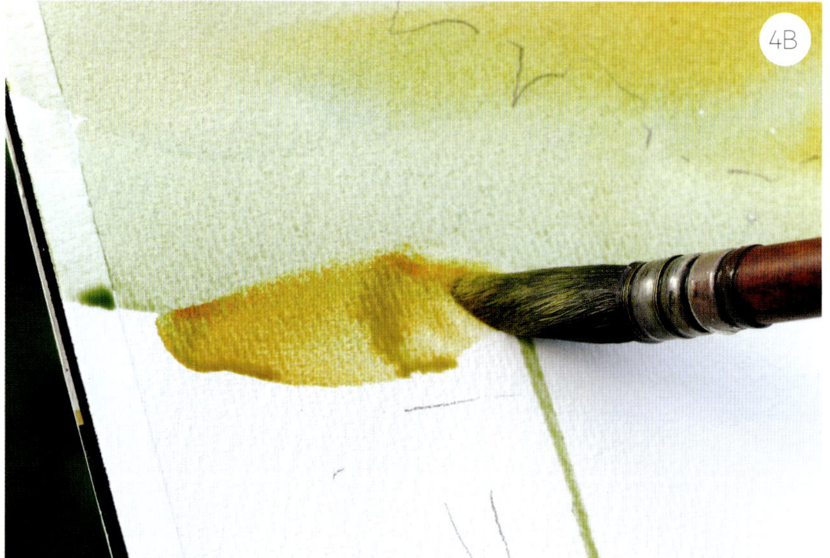

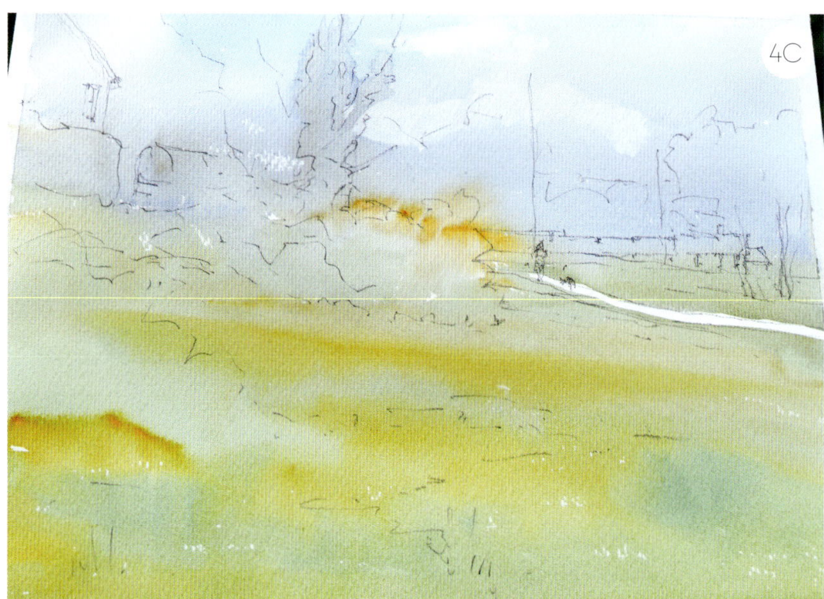

5. The distant buildings

Use a mix of ultramarine and brown madder for the distant purple-blues on the right-hand side. Follow this up with some burnt sienna in the mix to suggest the walls of the distant houses.

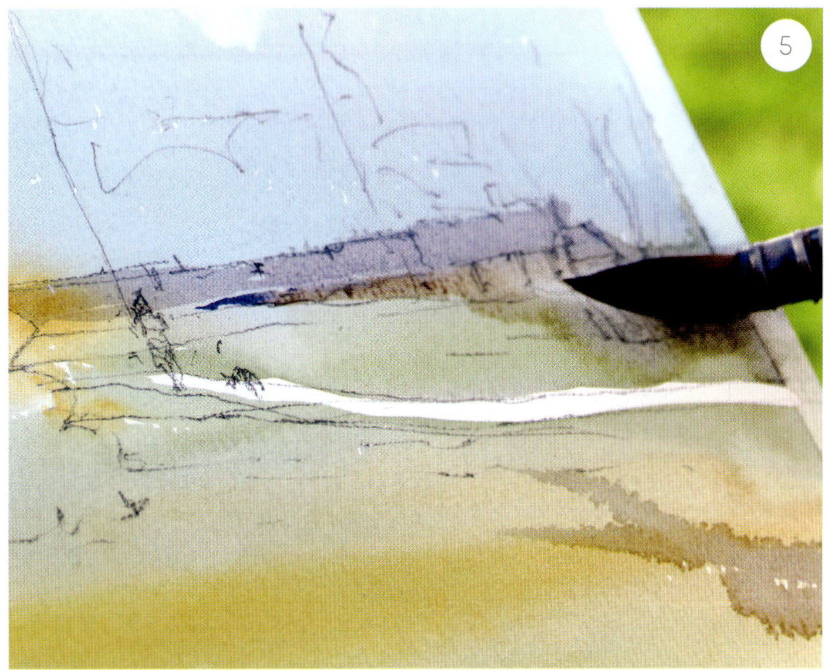

TIP: WORKING WITH 'MISTAKES'

Unfortunately my first wash wasn't quite dry and you can see the resultant cauliflower. As I almost always do, I leave it alone. I also accidentally dripped a huge blob of this mix just below the path, so I teased it out a little to suggest the direction of the grass. Don't be in a hurry to fix mistakes. Think of them first as opportunities to do something different. I will never fix a mistake unless I am as certain as I can be that the fix will be undetectable.

6. The distant trees

Use the same purple-blue mix that you used in step 5 for the distant trees. You'll need to keep these relatively simple so as not to compete with the foreground tree. To create a dry-brush effect, pinch the shaft of your mop brush between your thumb and forefinger, then use the side of it, held parallel to the paper, to stroke in the suggestion of the bare branches.

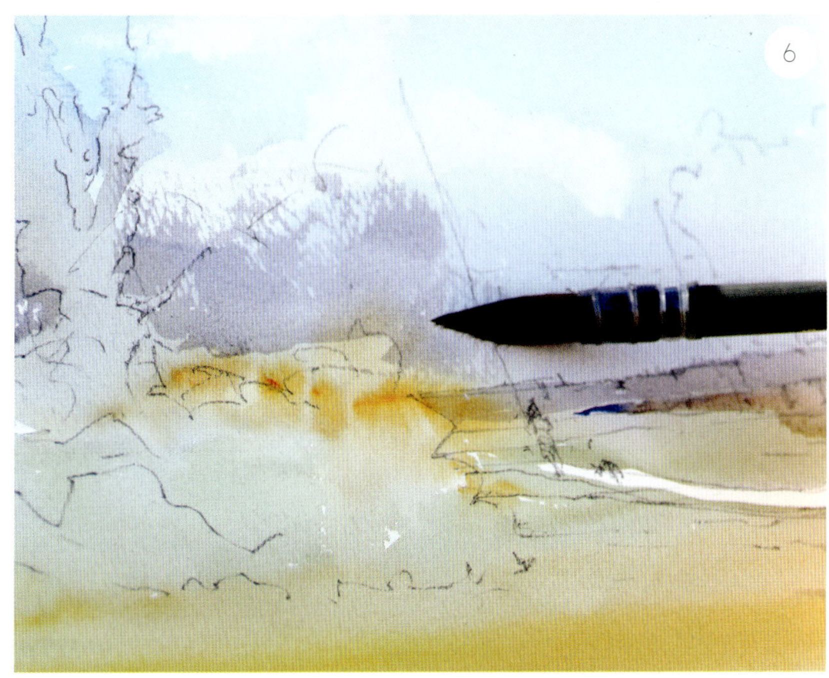

WORKING ORDER
My usual method of working is to begin with the most distant elements and work forward, but because the drying time was quite long, even on this relatively mild spring day, I had to jump around a little.

7. The house

Use a fairly strong mix of ultramarine, burnt sienna and brown madder for the house in shadow on the left-hand side. The aim is to make it strong enough to avoid the need for a second layer of paint, but without risking it becoming too obvious. Vary the mix, and leave a gap for the window.

8. The trees

On to the main trees now. These need to be strong in order to really stand out from the background. Use the same mix as you used for the house in step 7, but make it a little stronger and vary it as you work. Use a size 10 rigger to paint the finest branches, concentrating on creating a believable jumble of branches but keeping in mind how they grow (8A). Twigs are relatively straight and then suddenly change direction where the twig divides or where there is a side shoot. Try painting quick straight marks, pausing and changing directions. Slow curved marks will not work for the vast majority of trees with the possible exception of a weeping willow.

Using a mix of phthalo blue and burnt sienna, paint the ivy using the side of the rigger. Adding ultramarine to the mix will give you the shadow-side colour (8B). Continue on to the next stage without letting the paint dry.

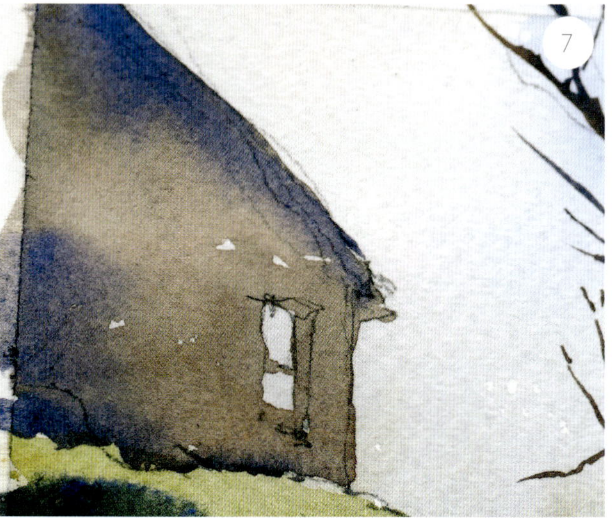

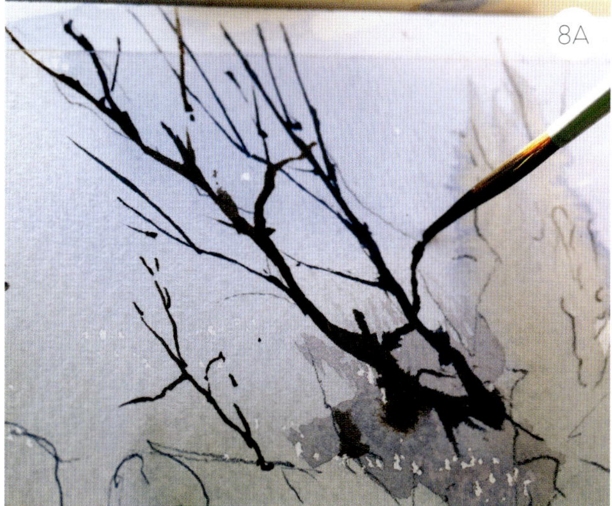

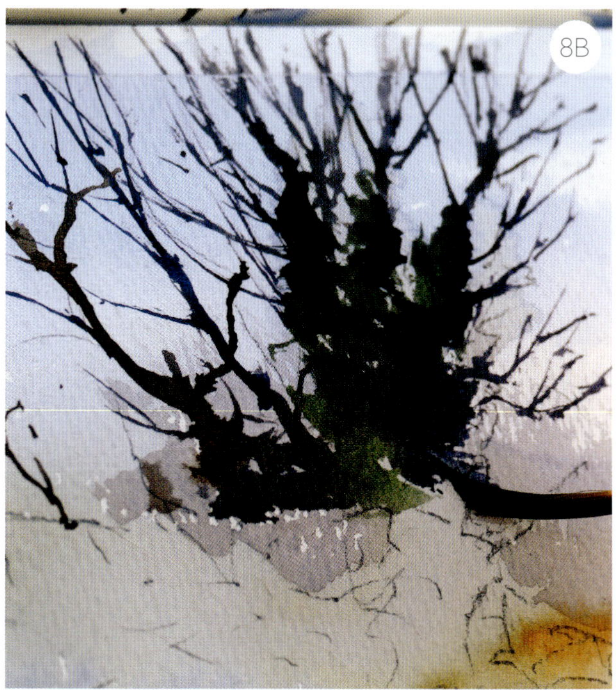

9. The gorse hedge

Continue on from the tree while it is still wet, using a size 12 round and some pure warm yellow to strengthen the colour of the gorse (9A).

Follow this with some of the shadow colour from the tree in step 8. The dark mix creates a strong contrast, allowing the yellow to glow. Create a bright green mix of phthalo blue and warm yellow and suggest the shrub in front of the gorse (9B).

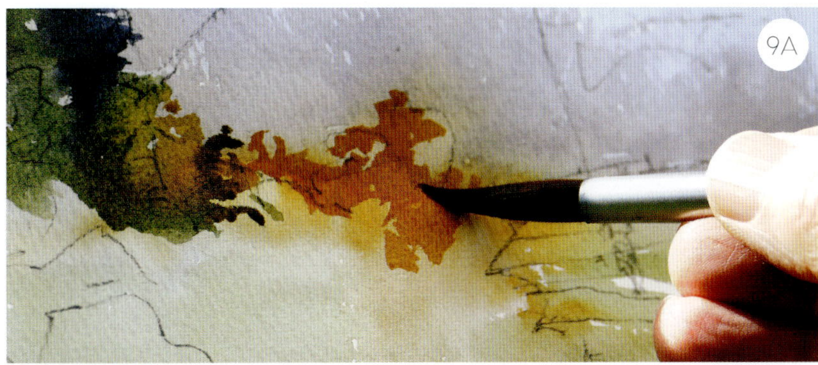
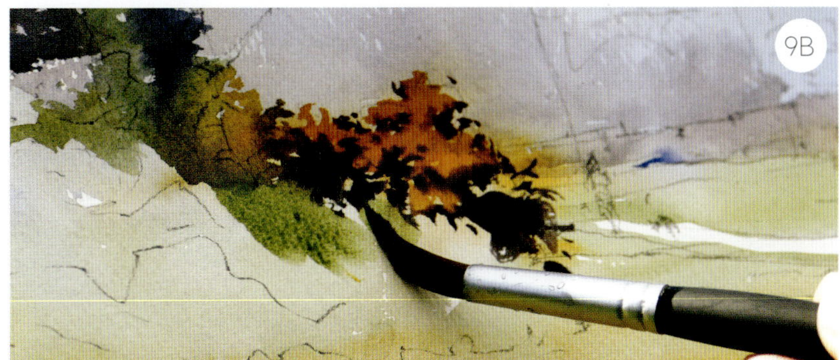

10. Strengthening the distant walls and trees

If the right-hand side is now dry, strengthen the colour of the walls of the buildings using burnt sienna (10A). Then slightly strengthen those distant trees (10B) using ultamarine and brown madder. You don't want to do too much – it is so important not to overdo the distance.

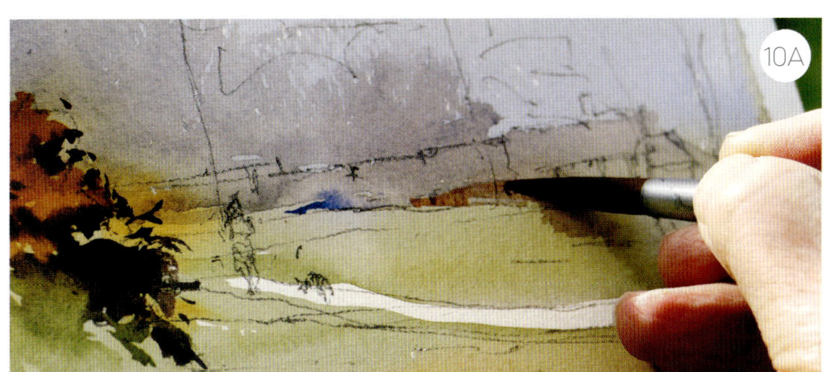
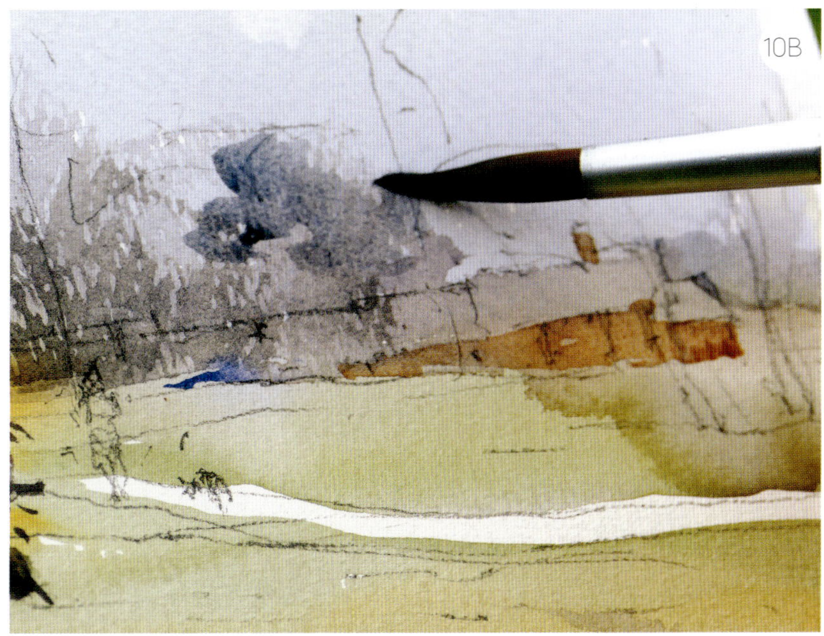

11. The hedgerow

Use a weak greenish-yellow to suggest the sunlight on the hedge, then follow this with a strong phthalo blue and burnt sienna mix to indicate the shadowed part of the hedge. The strength of this allows you to show a contrast against the lightness of the foreground shrub.

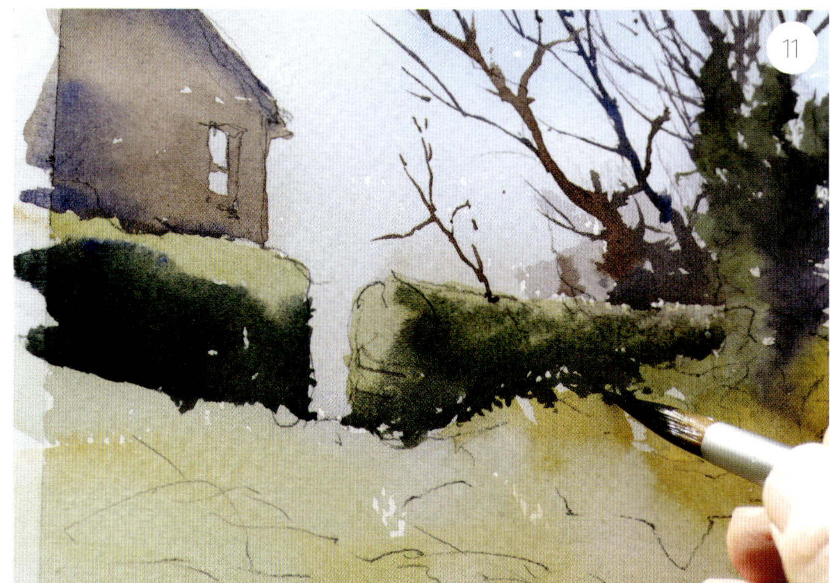

12. The figure

Use cobalt blue for the coat and add burnt sienna to this for the trousers and dog. To create a sense of distance it is important not to add in too much detail.

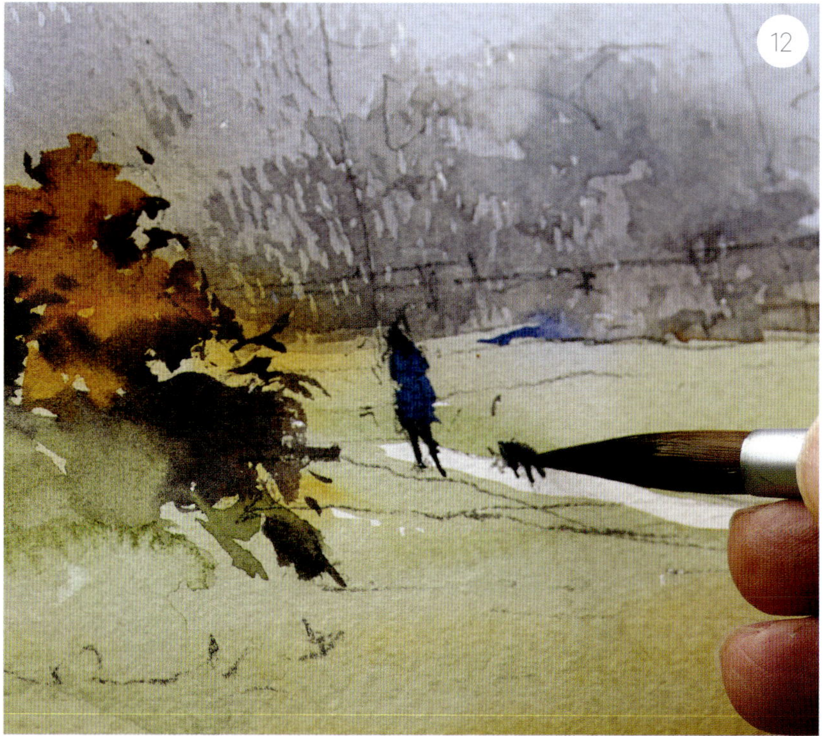

TIP: CREATING REALISTIC, DISTANT FIGURES

There were plenty of people around and so it was easy to check heights and proportions for my figure. The figure is quite far away so I really wanted no more than a suggestion.

13–16. Adding further details

I quite like telegraph poles. Landscapes can be very horizontal and the telegraph pole creates a welcome vertical. Add it in using ultramarine and burnt sienna with the size 10 rigger. Soften parts of it to avoid it being too dominant (13).

Use ultramarine and brown madder for the shadow mix on the right-hand buildings – begin with quite a weak strength (14).

Back to the foreground: add some stronger greens to create variety, together with some of the shadow mix at the bottom (15). Keep the brushstrokes organic, and bring them down the bank in the direction of the foreground grass at the same angle of the slope of the bank.

Soften a lot of the edges as you work.

Although the whole house is in shadow, it will always appear darkest under the eaves and in the window reveals, so add in further washes to darken these areas (16).

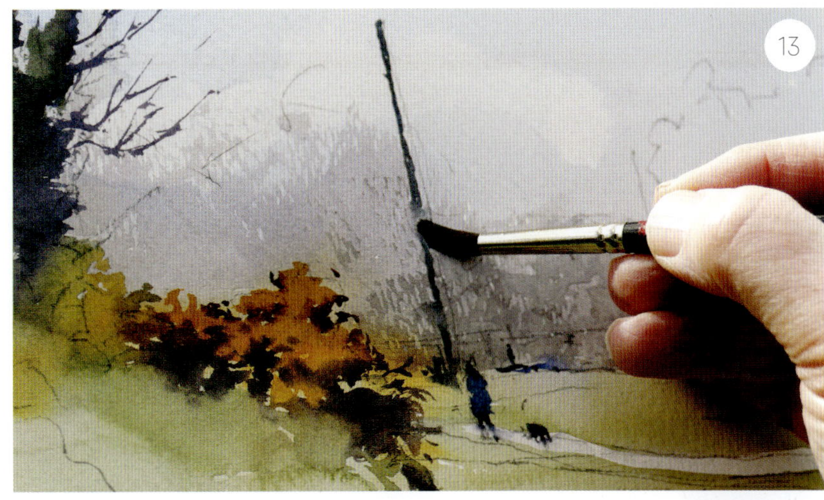

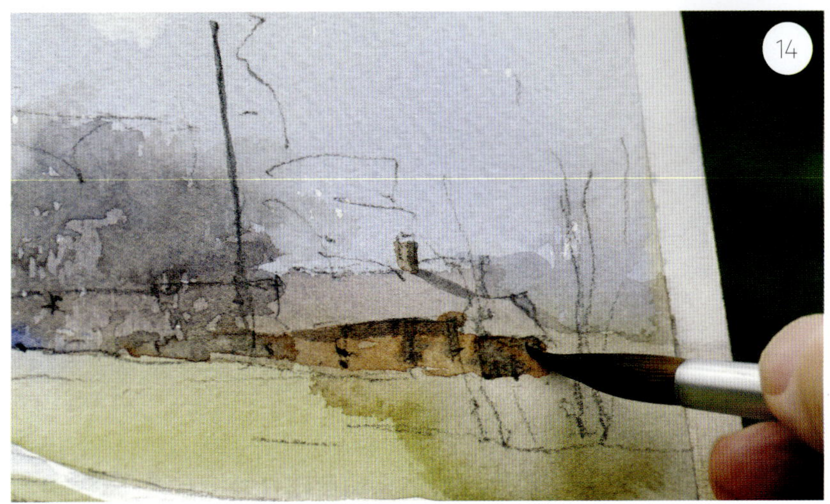

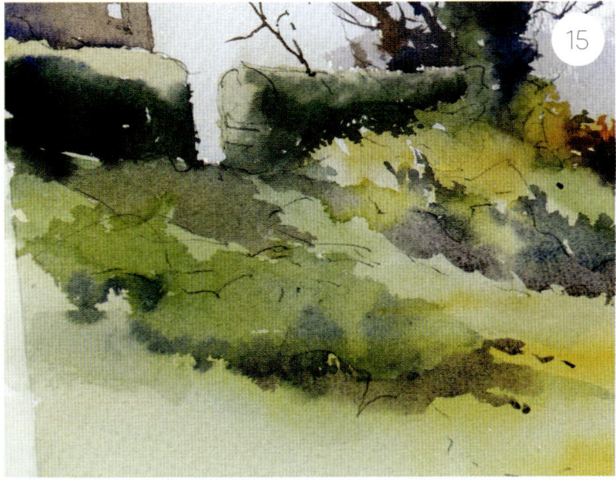

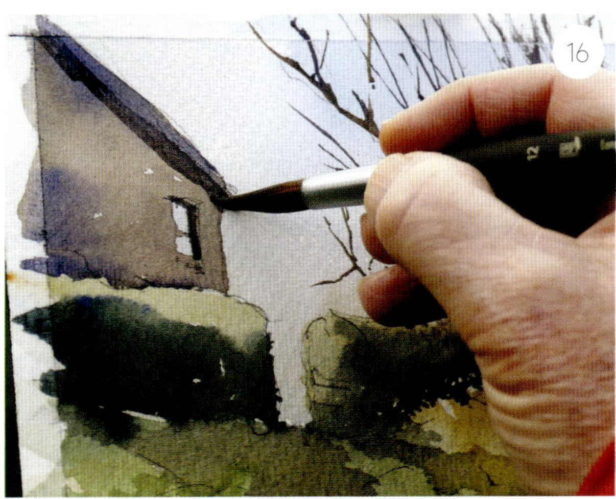

17. The midground trees

Add these with a stronger shadow mix (ultramarine and brown madder) using the side of a size 12 brush. Use a variety of strokes and soften quite a lot of them – you want to create the appearance of the leafless trees without painting hundreds of little lines (17A). Add a shadow under the trees to connect them together and avoid a disjointed appearance at the bottom of the trunks (17B).

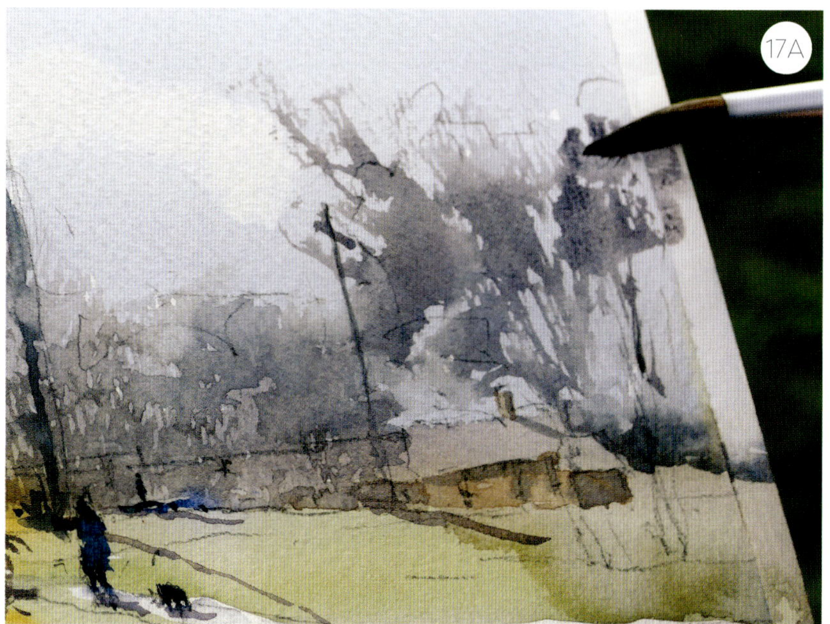

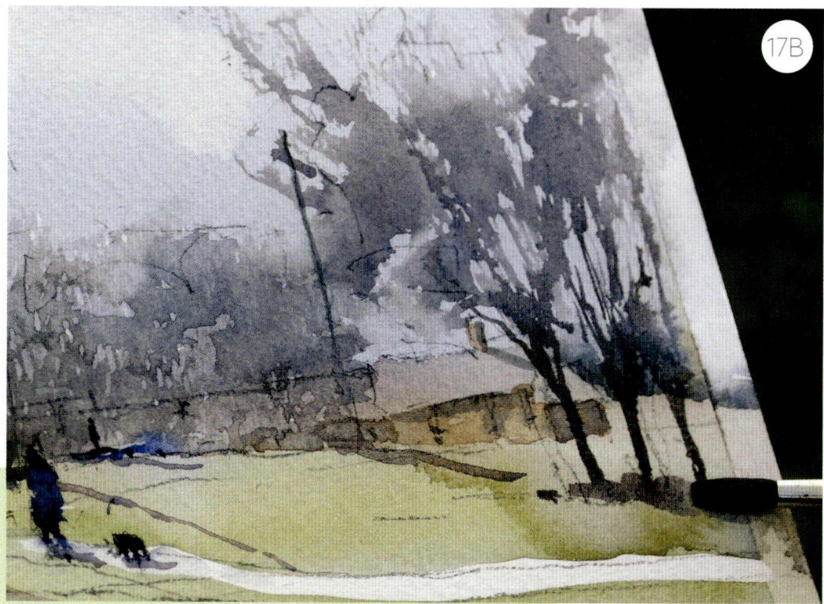

LOCATION INSIGHT

This was one of those perfect locations with toilets *and* an ice cream van close by.
My painting location was well off the public path and the grassy ground was quite soft, so that meant I didn't get a single passer-by stopping for a chat!

TIP: CREATING REALISTIC DAFFODILS

The furthest areas of flowers need to be little more than simple suggestions. This sounds quite easy but in practice it can be hit or miss. Too detailed and the flowers will advance, and too simple will be meaningless. I like to create almost random abstract marks that are roughly the size and shape of the groups of flowers. It is important to think of groups, not individuals. I use my finger quite a lot to soften or rather smudge the marks, as this helps to integrate them with the background washes.

18. The daffodils

Using a strong mix of warm yellow colour and your size 12 brush, begin to dab in uneven lines of daffodils so that they slope gently down the bank (18A). Use your finger to smudge the marks slightly as you go (18B). Continue to add further drifts of flowers as you go (18C), dropping in occasional touches of green to indicate where the stems and leaves will be (18D). At this stage do not try to paint any specific flowers.

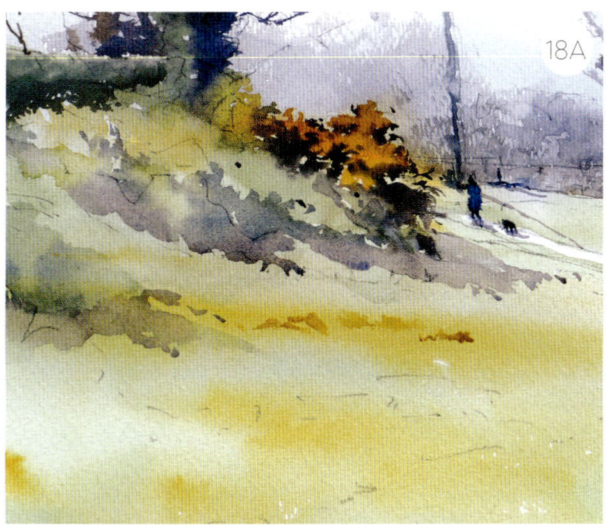

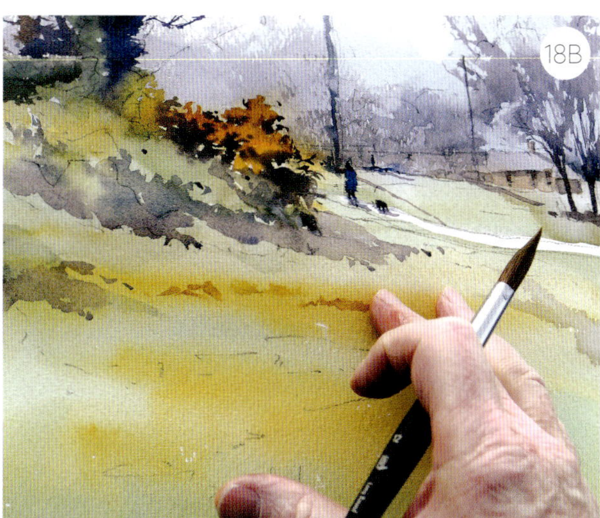

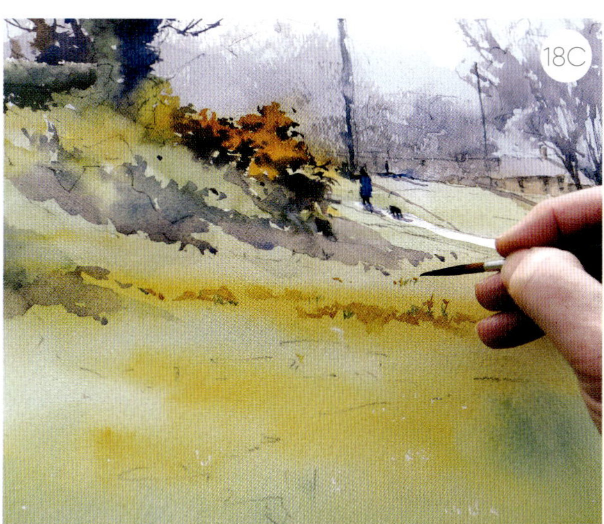

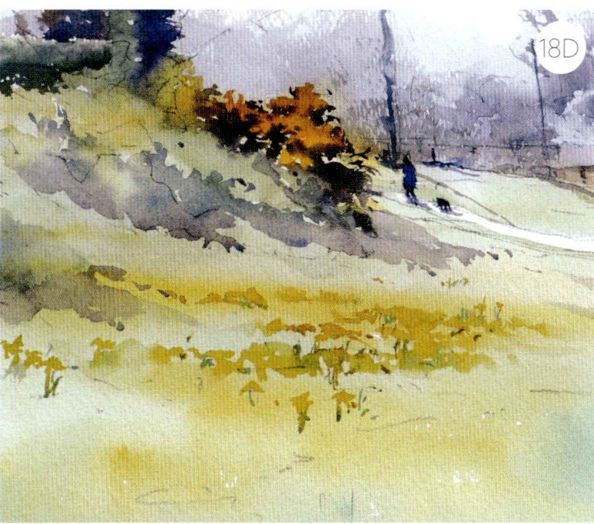

The daffodils continued

At the midway point between the most distant and the closest daffodils, start to make some more 'daffodil-like' marks, along with some distinct suggestions of leaves. You still don't want strong detail, so use some splatter, created by tapping a loaded brush, to keep things loose (18E).

In the foreground area, use stronger colour, harder edges, stronger shadows and more of an obvious flower shape in places. Use an orange mix made from warm yellow and warm red to simply suggest some of the flower trumpets (18F).

I feel that the original wash is a little too pale for the foreground, so I have tried to balance mine with some additional greens (18G). It's difficult to know when enough is enough, but, if you want to, add in few stronger suggestions of the foreground flowers using your strongest mixes yet.

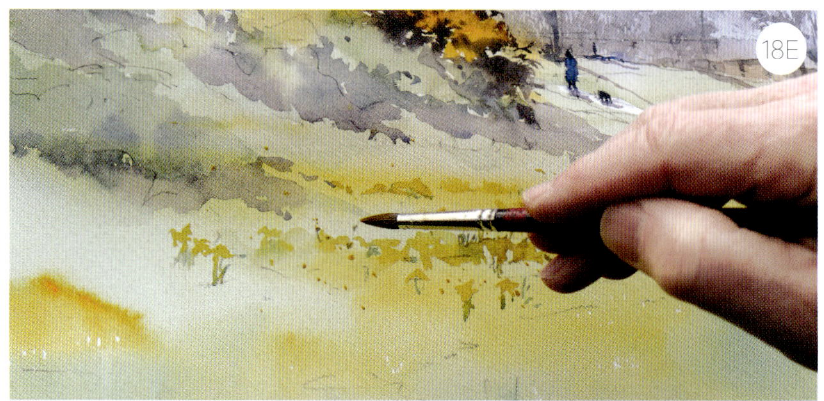

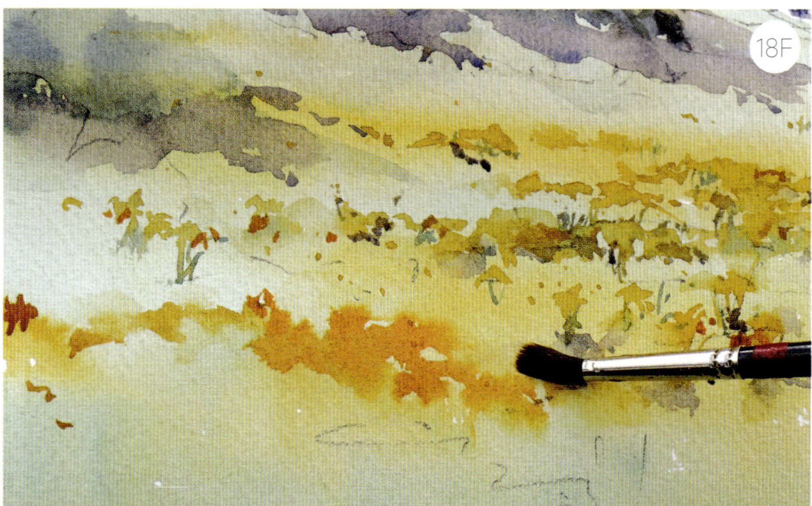

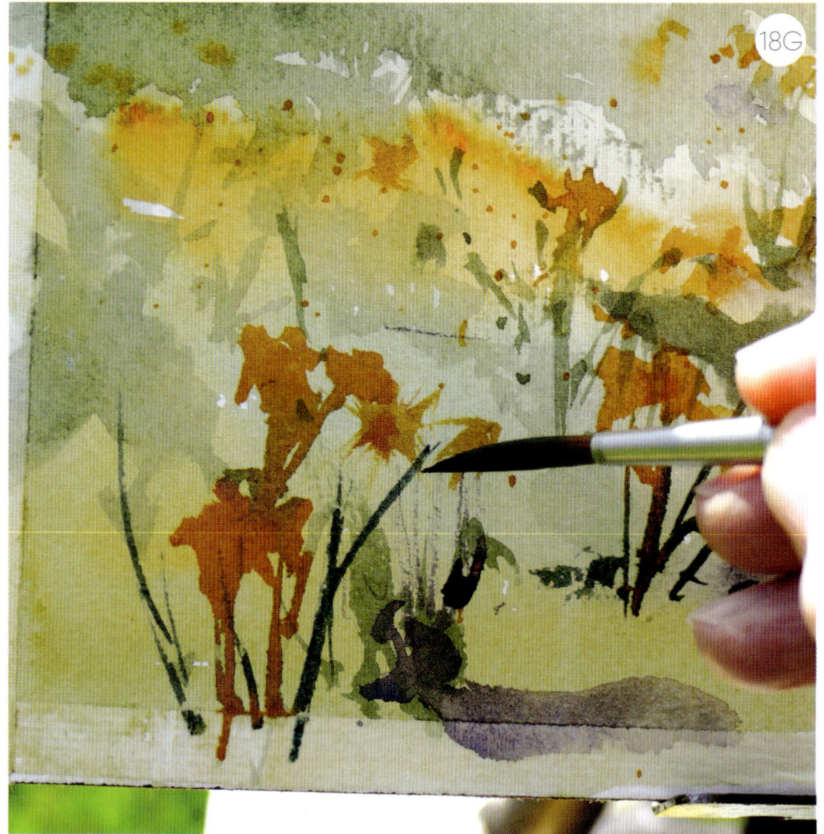

Use your shadow mix (ultramarine and brown madder and your size 8 or 12 brush) to add in some touches of shadow at the base of some of the clumps, and dotted naturally about in the drifts. If you want to pick out some of the paler daffodils, mix a little yellow into some pure opaque white and touch them in. These must be added over relatively dark areas or they won't be seen (18H).

Add the centres of the white daffodils using strong mixes of red or orange for contrast (18I).

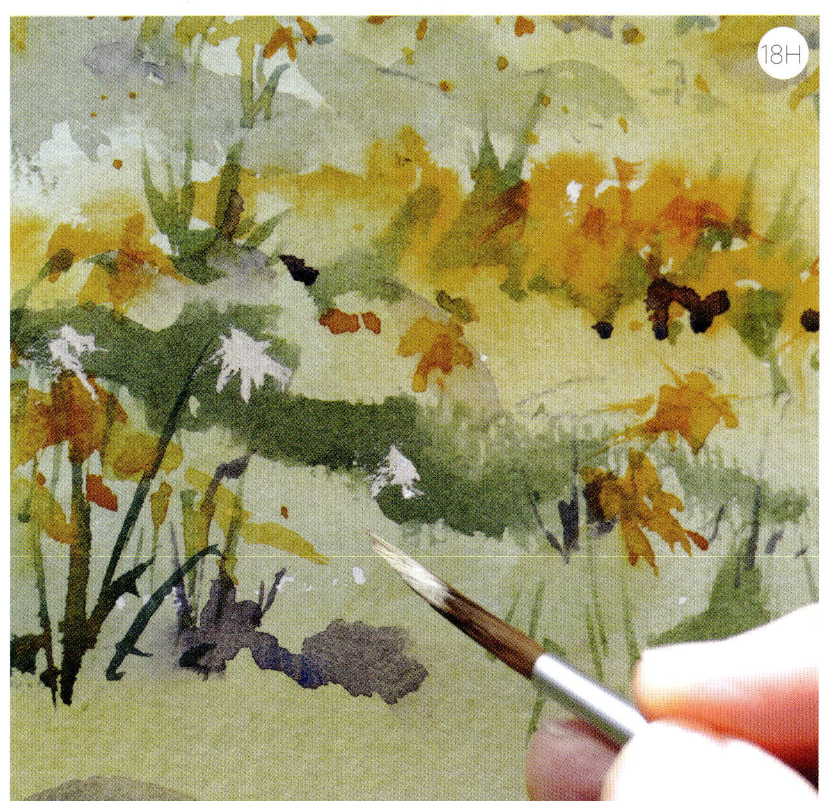

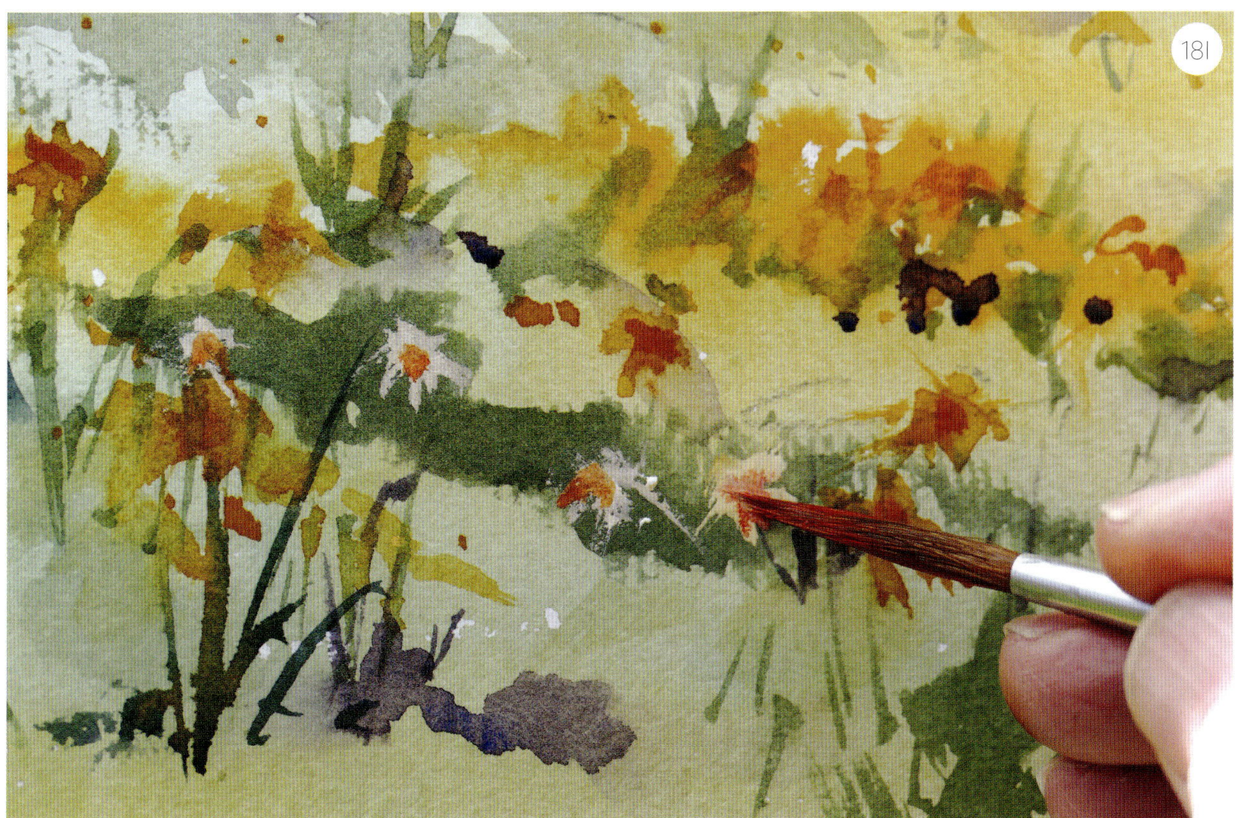

19. Final details

Use a very strong mix of ultramarine and brown madder to add some final branches to the main tree. Using your rigger, use the same mix to create the telegraph lines and add some simple detail on the poles.

To finish, you may want to use pure opaque white to add a simple 'halo' to the figure.

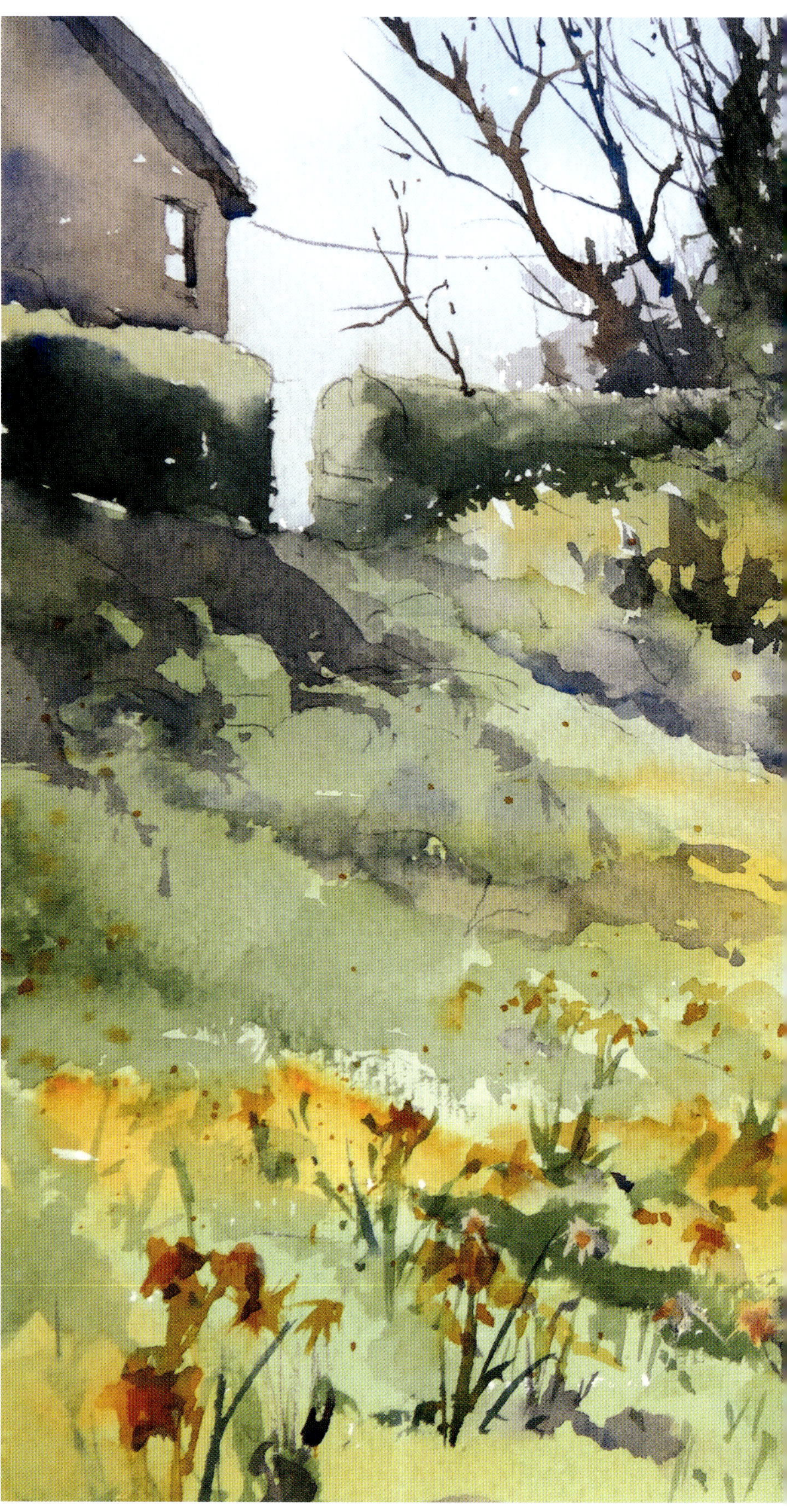

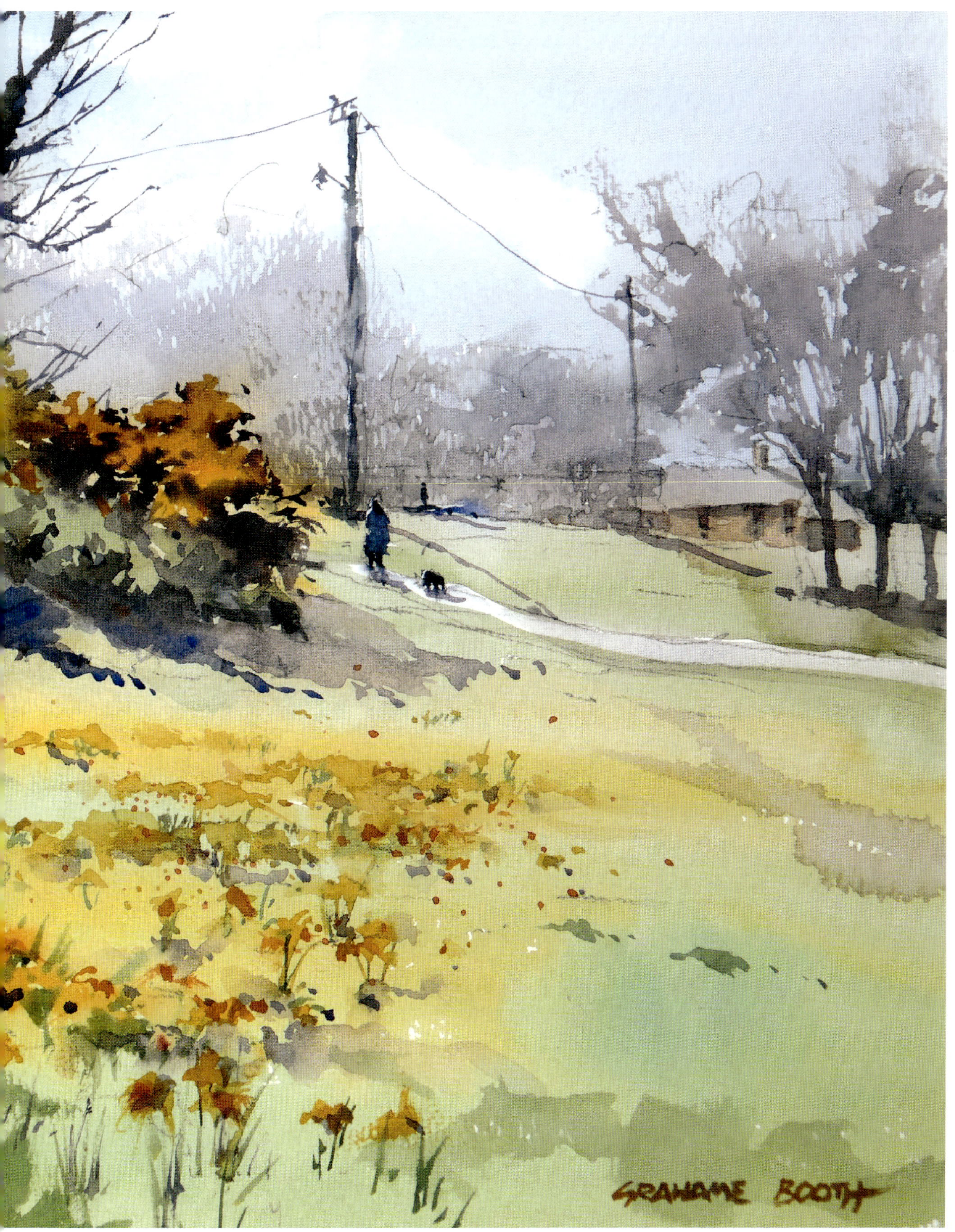
GRAHAME BOOTH

2. RNIYC, CULTRA

This was bright and blustery springtime weather and although the leaves were just about starting to appear on the trees, they are not really noticeable from this distance. Of course, the subject isn't really about trees; instead we have the rather nice clubhouse of the Royal North of Ireland Yacht Club (RNIYC) and lots of boaty clutter in the grounds.

YOU WILL NEED

PAINTS

- » **Cobalt blue**
- » **Ultramarine**
- » **Phthalo blue (green shade)**
- » **Warm yellow**
- » **Burnt sienna**
- » **Brown madder**
- » **Warm red**
- » **White gouache**

BRUSHES

- » **Mop or other large soft brush, squirrel or synthetic**
- » **Size 12 and 8 round, sable or synthetic**
- » **Size 10 rigger, sable or synthetic**
- » **Old size 8 sable for softening and lifting out**

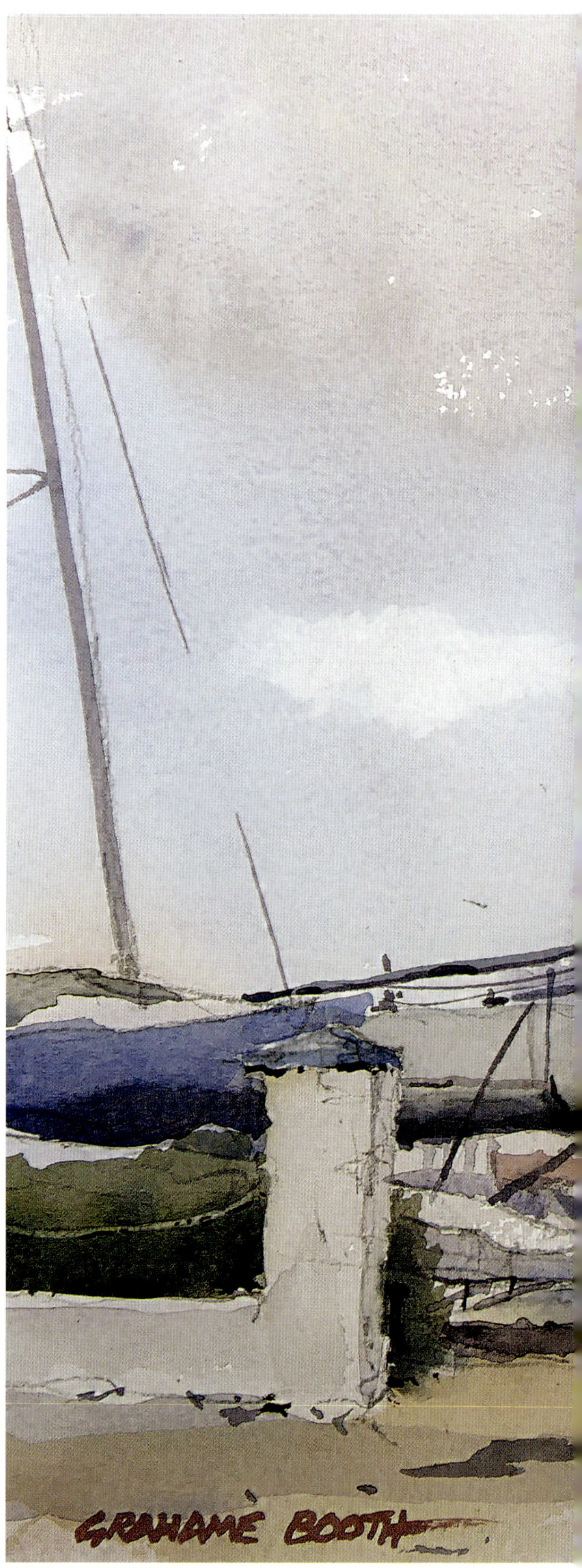

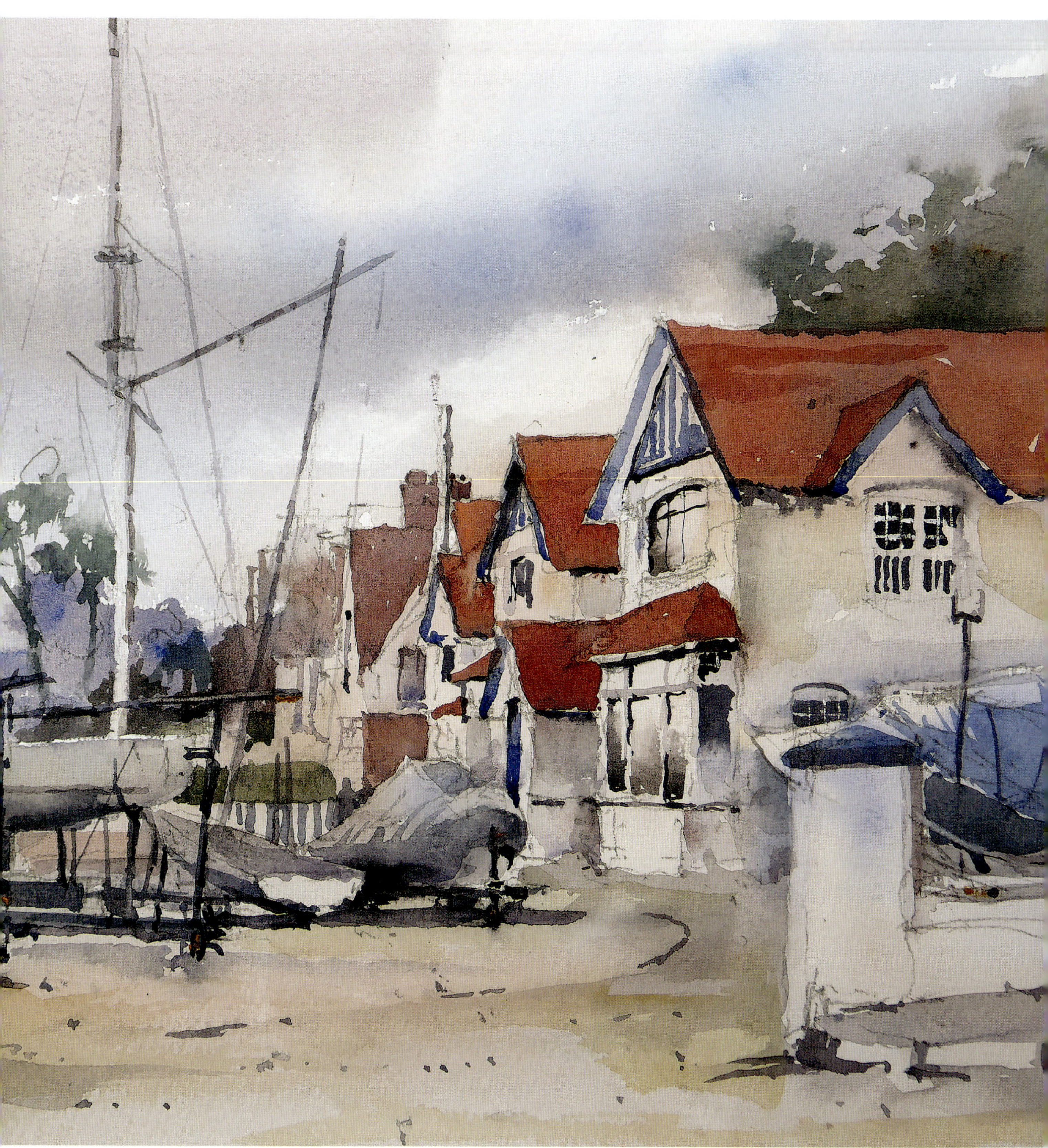

RNIYC, CULTRA
38 x 28cm (15 x 11in), Millford CP 300gsm (140lb)

1. The initial sketch

The sea is actually just to the left of the photograph, but, although I took my usual walk around, I couldn't find a position where the sea, the boats and the clubhouse were all arranged nicely, so the sea had to go. I kept things much as they are in reality but I did move a few things around. If you refer to the photograph (1A), you can see which parts of the original scene I chose to omit or change in the final sketch (1B).

» I greatly simplified the collection of boats and the distant buildings.

» I left out the benches in front of the main window and the yellow water hydrant indicator, following my usual question of, 'If it wasn't there, would I put it in?' – I certainly wouldn't have added the bright yellow marker.

» I wasn't sure about the position of the gateposts so I made them a little smaller and further apart.

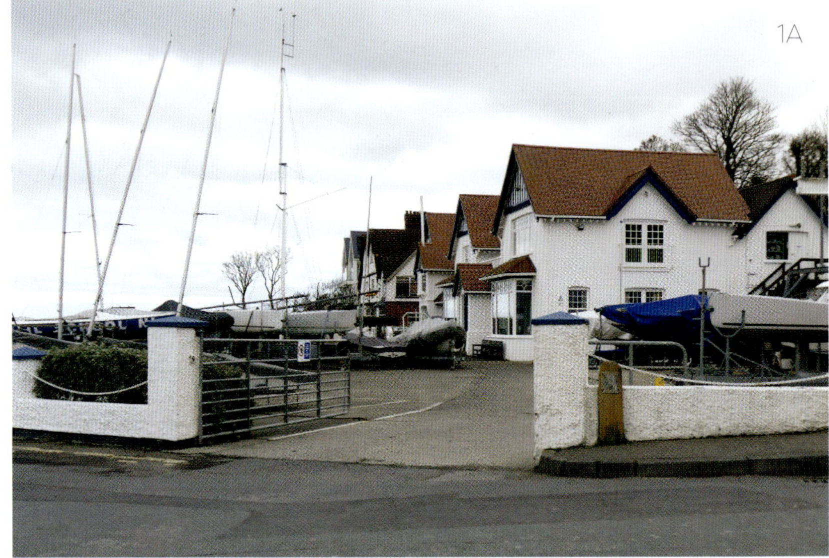

1A

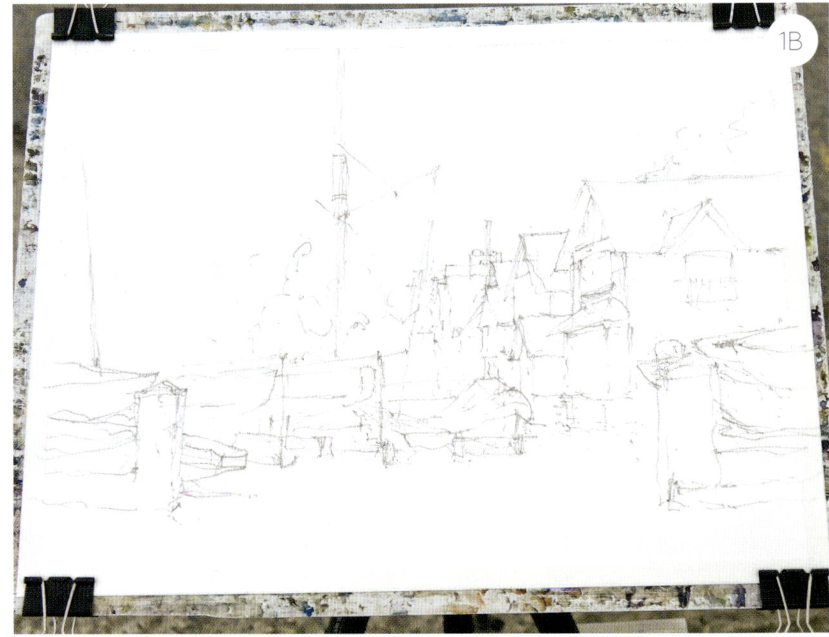

1B

LOCATION INSIGHT

I had just finished my drawing and was feeling quite pleased with myself when one of the club members decided to move his boat. I am always amazed at how apologetic people are for doing what they are perfectly entitled to do, and in my experience they always try to avoid getting in the way. As it was, he was finished in a few minutes.

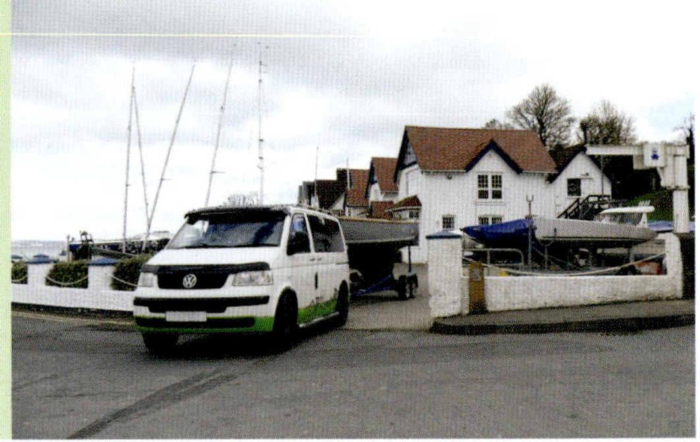

2. The first wash

Put in your first wash, working from the top of the picture down and blending the colours as you go using a soft mop brush. Mix a grey for the sky from ultramarine and burnt sienna, then use cobalt blue for the sky – don't leave areas of white paper to suggest cloud. Instead, use plain water for the cloud areas. This is important to allow the clouds to be lifted out later without too hard an edge. Wash on down the paper and add more burnt sienna to suggest the warmth of the buildings, a little more cobalt blue for the boats, then finish the foreground with a dull orange mixed from warm red and burnt sienna (2A).

While the sky is still wet, gently lift out a few suggestions of white cloud using kitchen paper (2B). Leave the painting to dry: although this wasn't a warm day, the drying time wasn't too long.

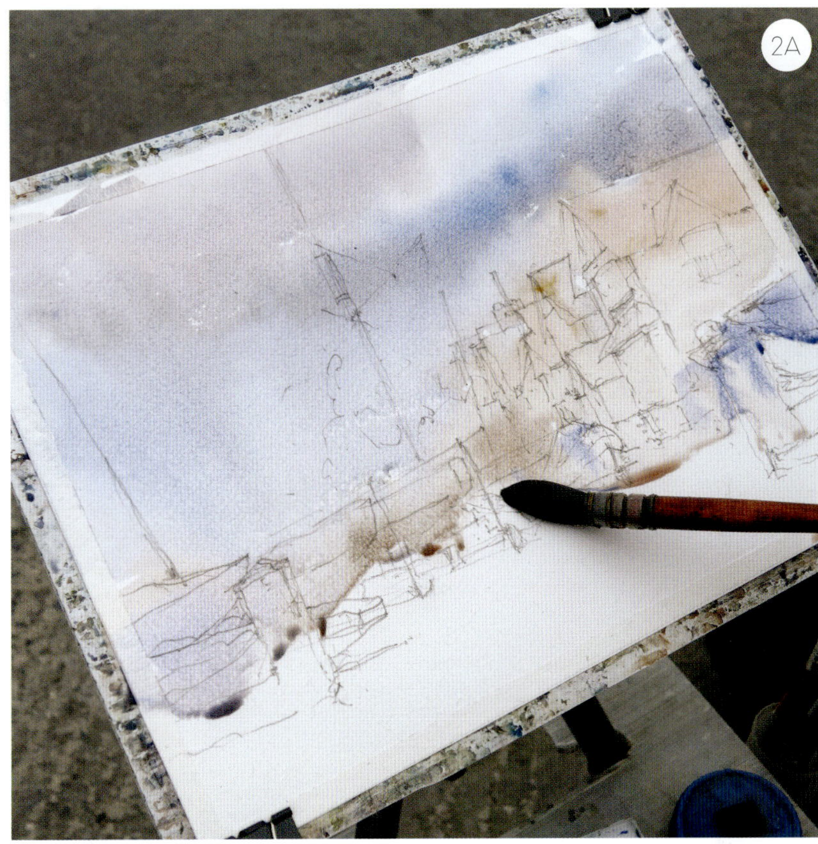

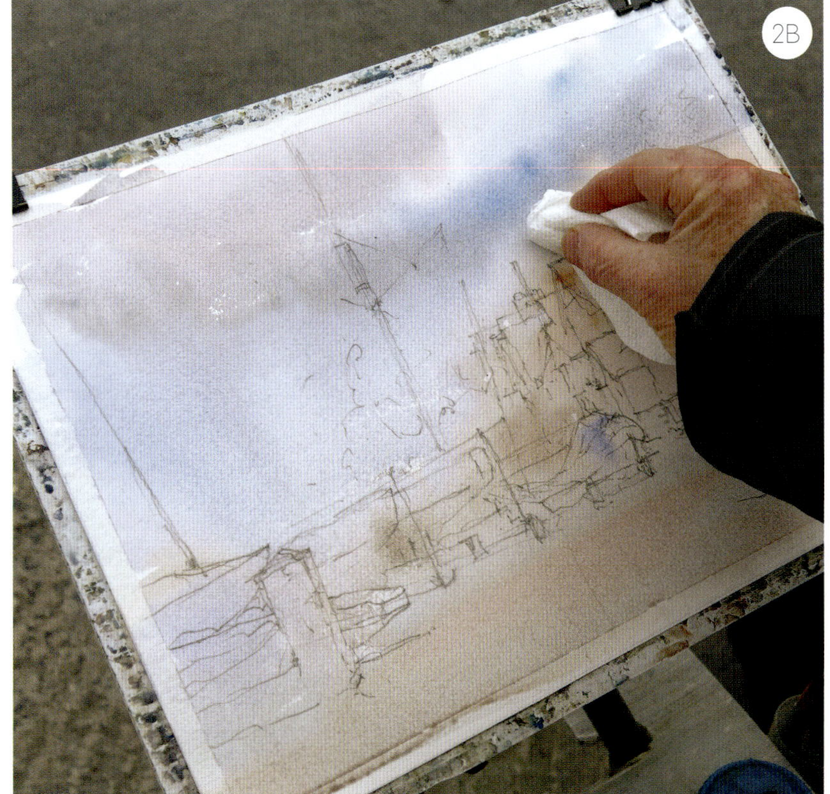

CHANGING CONDITIONS

The sky was changing constantly, with the grey clouds opening up to reveal some blue sky, but I rarely attempt to paint a frozen sky, preferring to go more for a general suggestion of the conditions. Because the sky changes constantly on a blustery day, there is little point in trying for a snapshot. Instead, try to paint an 'average' sky, indicating the general features you have noticed.

3. The distant trees and roofs

This is quite a complex subject so it's very important not to get bogged down in unnecessary detail. Begin by suggesting the distant trees with a size 12 round and cobalt blue with a touch of brown madder (3A). Then add in the distant buildings. Use mixes of cobalt blue, burnt sienna and brown madder for everything from blue through to the reddish colour. At this point, allow elements to run together as this helps give harmony and you will have plenty of time to adjust details later (3B).

4. The clubhouse roof

The roofs of the clubhouse are quite a bright orange. Mix this using warm red and warm yellow with just a touch of ultramarine to temper the brightness. At this stage, simply paint all of the roofs with the same mix, only varying it slightly. Where two roofs overlap, treat them as one single shape. It is better to do this and separate them later if necessary.

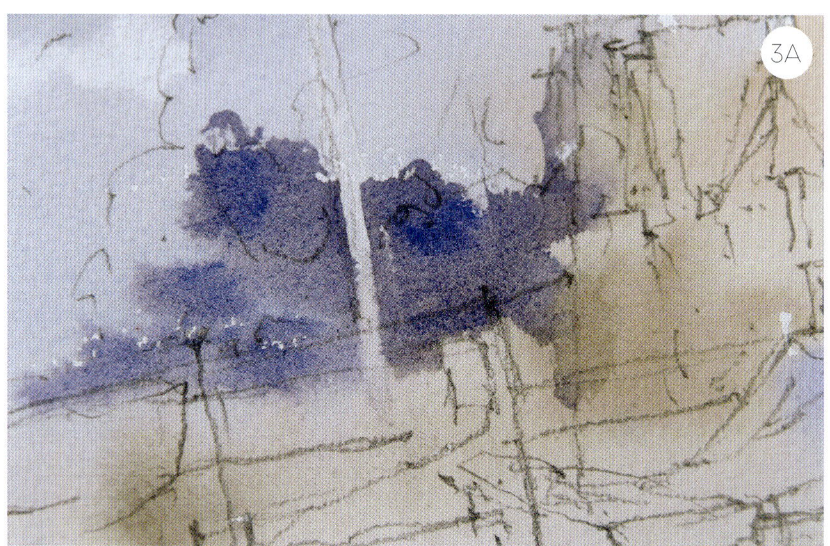

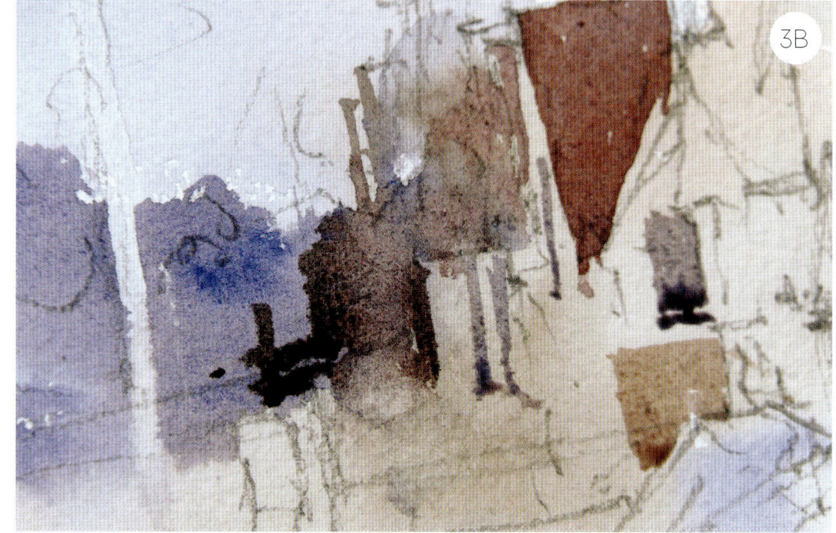

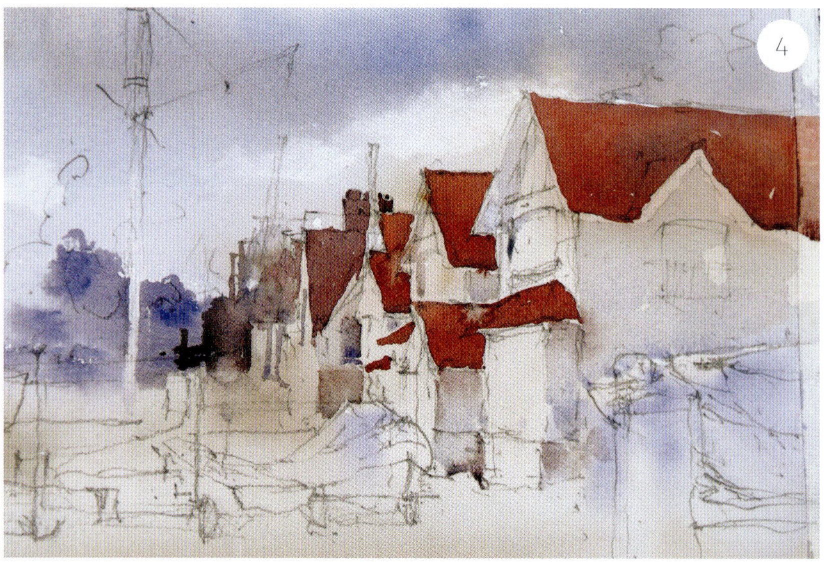

5. The boats

I was more interested in the arrangement of the boats than the individual boats themselves. With this in mind, paint an initial wash over all of the boats, allowing one to run into the next, creating the all-important connections. Vary the colour slightly using ultramarine, cobalt blue, burnt sienna and any other paint left over in your palette.

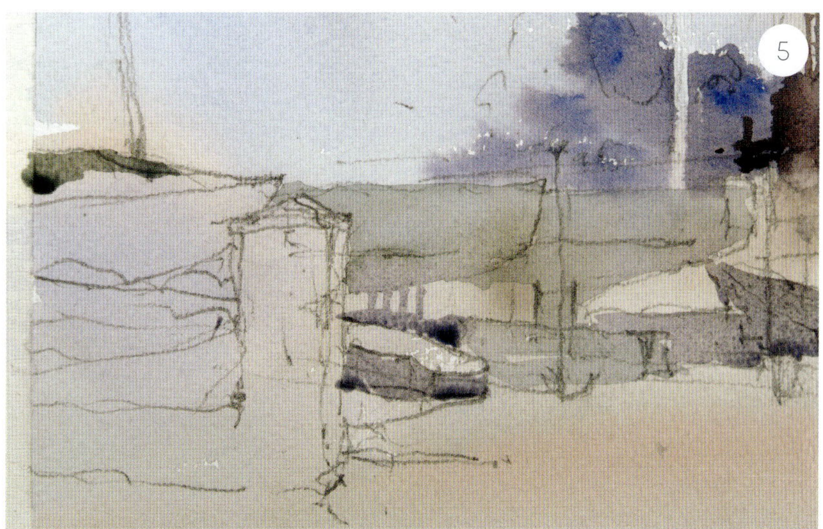

6. The distant trees

Use a mix of phthalo blue with warm yellow to create a dull green for the closer trees behind the clubhouse. A tree shape is enough for this – you don't need to create separate branches or leaves (not that there were any). Soften the edge of the tree shape slightly to avoid it being too eye-catching. Use this same mix to give just a slight indication of the two trees in the distance.

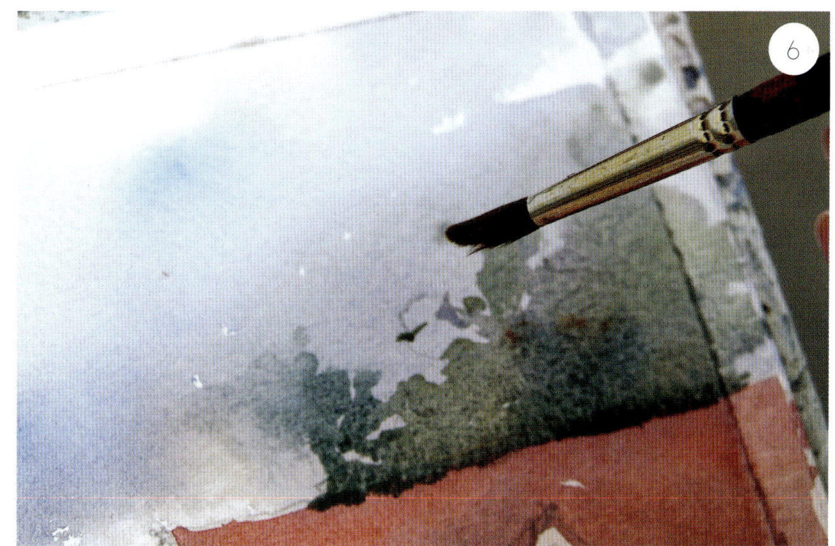

7. The paintwork

Use ultramarine and a size 8 brush to detail the rich blue paintwork.

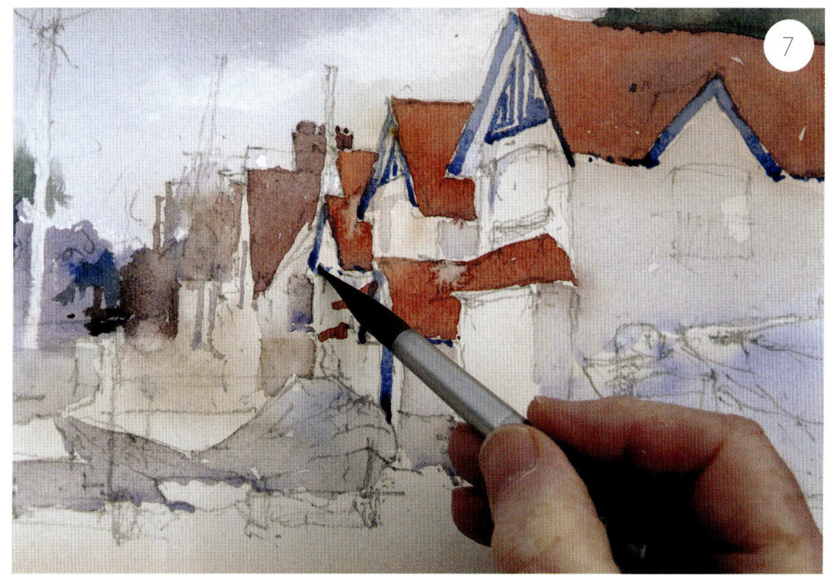

8. Defining the boats

It's time to define the boats a little more. Use ultramarine and burnt sienna to create a blue grey and use this for the darker areas of the boats and trailers. It is still important to connect things together, so don't differentiate between the darker parts of the boats, the trailers and the soft shadows below.

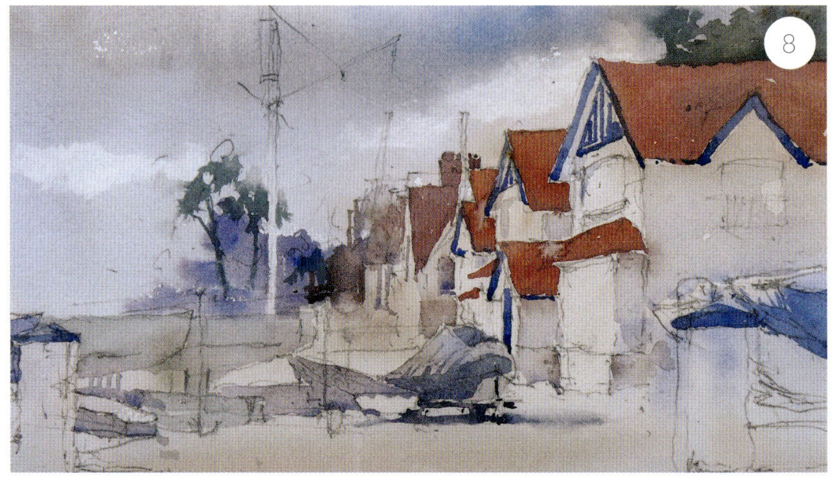

9. Adding straight lines

There are a lot of straight lines in this subject and they will look much better in the painting if they are at least reasonably straight. I used my watercolour mahlstick to paint the masts, which is much easier than attempting it freehand, but if you don't have one of these, you could try painting the edge of an old credit card and using it as a stamp. This will work better if you slightly abrade the edge using sandpaper.

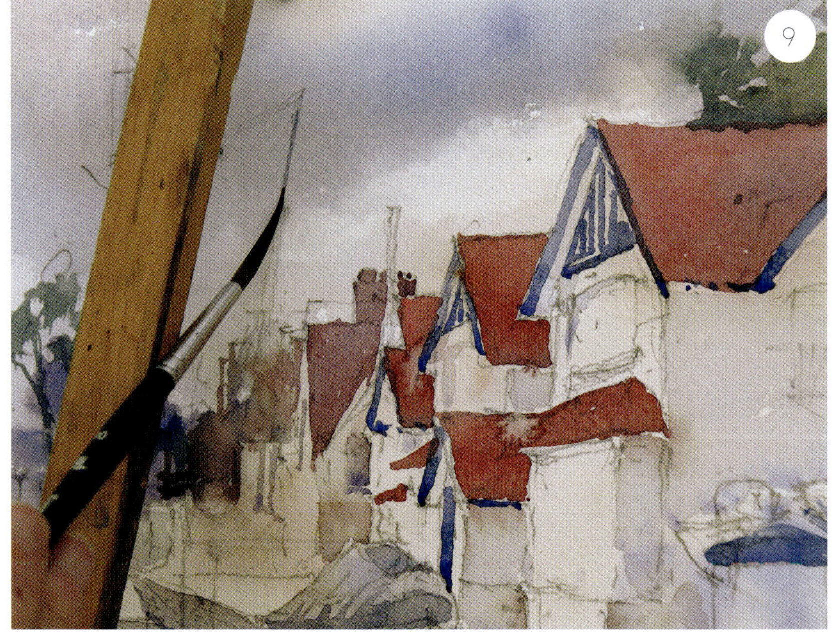

10. Curving the hull

Although we want to keep the boats simple it is still important to give a sense of the curvature of the hull. Simply darken the bottom of the hull and then soften the top of the dark mark to blend in with the topside.

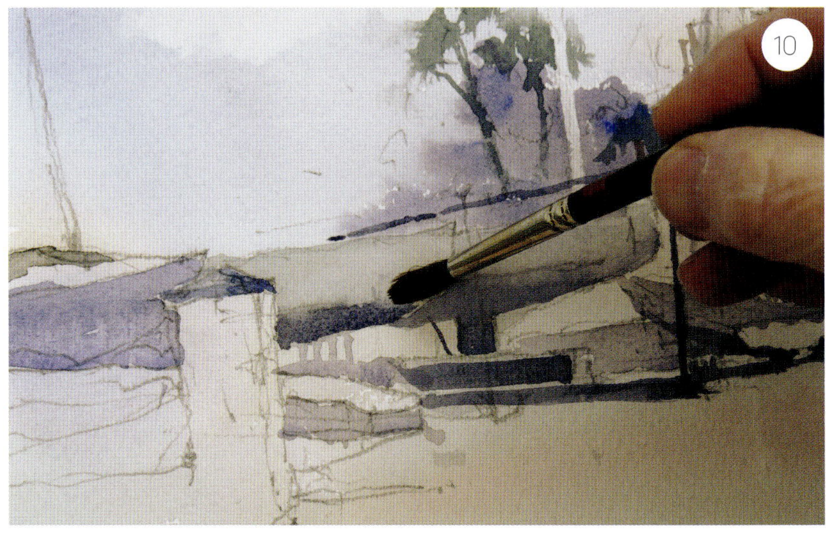

11. The hedge

Use a varying mix of ultramarine, phthalo blue and warm yellow to suggest the hedge behind the wall. This also provides some relief from the more formal structures in the boats and buildings.

12. The windows

Indicate parts of the windows using a strong mix of ultramarine and burnt sienna. (You will use white to suggest the glazing bars later.) I feel it is important not to repeat oblong shapes for windows. It is far better to create more abstract shapes by painting only part of the oblong for most of the windows.

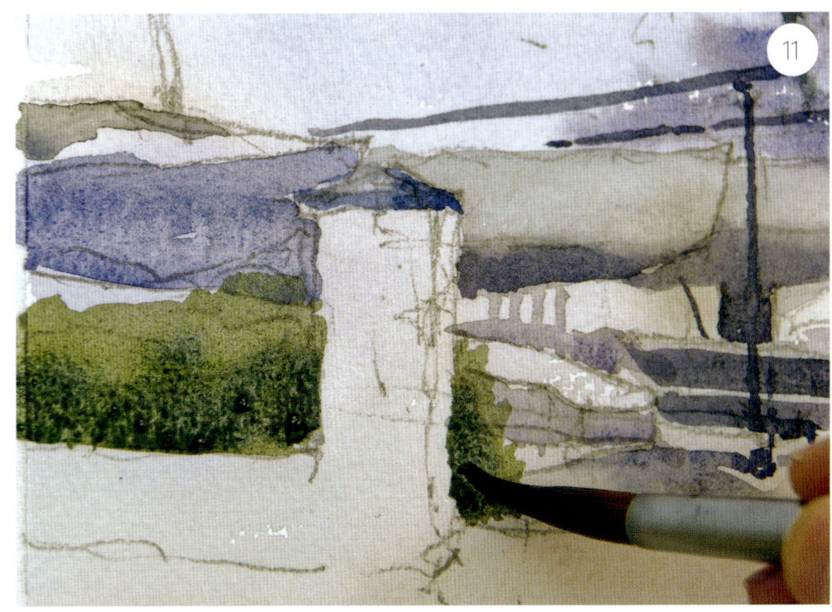

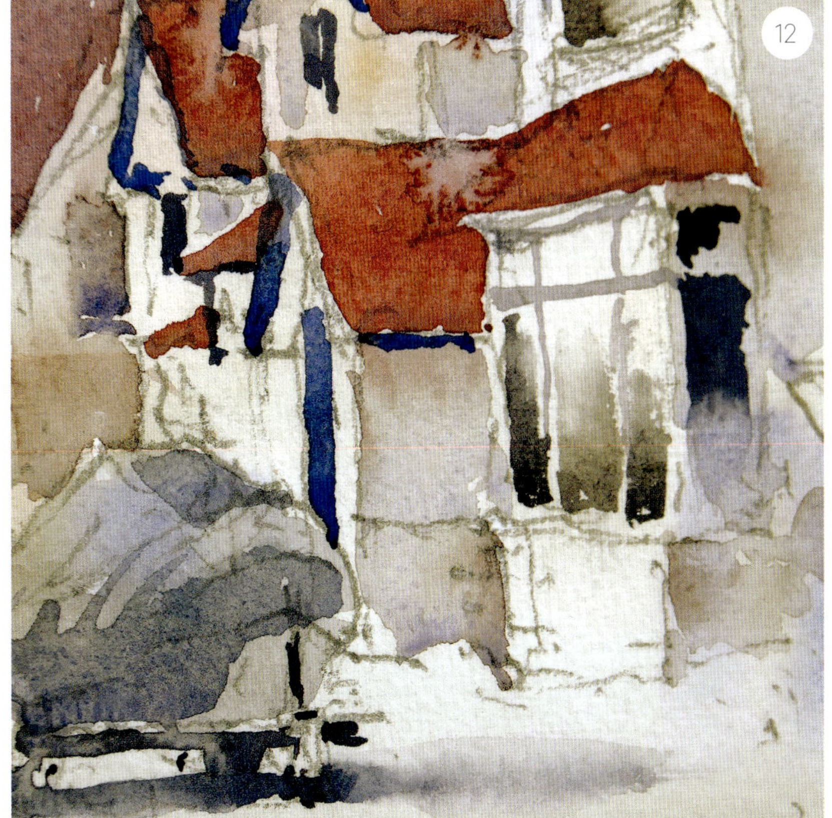

13. The gatepost

We need to separate the gatepost from the ground but we don't really want to darken either to any great extent. Instead, paint a sharp edge on the ground against the left side of the gatepost but soften it beyond – this gives the tonal difference we want but without any real increase in strength.

14. Darkening the windows

Indicate some of the darker parts of the windows using strong ultramarine and burnt sienna. Increase the strength of the walls and ground adjacent to the main window using a weaker version of the same mix, purely to make the main window look brighter.

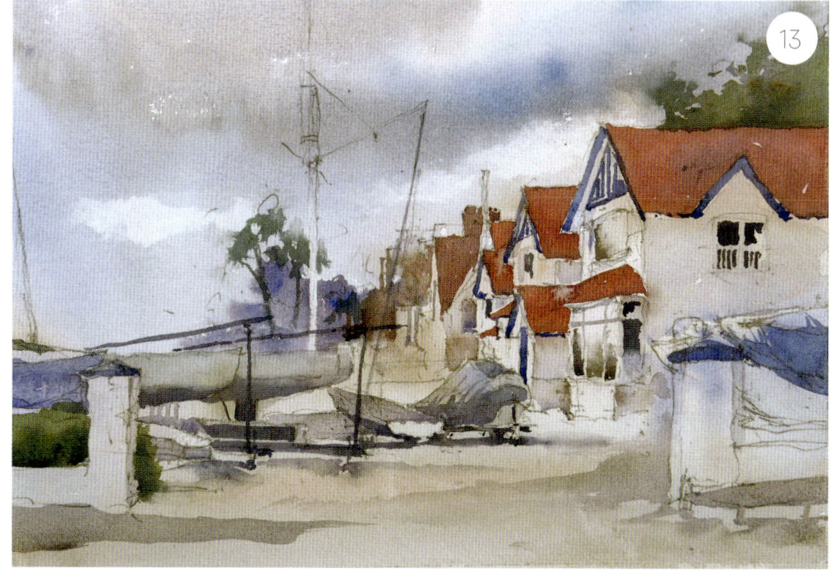

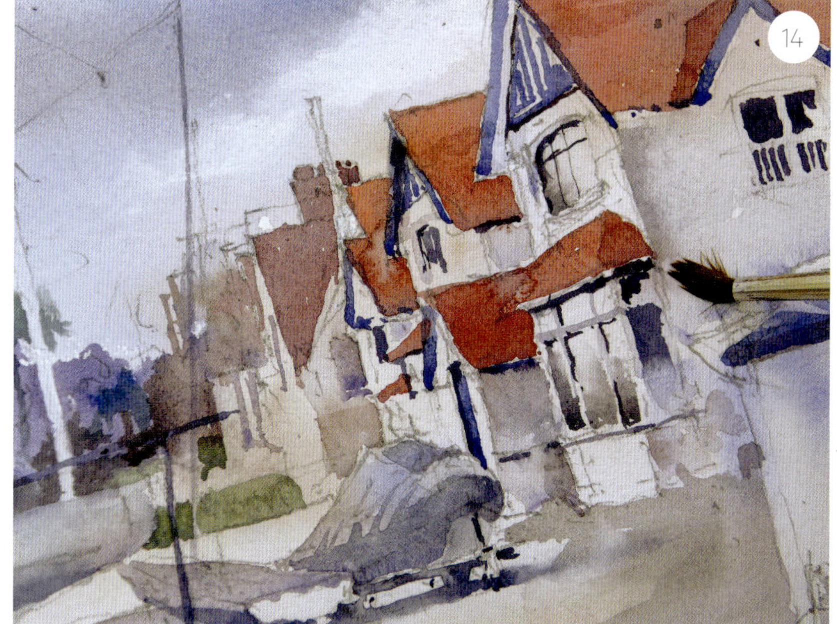

15. The flagpole and rigging

Paint the top of the club flagpole with the same blue grey that you have used elsewhere, but keep the lower part white. Although the flagpole is painted white in reality, it will appear dark against the light sky and light against the background trees. Add a few of the rigging lines using the same mix. I painted fewer than there were in reality: painting them all would have been overkill.

16. Lifting out

Use your lifting out brush to gently scrub out some light on the various poles. You could use opaque white for this, but it would make the poles far too obvious. Lifting out light creates a more subtle appearance.

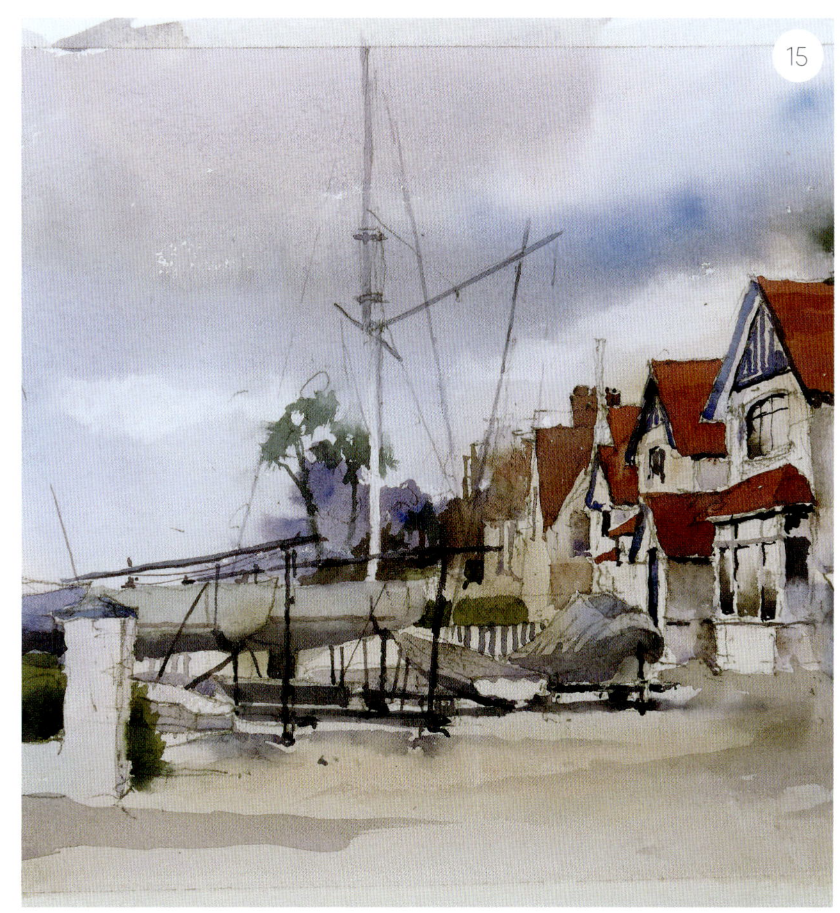

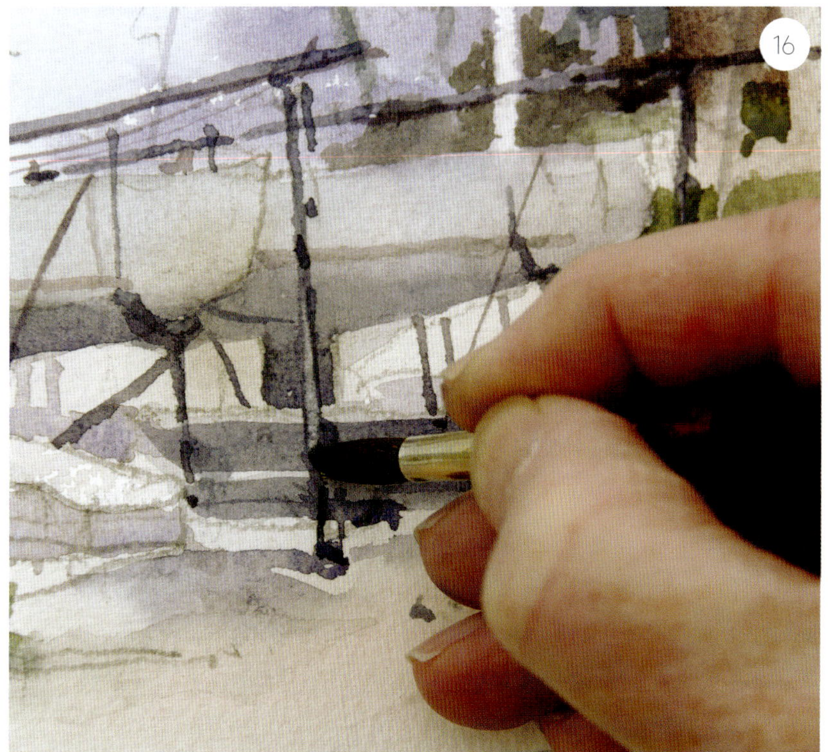

17. Final details

Finally, add some dark spots here and there on the ground, and on the gatepost and pavement. These little dark marks add interest to the painting. I could say they are deep shadows or stones but really they are just dark marks! Also add some pure white for the glazing bars.

I used a touch of the same warm red and warm yellow mix that I used on the roof to indicate the hubs of the trailer wheels. This was really to subtly spread out the red a little. It is best not to use red in only one place unless you really want to make a dramatic statement.

I am quite pleased with the finished painting. I feel I have simplified the subject quite well but with the benefit of hindsight I don't think I needed the gateposts at all. Oh well, we live and learn.

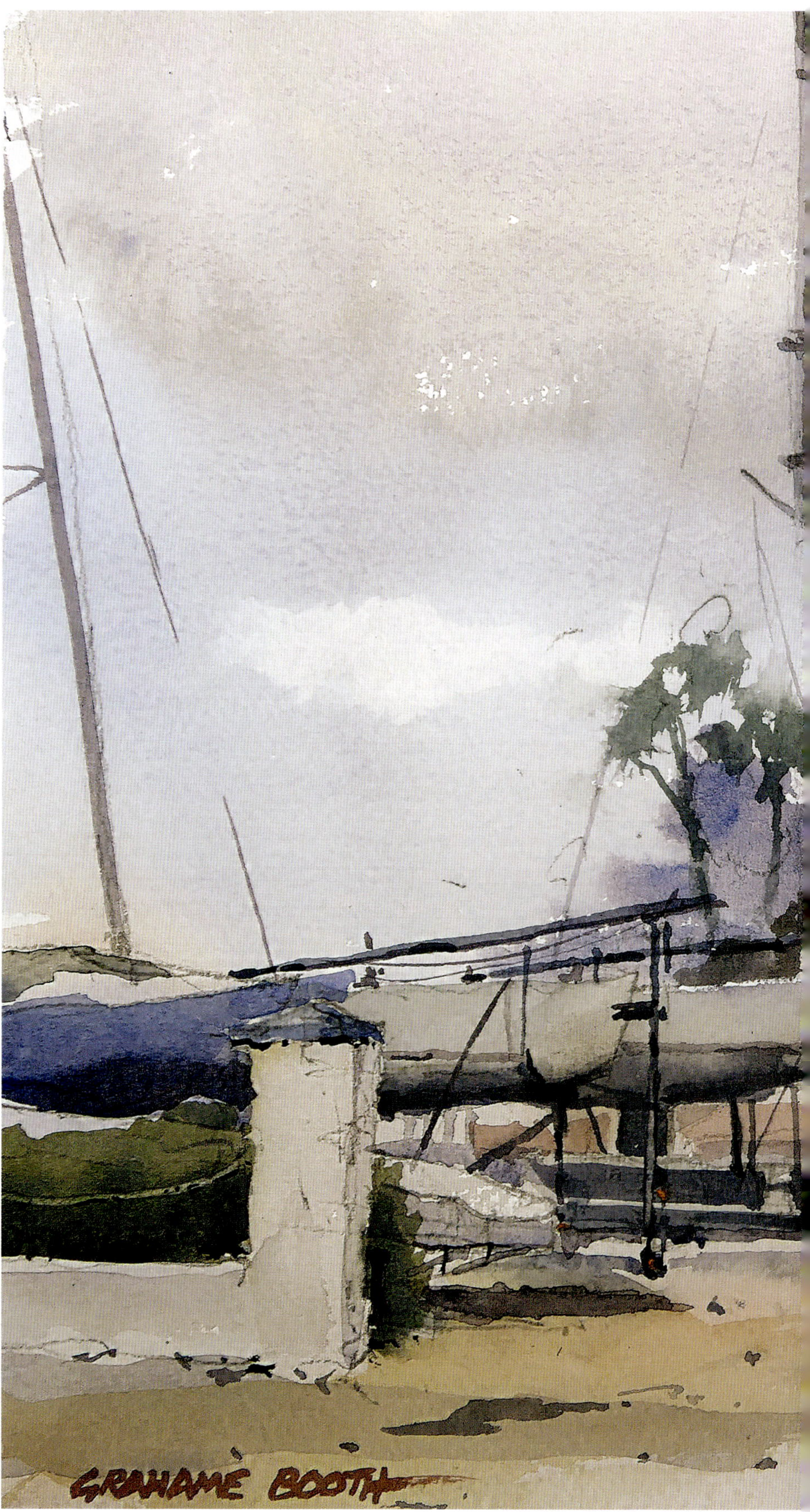

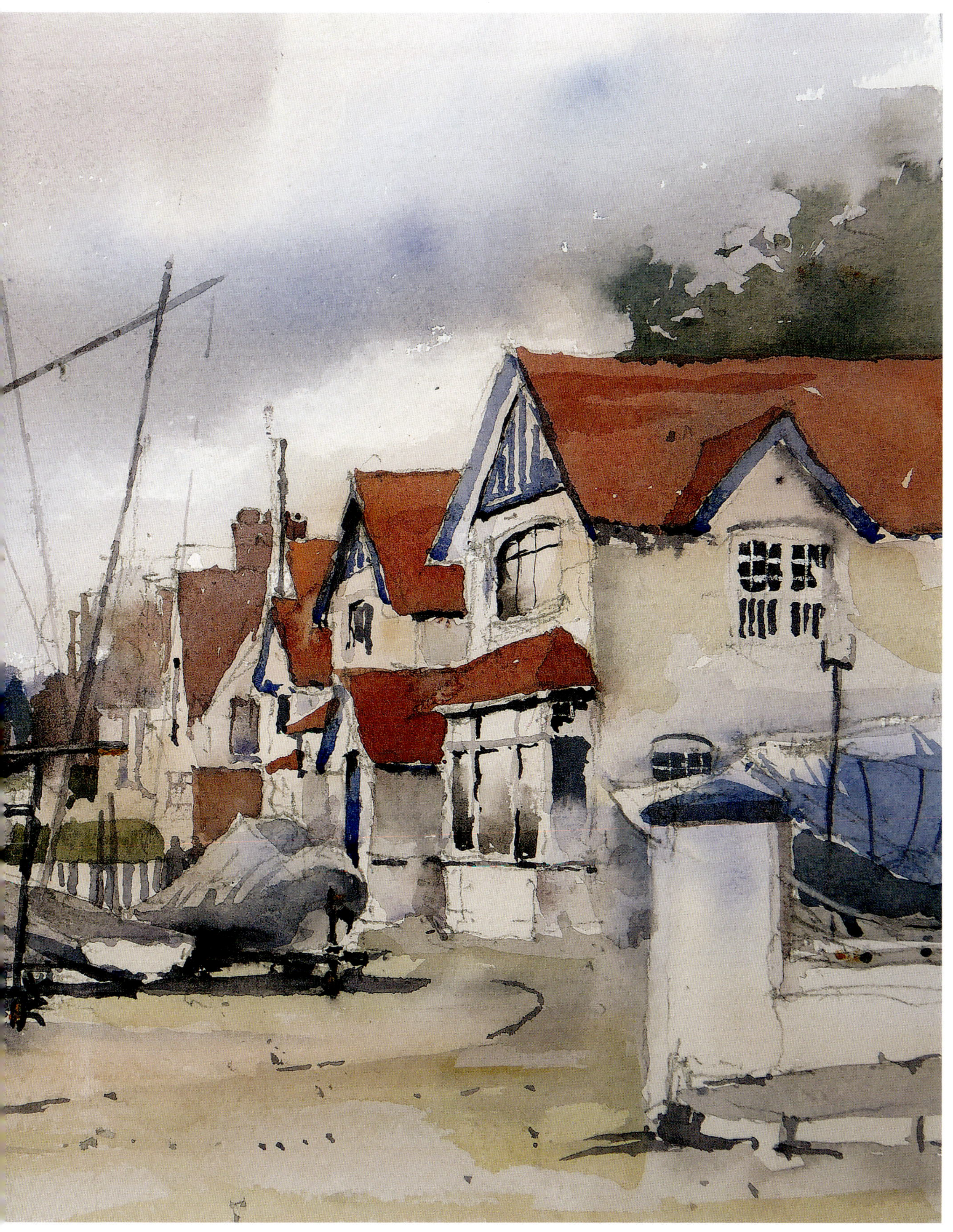

SUMMER

PAINTING OUTDOORS IN SUMMER IS a true delight. Days are longer and warmer so do take care to protect yourself from sunburn. In this season a hat is a must, especially for those of us who are follically challenged.

YACHTS AT ST. TROPEZ
38 x 28cm (15 x 11in), Bockingford CP 425gsm (200lb)

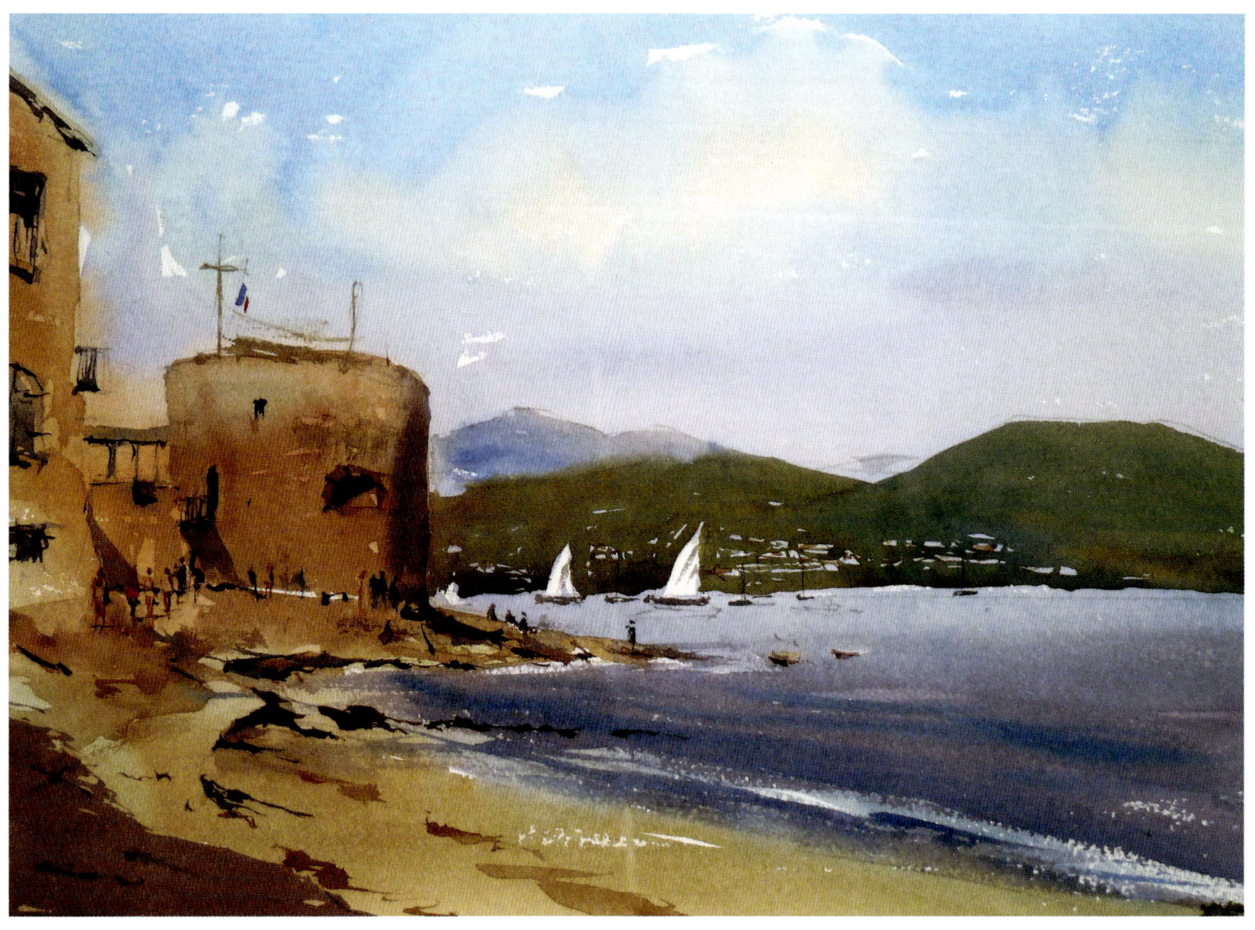

Light conditions

The sun reaches its highest point during this season and so around midday shadows will be very short and therefore less interesting. Painting earlier or later in the day is more comfortable. Heat can often generate a haze that can make distant parts of your subject more visually inspiring.

Potential weather conditions

There will likely be long, settled periods of good weather but this can often produce plain blue skies which really only work as a backdrop for bright white buildings. Don't be afraid to invent a few clouds.

Seasonal features

During summer there is a lot of green vegetation and often too much. Temper the greens by adding blues, yellows and greys. Blue skies will often produce some beautiful sea colours so coastal subjects are good for this season.

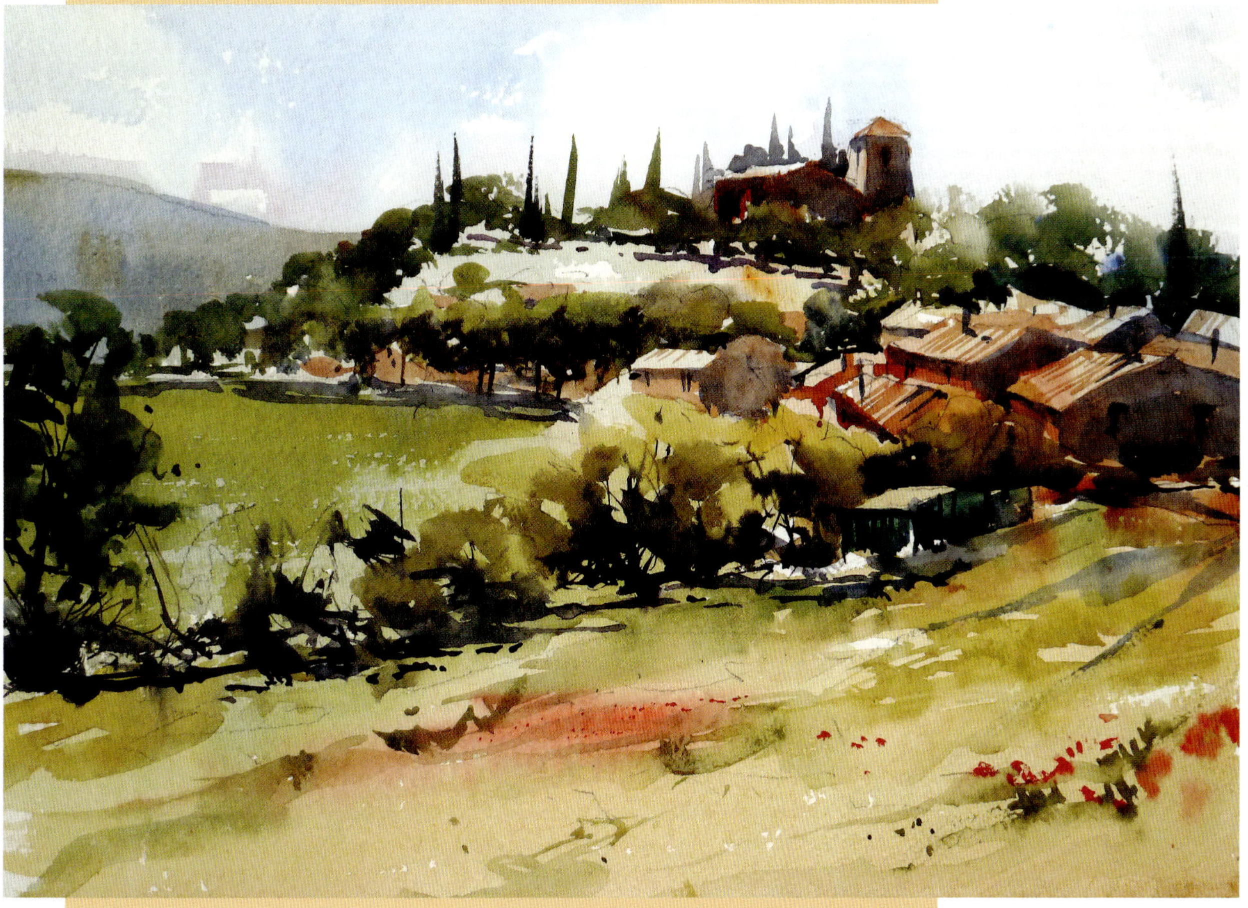

TOURTOUR,
PROVENCE
38 x 28cm (15 x 11in),
Bockingford CP 425gsm (200lb)

3. FARM BUILDINGS

This was a partly cloudy day with the sun coming and going – all fairly common for a summer in Northern Ireland. With buildings, I always find it is better to use a sunny situation with the sun positioned in such a way that it creates useful light and shade on the buildings to help them look more three-dimensional. Here, the sun was coming from the left, and, although most of the painting was painted in cloudy conditions, there was enough flitting sunshine to allow me to see the position and strength of the shadows.

YOU WILL NEED

PAINTS

- » **Ultramarine**
- » **Phthalo blue (green shade)**
- » **Cerulean blue**
- » **Warm yellow**
- » **Cool yellow**
- » **Burnt sienna**
- » **Quinacridone magenta**

BRUSHES

- » **Mop or other large soft brush, squirrel or synthetic**
- » **Size 12 and 8 round, sable or synthetic**
- » **Old size 8 sable for softening and lifting out**

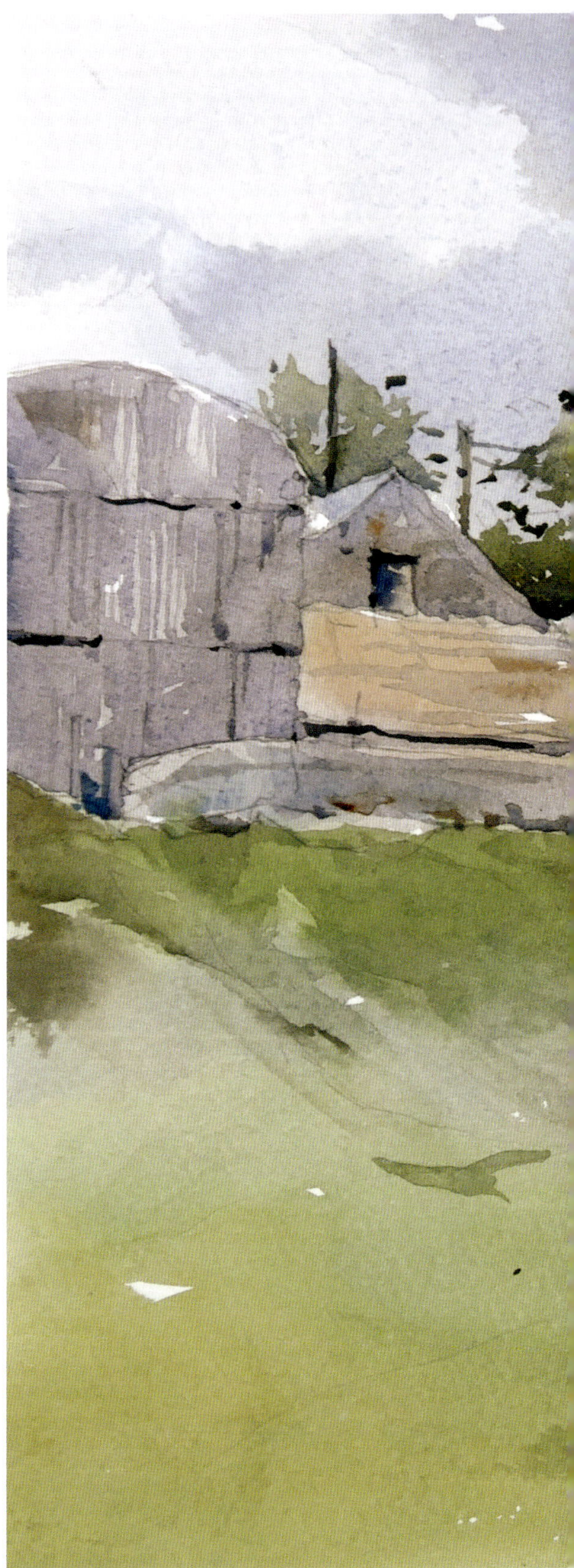

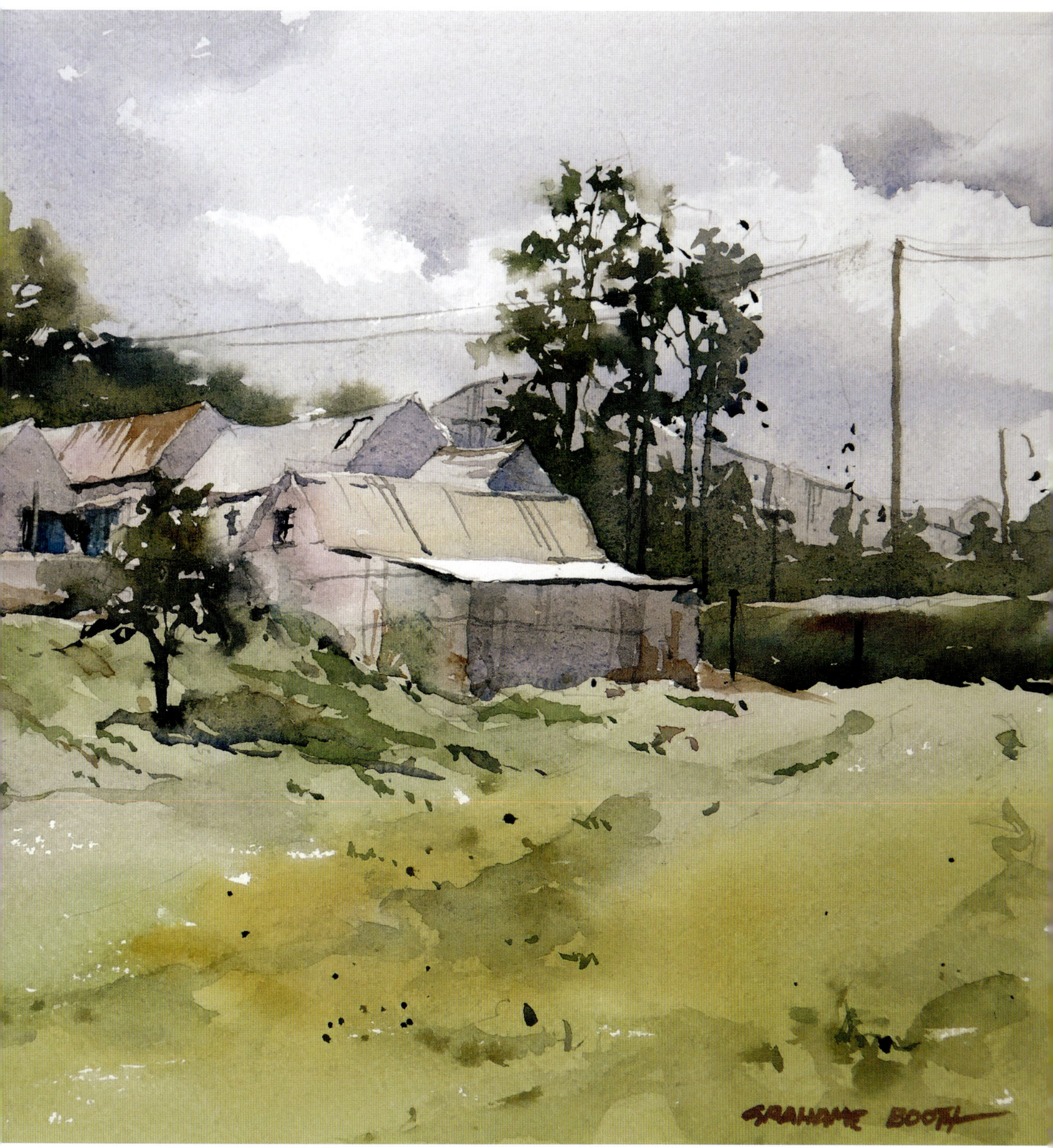

FARM BUILDINGS
38 x 28cm (15 x 11in), Millford CP 300gsm (140lb)

1. The initial sketch

Perspective is always very important with buildings and, with an eye-level line well below the buildings, it was important to get the perspective correct to give me the correct impression of looking up at them. Because of the high position of the buildings, all horizontal lines appeared to slope down as they receded. If you refer to the photograph (1A), you can see which parts of the original scene I chose to omit or change or accentuate in the final sketch (1B).

» I decided to stop the left-hand side of the painting part way through the gable end of the large barn. To show the side of the barn would have directed the eye out of the picture – not good.

» On the right-hand side, I wanted to leave a little relatively empty space to provide variety from the buildings.

» I felt that the telegraph pole was a good vertical element to give me contrast with the largely horizontal buildings.

» To accentuate the buildings being above my eye level, I placed them relatively high on the paper.

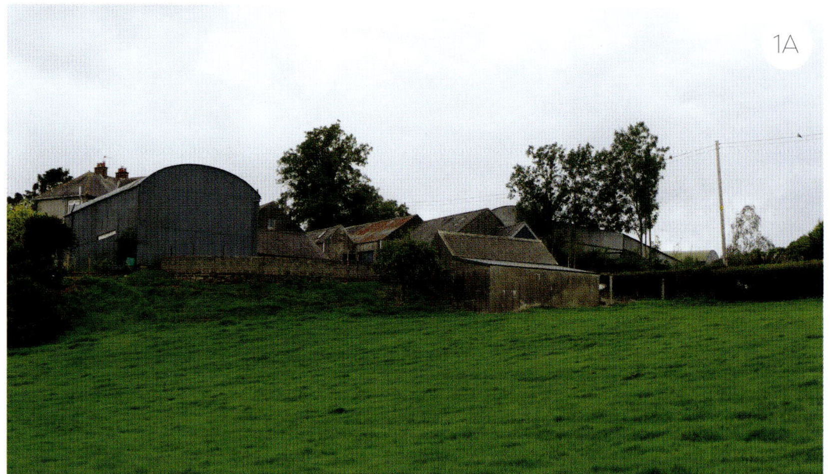

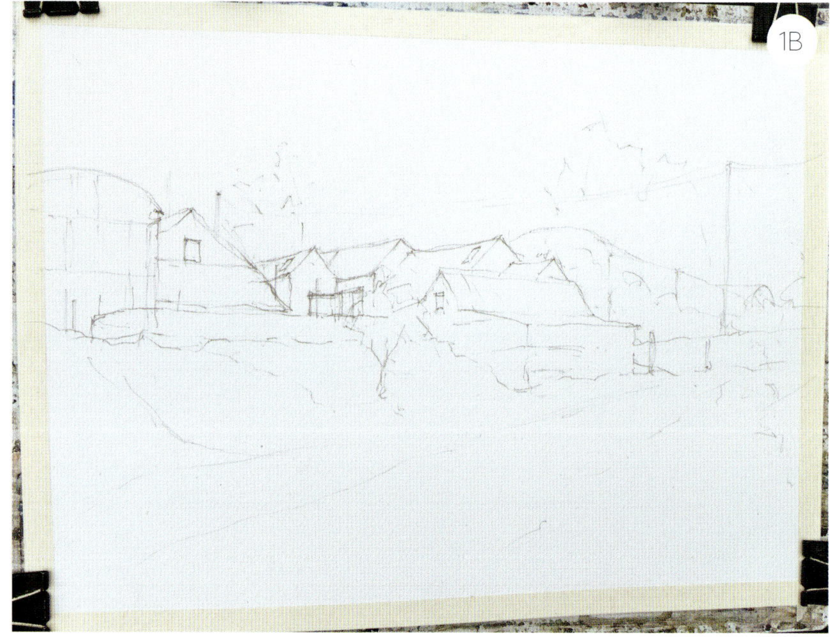

2. The sky wash

Use a large soft mop to paint the sky wash with a simple grey wash of ultramarine and burnt sienna with a little touch of quinacridone magenta just to give it a little bit more life (2A).

Use a lightly scrunched-up piece of kitchen paper to gently lift out some white clouds. With the sky still wet, drop in a darker version of the sky mix without the quinacridone magenta to suggest darker clouds (2B). Continue to the next stage without letting the paint dry.

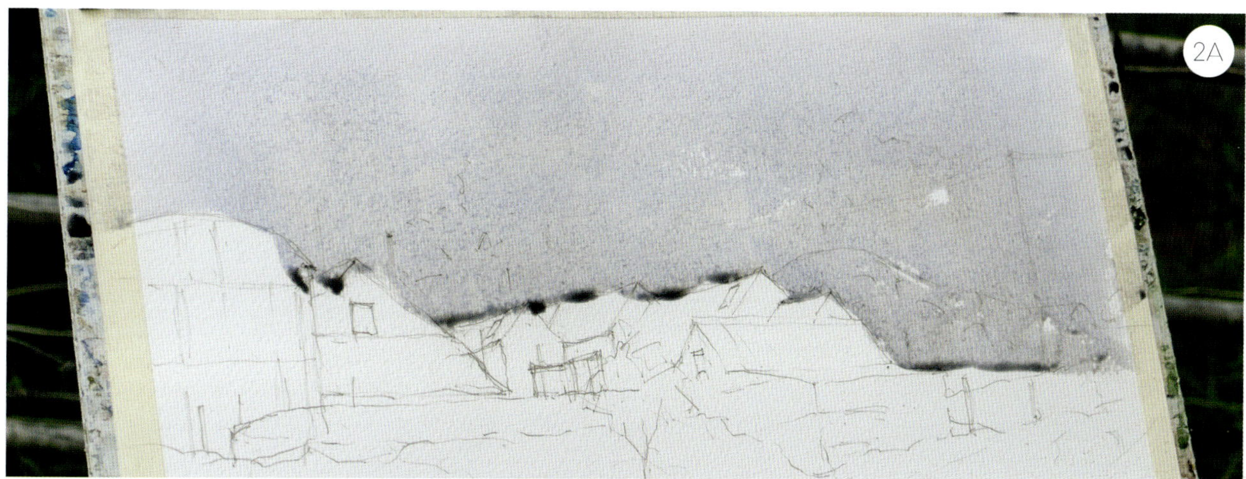

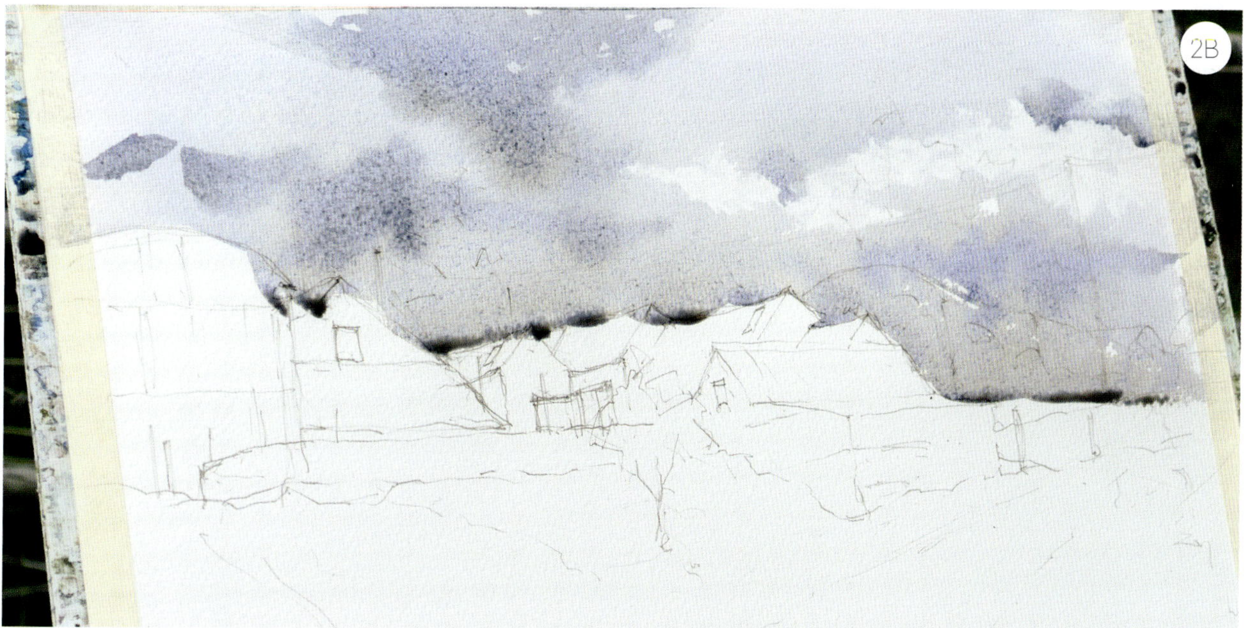

3. The buildings

With the sky still wet, continue the wash down the paper over the buildings using the same ultramarine and burnt sienna mix but with a bit more burnt sienna added (3A).

Because there are no hard edges at this stage, there is absolutely nothing defined, so freely add whatever colours you choose to create more subtle variety: I added a little touch of quinacridone magenta to bring some additional warmth to the buildings. Leave the roof of the nearest barn untouched so that you can suggest sunlight on the relatively flat roof (3B).

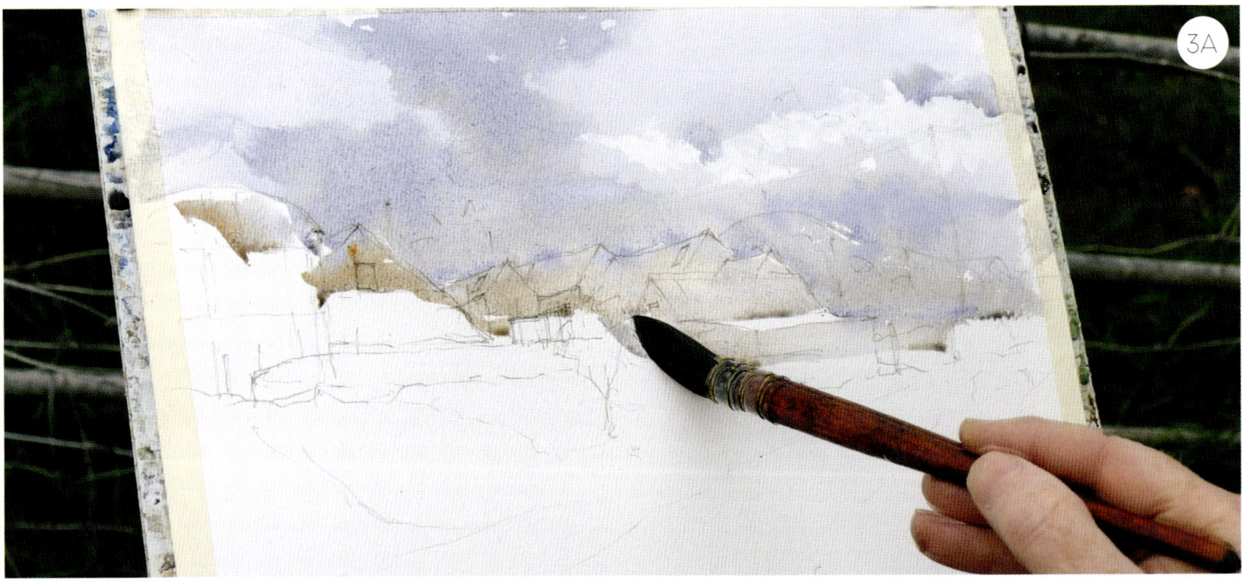

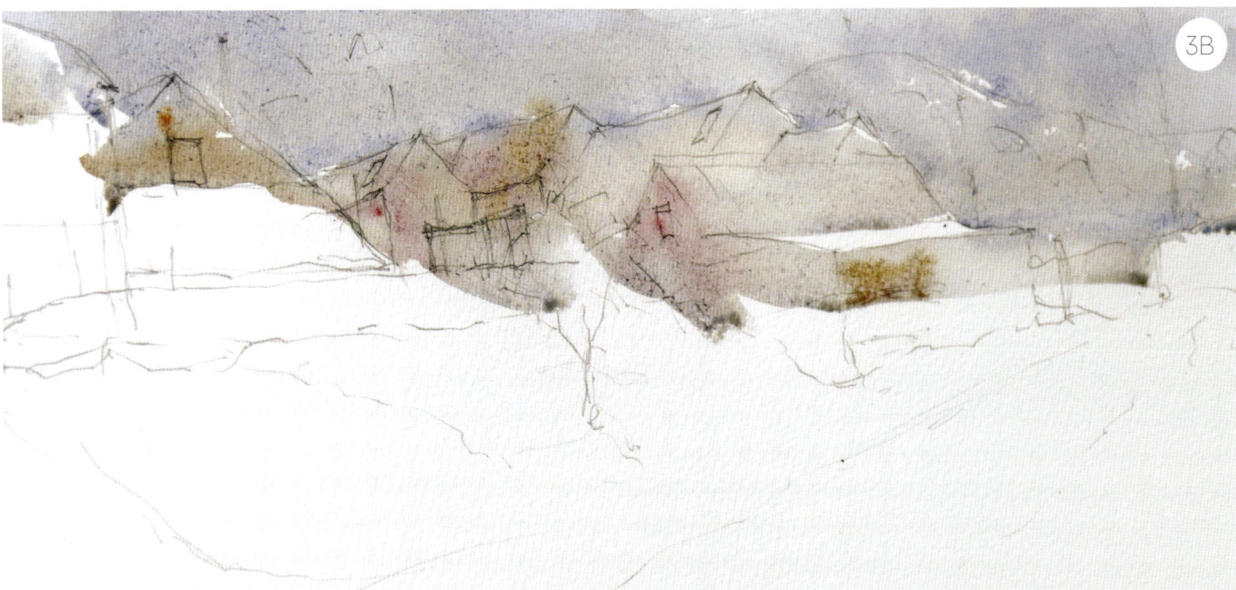

4. The grass

Continuing down into the grass, use a mix of ultramarine and warm yellow (4A), varying the proportions as you go and adding a little more yellow to the mix in the foreground (4B).

I am satisfied with this first wash. There is good variety in the colours of the sky, buildings and grass, but I still have plenty of options as I continue the painting (4C).

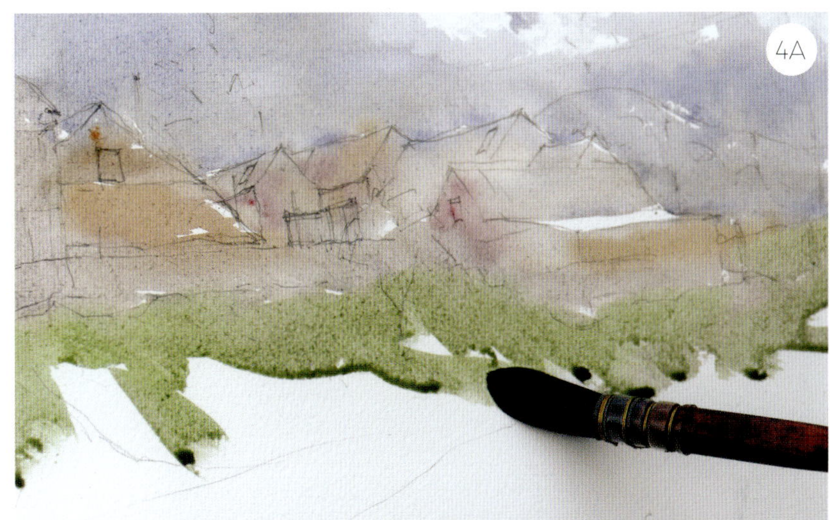

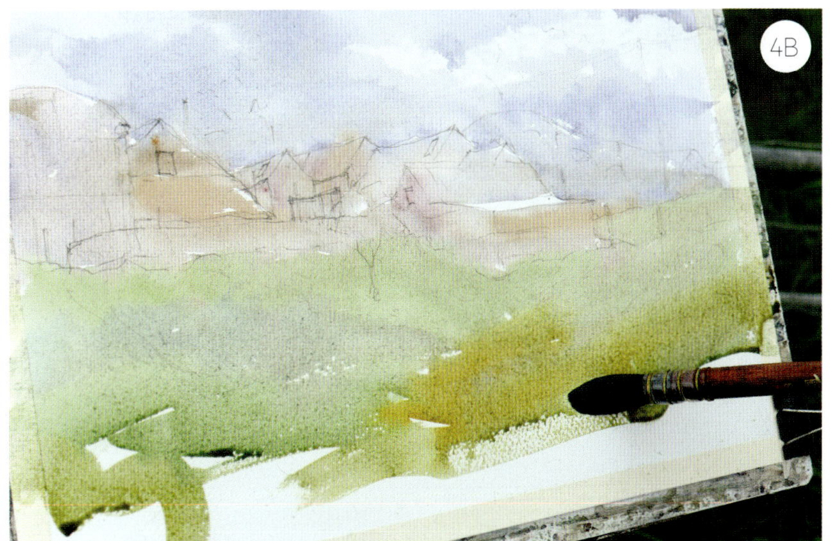

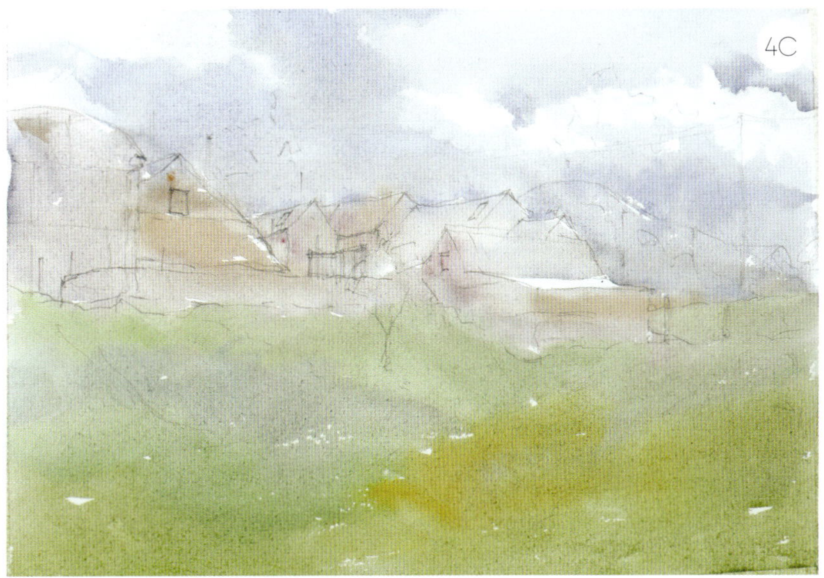

5. The distant barn

Begin to define the painting, starting with whatever is furthest away, in this case the grey barn behind the buildings. Although there is quite a lot going on here, at this point paint the entire area simply with a grey mix of ultramarine and burnt sienna using a size 12 round brush. There is no point trying to do too much at this early stage, particularly in the distant areas.

6. The background trees

Use the fine point of a size 12 round to create a very uneven edge, exactly what you expect on a tree. Use a mix of ultramarine with warm yellow for the areas of the tree in sun, and a mix of phthalo blue with burnt sienna to suggest the darker areas of the tree (6A). As the sun is on the left, most of the darker areas of the tree will be on the right.

Try to avoid a completely hard edge by gently softening parts of the outer edges of the tree.

Continue the wash, varying it as you go, down to the top edge of the roofs. Here you definitely want a crisp, hard edge (6B). Although you are painting the trees, you are also in effect painting the top line of the roof and you need a clear distinction between them with no softening.

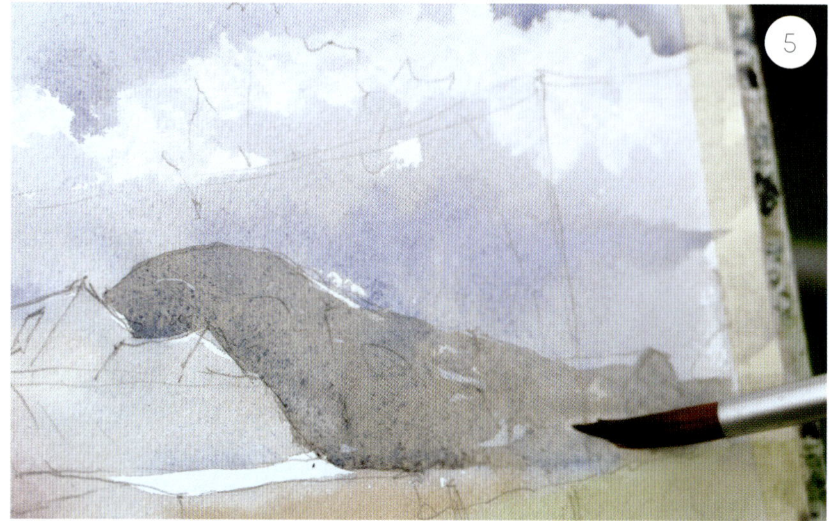

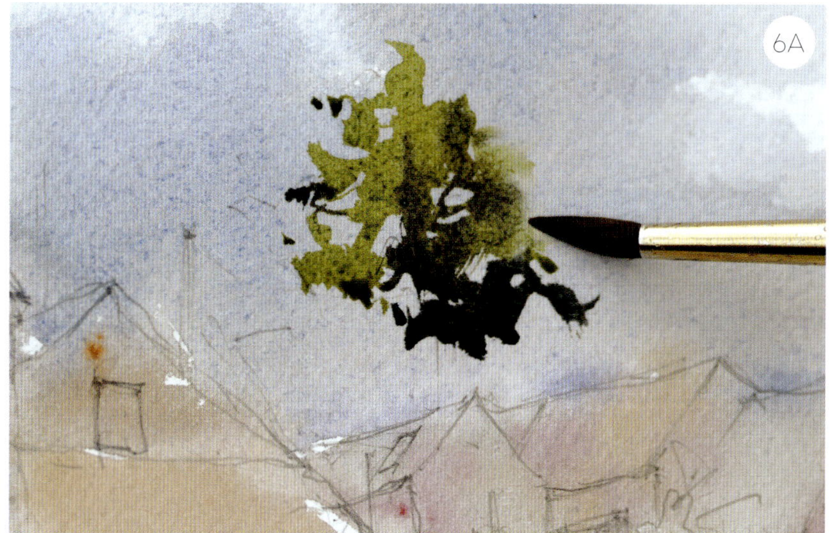

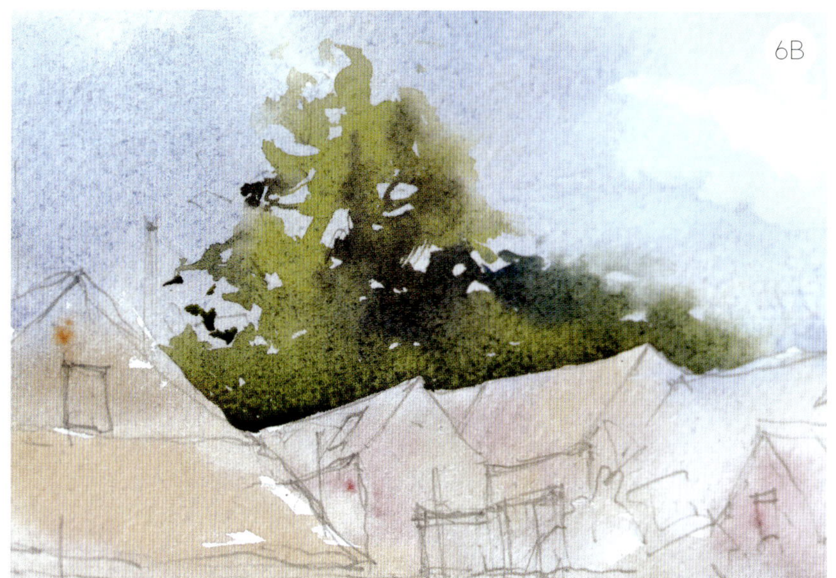

7. The right-hand trees

Paint the trees further to the right in the same way, changing the blend of colour in the mix (7A). Add in suggestions of their trunks, and dark shadowy areas at the base to connect them all (7B). Also paint in the hedge using the same mix with a little burnt sienna added, and leaving a little light band to suggest the light catching the top of it.

Paint the telegraph pole at the same time using ultramarine and burnt sienna and allow it to connect and blend with the vegetation (7C). This gives one single interesting shape instead of several less interesting ones.

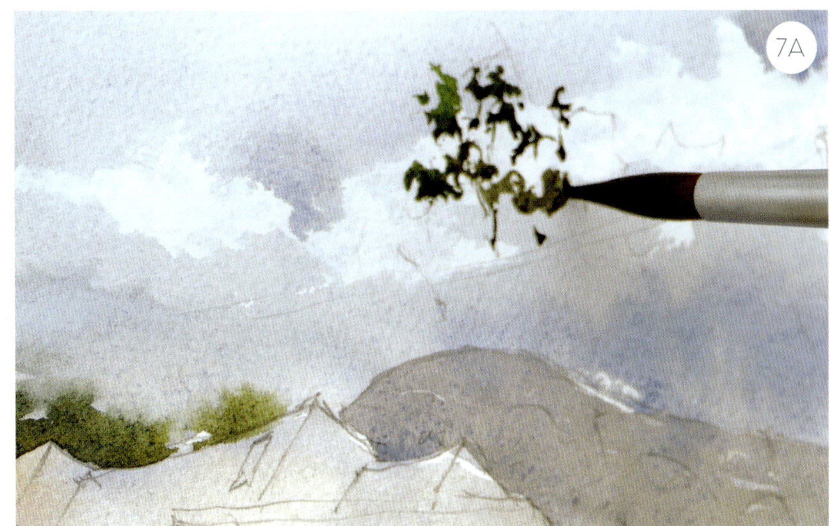

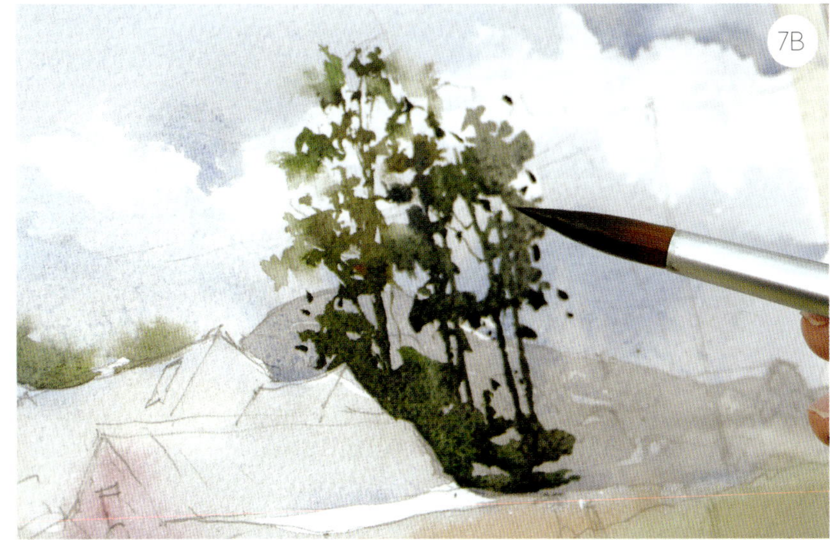

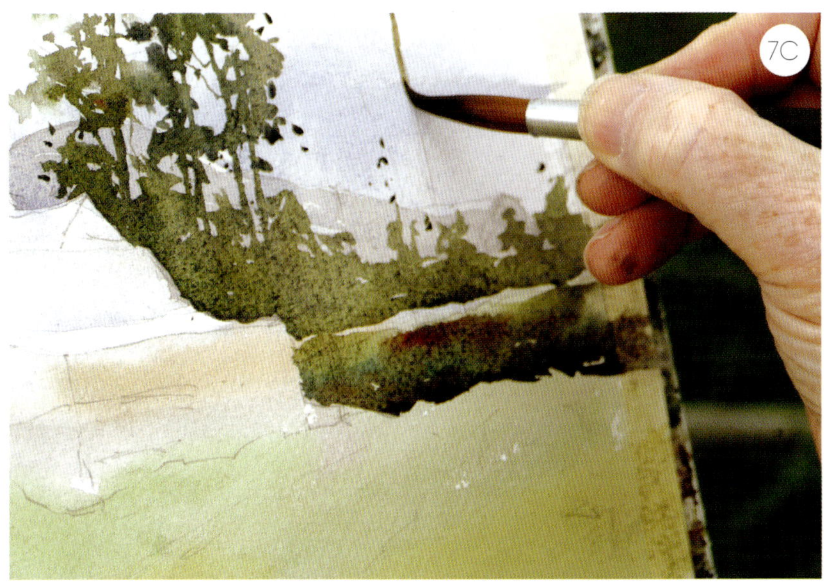

8. The buildings

Add a little quinacridone magenta to your standard grey wash and try to suggest both the shadow areas of the barn as well as hinting at the corrugations in the metal. Soften this a little bit, as we don't want to attract too much attention to this area close to the edge of the painting (8A).

Continue to paint this same wash over the shadow areas of all of the buildings. Where possible, try to link one shadow area to the next. It isn't always possible, but we want to avoid too many disconnected shadow shapes. Notice how the underlying colour variations from the first wash add subtle variations to the shadow (8B).

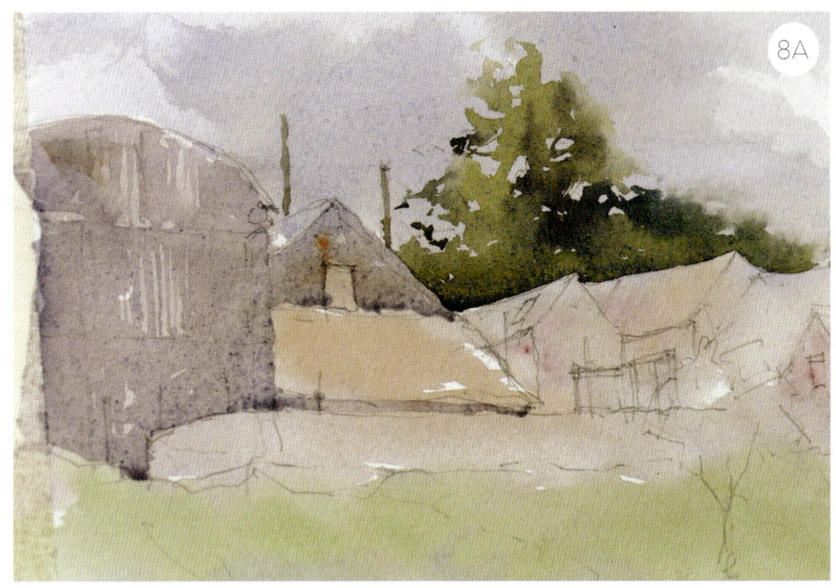

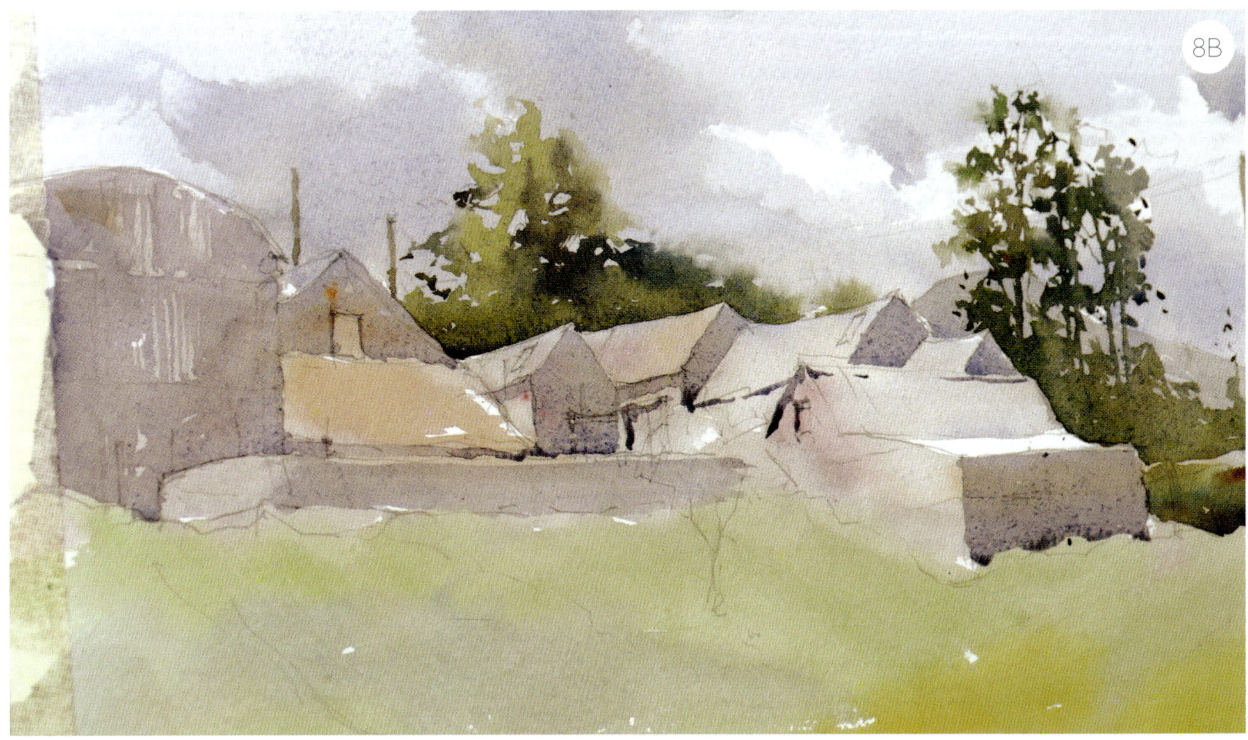

9. The grass

We now need to get some shape and direction to the grass. Begin with a wash of ultramarine and cool yellow, which creates a rich green, well suited to the grass. Use your brushstrokes to follow the slope of the field, creating connections as you go and softening in parts to connect this new grass wash to the old (9A).

Add a little bit of random splatter to quickly and simply hint at variations in the closer grass. The size of brush largely dictates the size of the splatter. Fully load the brush with paint and tap it smartly on the ferrule (9B).

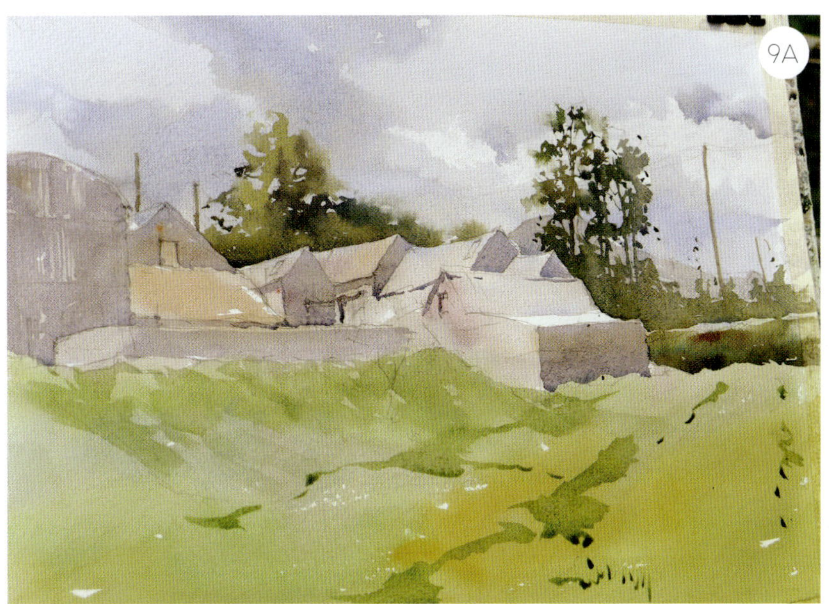

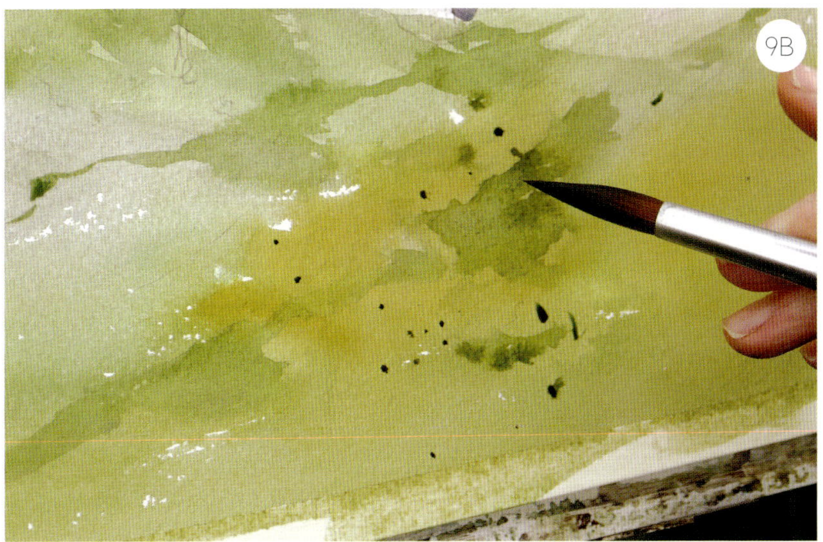

LOCATION INSIGHT

Although I was in a fairly remote area here, I had a few people stop to say hello. For some plein air painters this is a distraction from the painting but I quite enjoy it (at least if the painting is going well!). One woman was delighted to have seen her first ever working artist, and a passing gentleman informed me that the sheep in the adjacent field were a very rare variety. You won't find that out from a photograph!

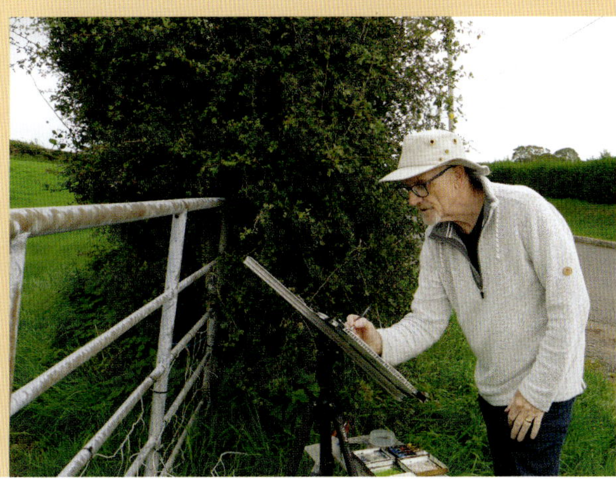

10. The skylight

We want to make the skylight on the roof of this building lighter than the roof itself but we don't want to substantially darken the roof. This can be simply achieved by painting a dark edge around the window and then softening it into the roof. Our brains are not very good at recognizing subtle variations in tone, but better at noticing abrupt changes. This allows us to create the light skylight without substantially darkening the roof.

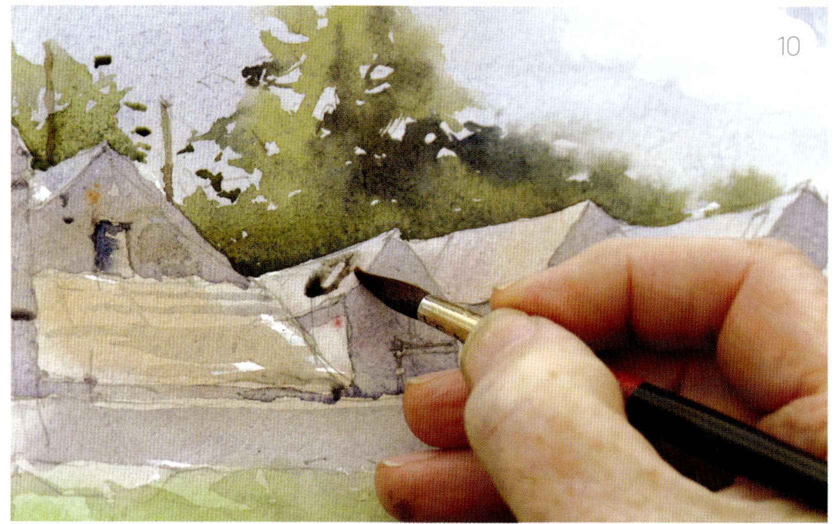

11. The rooftops

Continue to add more definition to the rooftops using a variety of mixes – enough to provide interest but not so much as to attract the eye too much.

12. The wall

Add further little hints of definition on the retaining wall using a dark mix of ultramarine and burnt sienna – break the dark line up to prevent it from becoming too obvious.

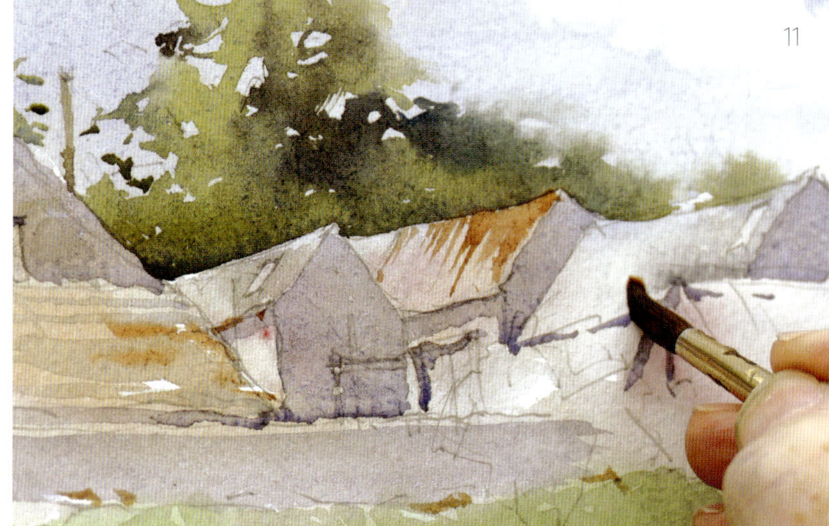

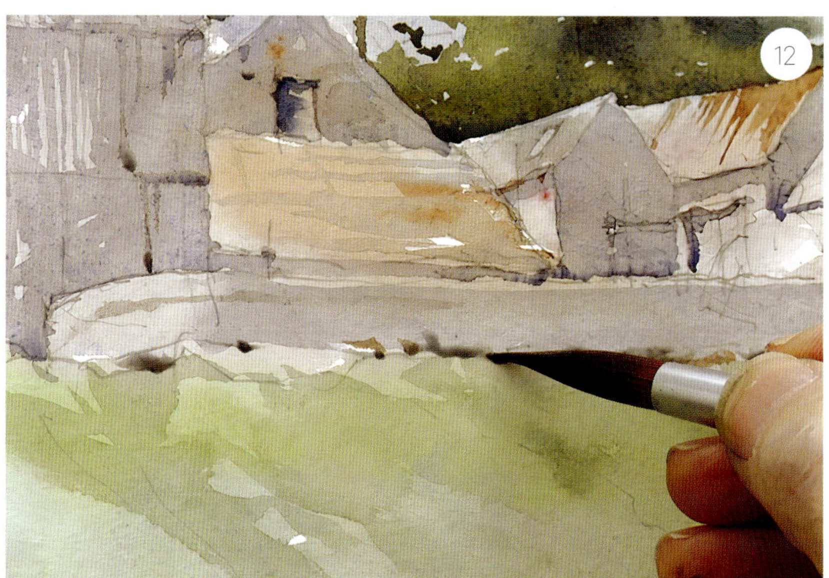

13. The foreground tree

Paint the foreground tree in a similar way to the background trees but using stronger mixes (13A).

It is a good idea to allow the base of the trunk to blend with the tree shadow as this helps connect it to the ground (13B).

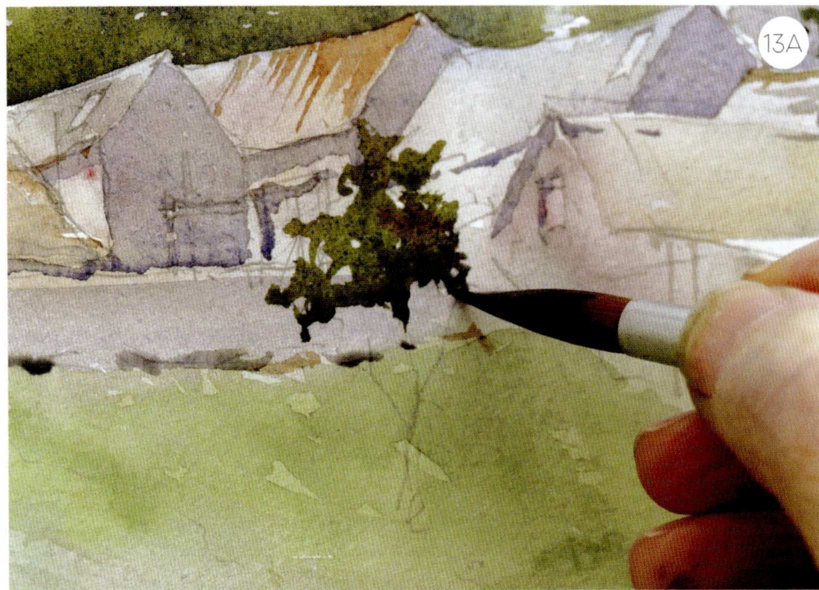

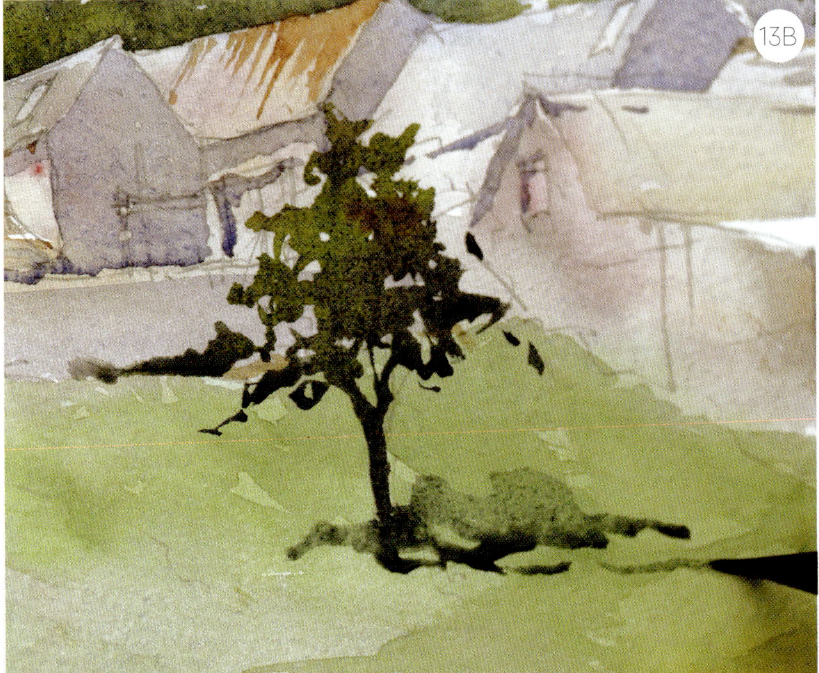

14. Final details

For me, the finished foreground tree is a little too obvious and draws too much attention. If you want to, soften the edges a little to blend it in to the general buildings area.

Finish the buildings area by adding a little more texture to the walls and some cerulean blue to the doors. When I use such a strong colour in a painting, I like to add it here and there in other parts of the painting too. This helps to prevent it from being too obvious. Lift out a couple of light areas to break up some of the stronger darks in the doors.

Repeat step 9 to give the grass a little more strength. Essentially, repeat what we did earlier but leave a few more hard edges. It is fun to create little tufts of grass but important not to overdo this.

Finally, use a ruling pen to create fine consistent lines for the power cables.

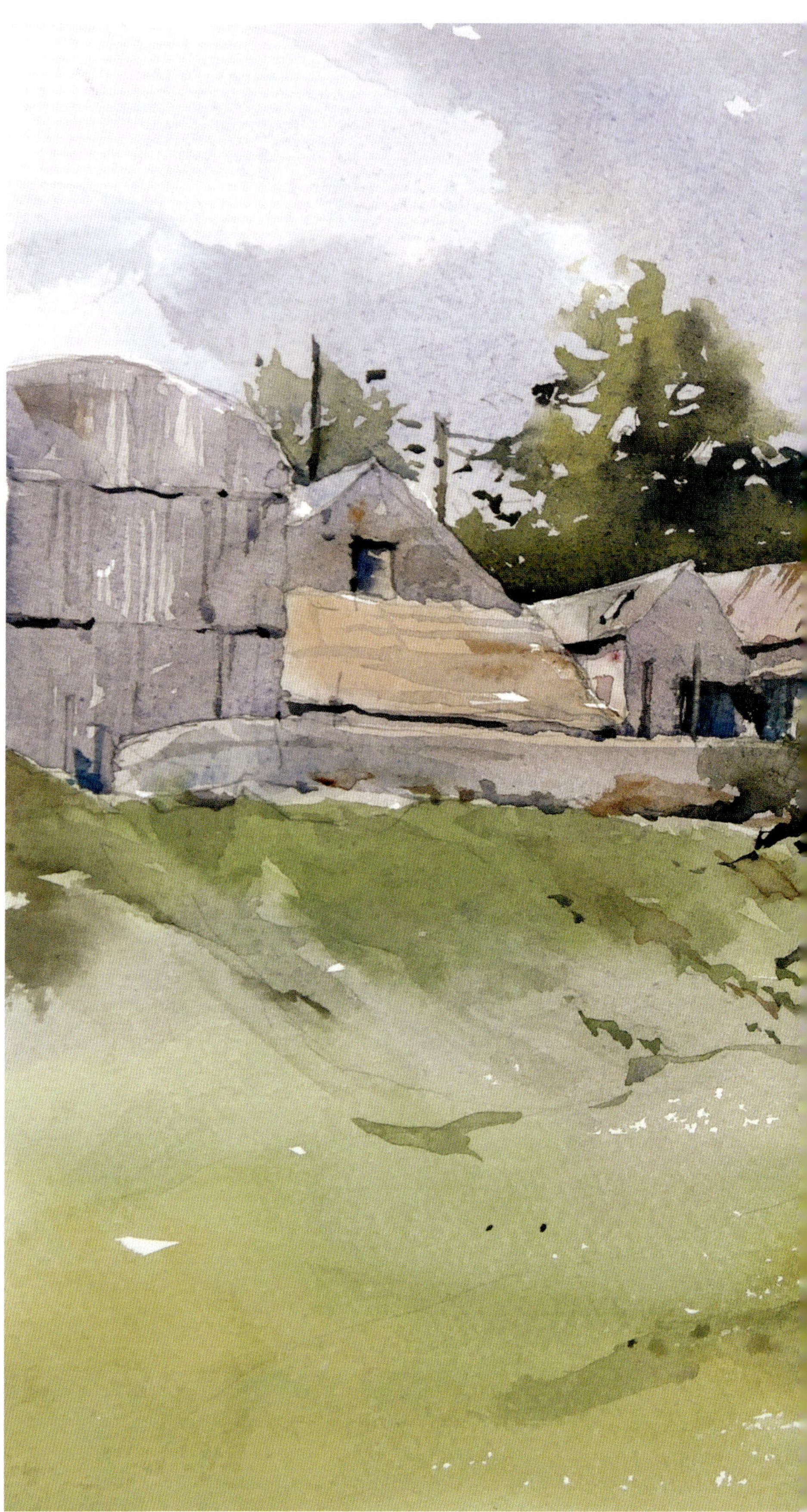

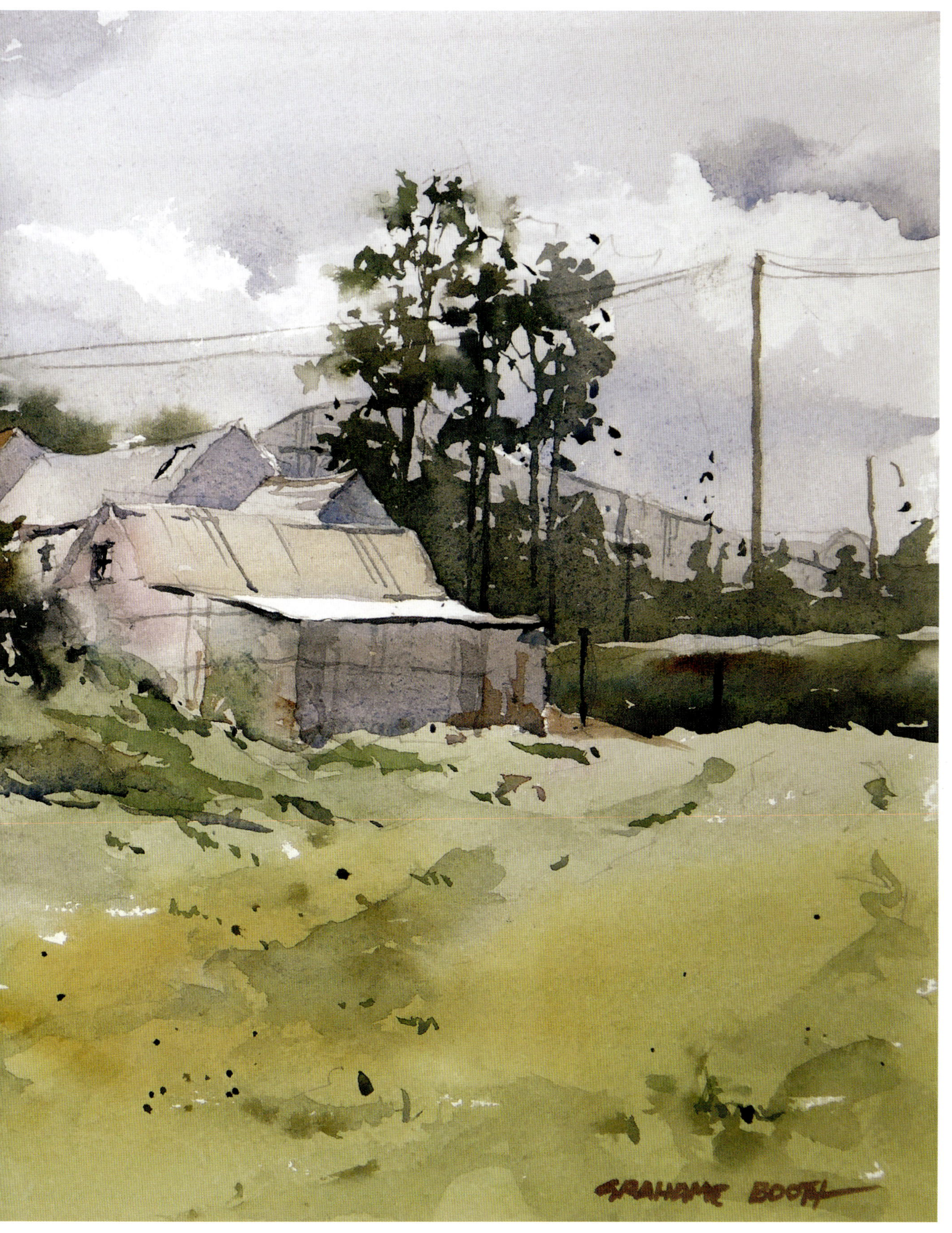

4. SUMMER LANDSCAPE

This is a fairly typical open landscape and it was a very hot (in British terms) summer day. These landscapes do not present much of a challenge to draw, but be warned: I usually find that the subjects that are easiest to draw are the most difficult to paint!

YOU WILL NEED

PAINTS

» **Ultramarine**
» **Cobalt blue**
» **Burnt sienna**
» **Cool yellow**
» **Warm yellow**

BRUSHES

» **Mop or other large soft brush, squirrel or synthetic**
» **Size 12 round, squirrel or synthetic**
» **Size 12 and 8 round, sable or synthetic**
» **¼in (5mm) swordliner, sable, squirrel or synthetic**
» **Old size 8 sable for softening and lifting out**

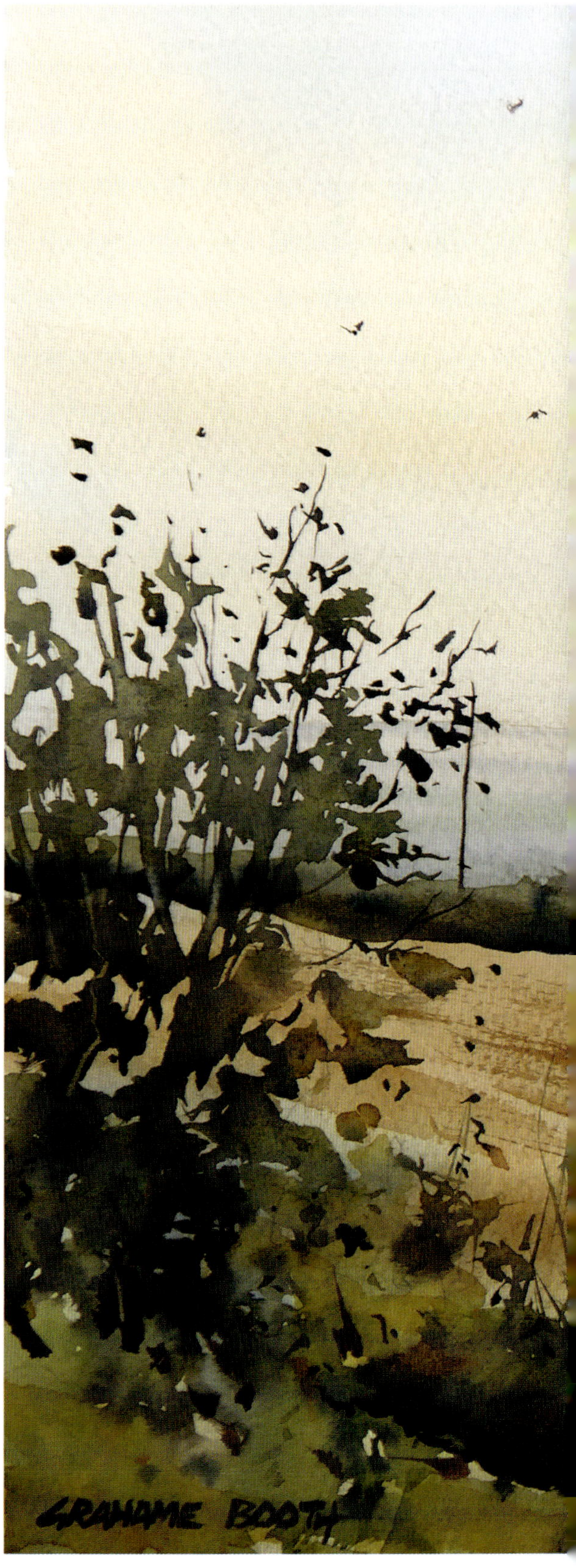

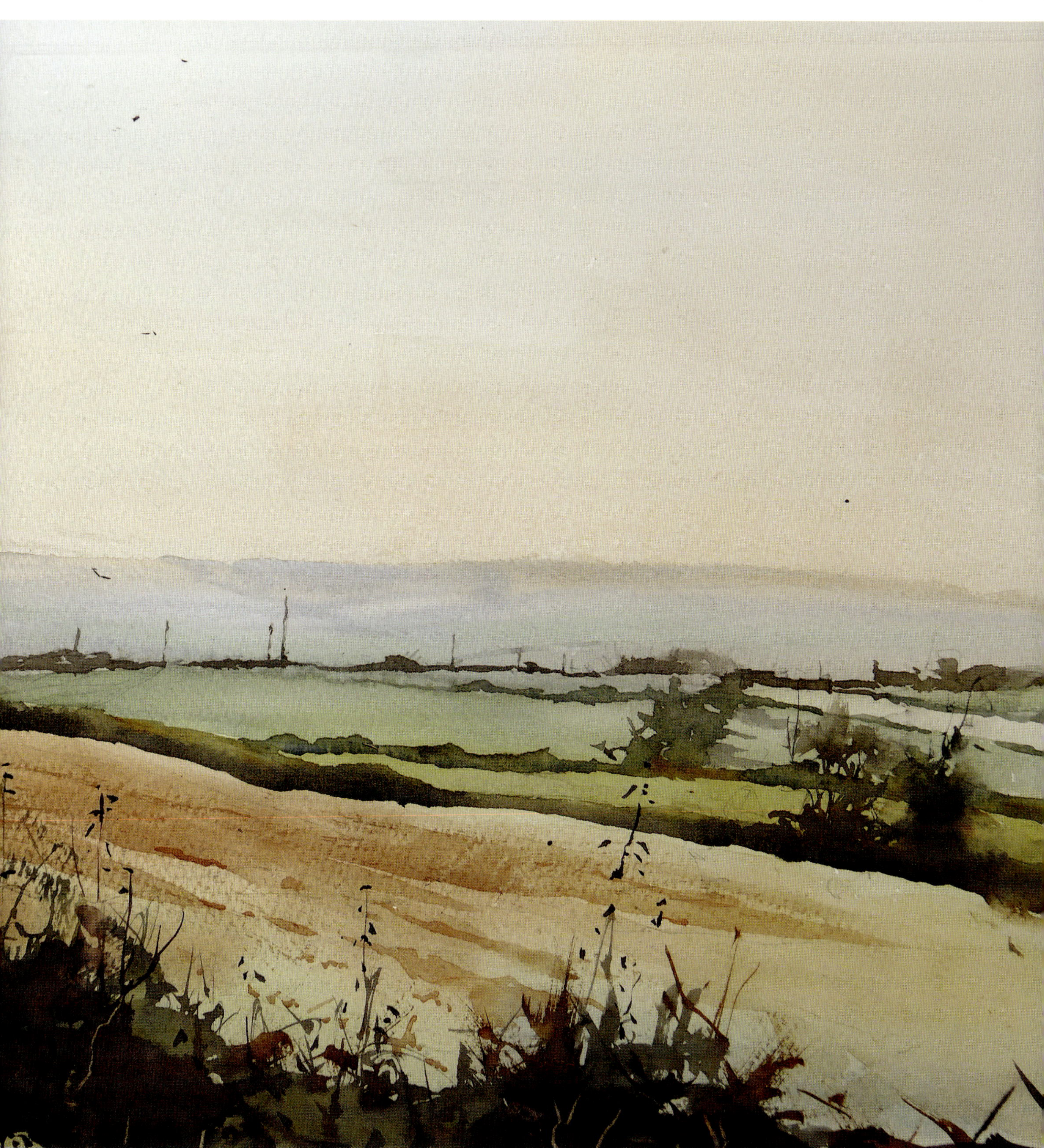

SUMMER LANDSCAPE
38 x 28cm (15 x 11in), Millford CP 300gsm (140lb)

1. The initial sketch

The drawing is not really much more than a few squiggles. I only ever indicate the trees very simply. Putting in too much detail can risk a painting by numbers approach and I try to avoid any pencil work in the extreme distance, especially today with a very obvious heat haze. Any pencil lines remaining in this area after the painting was finished would be very obvious to the eye. Such lines can sometimes be erased afterwards, even after being washed over, but there is no guarantee.

If you refer to the photograph (1A), you can see which parts of the original scene I chose to omit or change or accentuate in the final sketch (1B).

» I kept all the elements in front of me, but shifted hedgerows and trees slightly to make for the most pleasing composition.

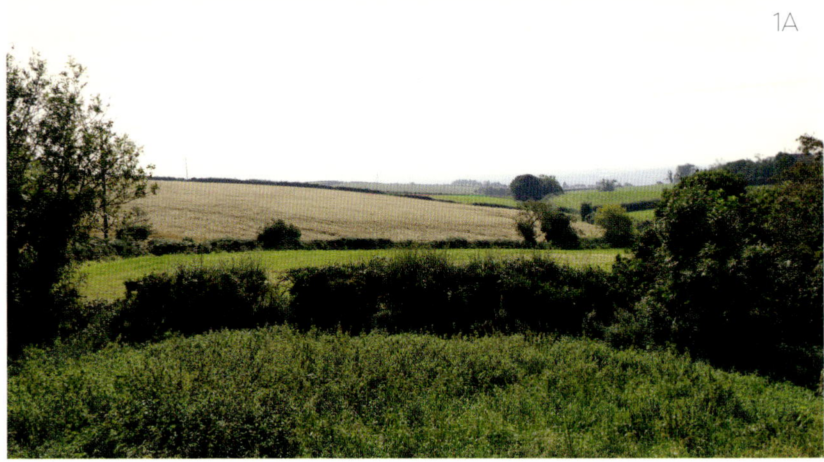
1A

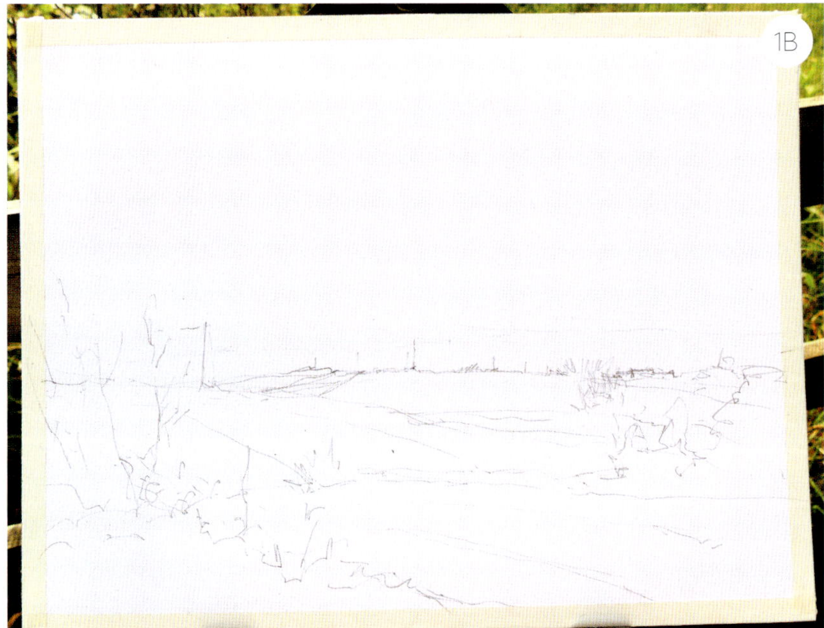
1B

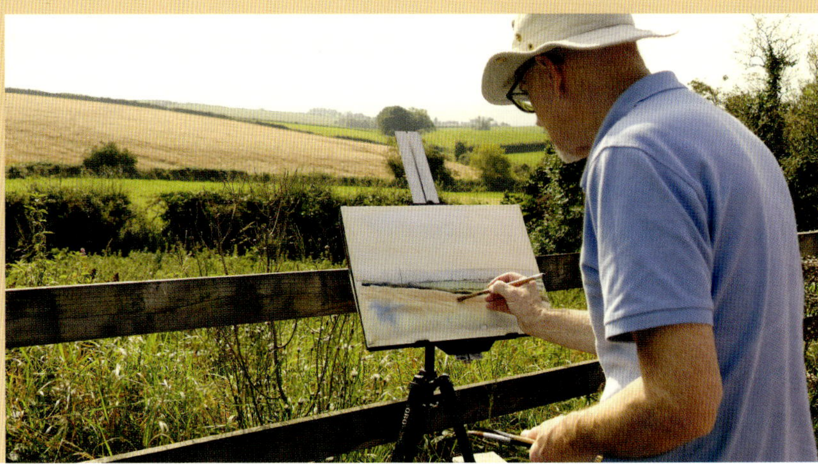

LOCATION INSIGHT

This was one of those really warm summer days, not too hot, but just perfect for plein air. I was also able to set my board up so that it was shaded from the sun – much easier on the eyes.

2. The first wash

Use a large soft mop for the first
wash, using cobalt blue for the
sky and a weak burnt sienna
to suggest clouds. (Leaving
the clouds as pure white paper
can make them appear very
cold.) Blend everything together,
leaving no hard edges.

Add a little cool yellow to hint
at the greens in the distance
(2A). In the foreground, drop
in some pure ultramarine and
burnt sienna (2B). I'm not entirely
sure why I did this, but it seemed
like a good idea at the time.
Summer landscapes tend to be
dominated by green so I was
trying to avoid too much in the
early stages.

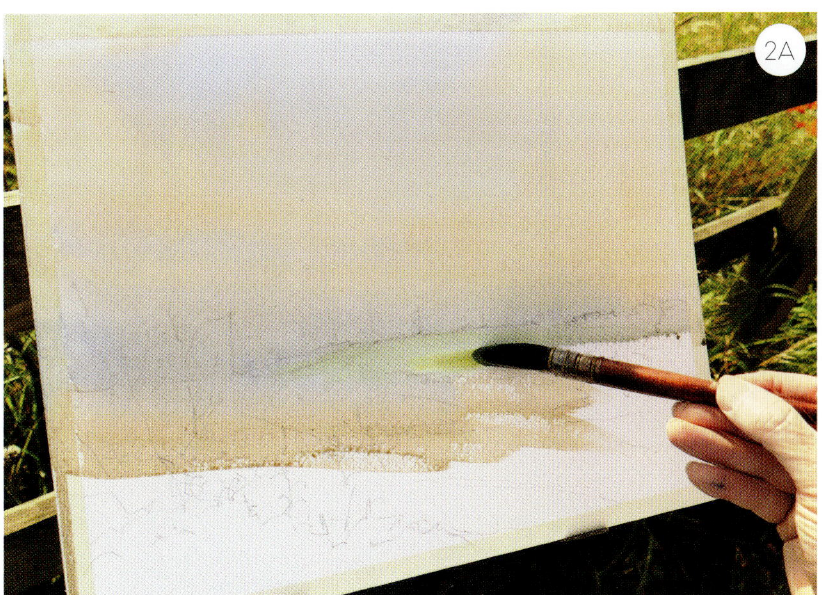

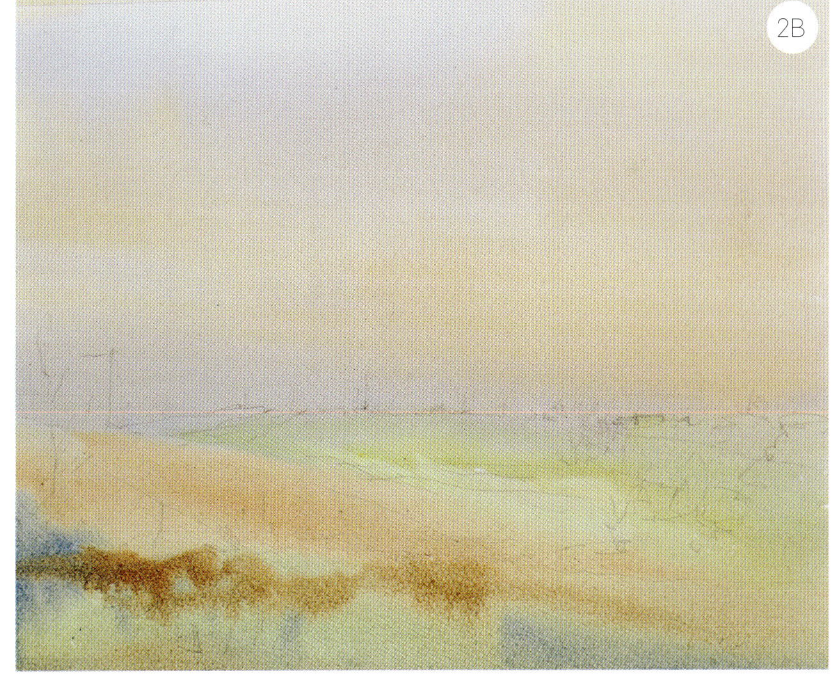

3. The heat haze

Before the first wash dries, paint some pure cobalt blue into the distance to simply suggest the heat haze. I found that the edge wasn't quite soft enough, so I used an almost dry Chinese brush to gently scrub the edge. (Using a damp brush to soften the edge would have risked creating a cauliflower.)

4. The distant fields

Continue with a size 12 brush and loosely indicate the distant fields using cobalt blue (4A). You want the previous wash to be just damp enough to soften the marks a little but not wet enough to let them disappear.

Use almost pure cobalt blue with just a touch of cool yellow here and there (4B).

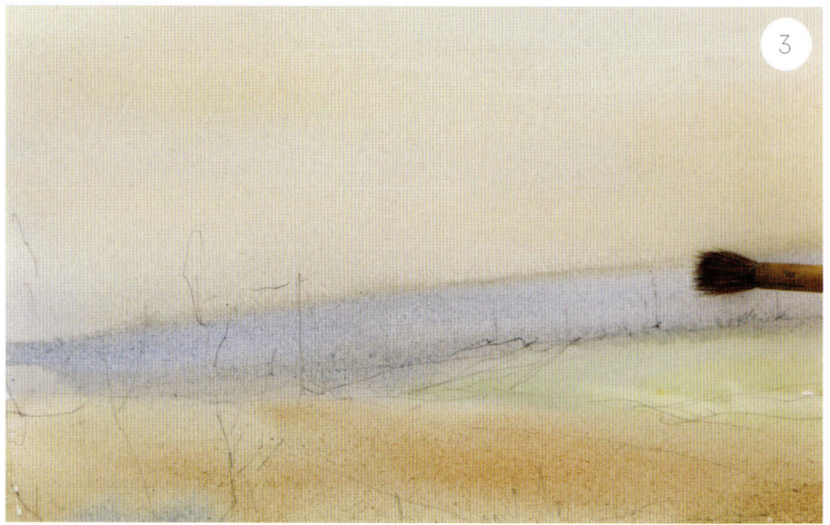

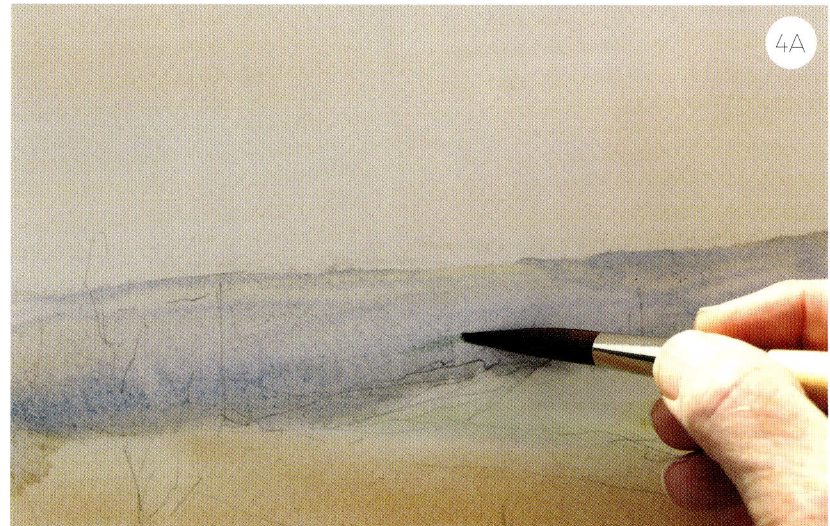

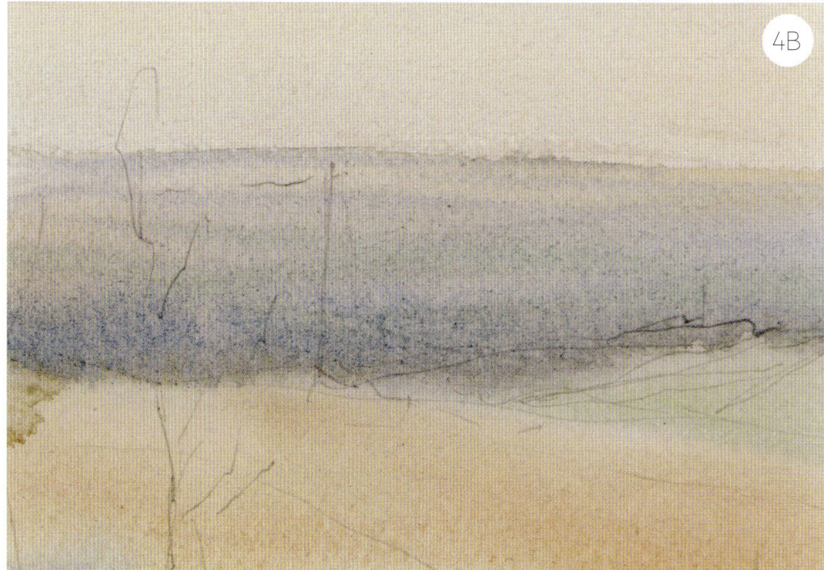

5. The fields

Continue down into the far field with a little more cool yellow in the mix. Continue to add more cool yellow as you create further distinct bands of paint for the fields (5A).

Use some stronger burnt sienna for the nearer golden field (5B), stroking in the paint to indicate the slope of the ground.

6. Distant features

Wait for the wet paint to dry, then simply suggest some of the more distant features with a mix of ultramarine and burnt sienna, making a broken, irregular line along the far field line. Here and there, soften the edge using a damp softening brush. Softer edges will help to suggest distance.

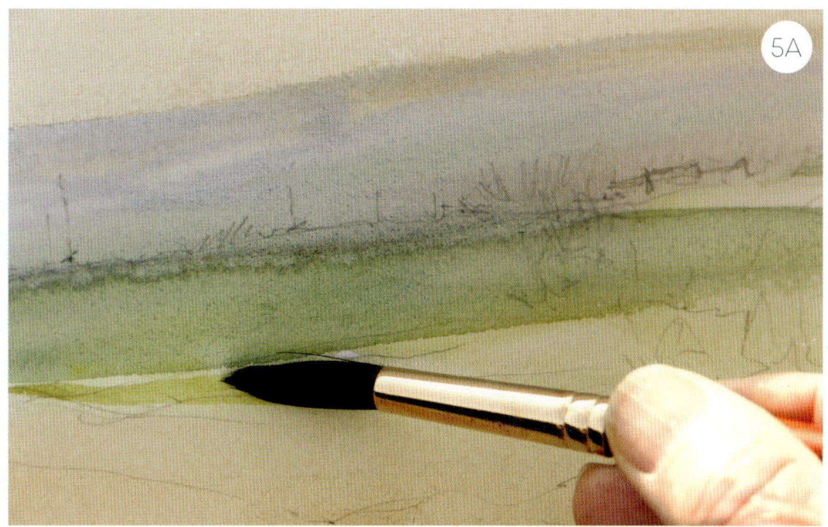

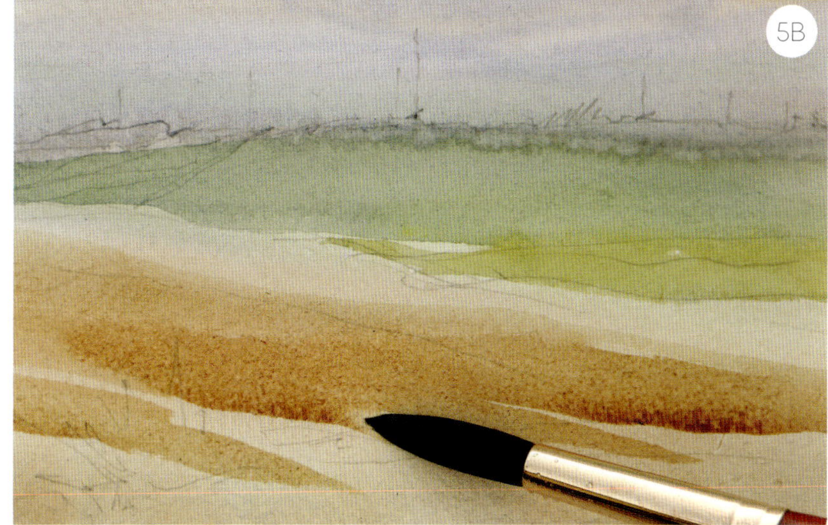

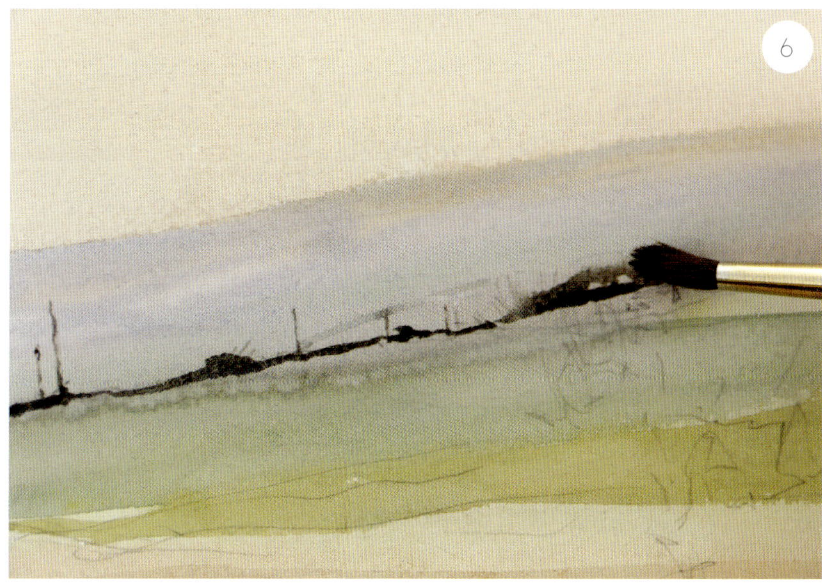

7. The hedgelines

Use a dark green mix of ultramarine with both cool and warm yellow to paint in the hedgelines (7A). Make irregular marks that hint at the shapes in front of you and resist any temptation to add detail (7B).

8. Hedgeline shadows

Drop in a strong mix of ultramarine and burnt sienna to the base of the closer hedges – this helps to give an impression of three dimensions as well as creating a strong dark/light counterchange with the field.

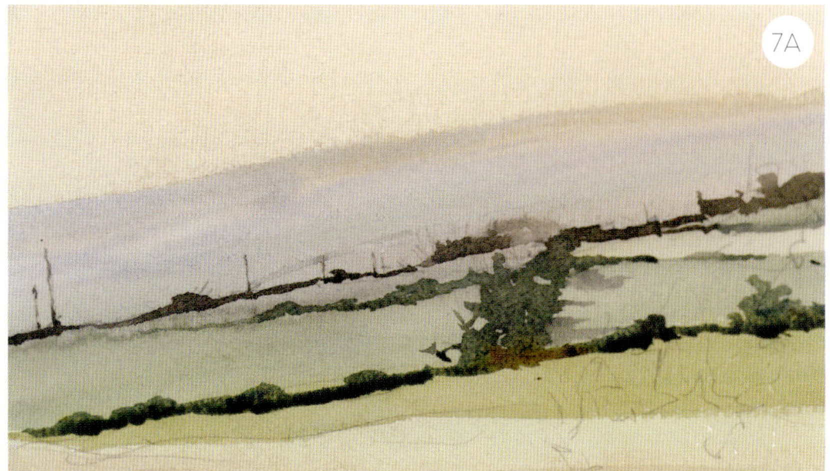

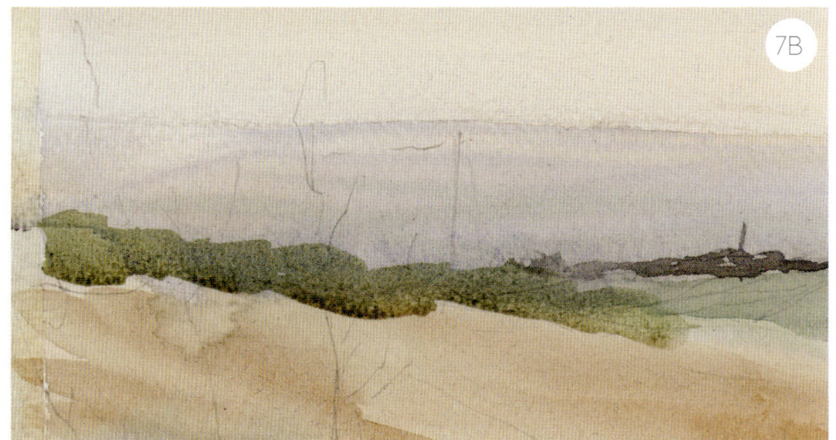

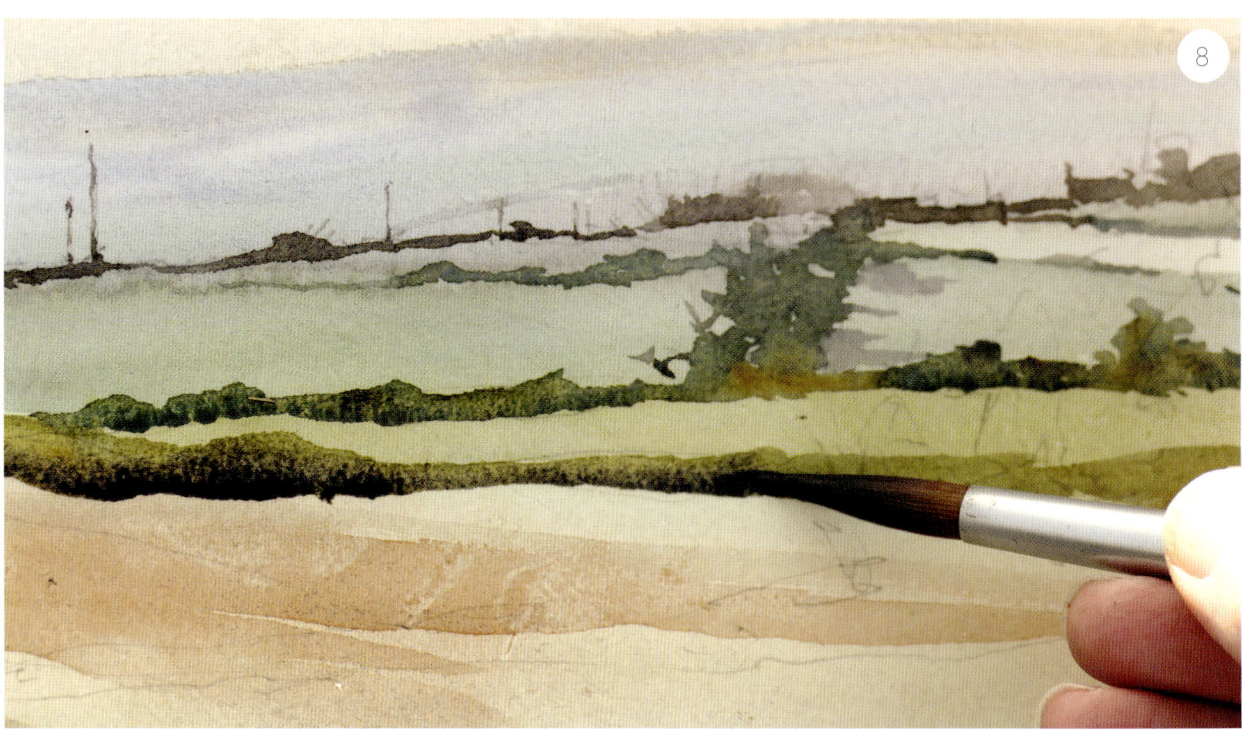

9. Simple trees

With a little more burnt sienna in the mix, create two simple trees to the right-hand side, allowing the marks and colours to soften into the surrounding fields a little, and then allow everything to dry (9A). The painting so far (9B).

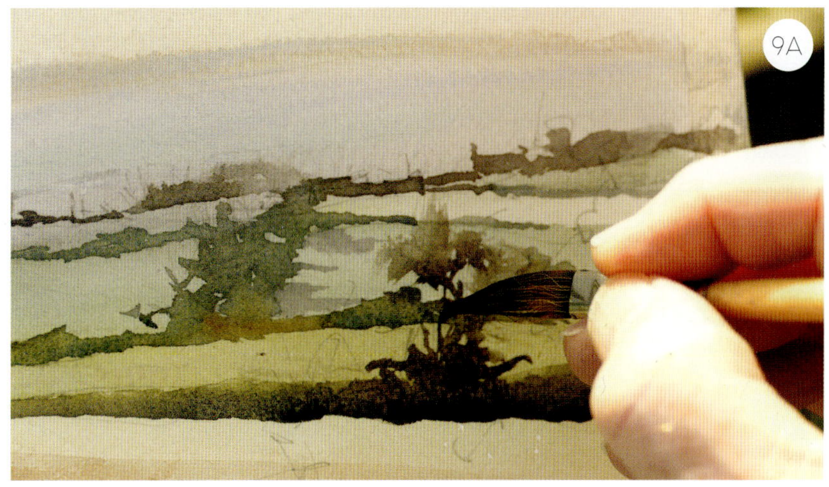

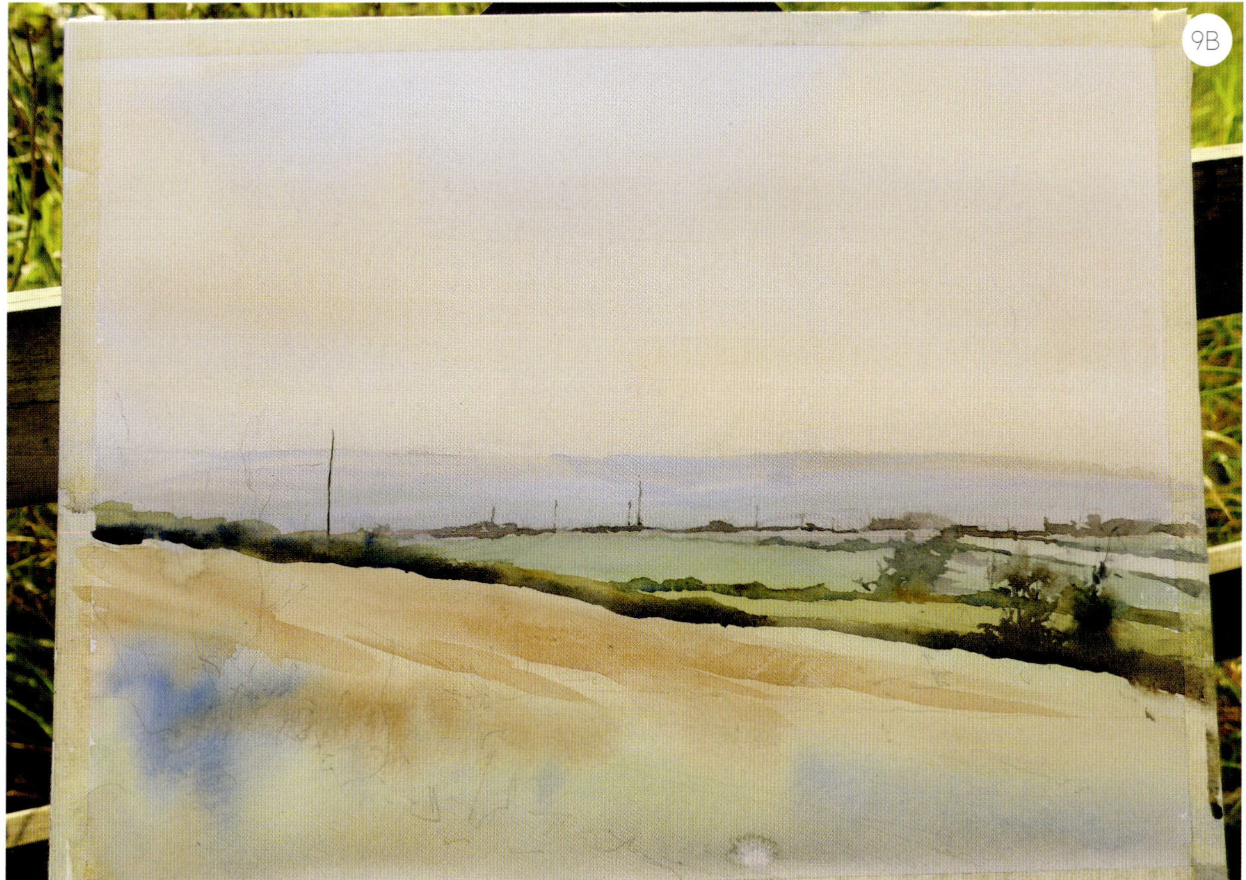

10. The field

To add a little more subtle definition in the golden field, create a few dry-brushed strokes, following the contours of the ground using the Chinese brush.

11. The left-hand tree

Start at the top of the tree: this may seem counterintuitive but beginning at the bottom and working up results in your fresh application of paint running down into the previously applied wash. Starting at the top and working down allows much more control.

Aim to produce lots of simple, varied brushstrokes and avoid any straight or rounded edges. Use a size 12 brush and various mixes of ultramarine and both warm and cool yellows to create the variety of greens needed (11A). Use ultramarine and burnt sienna to create the darkest areas. With trees it is very important to keep the edges as convoluted as possible. In reality, the bottom of the tree merged in with the grasses so I did exactly the same thing (11B).

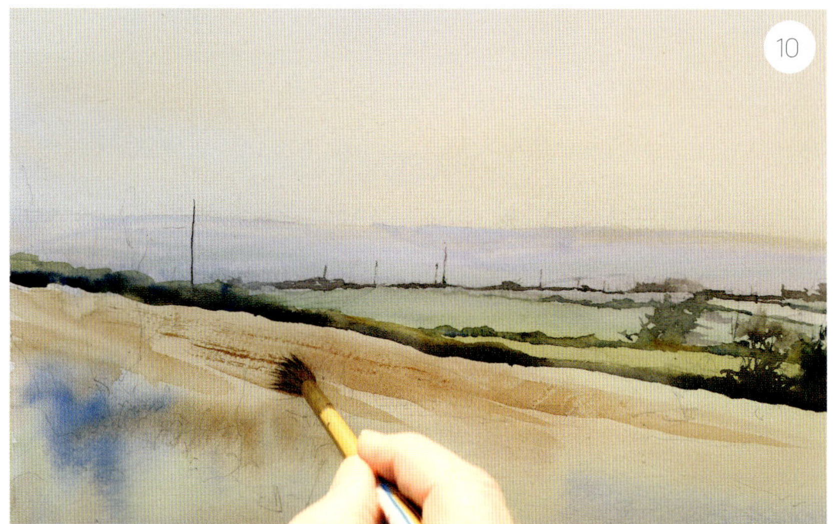

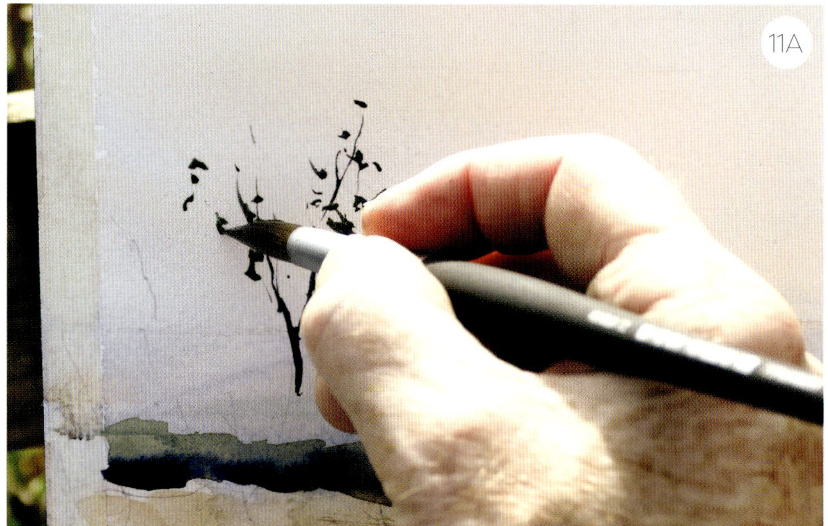

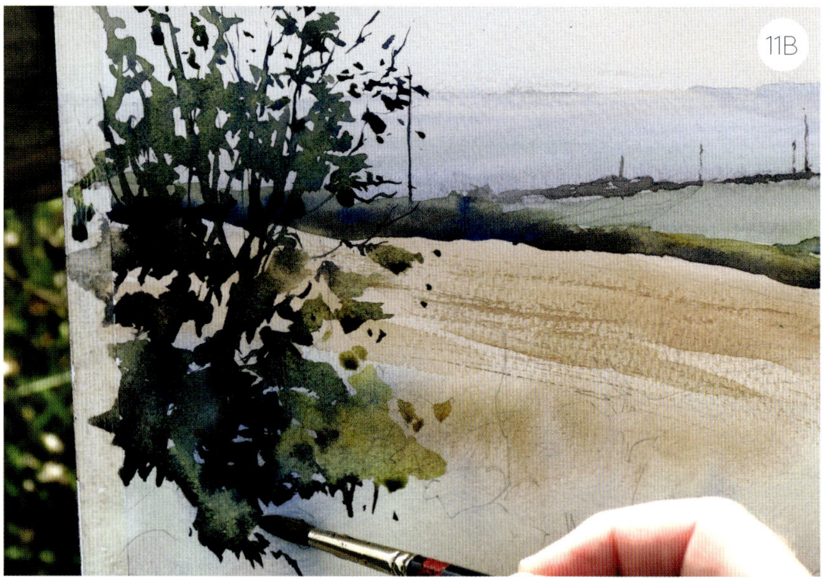

12. The foreground

For the foreground, use a paler green mix, allowing it to soften into the base of the tree. Work it down to the bottom of the painting and then towards the right. Continue onto step 13 before the paint dries.

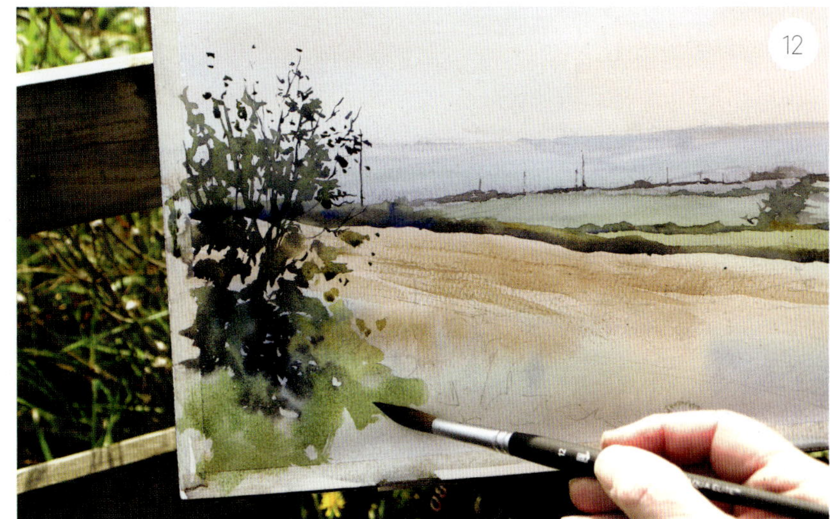

13. Foreground grasses

Using those same varied mixes as in steps 11 and 12, continue along the bottom of the paper, suggesting grasses and little twigs as you go (13A). Use the dry Chinese brush to create some grassy shapes (13B).

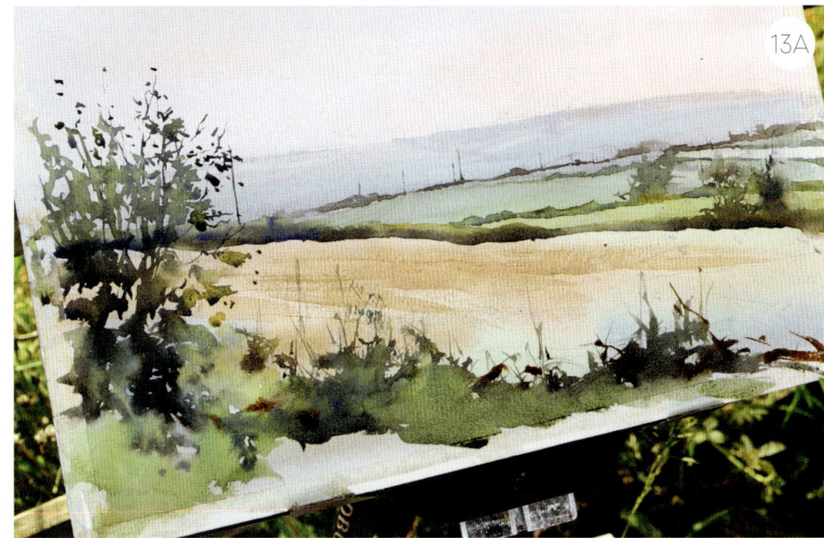

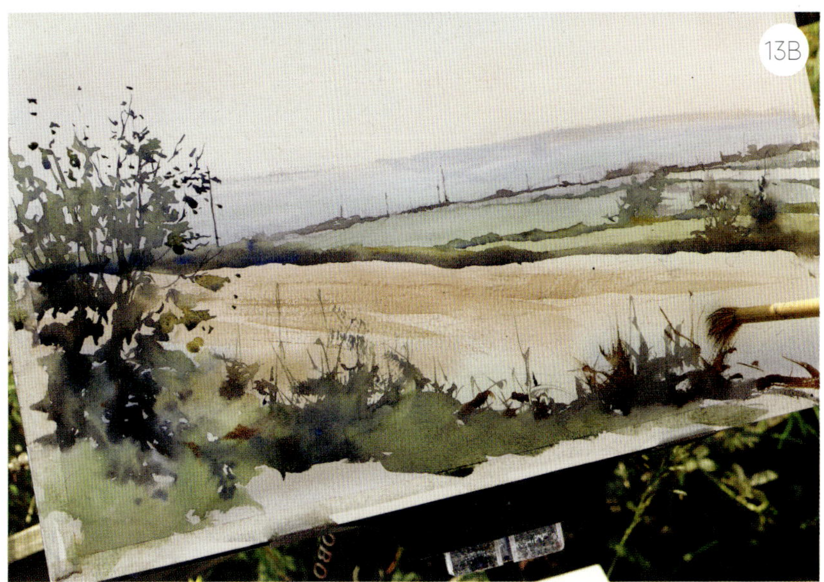

14. Final details

If you want to add a few finishing touches, lift out a few light branches with a damp softening brush. Scrape out some light twigs from the wet wash with a palette knife and then add some darker marks to the field and hedgerow. Finish off with a few flying birds. It is important to vary the marks for the flying birds so that no two are the same.

I was happy enough with the final result, and what's not to like about a couple of hours in the countryside on a beautiful summer's day?

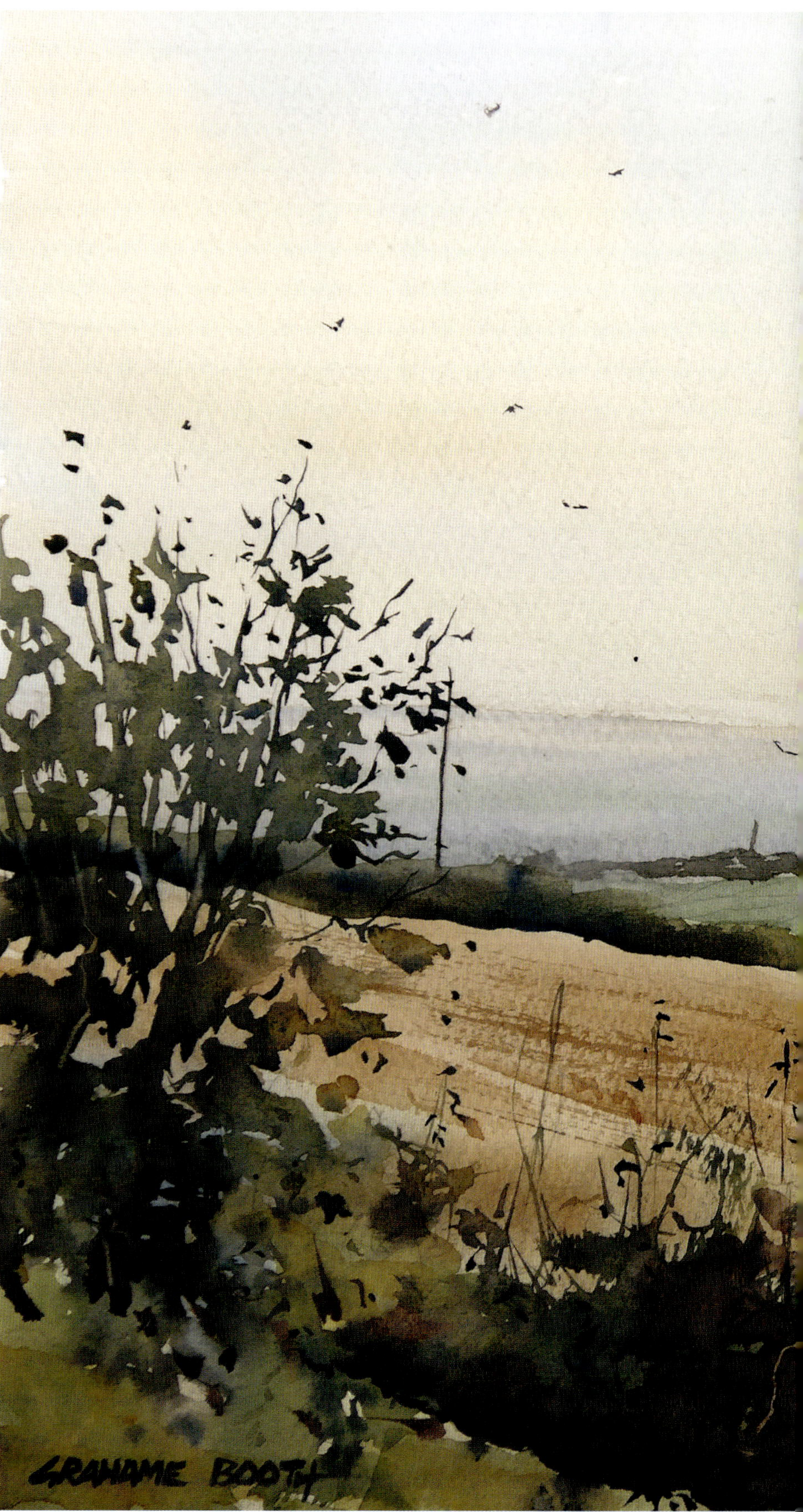

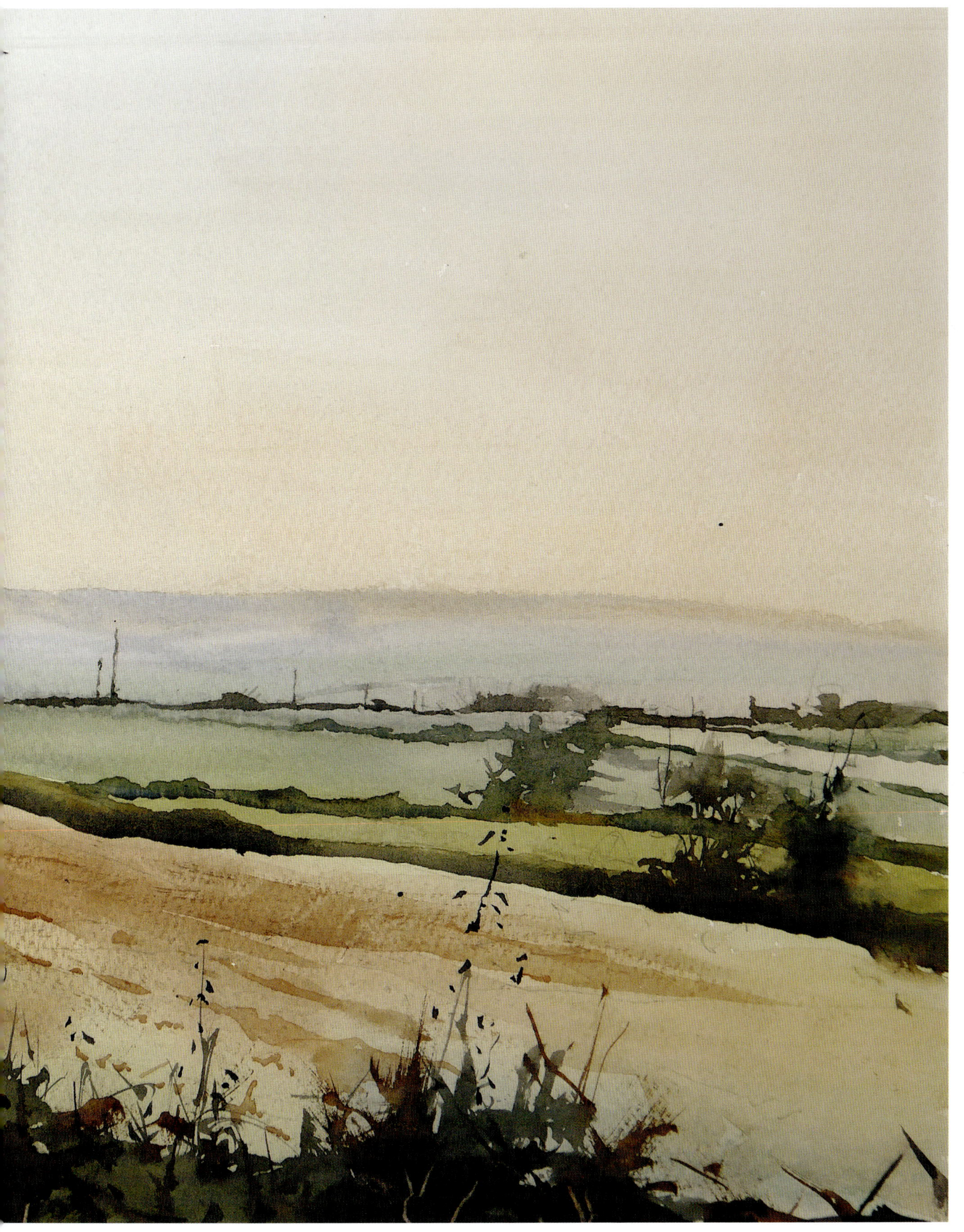

AUTUMN

THERE IS AN AWFUL LOT of green in summer landscapes and it is quite a relief when the beautiful colours of autumn start to appear. Of course, with the autumn colours comes a drop in temperature, and certainly in my part of the world an increase in humidity too. The extra humidity means that washes can take an age to dry. This is both an advantage and disadvantage. The advantage is that we have a great opportunity to work wet-in-wet, but the disadvantage is that paper can get so wet that it really doesn't dry at all outside.

I have a small hairdryer that plugs into my car accessory socket. I suspect this is absolutely hopeless for drying hair, but it does move the air enough to dry the paper. If I am painting at a distance from the car, I also have a gas-operated hot air gun that works pretty well. Care is needed with this, as the temperature could theoretically burn the paper, although this hasn't (yet) happened to me.

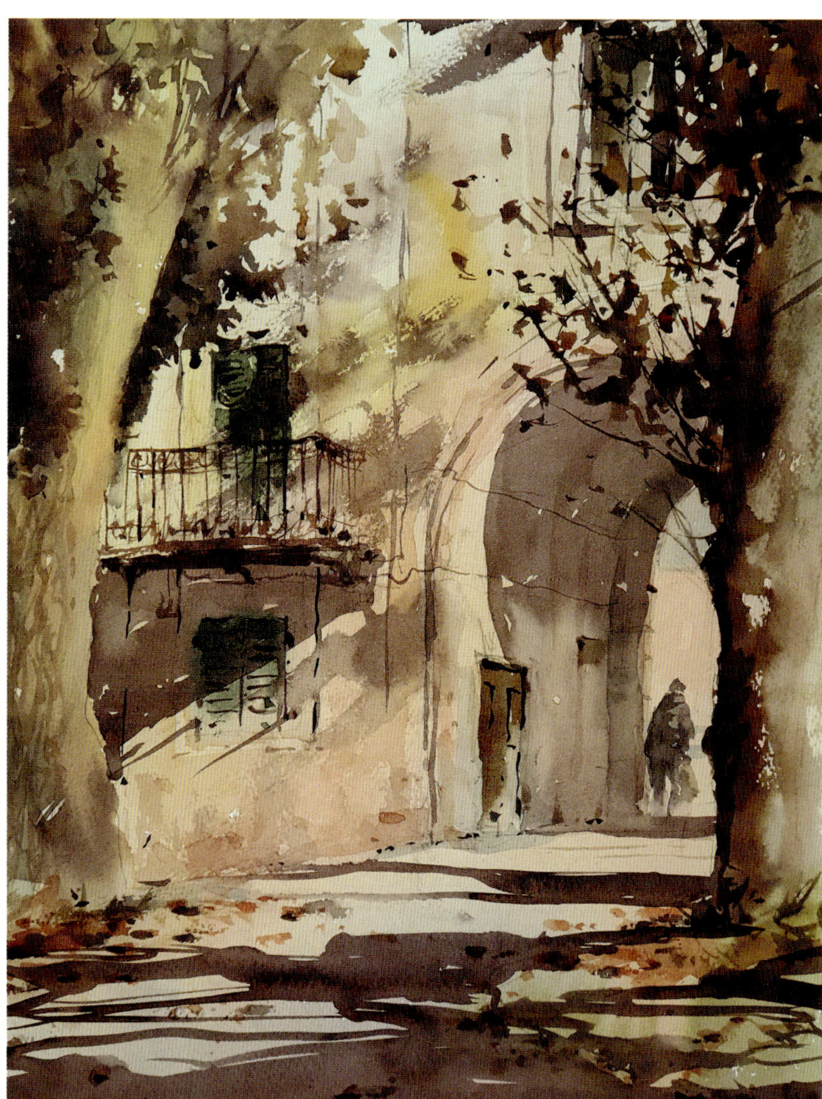

ENTRANCE TO FIVIZZANO, TUSCANY
38 x 51cm (15 x 20in), Millford CP 300gsm (140lb) (also on page 21)

Light conditions

Autumn has a much warmer light because the sun is much lower in the sky. Soft mists are common.

Potential weather conditions

A little of everything: early autumn can be very like summer, but as the days shorten and the sun lowers, the feel of winter approaches. Autumn has probably the greatest range of seasonal weather conditions.

Seasonal features

Autumn leaf colour is far and away the most obvious feature. The rich greens of summer mellow to provide a huge variety of leaf colour.

AUTUMN COLOURS
38 x 28cm (15 x 11in),
Bockingford CP 425gsm (200lb)

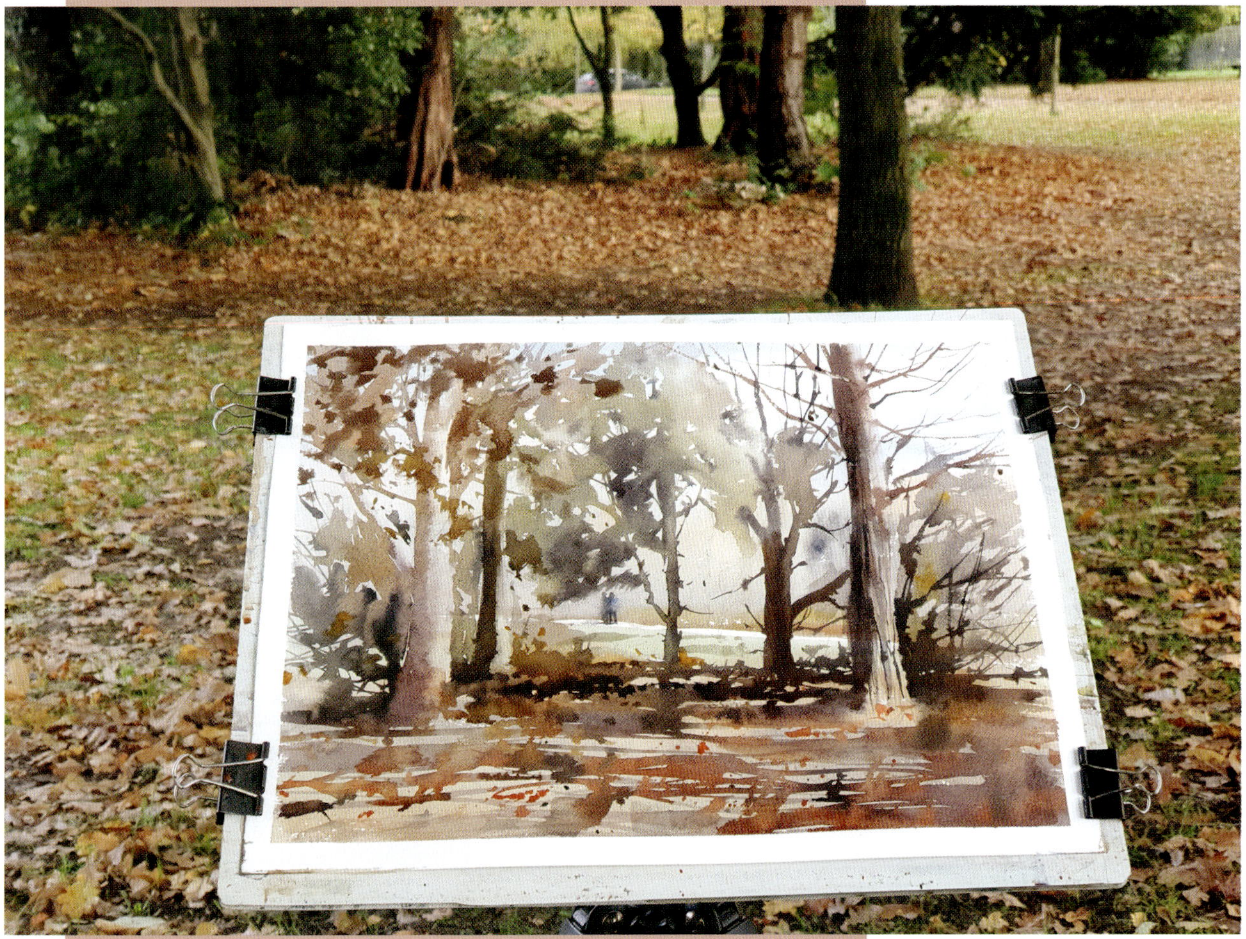

5. STRANGFORD LOUGH

This is Strangford Lough, a sea inlet on the east coast of Northern Ireland – a wild, beautiful place where you will find many more birds than people. Large open coastal landscapes are not very comfortable subjects to paint if the weather is cold, and, although on this day there was hazy early-autumn sunshine, a cool breeze blew up the lough. With this type of subject, strong sunshine is not so important as there are very few cast shadows.

YOU WILL NEED

PAINTS

- » **Ultramarine**
- » **Cobalt blue**
- » **Warm yellow**
- » **Quinacridone magenta**
- » **Burnt sienna**
- » **White gouache**

BRUSHES

- » **Mop or other large soft brush, squirrel or synthetic**
- » **Size 12 round, squirrel or synthetic**
- » **Size 12 and 8 round, sable or synthetic**
- » **Old size 8 sable for softening and lifting out**

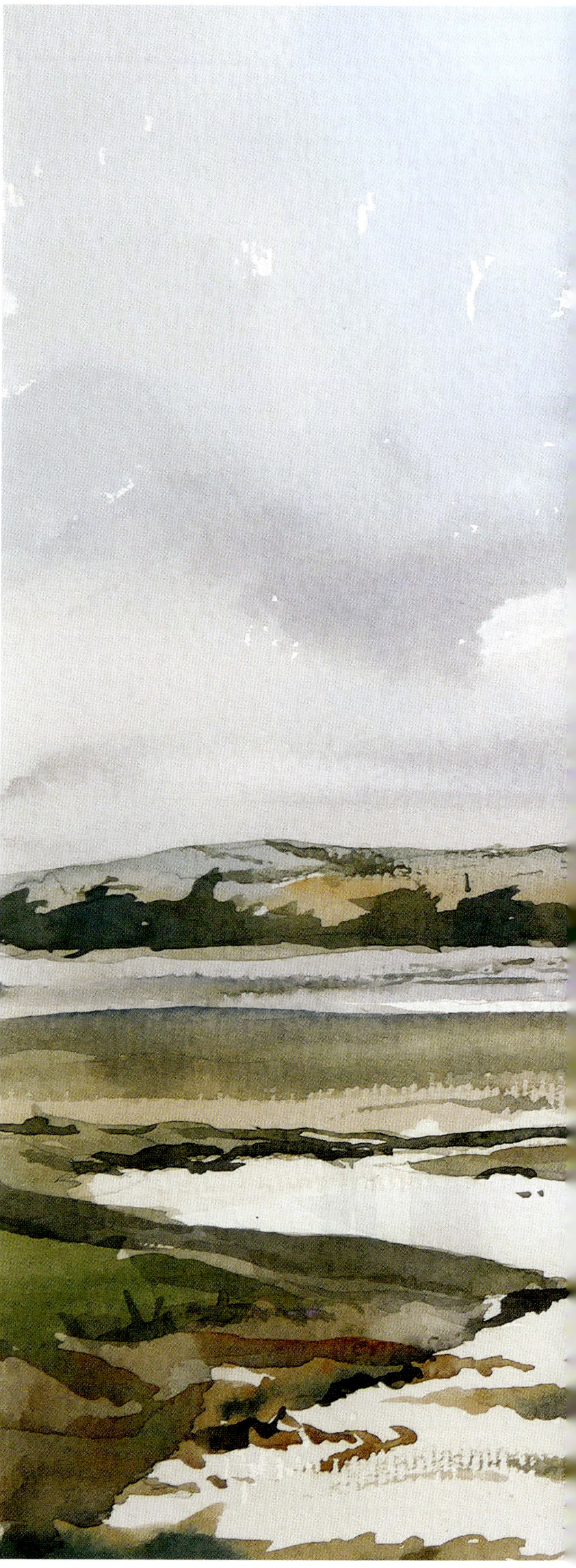

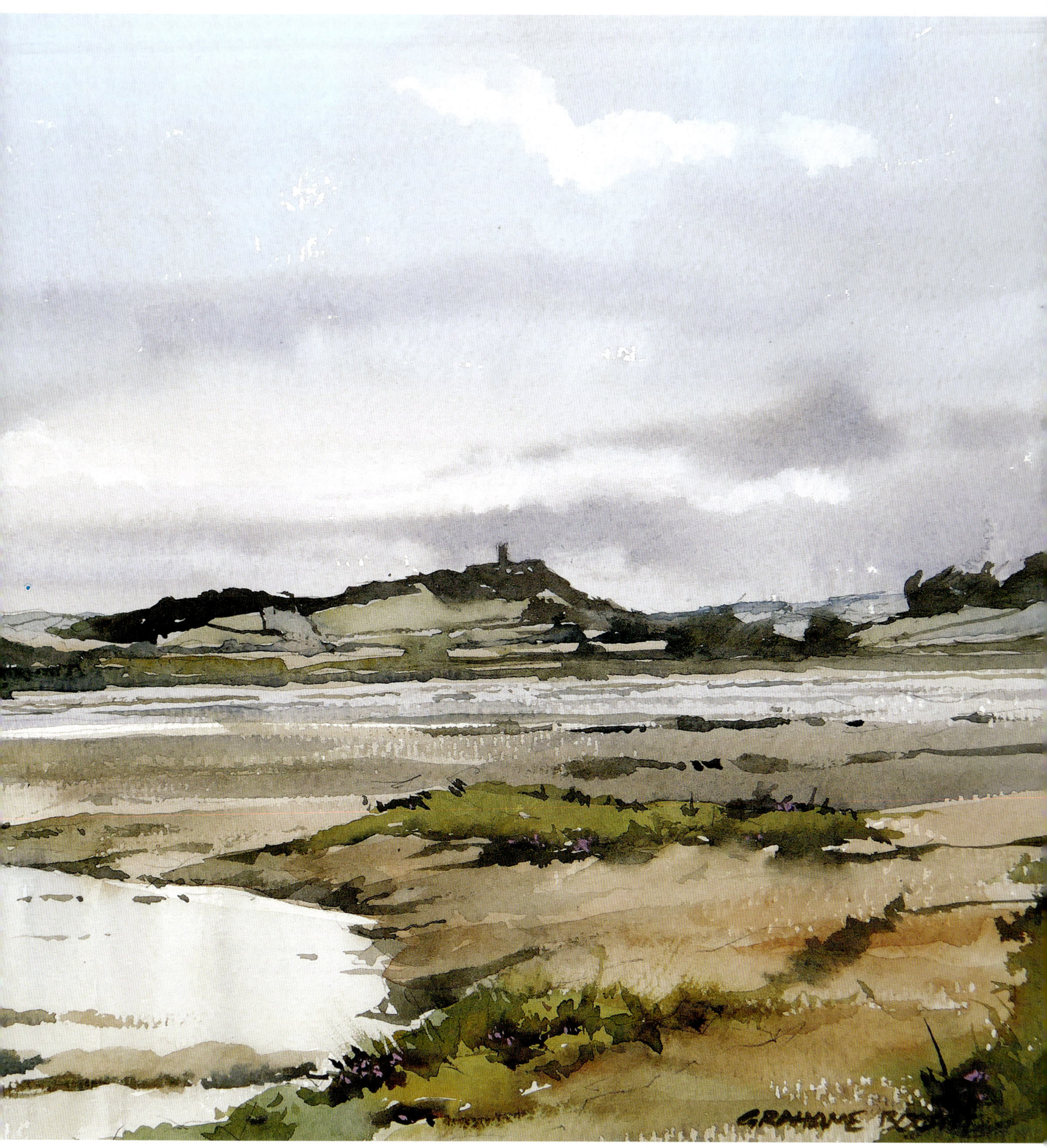

STRANGFORD LOUGH
41 x 31cm (16 x 12in), Saunders Rough 300gsm (140lb)

1. The initial sketch

This type of subject doesn't really require many drawing skills. Get the horizon on first and then build the rest of the drawing around it. I suppose the main problem is in ensuring the correct relative sizes of the foreground and distant areas. If the distant shore is drawn too large in relation to the foreground, it will appear closer than it really is and if drawn too small, it will seem to be much further away.

If you refer to the photograph (1A), you can see which parts of the original scene I chose to omit or change or accentuate in the final sketch (1B).

» There was quite a strong shadow being cast from the wall beside which I was standing, but, in the end, I decided not to put that in the painting as it would have been too distracting.

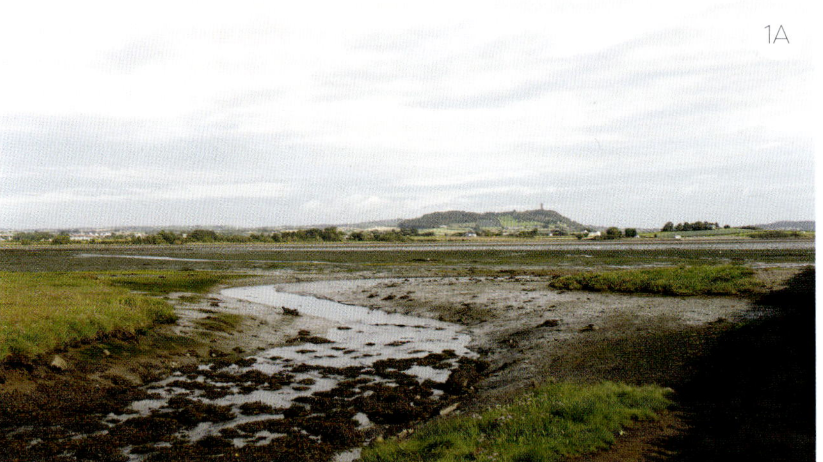

2. The first wash

Use a mop brush and cobalt blue for the sky (2A) but mix in small amounts of burnt sienna as you work down the paper (2B). Use more horizontal strokes as you approach the horizon. This helps to suggest the distant areas of the sky, relatively so far away that any clouds will appear to be in lines. Use some kitchen paper to lift out some lighter clouds (2C).

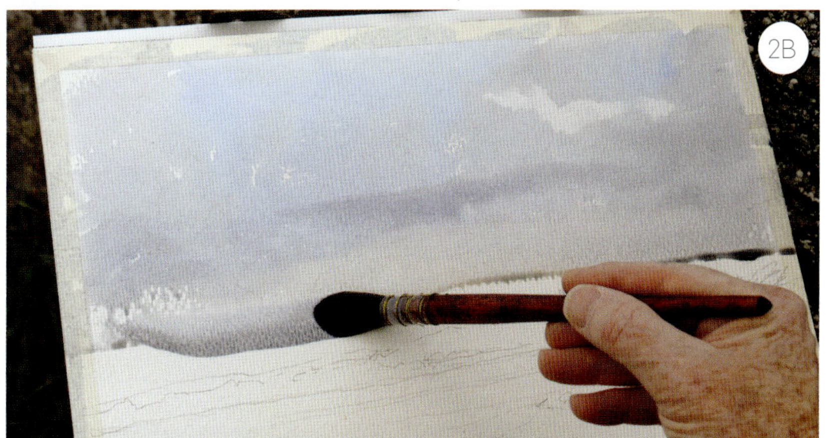

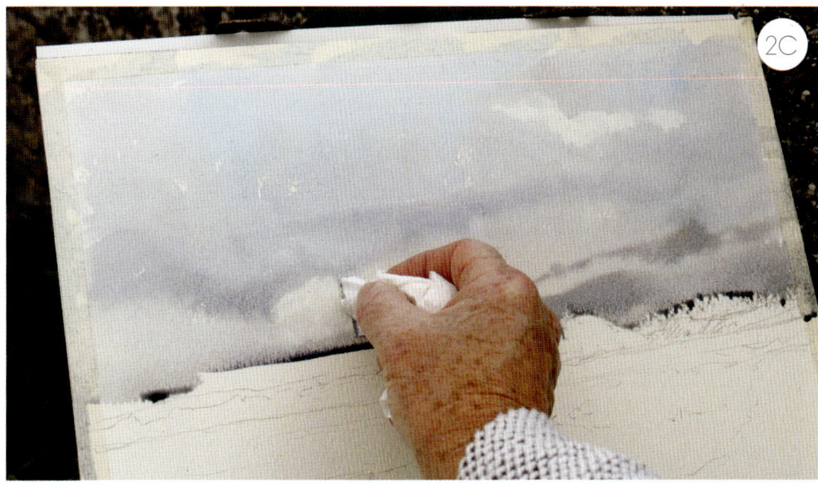

3. The mud flats

Continue down past the horizon, increasing the proportion of burnt sienna in the mix in order to suggest the mud. Continue this down to the bottom of the paper (3A).

I initially left white paper to suggest the shape of the water, but before the foreground wash dried, I decided to soften the edges a little. I prefer to avoid too many hard edges in the early stages of a painting. Hard edges commit you to certain actions whereas soft edges give you plenty of different options. The big problem with hard edges in watercolour is, being transparent, additional layers will not eradicate unwanted edges (3B).

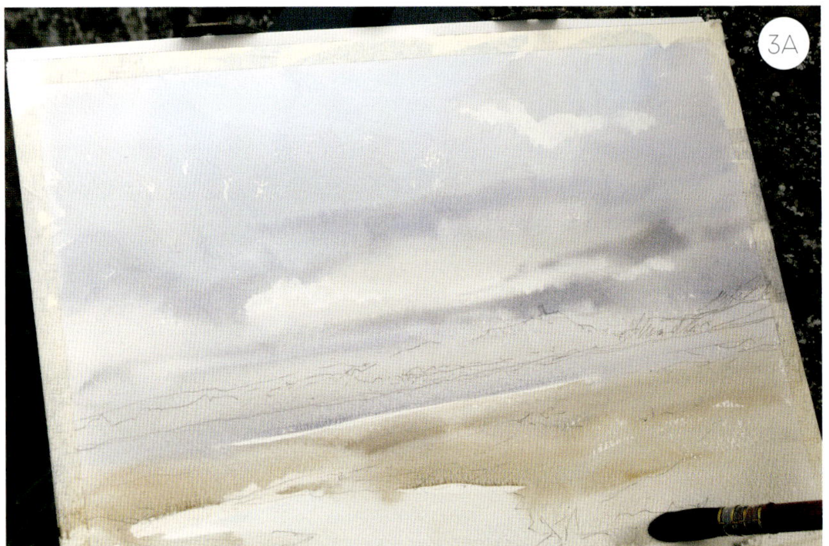

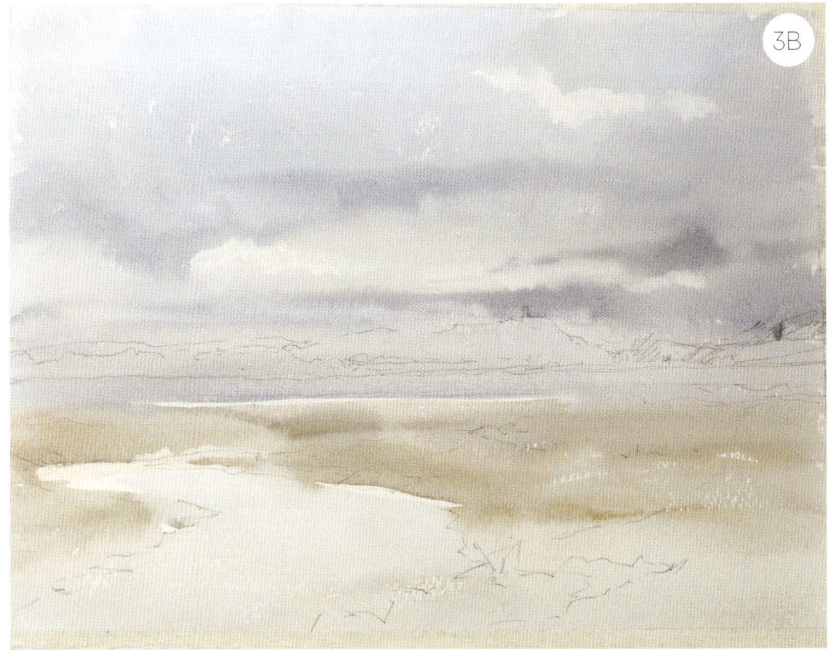

LOCATION INSIGHT

I paused at this point to make room on the path for two young horsewomen to pass. They stopped to take a look and were very kind about my efforts. The women that is, not the horses. The horses didn't seem to be very impressed at all!

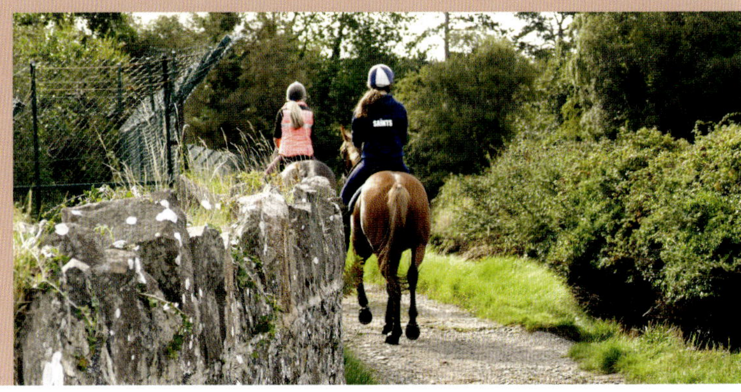

4. The distant shore

Use a size 12 synthetic squirrel brush with a mix of cobalt blue and a touch of warm yellow to paint the distant shore area (4A). Keep this area quite blue (4B) but then vary the mix a little and add some burnt sienna for the closer areas of the shore (see step 5 image). Make no attempt to paint any details. At this stage, it is all about capturing some of the local colour. The details will come later.

5. The distant water

As with the sky, features on a flat surface far away will always appear to be in horizontal lines. Begin the distant water and beach with a strong mix of cobalt and burnt sienna. Then use a softening brush to lighten and soften these marks.

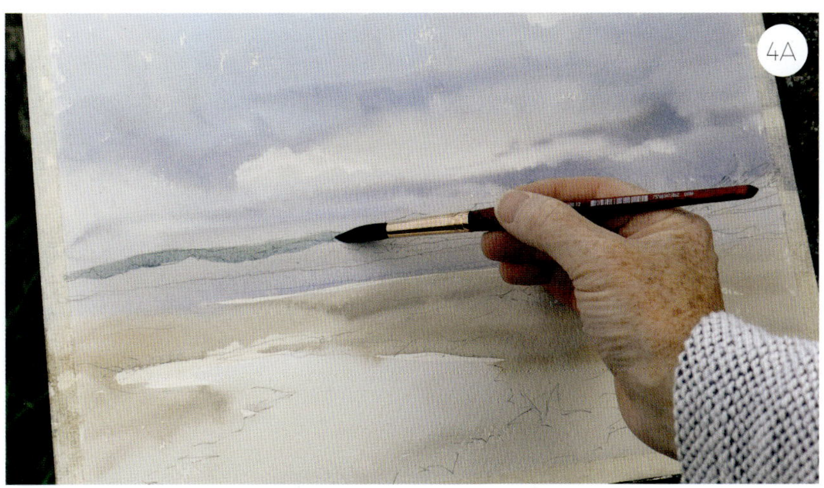

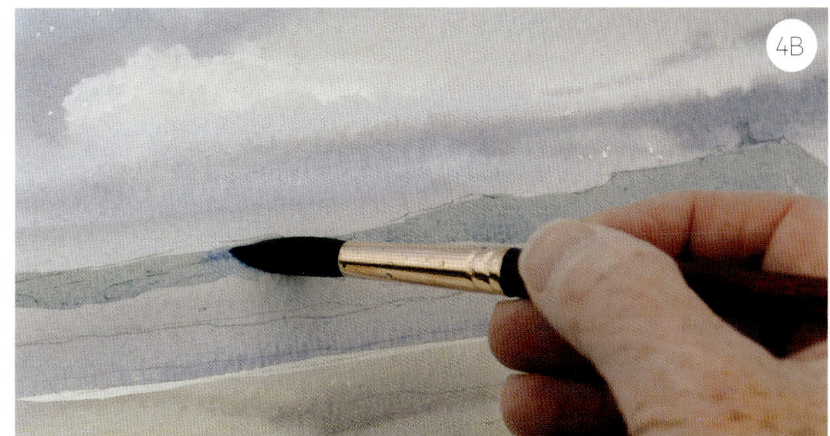

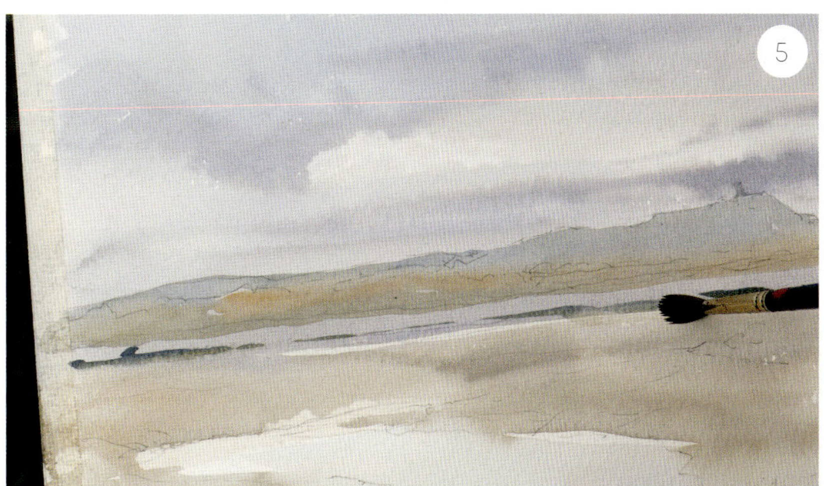

6. The distant water

Continue with these thin horizontal marks in the distance, using your finger to soften them here and there. The effects of aerial perspective include an apparent softening of edges, so on balance your distant areas should have a greater number of softer edges than your closer areas.

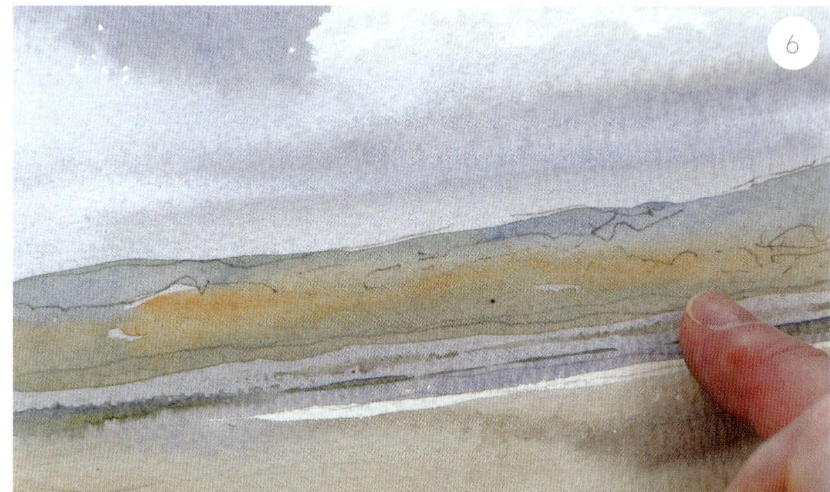

7. The middle ground

Continue down the paper in the same way, but make the marks thicker and warmer as you go. This is just a simple perspective device. If there are thin lines in the distance, then we would expect thicker lines closer. Use more burnt sienna in your cobalt blue to warm the mix.

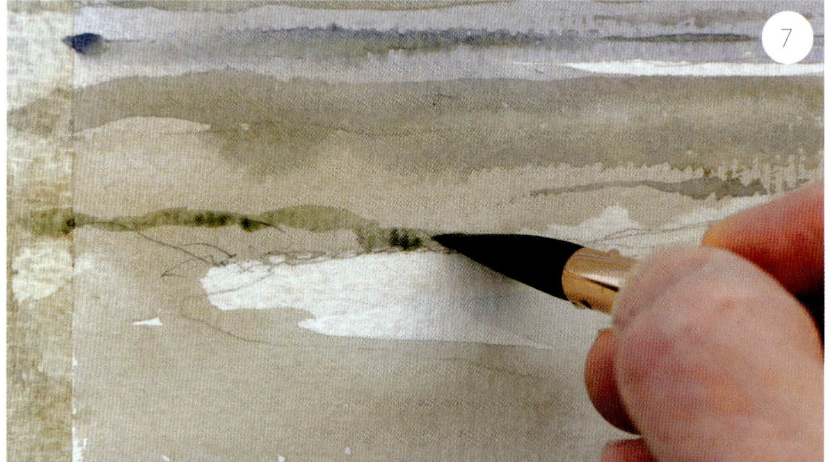

8. The foreground

As you approach the foreground area, more varied marks are needed, in this case to suggest the slight slope of the beach down to the water. Continue to use the cobalt blue and burnt sienna mix, but strengthen it even more for this area. Although I am leaving a greater number of hard edges here, I still soften them to some extent. It is important however to begin creating an obvious tonal counterchange between the water and the bank.

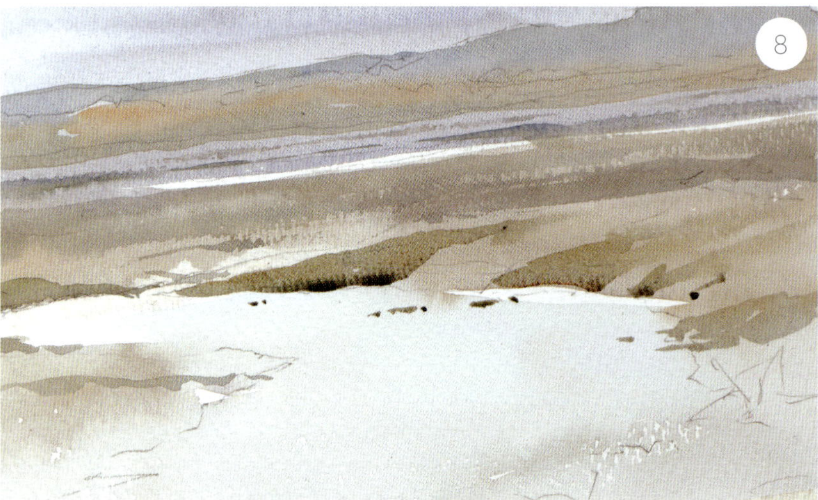

9. The extreme foreground

In the extreme foreground, use some stronger colours – use pure burnt sienna, but also a green mix of ultramarine with warm yellow. Continue to make varied, irregular marks to suggest the shape of the bank.

10. The sandbank

Continue to make varied marks in this foreground area, changing the mix as you go, varying the proportions of ultramarine and burnt sienna. Use a dry brush to suggest tufts of grass and to create more tonal variety in the grass covering the top of the bank.

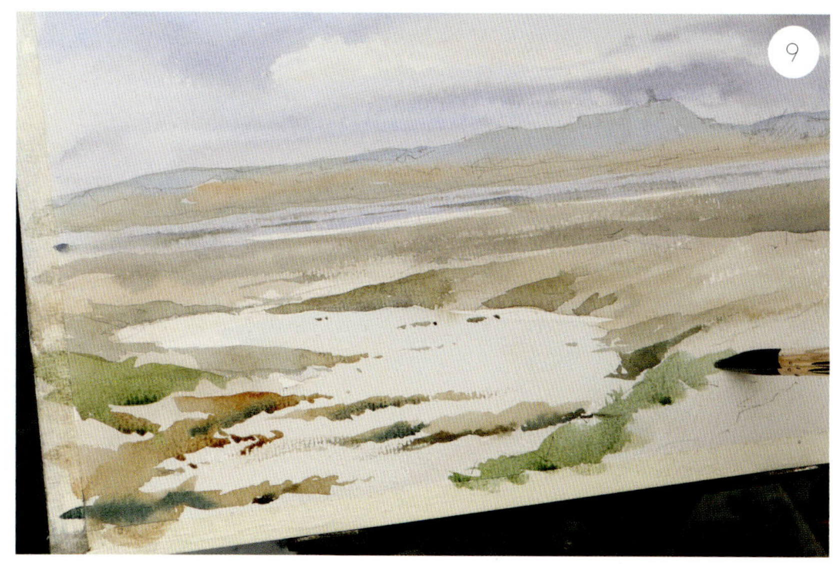

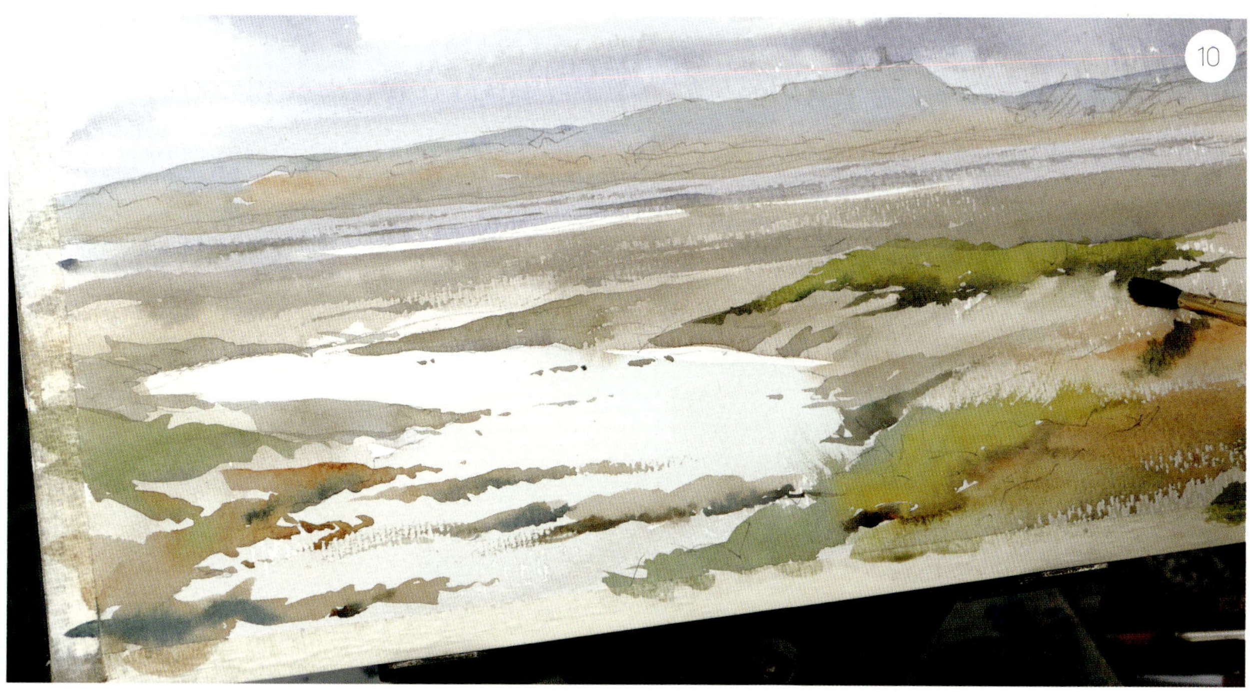

11. The distant hills

Use a size 12 pointed synthetic sable brush with some cool blue-greens mixed from cobalt and warm yellow to hint at the extreme distance. Create directional marks that run along and down the sides of the distant hills to suggest the form and slope. It is very important that these marks are softened either with a brush or with a finger in order to suggest distance.

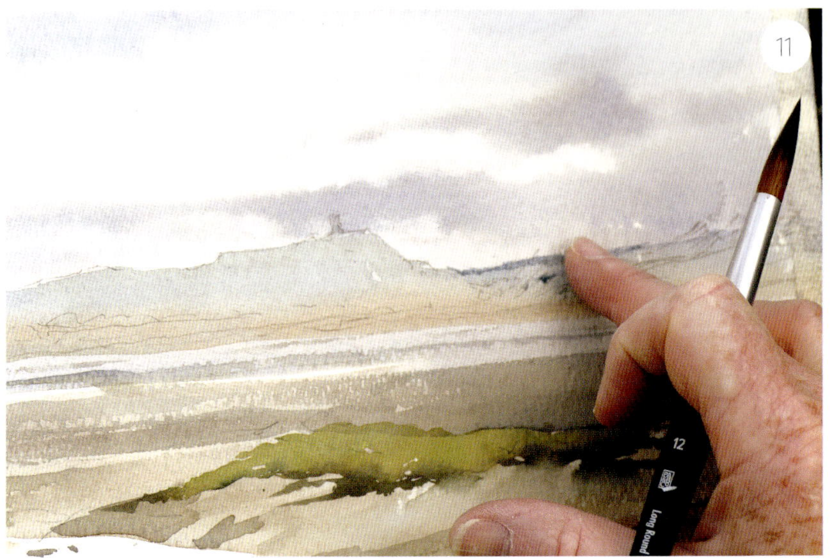

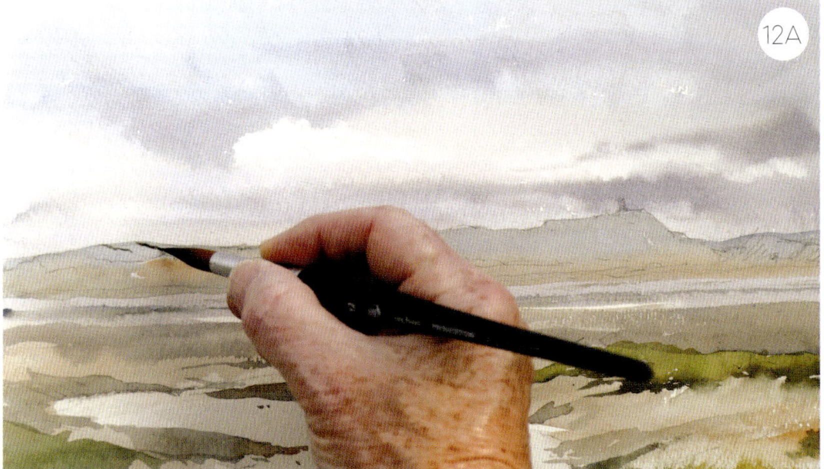

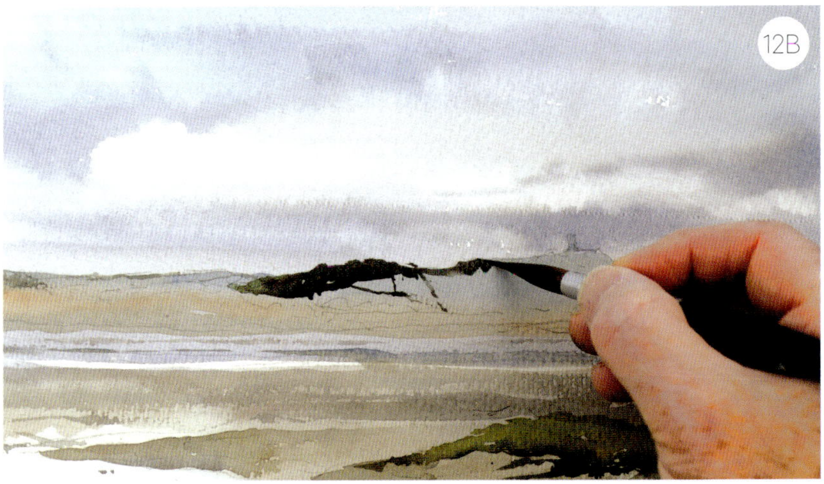

12. Adding details

It's time to take a bit of a chance now with some stronger grey greens. Using a varying mix of cobalt blue, burnt sienna and warm yellow gives plenty of variety in this section. Hint at some of the structures present but don't get bogged down in detail. Create the distant hilltop and hedgerows (12A and 12B).

There is a large tower on the top of the hill – simply paint that as part of the vegetation. We want it to be part of the hill, not looking like something stuck on top. Work down the hillside towards the water, adding the suggestion of distant trees (12C) and closer hedgerows (12D).

Add some softer greens to some of the distant fields to add variety (12E).

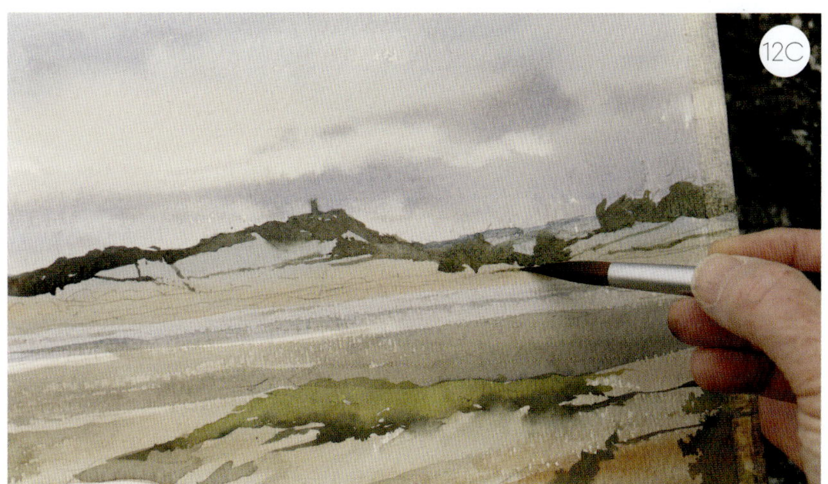

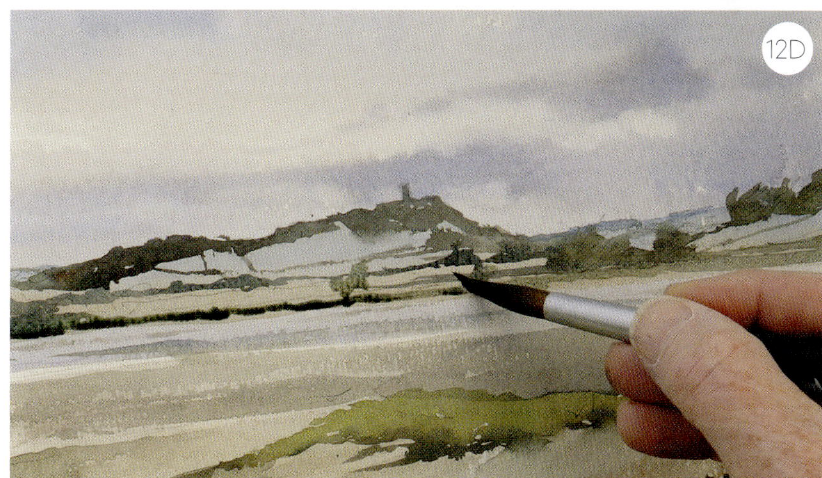

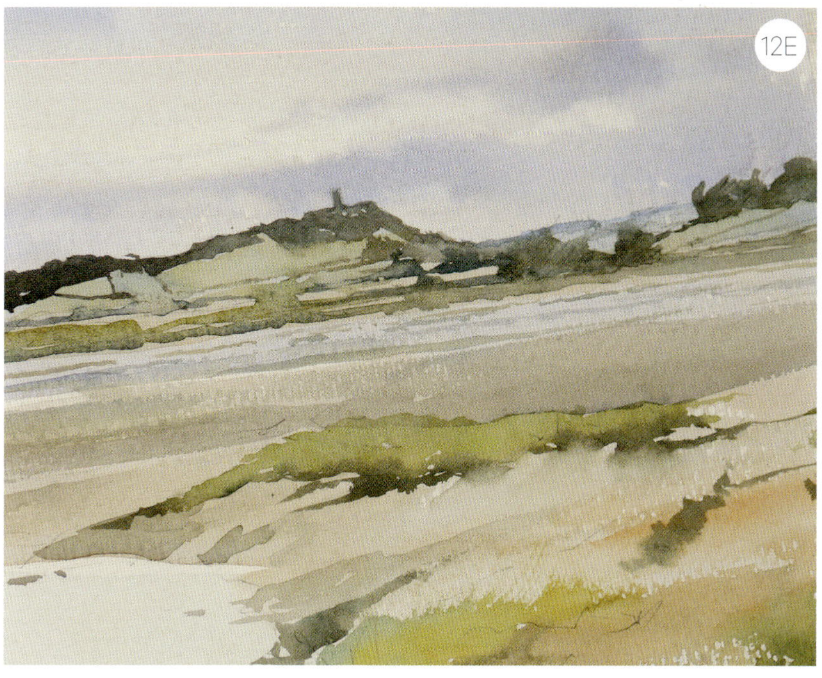

13. Adding dark touches

Continue down into the middle ground with a stronger version of the cobalt blue, burnt sienna and warm yellow mix, making almost all random marks. As well as adding darks, this has the added effect of making the lights appear lighter.

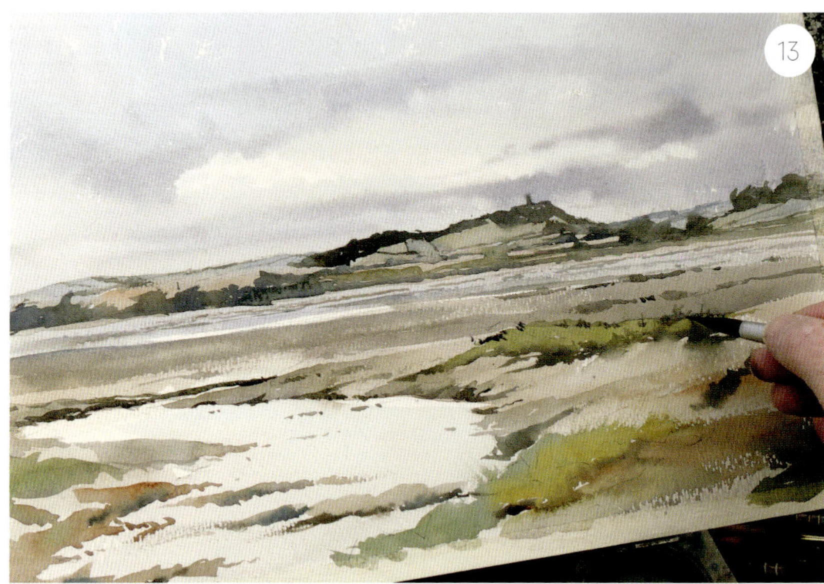

14. Adding foreground details

In the foreground, continue in a similar vein, varying the cobalt blue, burnt sienna and warm yellow mix, creating variety but only hinting at detail. Use the same colour blend to add a suggestion of sea grasses (14A) and continue to add further shadowy touches around the water line (14B).

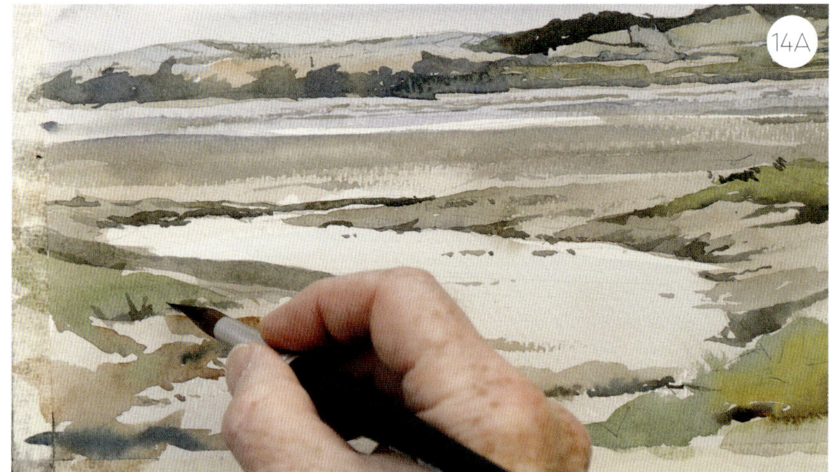

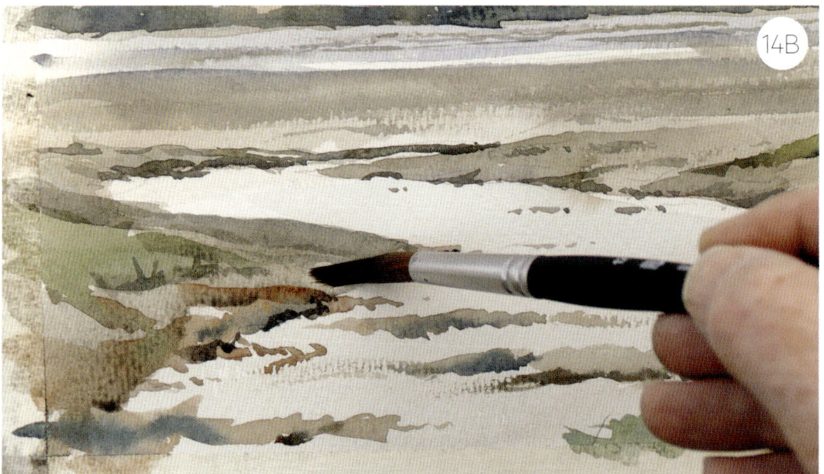

15. Grasses

Painting tufts of grass is as much down to luck as judgement. In general, I will try out different tuft-like marks. If I don't mind them, I will leave them, and if I don't like them, I soften them. Use the same varied blend as in the previous step to create a variety of grass-like shapes in the foreground.

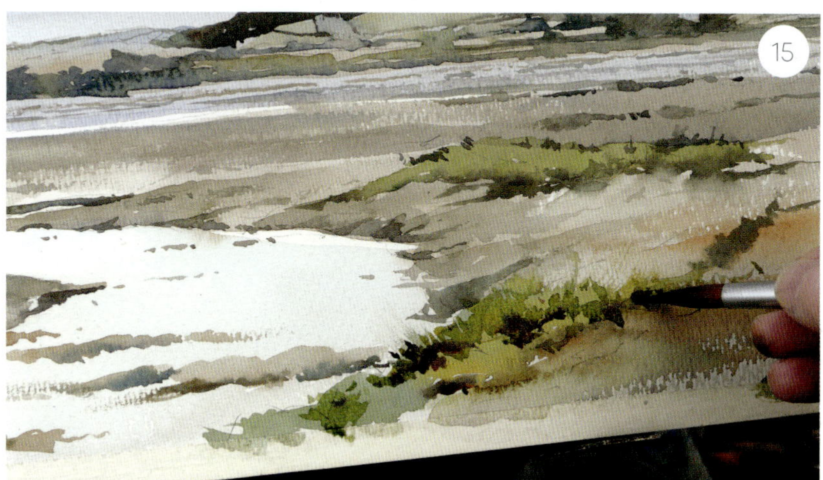

16. The sandbank

Here, I feel that the foreground area beside the water needs to be stronger and warmer. Add a simple wash of burnt sienna.

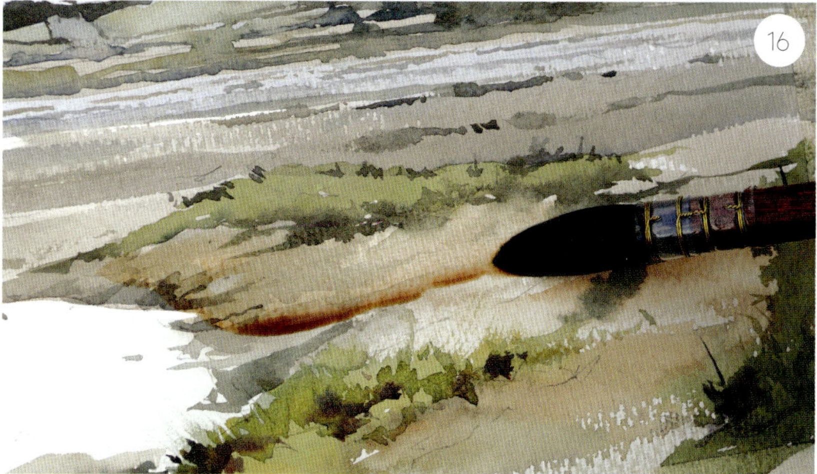

17. The water

To make the water appear a little less bland, add some soft vertical marks using cobalt blue to suggest some subtle sky reflections. Go easy here – we have spent time making the water look light by placing dark tones around it, so we don't want to risk over-darkening it.

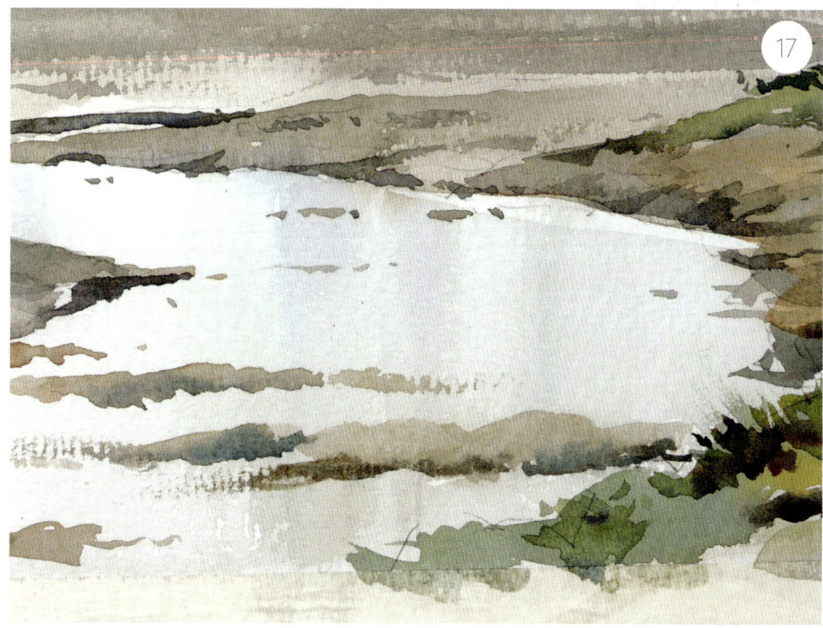

18. Final details

Add a few vibrant sea asters with
a mix of quinacridone magenta
and opaque white. Dot a few
about amongst the sandbanks
to balance the use of such
a vivid colour.

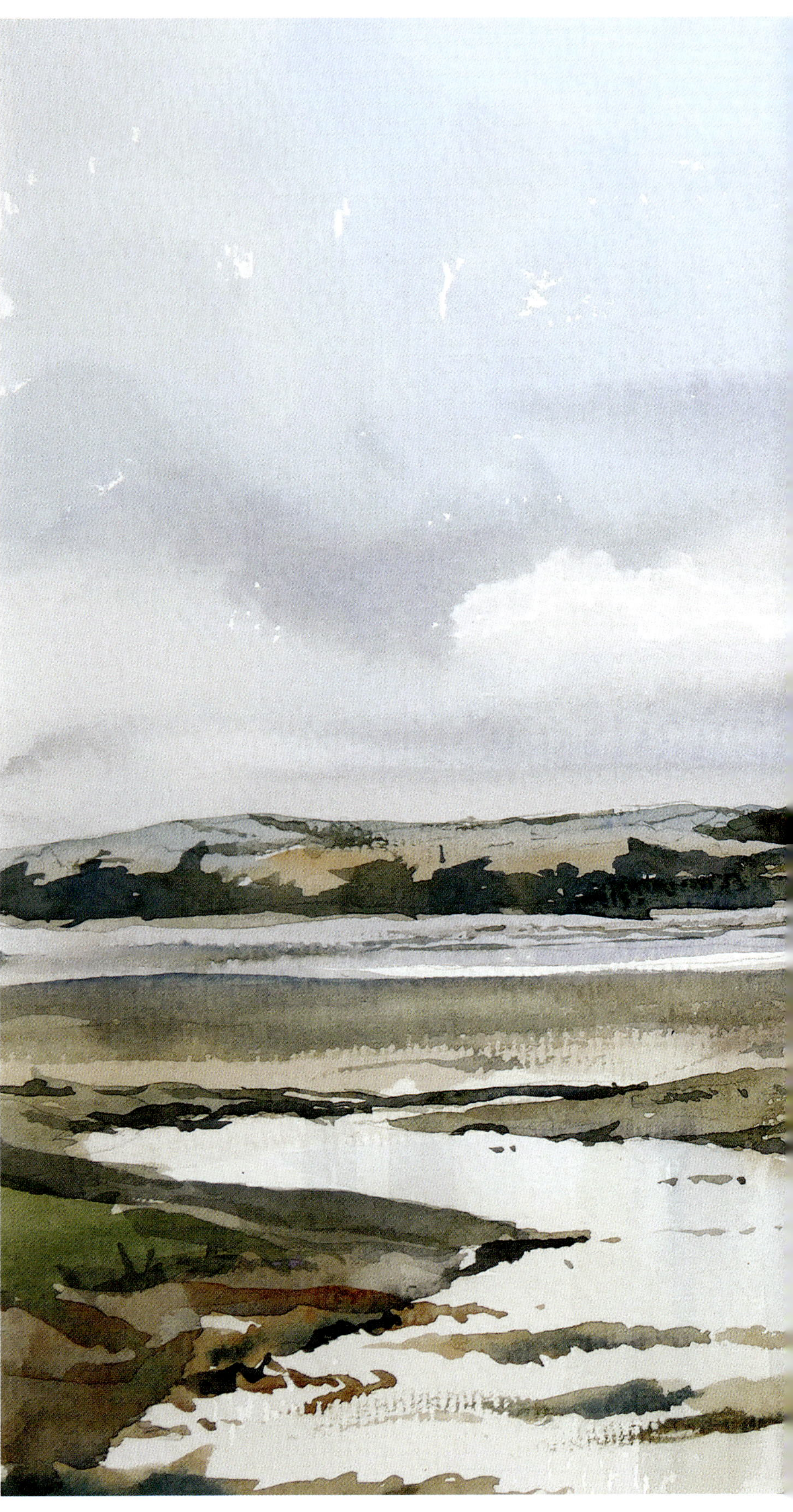

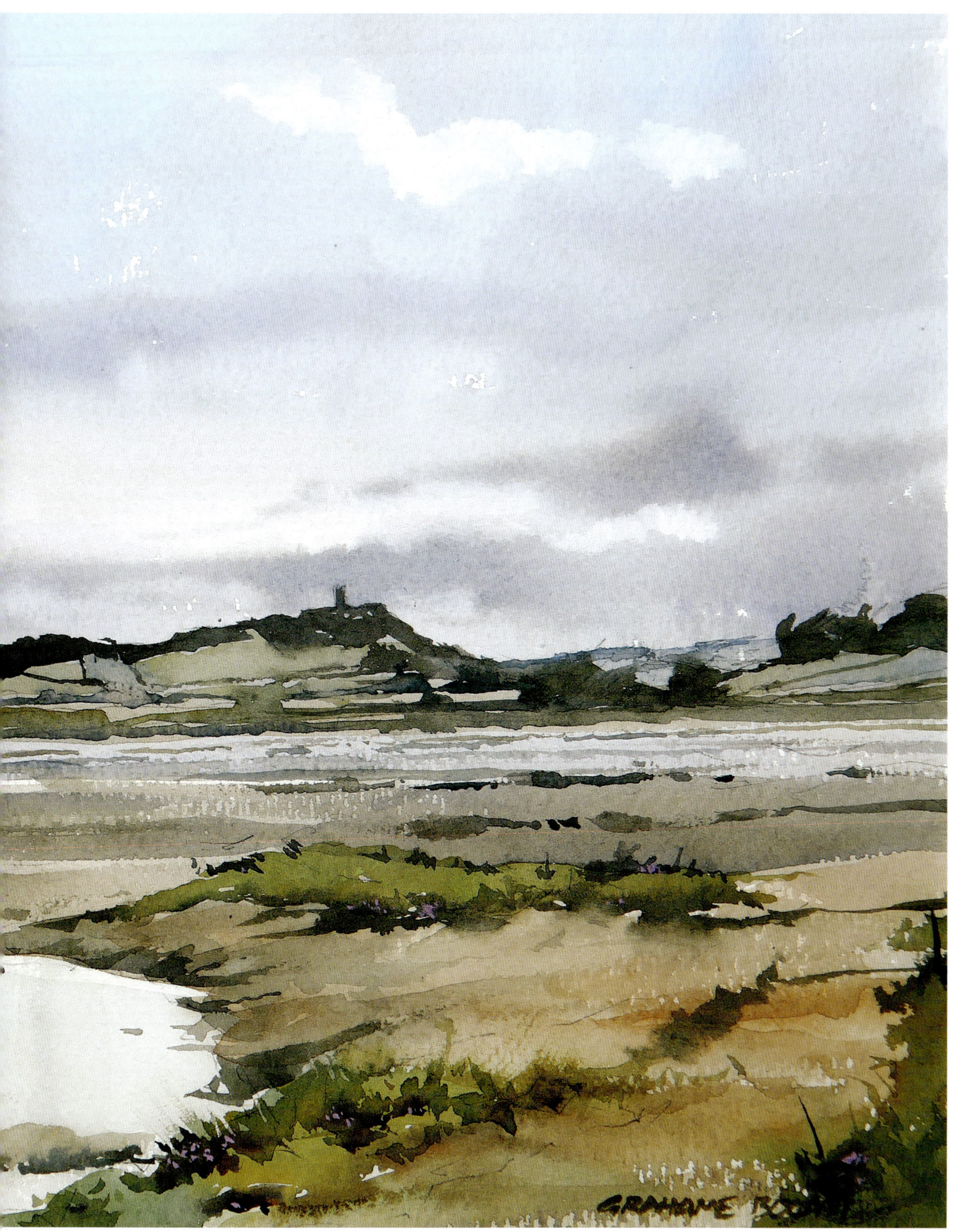

6. MINNOWBURN

This is a fairly typical river scene with a bridge and a variety of trees at different distances, but it is the autumn colours that really set this subject apart. In the photograph, the autumn colours don't appear that strong, but standing there at the riverbank I was aware of much more golden colour in the beech trees across the river and so resolved to enhance the colours to better suggest the autumn day.

YOU WILL NEED

PAINTS

» **Cobalt blue**
» **Ultramarine**
» **Phthalo blue (green shade)**
» **Warm yellow**
» **Warm red**
» **Quinacridone magenta**
» **Burnt sienna**
» **White gouache**

BRUSHES

» **Mop or other large soft brush, squirrel or synthetic**
» **Size 6 pointed mop, sable or synthetic**
» **Size 12 and 8 round, sable or synthetic**
» **Size 10 rigger, sable or synthetic**
» **Old size 8 sable for softening and lifting out**

MINNOWBURN
26 x 36cm (10 x 14in),
Millford CP 300gsm (140lb)

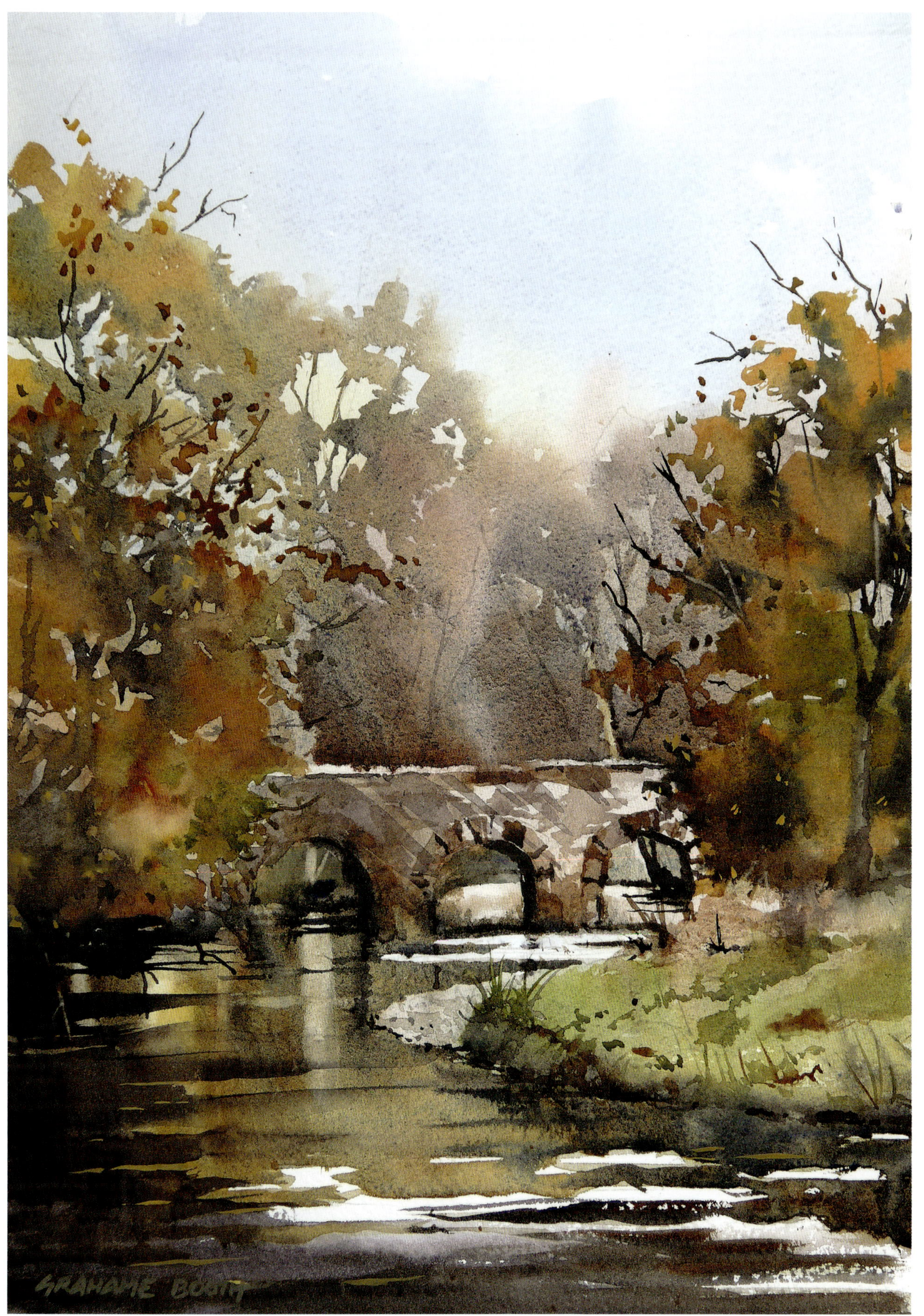
GRAHAME BOOTH

1. The initial sketch

There isn't a lot of point in drawing the trees too carefully. Drawn carefully, there is a risk of the painting becoming a colouring-in exercise, so instead I merely indicate the main branches and I can then have some fun with the paint later. I take some care over the bridge and the edges of the river. If you refer to the photograph (1A), you can see which parts of the original scene I chose to omit in the final sketch (1B).

» The scene is largely unchanged, but I left out the near riverbank, as it makes for a more pleasing composition. Triangle shapes in the corners will distract the eye too much.

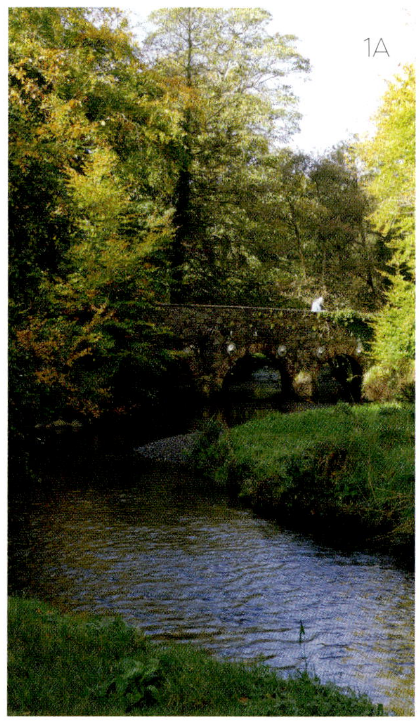
1A

1B

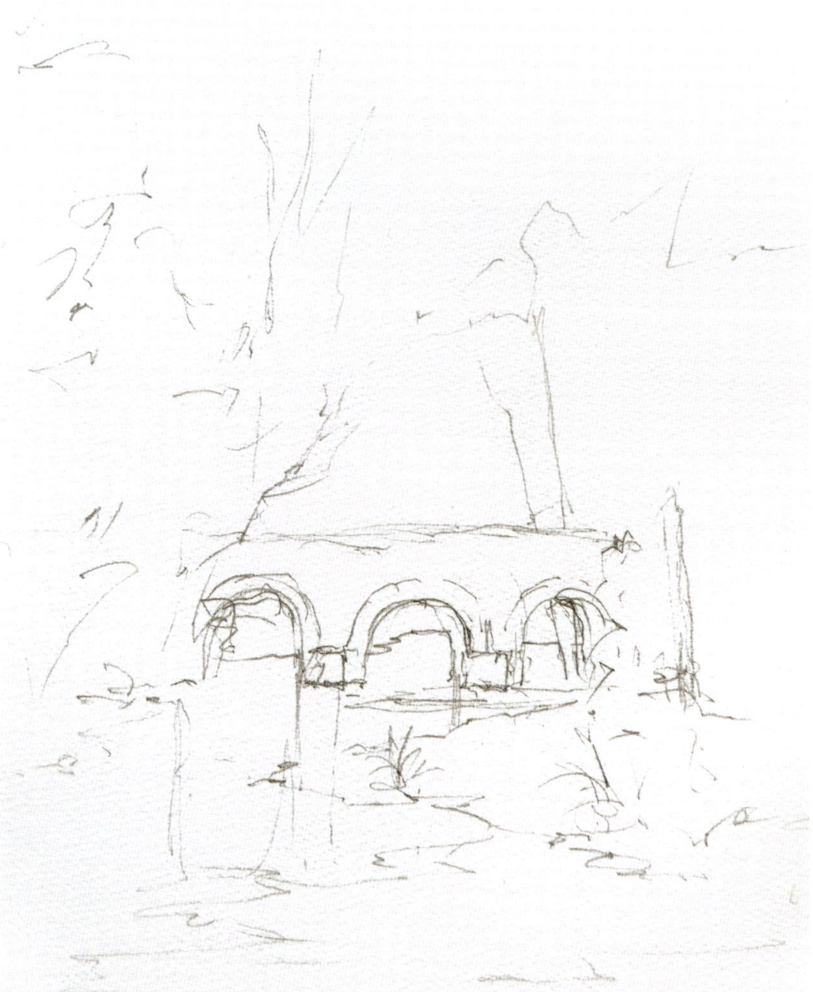

2. The sky wash

The sky is not very important in this painting, serving only as a pale blue background for the trees. Wash a mix of cobalt blue over the paper starting at the top and working down, changing the strength slightly as you go and adding a little warm yellow and warm red into the blue, which begins to suggest some tree colour. Use a soft mop at this stage.

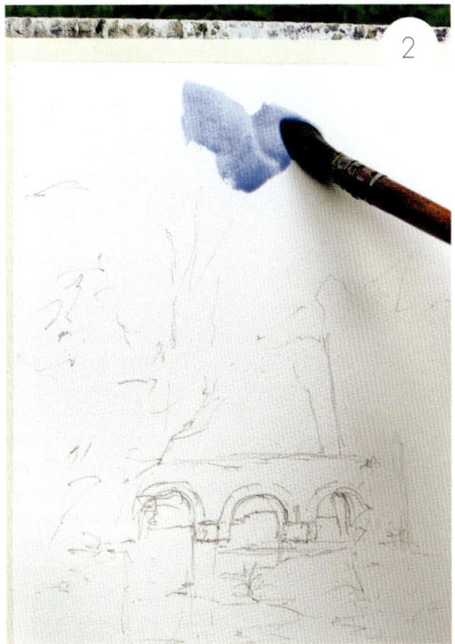
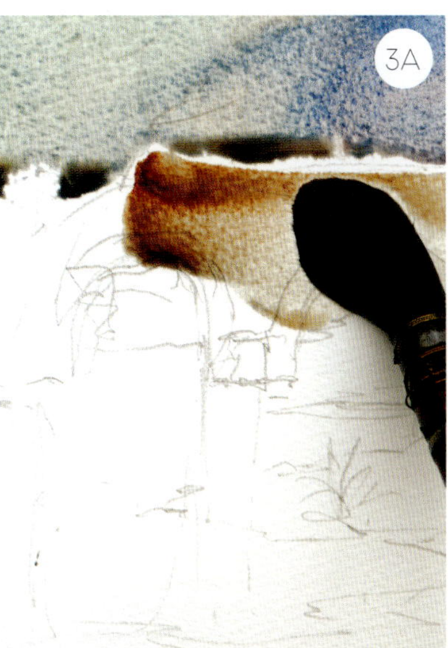

3. The middle ground

Leave a little gap at the top of the bridge to suggest the light hitting this area (3A) and continue down with burnt sienna, adding a green mix from ultramarine and warm yellow in the grassy area. Leave some of the area below the bridge untouched too. This will hint at sunlight on the water (3B).

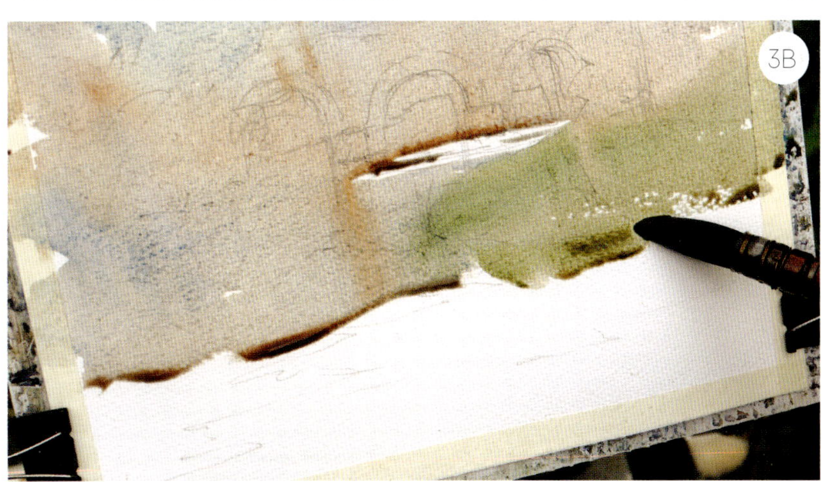

4. Reflections

Suggest reflections in the water by dragging down some of the colours that you will use for the trees: pure warm yellow is suitably warm for this purpose, as is burnt sienna. Also introduce some darks mixed from ultramarine and burnt sienna to provide tonal contrast. Here I changed to my synthetic Kolinsky mop, which allows more control.

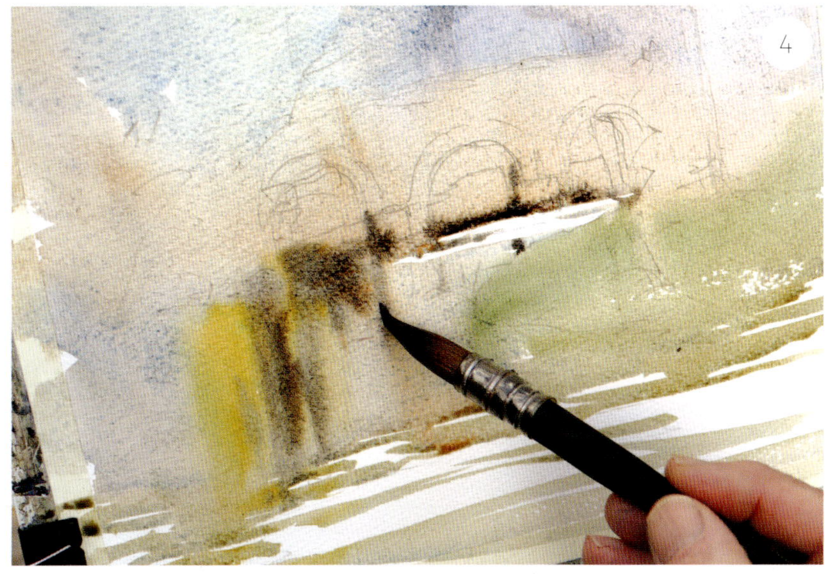

5. The river

Continue the river wash down the paper using horizontal strokes to suggest rippling in the water. Use the same colours as mixed in step 4. Leave some areas of the paper unpainted to suggest the light reflecting on the water.

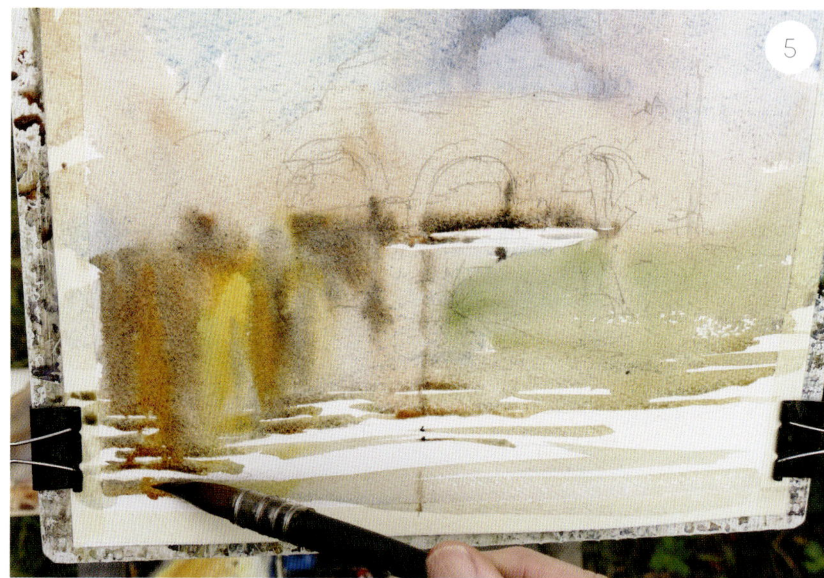

6. The trees

You can pretty much go to town with your colours when painting autumn trees. Almost anything goes. The colours are so varied that you can use up some of those pigments you seldom use! Start at the top, and touch in a tree-like area of paint (6A). Change the colour slightly, then paint the next few trees, overlapping and butting up to each other (6B).

The first wash hadn't dried completely, so I got a little softness in the second wash. I was quite happy with this as I would have softened the edges anyway. Leave as crisp a line as you can at the top of the bridge. It is important to remember that it is never a problem for the paint to merge and blend. If a hard edge is needed, then just wait until the earlier wash is completely dry and add it then.

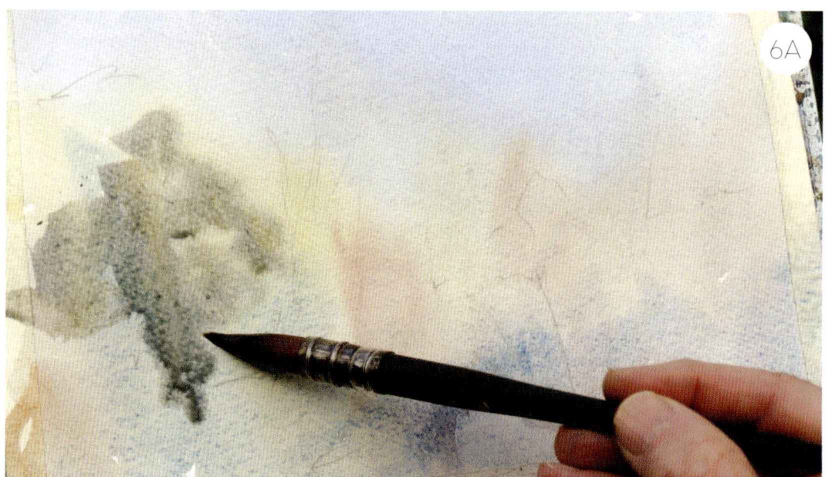

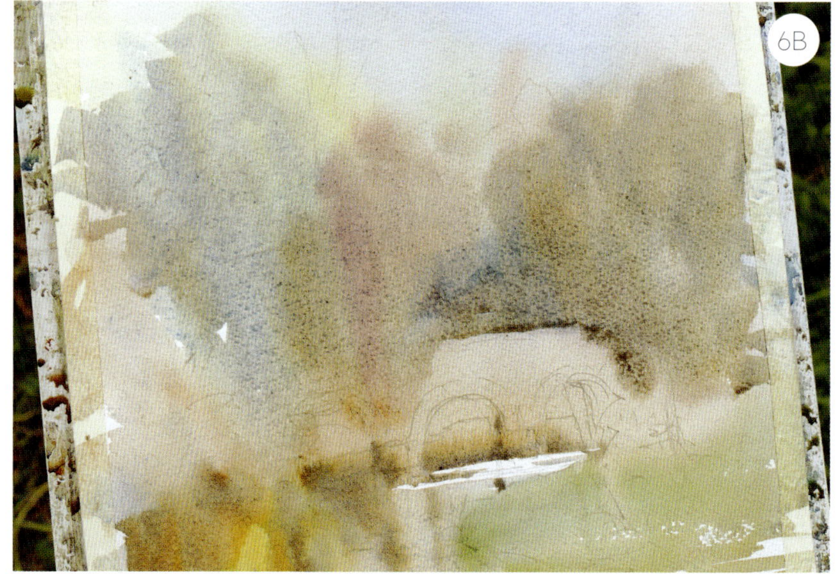

7. Lifting out

Use your lifting-out brush to create a few light-coloured trunks.
It is very easy to lift out colour from a damp wash. Just be sure that
your brush is barely damp. Too wet and you are likely to create
cauliflowers or runbacks. Rinse and dry your brush frequently.
As you lift paint, your brush will become wetter.

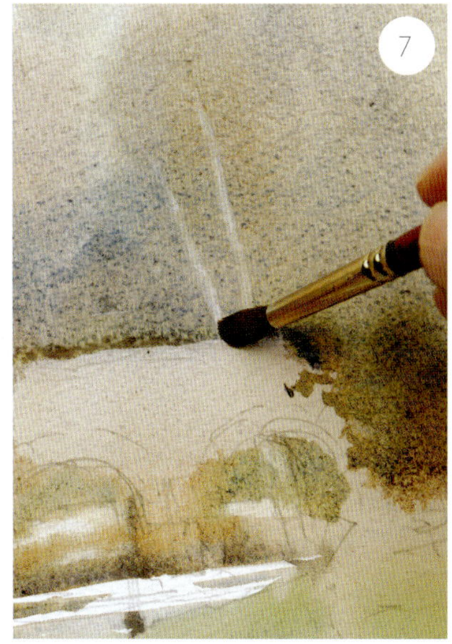

8. Fixing a cauliflower!

Hmm. This is a cauliflower
caused by my wet second wash
flowing down into my not-quite-
dry first wash. You might not
encounter this problem, but in
case you do…

First I tried to gently lift the
excess moisture at the edge, but
the paint continued to flow down
(8A and 8B). My best option was
to add stronger paint into this
edge. By doing so I was able
to arrest the cauliflower and
increase the strength of my
reflections. The paint flowing
down was weaker than the paint
that was already there and that
is why the cauliflower formed.
By adding strong paint into
weaker paint I was able to fix the
problem (8C and 8D).

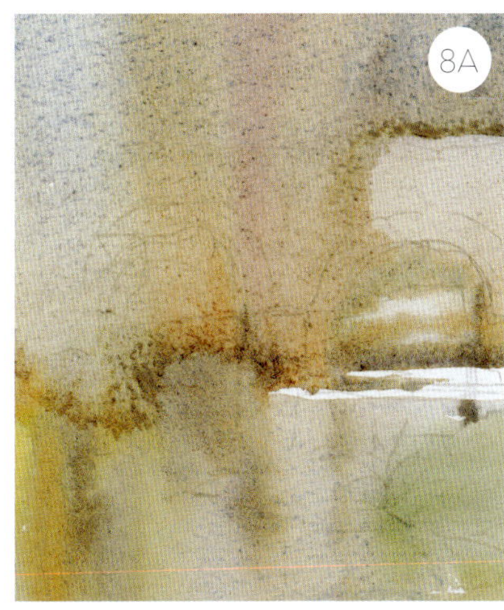

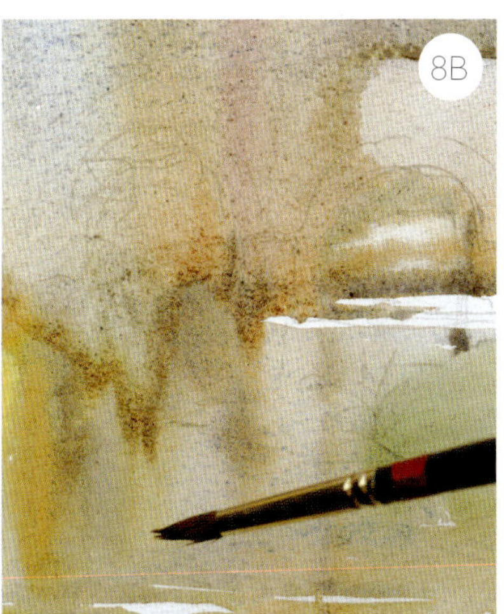

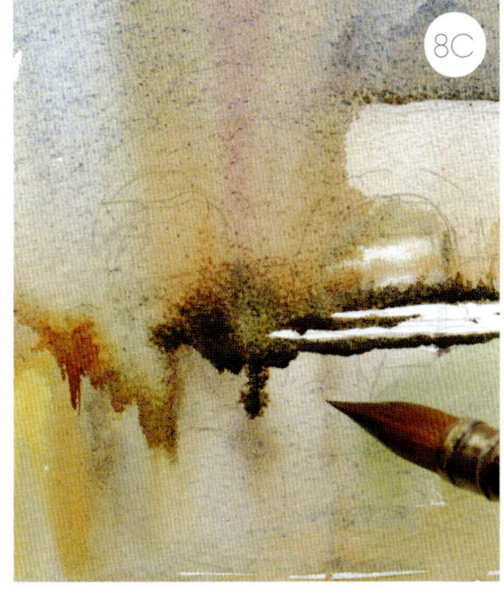

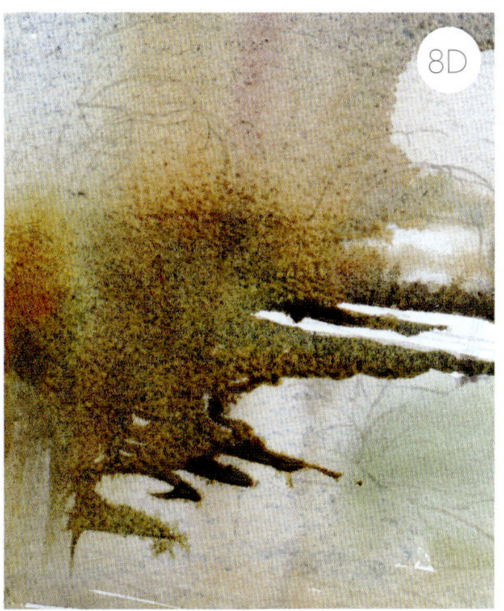

9. Lifting out reflections

Lift out some light reflections from the damp river wash (9A). This creates some useful tonal variety in this area (9B).

10. Shadows

Use a strong mix of ultramarine and burnt sienna to paint the dark shaded areas underneath the arches of the bridge. On the left-hand arch, allow the dark shadow to continue down into the water as a reflection.

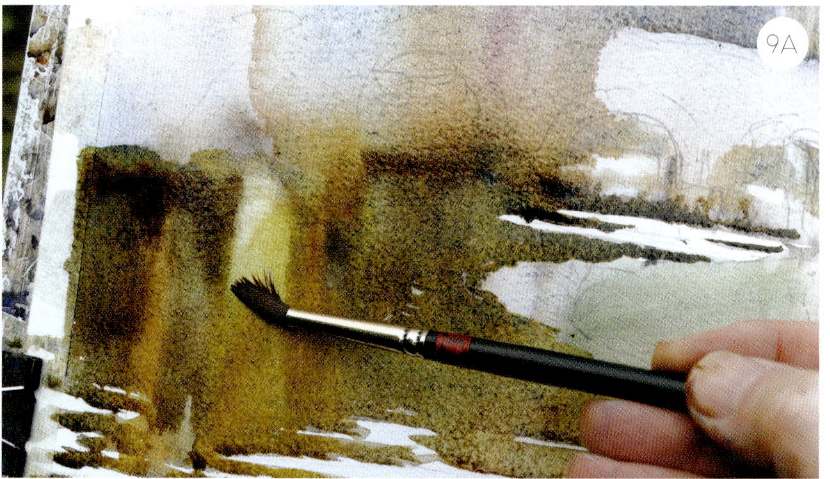

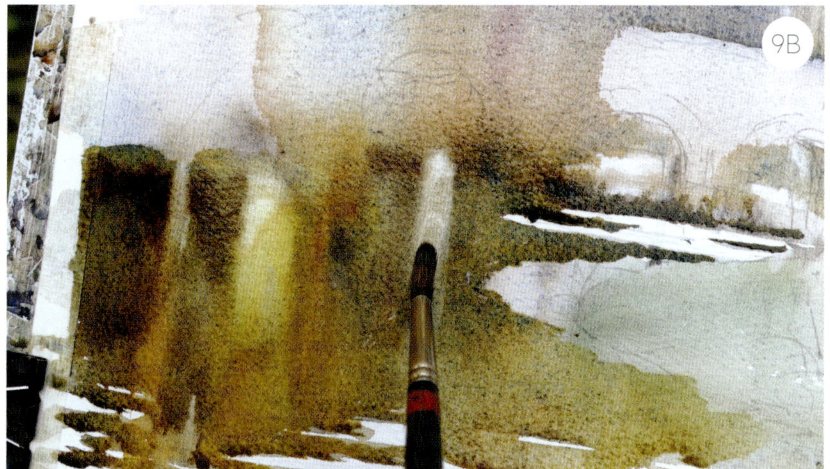

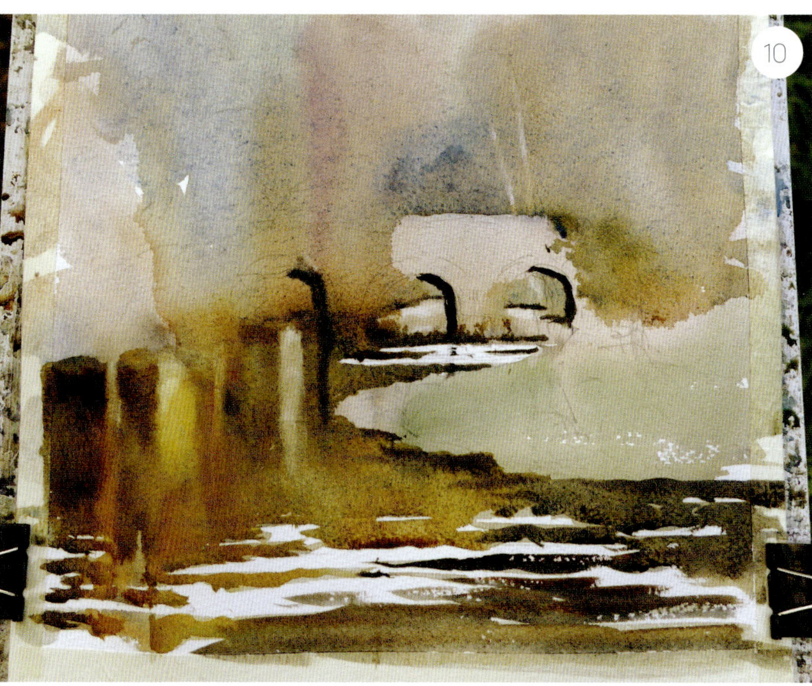

11. Refining the trees

The vague background trees are fine but we now need some more strongly defined trees in the middle ground. Wait until the wash is dry enough to continue without being completely dry.

Change to a size 12 round brush and use a varied mix of burnt sienna, ultramarine and warm red. Suggest a few branches, but not too many, as there is still considerable leaf cover (11A). The branches must be painted while the leaves are still wet so that the two merge together. Vary the colours as you work through the canopy (11B).

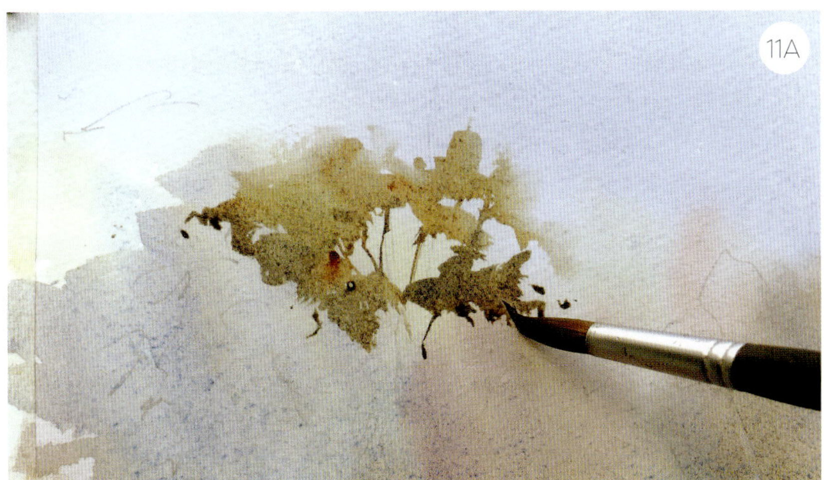

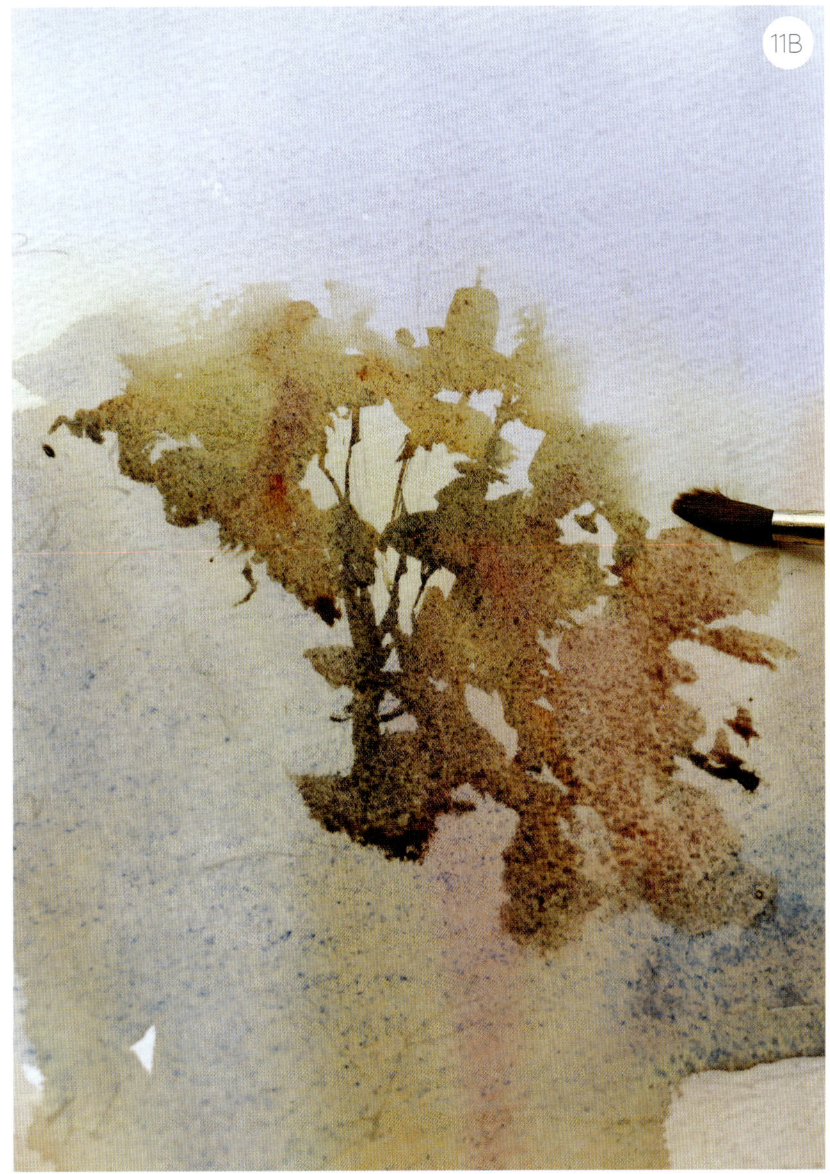

12. Tweaking a few details

If you need to, lift a little more light from the top of the bridge to separate it from the background (12A).

Drop in some pure burnt sienna to suggest clumps of dried grass on the right-hand bank (12B).

Darken the waterline on the right-hand bank using a strong mix of ultramarine and burnt sienna to create a stronger contrast with the grass (12C).

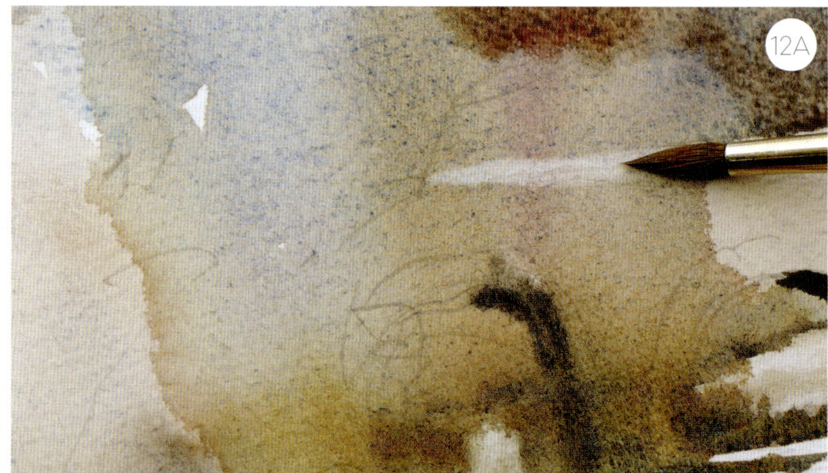

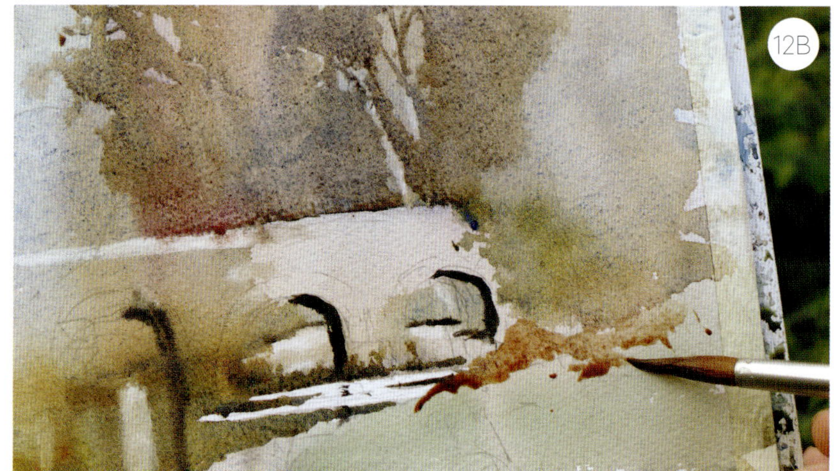

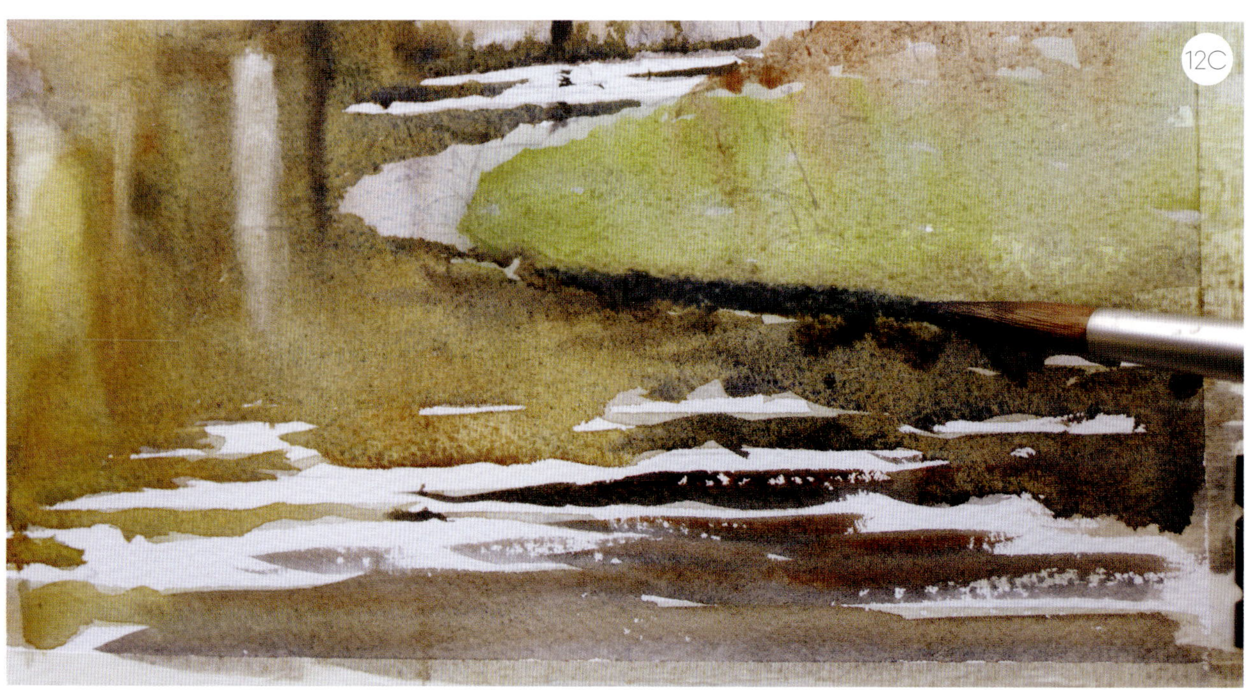

13. The far left-hand trees

Use a mix of warm yellow and warm red along with burnt sienna to give a range of varied oranges for the foliage; for contrast, use a strong mix of ultramarine and warm yellow to suggest the green leaves that are still there (13A).

For the branches, use a rich ultramarine and burnt sienna mix and apply this using a size 10 rigger. The bright autumn colours always make trunks and branches appear darker (13B). Introduce the branches while the leaves are still wet (in my case, there was not that much I could do about it, as everything was taking an age to dry!). Soften off this tree about halfway down to leave room for the tree in front (13C).

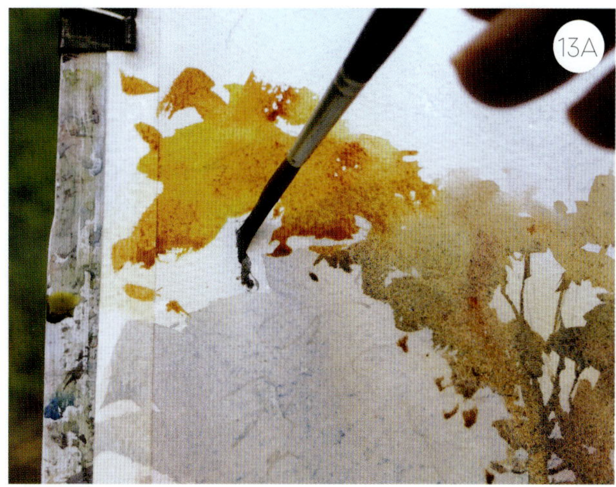

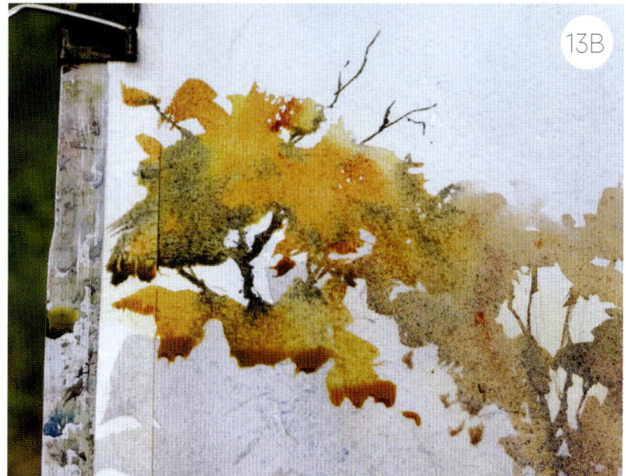

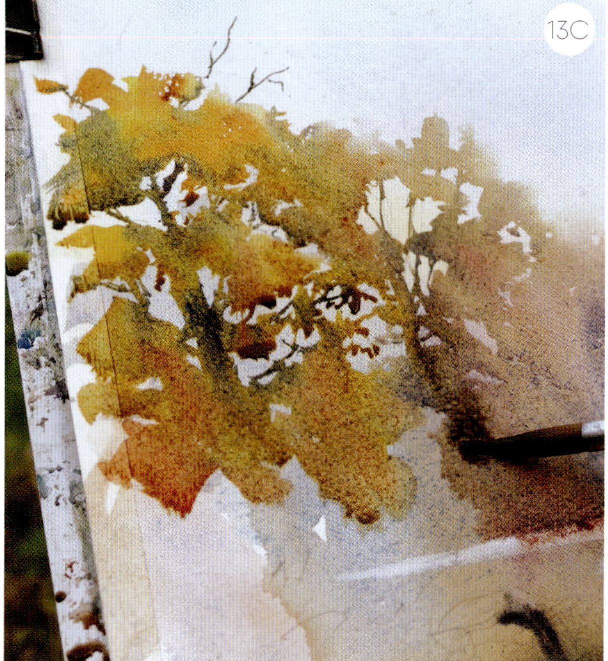

LOCATION INSIGHT

Although very much a rural location, this National Trust property is popular with walkers and dogs so usually the dogs came over first to investigate followed closely by their owners. I even had an enquiry about a sale!

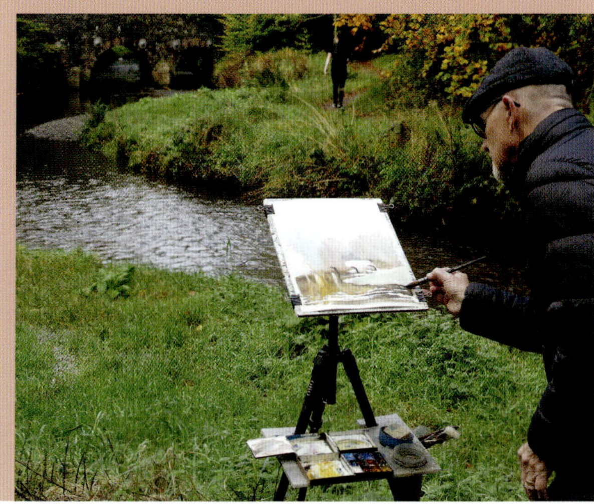

14. The waterline

A mix of phthalo blue and warm red creates a rich strong dark – use this for the waterline on the left-hand side, continuing it into the water to suggest dark reflections. At this point, leave your painting to dry. (I returned to my car to use the hairdryer and to collect my gas hot air gun which I'd forgotten. A hot coffee goes down well too!)

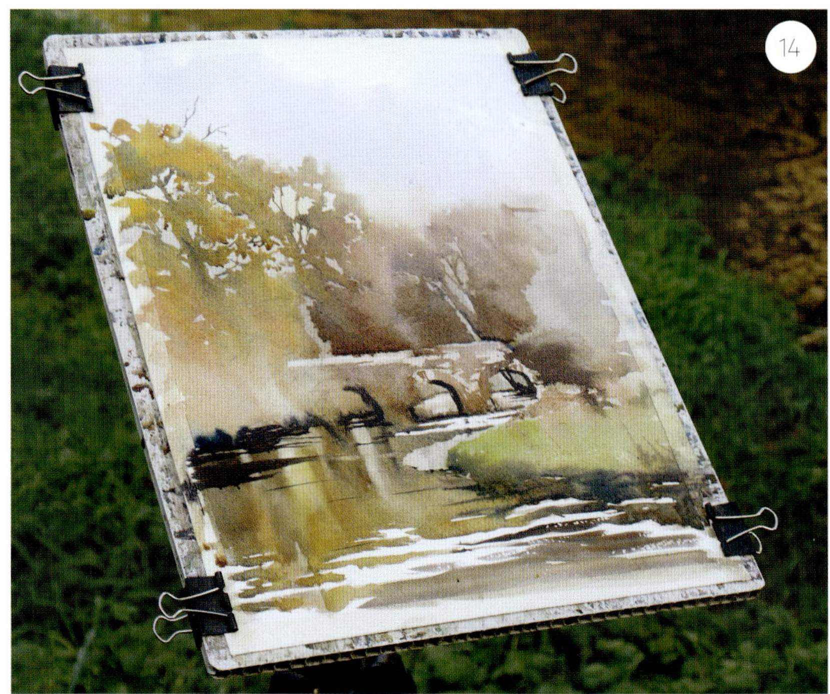

15. The right-hand tree

Dry paper will allow you to create much sharper-edged foreground trees. Mix your colours as for the previous trees in step 13, but use slightly stronger mixes of each (15A). Continue down the tree, creating areas of deep shadow, branches and beautiful splodgy colourful foliage (15B).

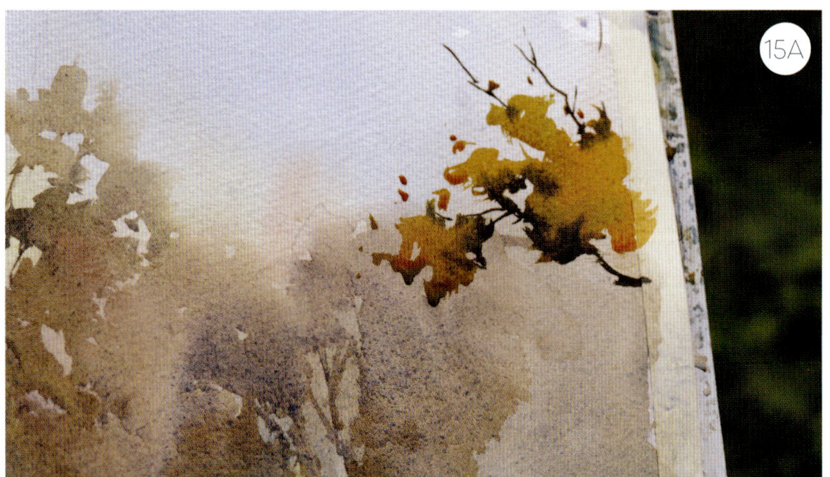

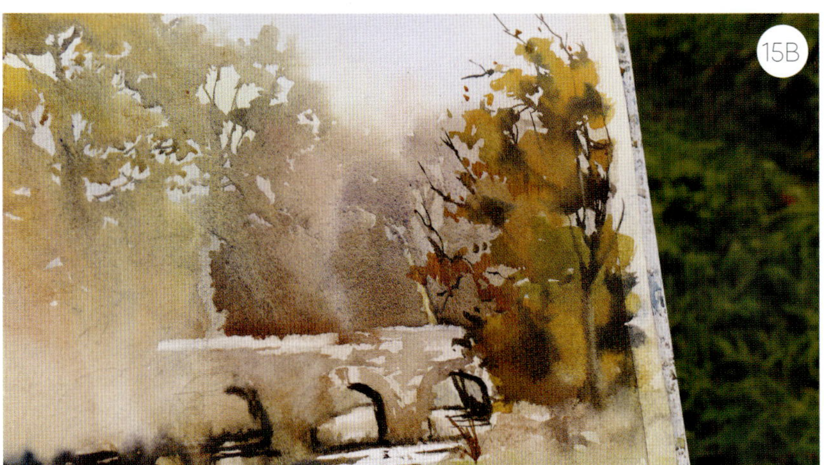

16. Grassy tufts

Phthalo blue is an exceptionally strong pigment that many people avoid, but it really is an excellent mixing colour. Create little tufts of grass with warm yellow and just a touch of the phthalo blue. (Too much phthalo blue would give a very unnatural-looking green.) Continue to add touches to the riverbank using little touches of burnt sienna.

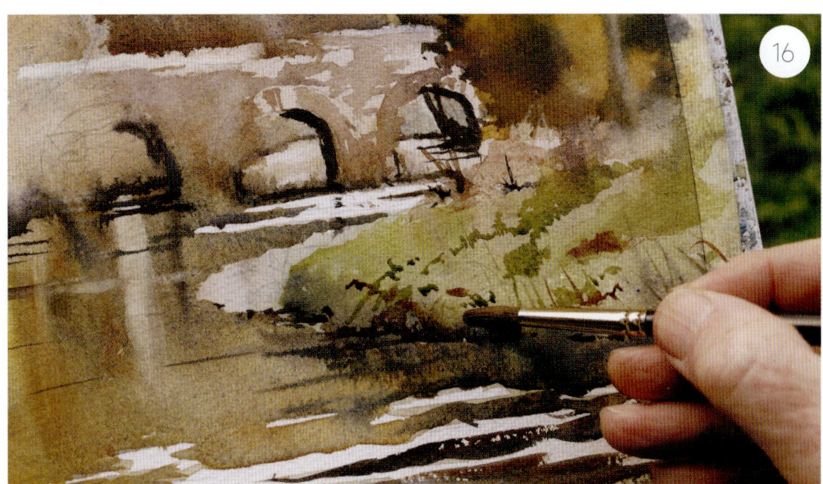

17. The left-hand tree

Paint the left-hand tree in the same way as the right-hand tree, but use slightly different proportions of paint in the mix to give it a slightly different appearance. Allow this tree to merge with the dark shadows at the bottom.

18. The bridge

Use a brownish mix of ultramarine and burnt sienna to paint the voussoirs and keystone of the arches (voussoirs are the wedge-shaped stones that make up the curve of the arch and the keystone is the stone at the top centre). We don't want to be too precise here – we definitely don't want to paint every stone, as this would draw far too much attention to the bridge. We want the bridge to be part of the landscape but not to overpower everything else.

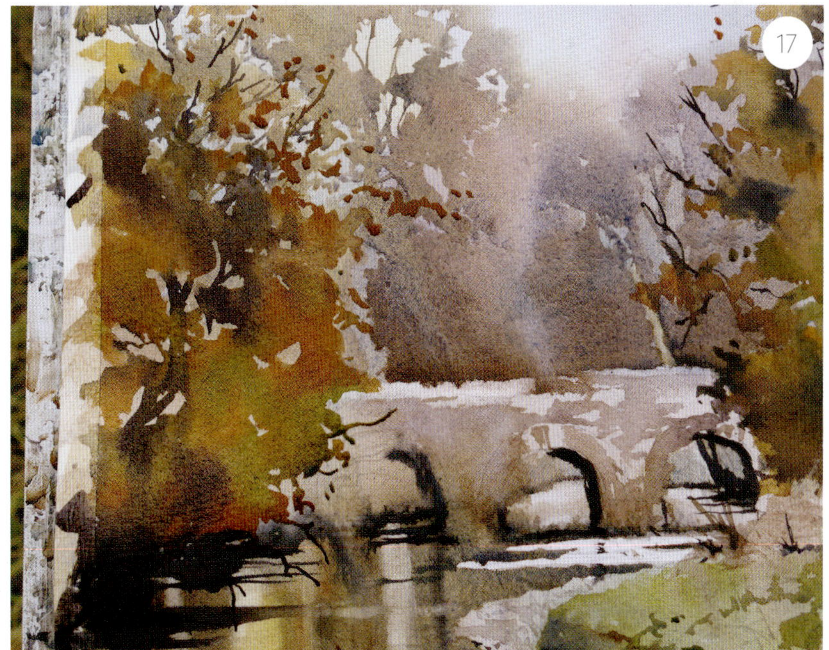

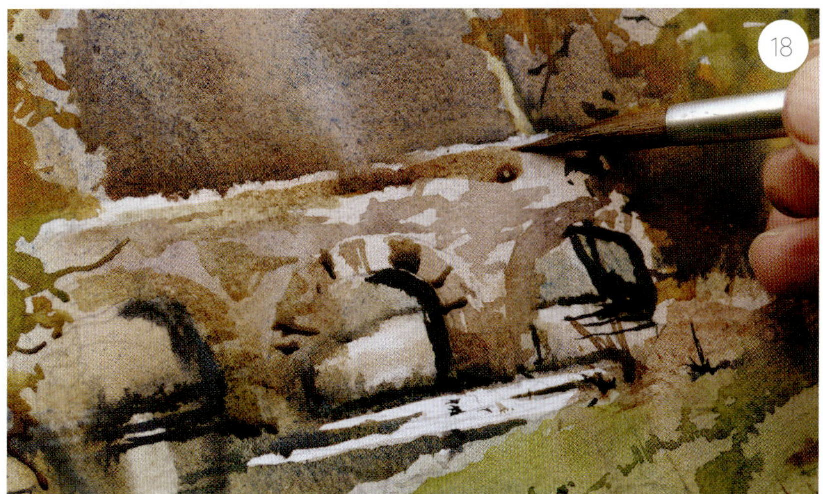

19. Lifting out branches

Lift out some lighter branches
to create contrast against the
darker branches.

20. Darks and lights

Use a blue-green mix of
ultramarine and warm yellow to
strengthen the riverbank visible
through the arches. This will
accentuate the light in the water
in the distance. Remember that
in order to create light we must
add dark.

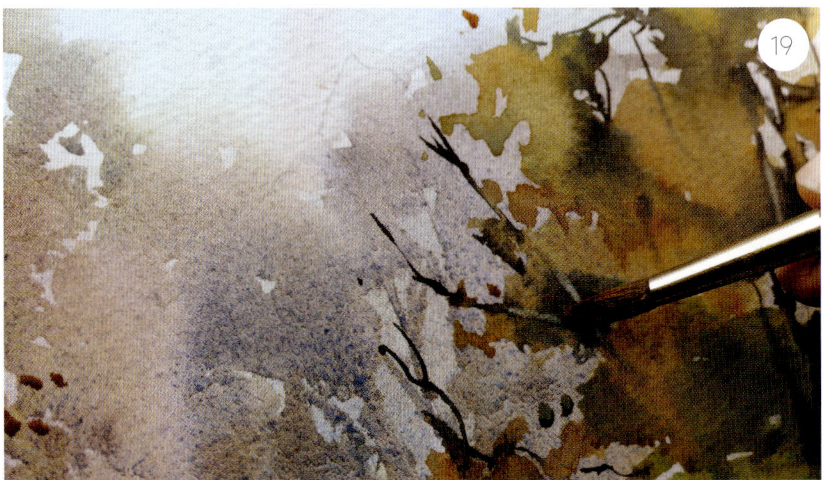

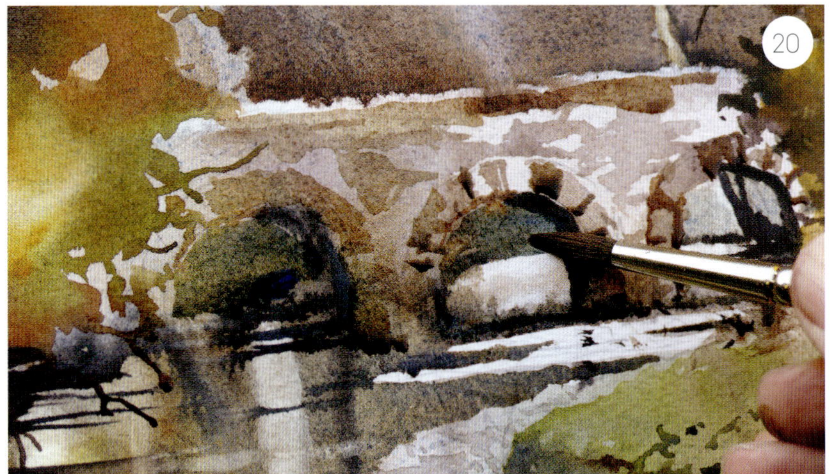

21. Final details

The painting is almost finished now and I am looking at ways I can
increase the impact. This will always involve creating rich tonal
contrasts. For me, the dark reflections would be better taken further
down. Continue these dark reflections across the bottom of the
painting to help to concentrate the light in the lower mid-section.

Use a mix of opaque white with warm yellow to introduce some
lighter leaves into the dark areas of the trees as well as some lighter
reflections into the dark reflections. Don't use too much water in a
gouache mix or the opacity will suffer greatly. Diluted gouache is
only marginally more opaque than watercolour.

Finally, paint a few diagonal shadows on the bridge using
ultramarine and burnt sienna to help give the impression of rays
of sunlight.

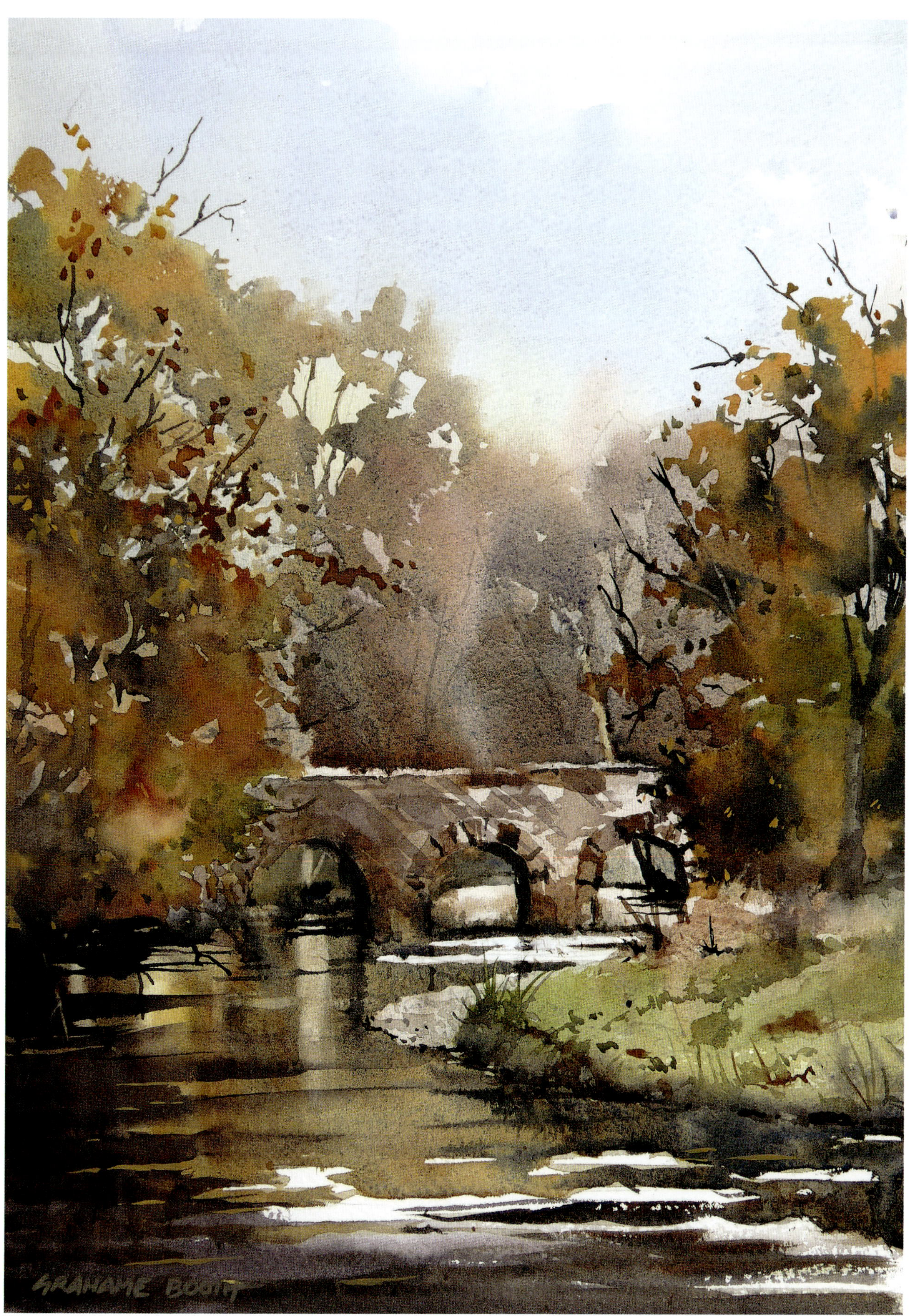
GRAHAME BOOTH

WINTER

I N WINTER, ONE OF THE few things a painter can look forward to is snow. Snow completely changes a landscape, turning even the most mundane subject into a wonderland. It probably isn't a great idea to go driving too far in snowy conditions, but if you have suitable subjects within walking distance (and, let's face it, almost all subjects are improved by snow), you definitely won't want to miss them. Adding sunshine to snow makes it even better. Care is needed both in getting to your subject but also in not outstaying your welcome. Temperatures will be low, so planning a short session is probably wise. This can be helped by painting small, especially as the usual winter problem of slow drying will be present. Remember the sage advice: 'there is no such thing as bad weather, only bad clothes'.

SNOWDROPS
51 x 38cm (20 x 15in),
Bockingford CP 425gsm (200lb)

Although this was painted a few years ago, I can clearly recall just how cold that morning was! The snowdrops are just varying marks of pure white gouache.

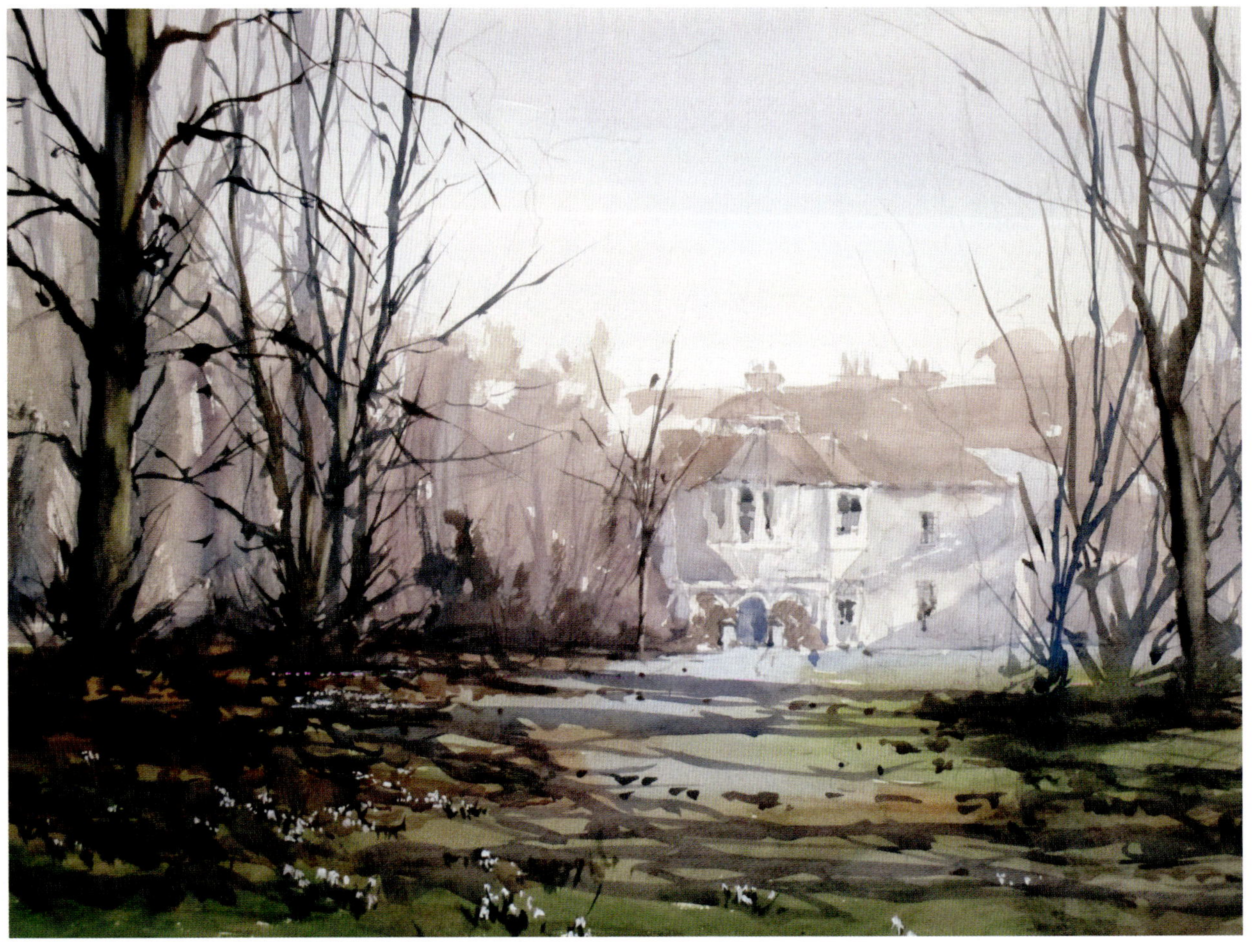

Light conditions

The sun is lowest in winter and this often means that parts of the landscape never see sunlight at all. That's the downside. The upside is that the low sun means very warm light and that can really help to make almost any subject attractive.

Potential weather conditions

First off, it can be cold, so dress suitably and don't spend too much time on site – good for simplifying those paintings. Winter haze, mist and fog are common and can be beautiful additions to a morning landscape.

Seasonal features

The obvious one is snow, but even if snow is relatively uncommon, a crisp winter frost can give some lovely effects. Don't disregard the rain. Painting from your car is still plein air in my book!

WEXFORD SUNSET
51 x 38cm (20 x 15in),
Saunders CP 425gsm (200lb)

Sunsets can be problematic as they don't last too long. The trick is to have everything ready, including the drawing, and to start painting 20 minutes or so before what you might consider to be the ideal light conditions.

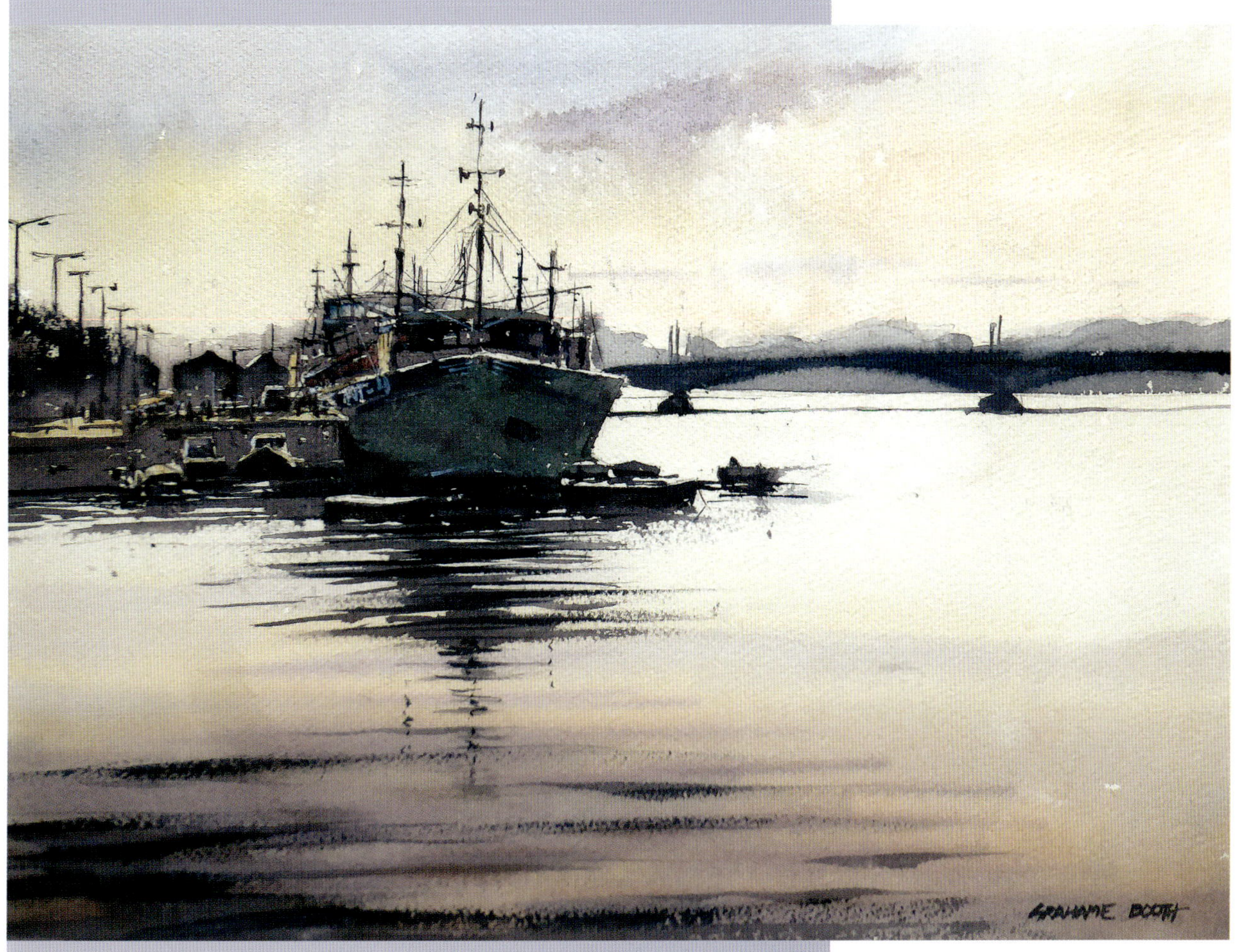

7. WINTER SNOW

I struggled into my layers, picked up my light sketching kit and off I went up into the hills behind where I live. I wasn't the first to arrive. Halfway up the hill I could already hear the cries of excited children (and adults) with their toboggans. I am very familiar with this area and already had an idea of what I would paint. The sun was in the right position and so I didn't have to waste too much time selecting a subject. Nothing too onerous, just a view through the trees and across the field of snow. There was a nice splash of warmth in the beech leaves still attached to one of the trees.

YOU WILL NEED

PAINTS

» **Cobalt blue**
» **Phthalo blue (green shade)**
» **Ultramarine**
» **Quinacridone magenta**
» **Burnt sienna**
» **Warm red**
» **Warm yellow**

BRUSHES

» **Size 12 round synthetic travel brush**
» **Small Chinese brush (approx. size 6); a size 6 rigger would be similar**

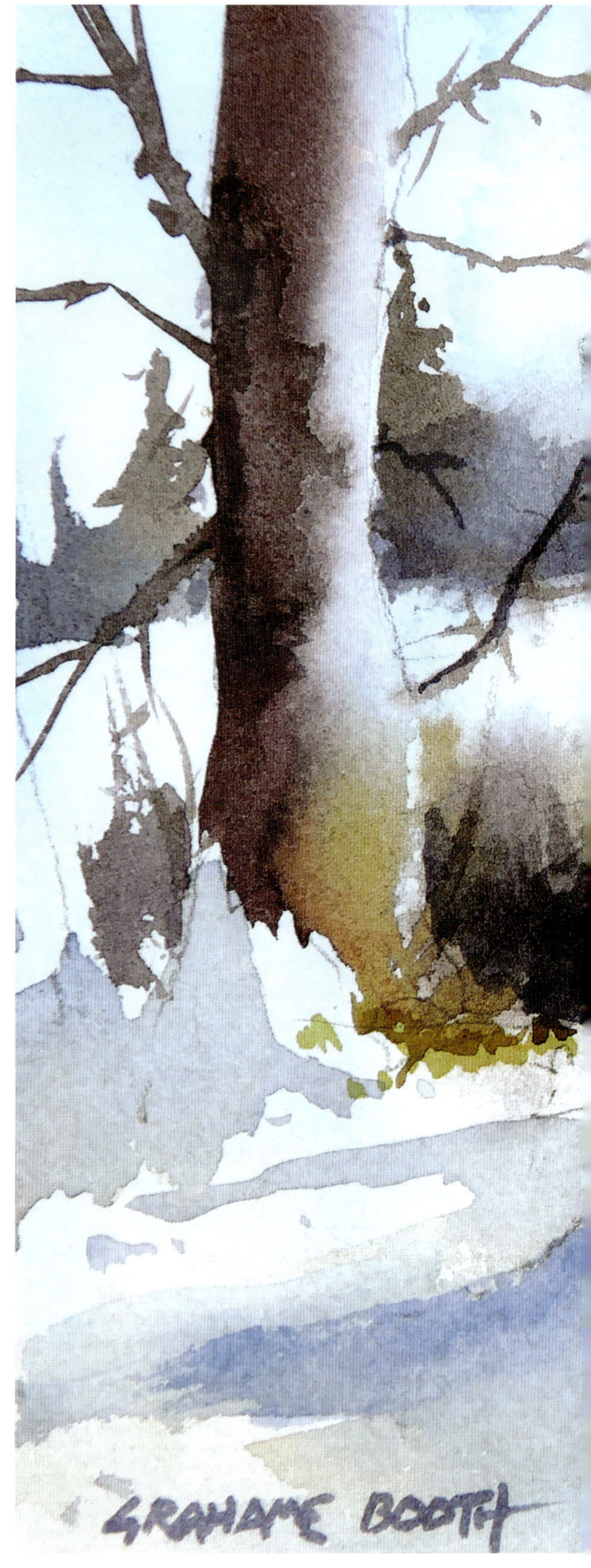

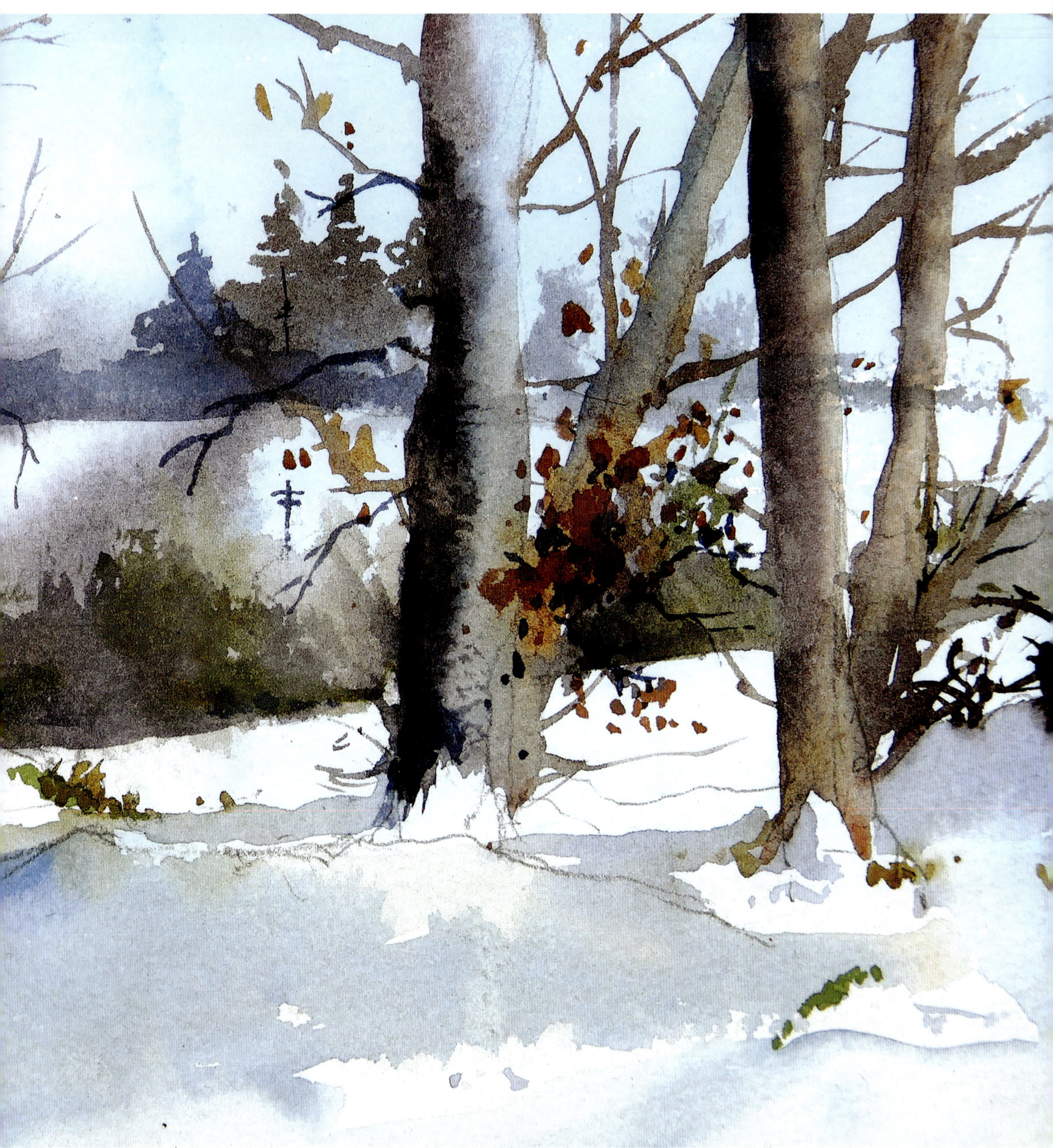

WINTER SNOW
22 x 17cm (9 x 7in), Millford CP 300gsm (140lb)

1. The initial sketch

I have kept the sketch relatively loose and simple, only marking in tree trunks and the top edges of fields or snow banks. If you refer to the photograph (1A), you can see which parts of the original scene I chose to omit, change or accentuate in the final sketch (1B).

» I reduced the number of trees by focussing in on the largest three, to give a better balance to the composition.

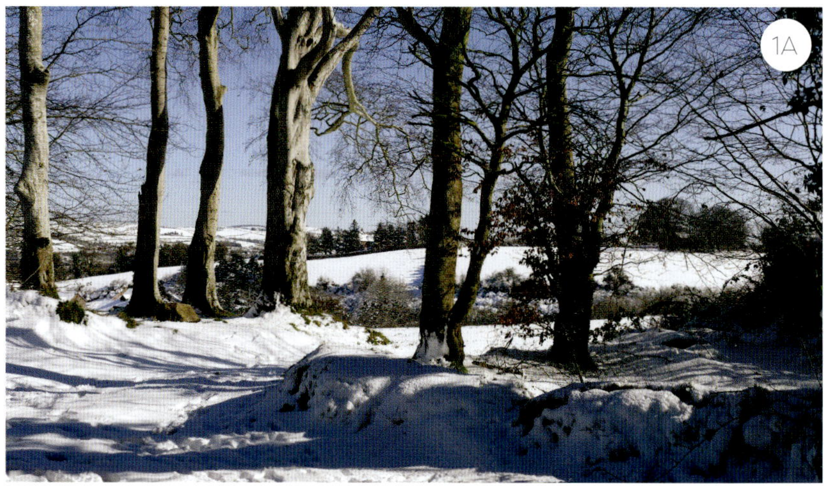

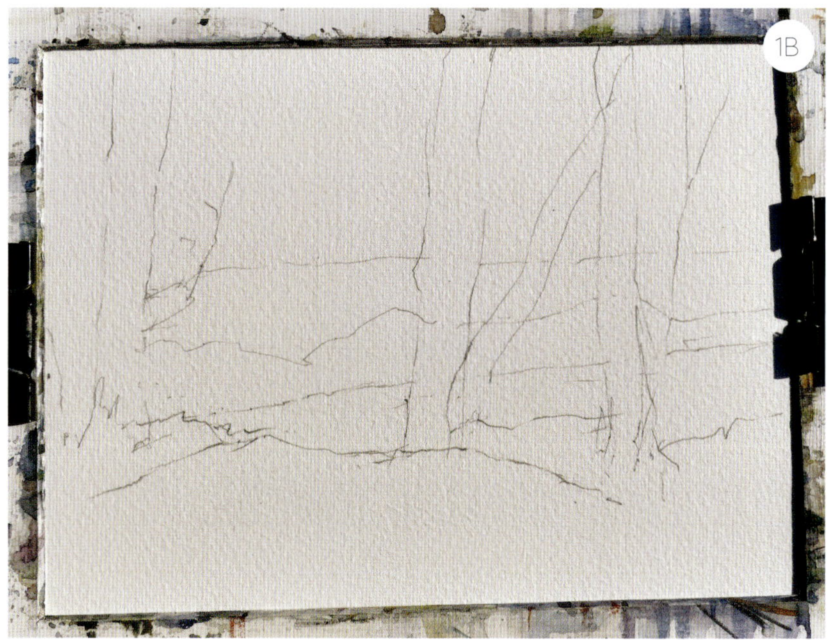

PAINTING SNOW

In a snow painting there are two important things to consider. First, the snow must be lighter than almost everything else, but second, the snow mustn't be pure white. This might seem a little strange – after all, snow is very obviously white. However, when we view it, it is affected by all sorts of things, chiefly the warm light from the winter sun, which actually makes it slightly warm in colour. On the other hand, shadows on snow are clearly blue and cool. This is why it is best not to leave the snow as white paper – the white paper is much too stark.

2. The first wash

Starting at the top of the paper and using a size 12 round brush, use a mix of phthalo blue (green shade) with a touch of quinacridone magenta for the sky. This mix produces a very lively transparent sky blue, ideal for snow and for subjects requiring a really rich sky colour. Lighten the blue as you go down the paper past the furthest fields, but then gradually add a little burnt sienna to the mix (2A). See, no white paper (2B)!

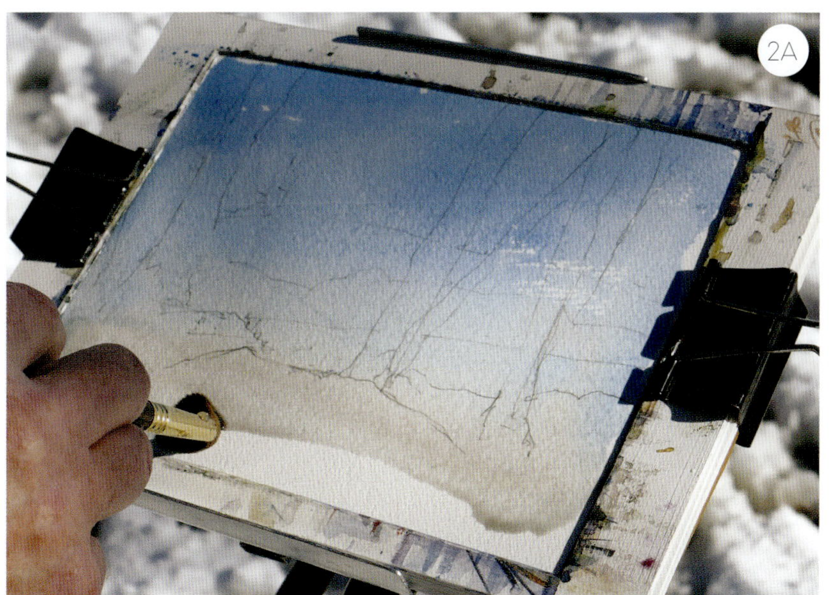

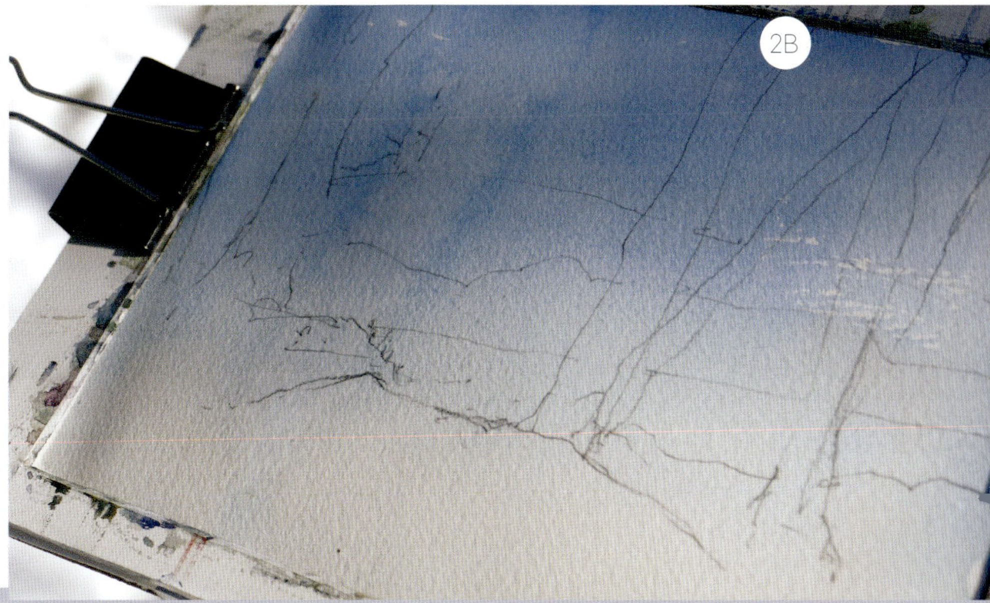

LOCATION INSIGHT: THE PERILS OF SNOWFALL!

Aaarrrrgh! I'm not sure if I actually said this out loud, but it's certainly what I felt as a lump of snow fell off the tree above and landed squarely down my neck. Suitably wakened up, I hopped around for a few seconds, as you do, and then got back to work. You would have thought I would have learned from that, but no, a few seconds later a blob of melted snow landed on my paper. You can see the edges of the incipient cauliflower just forming over to the left in the image in step 4. This is probably a good opportunity to make a couple of suggestions: a) never touch a cauliflower: it will almost certainly make it worse; and b) never stand directly under a tree when there is melting snow on it.

3. The distant treeline

Sticking with the phthalo blue, add some warm red to form a rich dark blue-grey, ideal for the distant treeline. Make the mix quite strong. Use the side of a rigger to give a varied line (3A).

Once the first wash has just about dried but before the treeline dries, add a few simple conifer shapes with a slightly darker mix to blend nicely into the rest of the trees. Create more defined, tree-like shapes using the tip of your rigger and working down from the tip of the tree in loose, side-to-side, diagonal movements (3B).

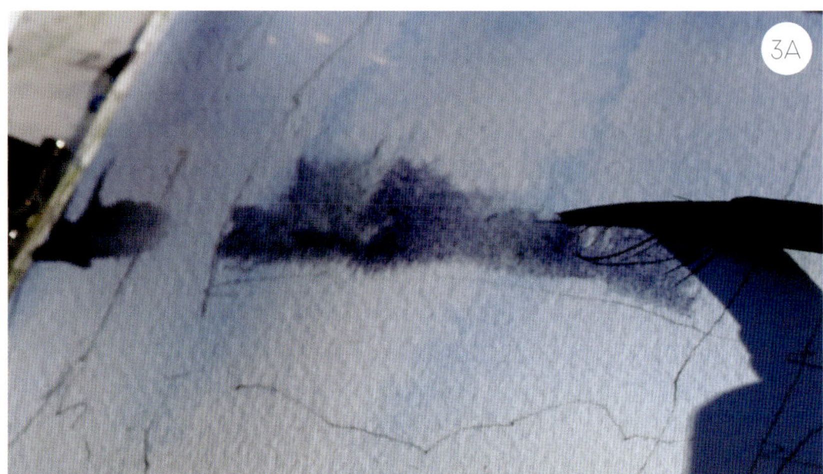

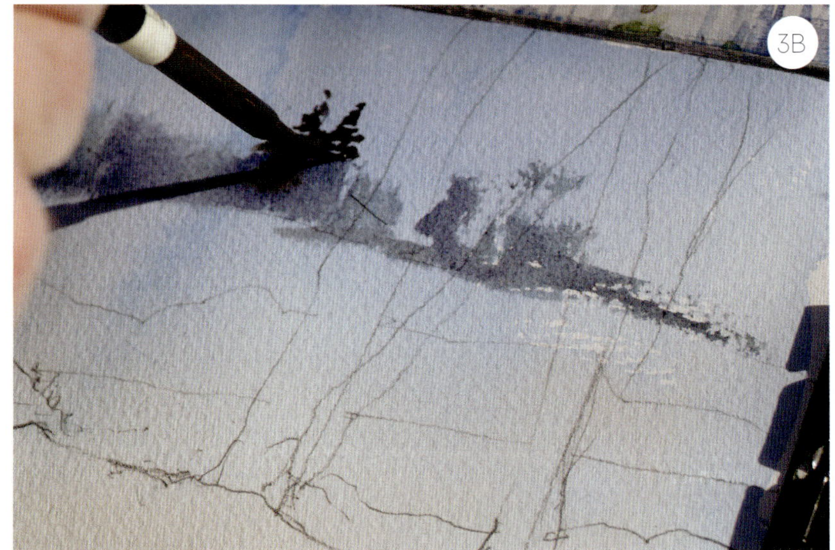

4. The shrubs

Add a little warm yellow into the step 3 mix, and then repeat the same loose, varied brushstrokes created in step 3A to create the nearer line of shrubs.

You can see how the cauliflower area is still wet but there isn't much I can do. Leave the painting to dry for as long as you can bear before moving on to step 5.

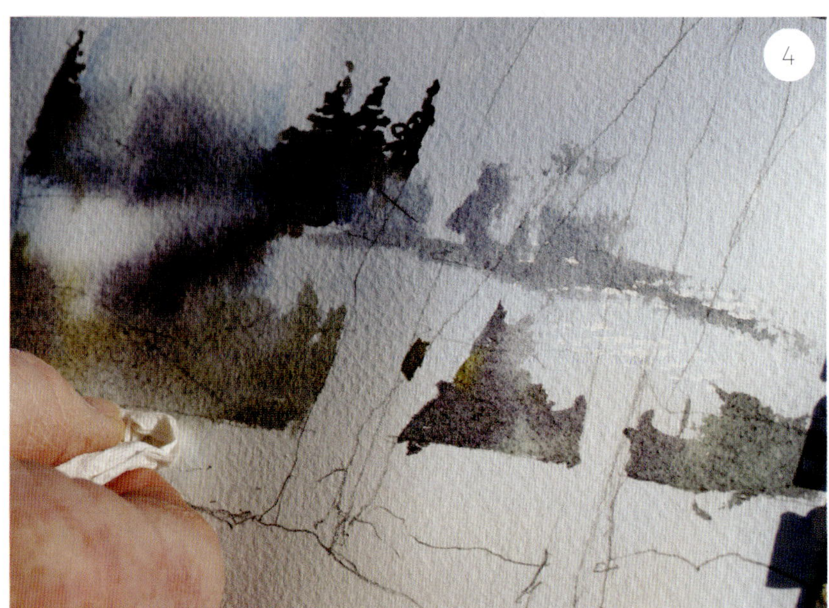

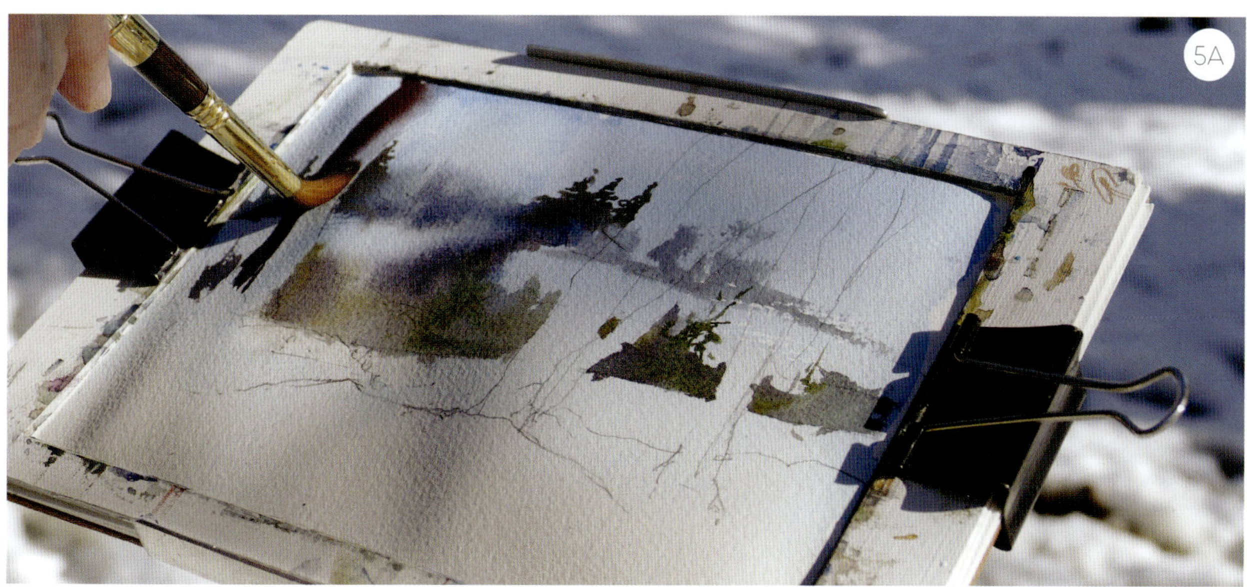

5A

5. The trees

The trees need a sense of their cylindrical shape, and this can be suggested with a stripe of dark paint on the shadow side (phthalo blue (green shade) plus warm red) immediately followed with a damp brush down the light side (5A). All being well, the dark will gently drift across into the light giving a soft dark-to-light transition. Sometimes it can drift too much, in which case you'll need to use a drier brush to lift off some of that excess colour on the light side. Equally, it may not drift enough, in which case you'll need to tease it across using a barely damp brush.

Repeat for the other trees, changing the mix slightly purely for variety (5B). Because of the low temperatures the painting was drying so slowly that I worked all of the trunks before starting on the side branches.

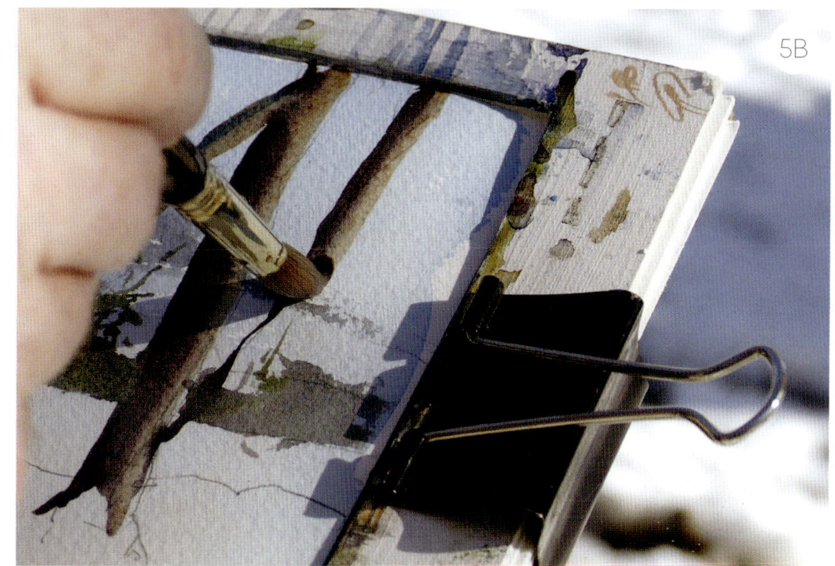

5B

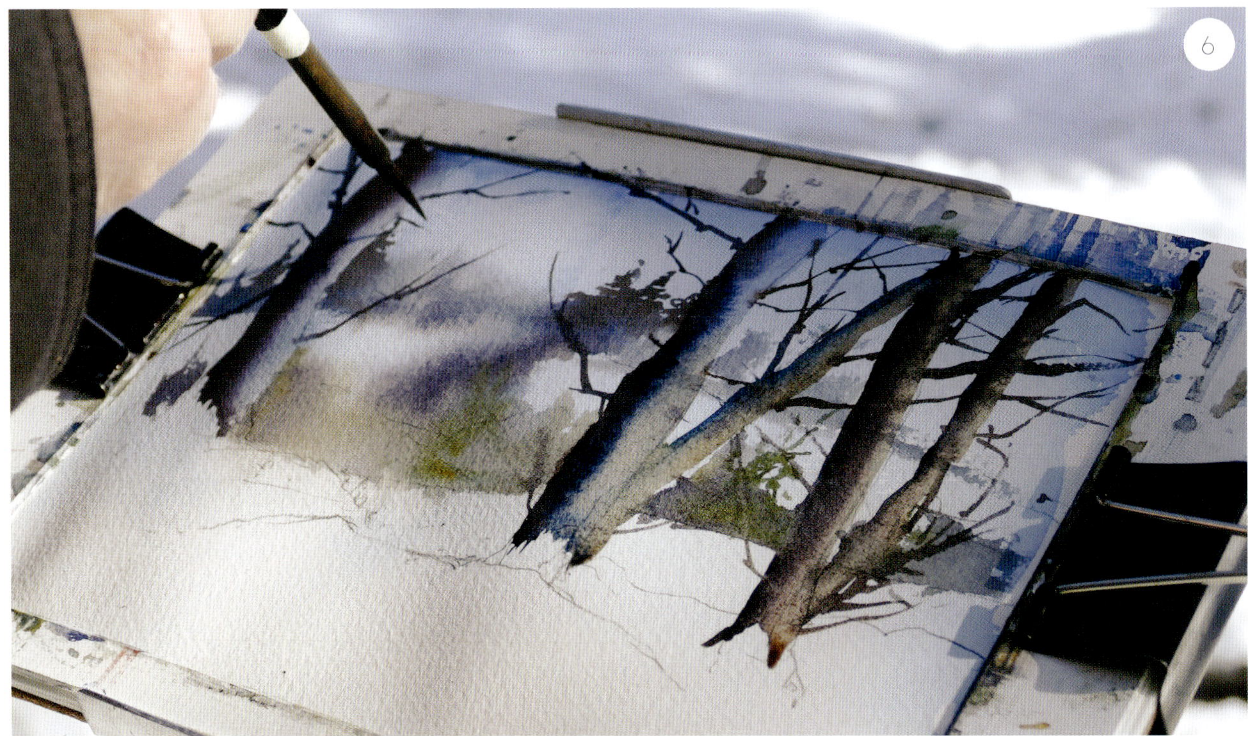

6. The branches

Using the very tip of your rigger and the same phthalo blue/warm red mix, add the side branches, taking care to vary their shape and trying to make sure they get narrower as they move further away from the trunk. Keep a loose grip on the brush to ensure loose, more realistic-looking strokes.

7. The beech leaves

Add a splash of pure burnt sienna with loose, leaf-like marks around one of the trunks and at the base of some of the branches – this adds that all-important touch of warmth to suggest the beech leaves.

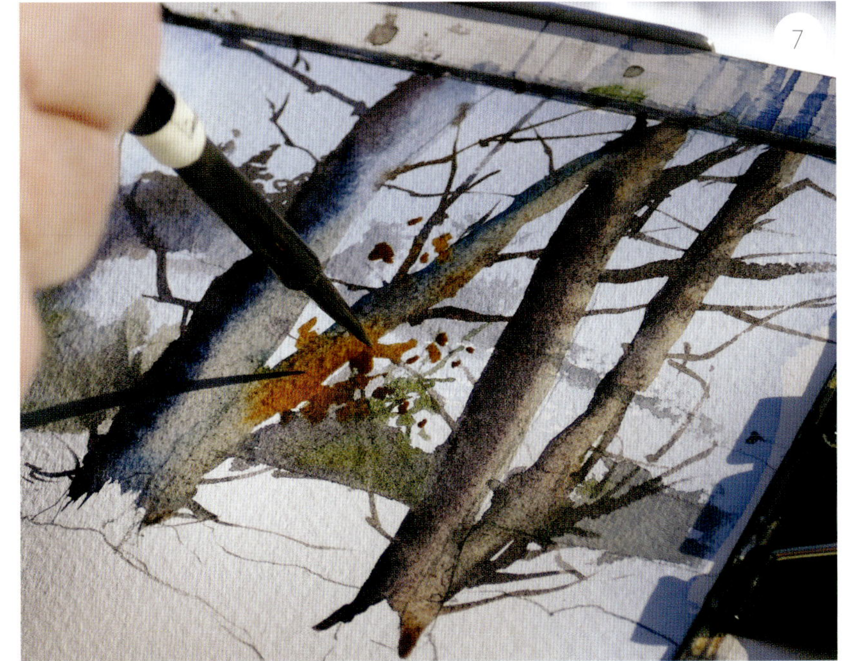

8. Adjusting the tone

Assess the tone of your foreground snow, and adjust it slightly if you need to. As often happens, almost all of my warm tone in the first wash disappeared as it dried, so I reinforced this with a weak burnt sienna mix with a touch of ultramarine to kill the orange.

Add some touches of green mixed from ultramarine and warm yellow to the base of the right-hand tree and on the ground between the trees, to add a touch more warmth.

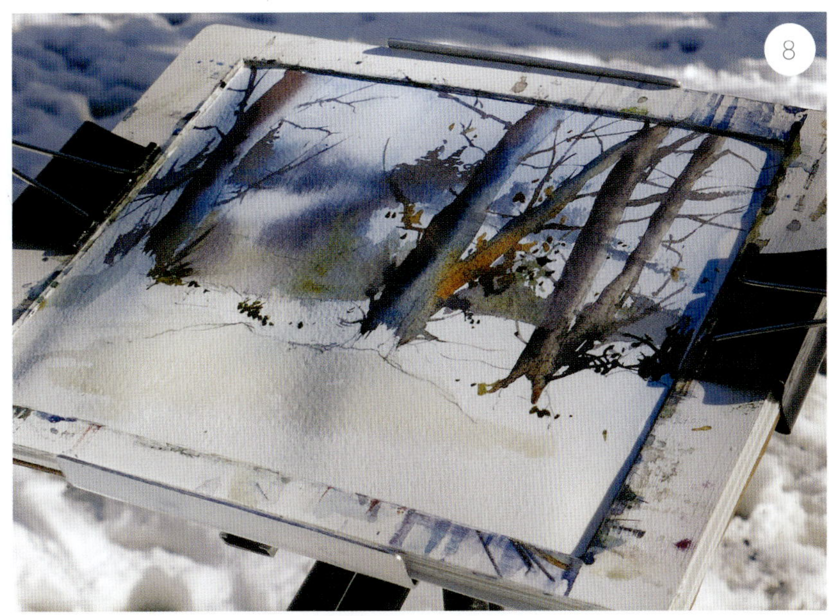

9. The shadows

Shadow time now, and cobalt blue works a treat for snow shadows. Keeping in mind the soft undulations of the snow, try to echo that with your brushstrokes. Work around the bases of the trees, creating shadows cast by the trunks too (9A). Continue to work into the foreground, creating the illusion of drifted snow (9B).

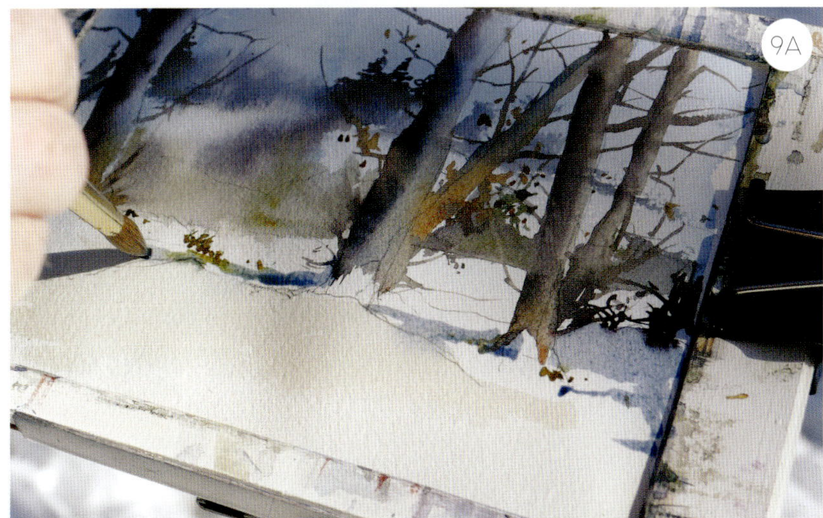

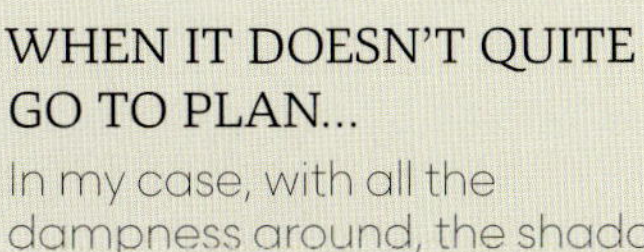

WHEN IT DOESN'T QUITE GO TO PLAN...

In my case, with all the dampness around, the shadows don't really work as well as I would have liked. At this point I have two options: either live with it or fiddle with it, trying to fix it. I almost always choose option one. On the rare occasions I take option two I always ruin it. It is much more important for your watercolour painting to be interesting and fresh.

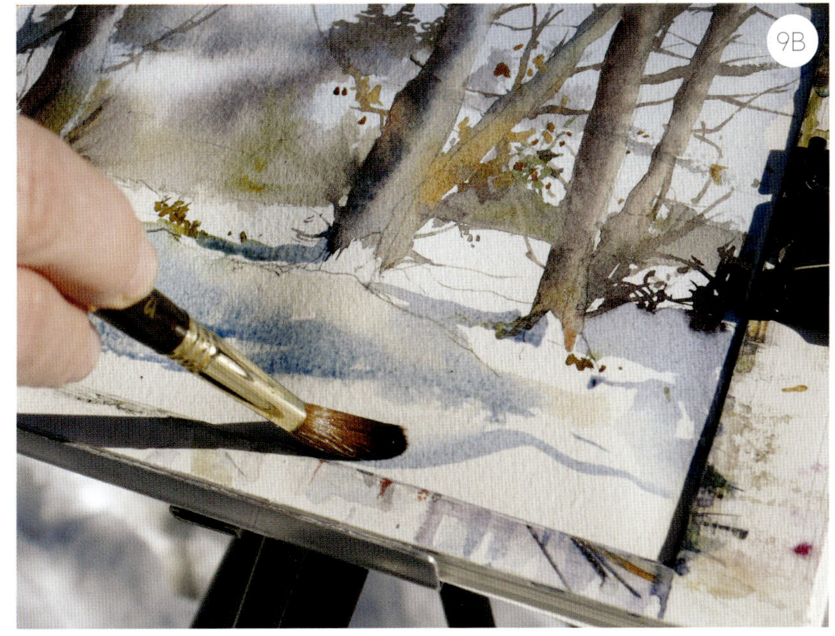

10. Final details

Add in a few final dabs of warmth to the middle and foreground using a variety of greens, to suggest greenery peeking through the snow.

There really isn't much more I can do. The paper is really too wet to continue, so it's time to head for home. I might add a few finishing touches back in the studio, hoping I won't get a call from the plein air police! Note that the huge cauliflower really isn't too noticeable now.

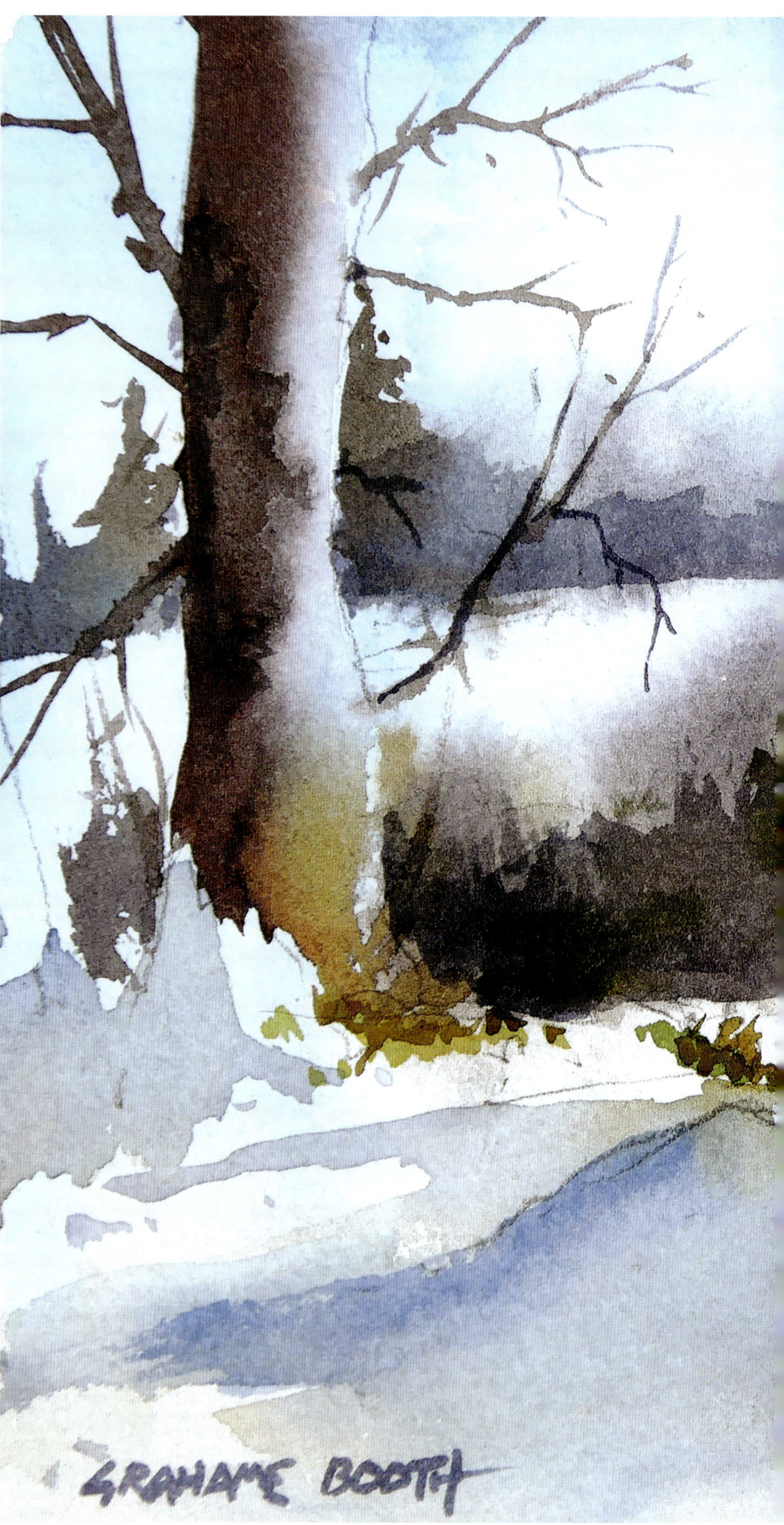

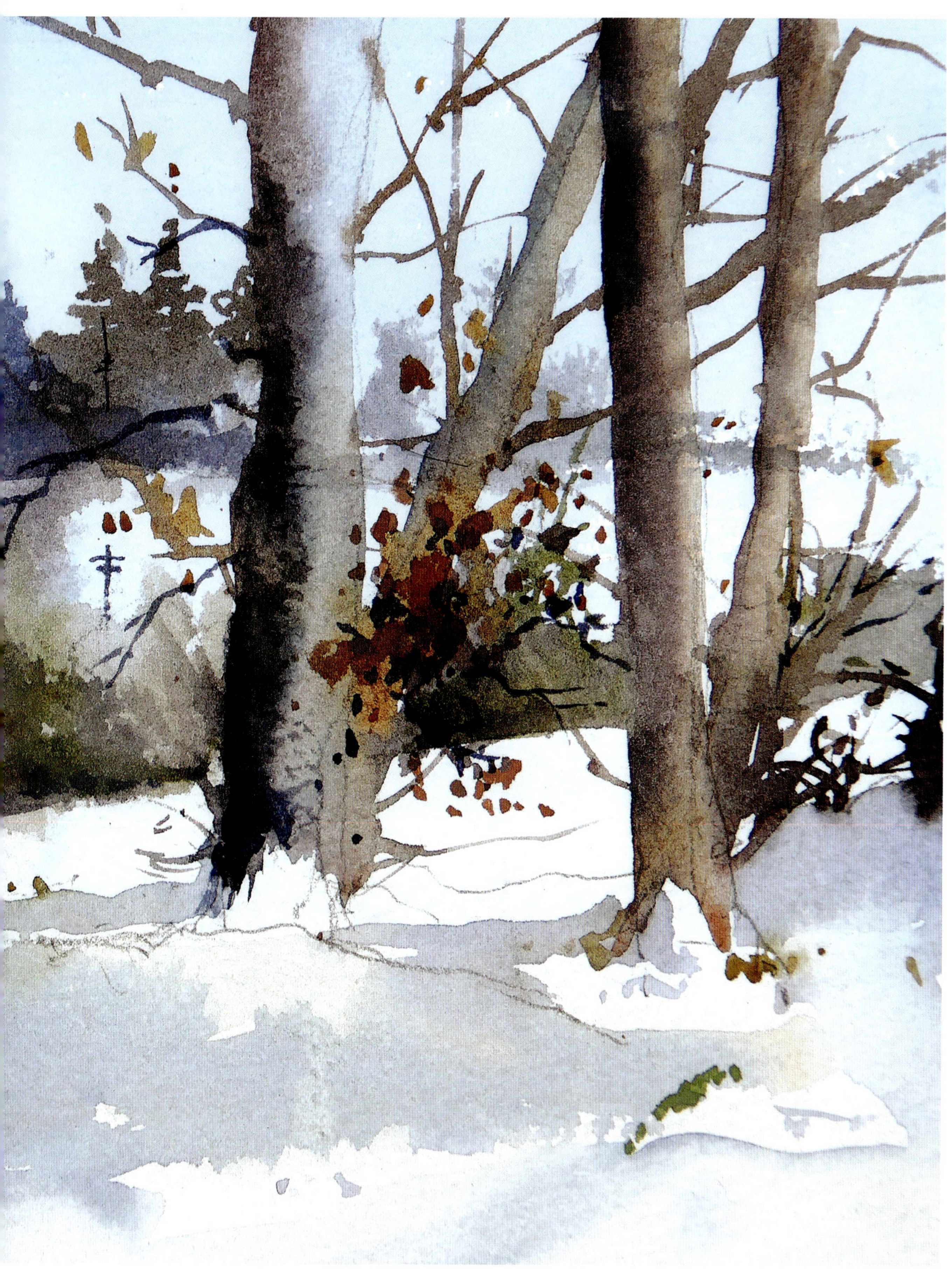

8. WINTER SUN

In winter you may have to wait for a while to get a day with some consistent sunshine. This late February day was just perfect, and the added bonus was that I was out and about painting with members of my plein air group. The location is a large public park – it's actually a botanical garden, but in the depths of winter there isn't much colour. I chose this subject simply because of the beautiful little streak of pure light on the ground in front of the bandstand and this was emphasized by the sun being right in front of me, creating lots of strong dark shade. I remembered to bring a hat to keep me warm but forgot about the need for a brim so there was quite a bit of glare to deal with. I set up on one of the paths beside the field. This was a little further away from the main subject than I would have liked, but recent heavy rain would have made a trip to the centre of the field a very muddy experience, something I was happy to avoid.

YOU WILL NEED

PAINTS

» **Ultramarine**
» **Warm yellow**
» **Burnt sienna**
» **Brown madder**
» **Warm red**
» **White gouache**
» **Cool yellow**

BRUSHES

» **Mop or other large soft brush, squirrel or synthetic**
» **Size 12 and 8 round, sable or synthetic**
» **Size 10 rigger, sable or synthetic**
» **Old size 8 sable for softening and lifting out**

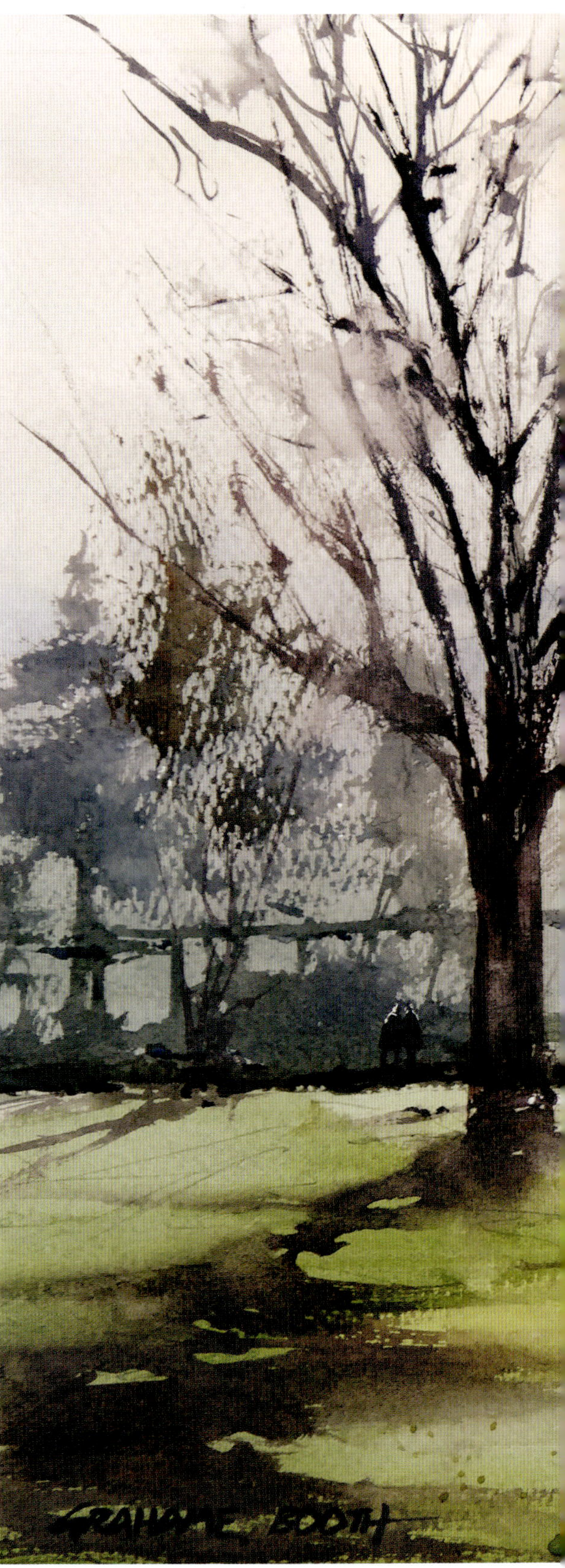

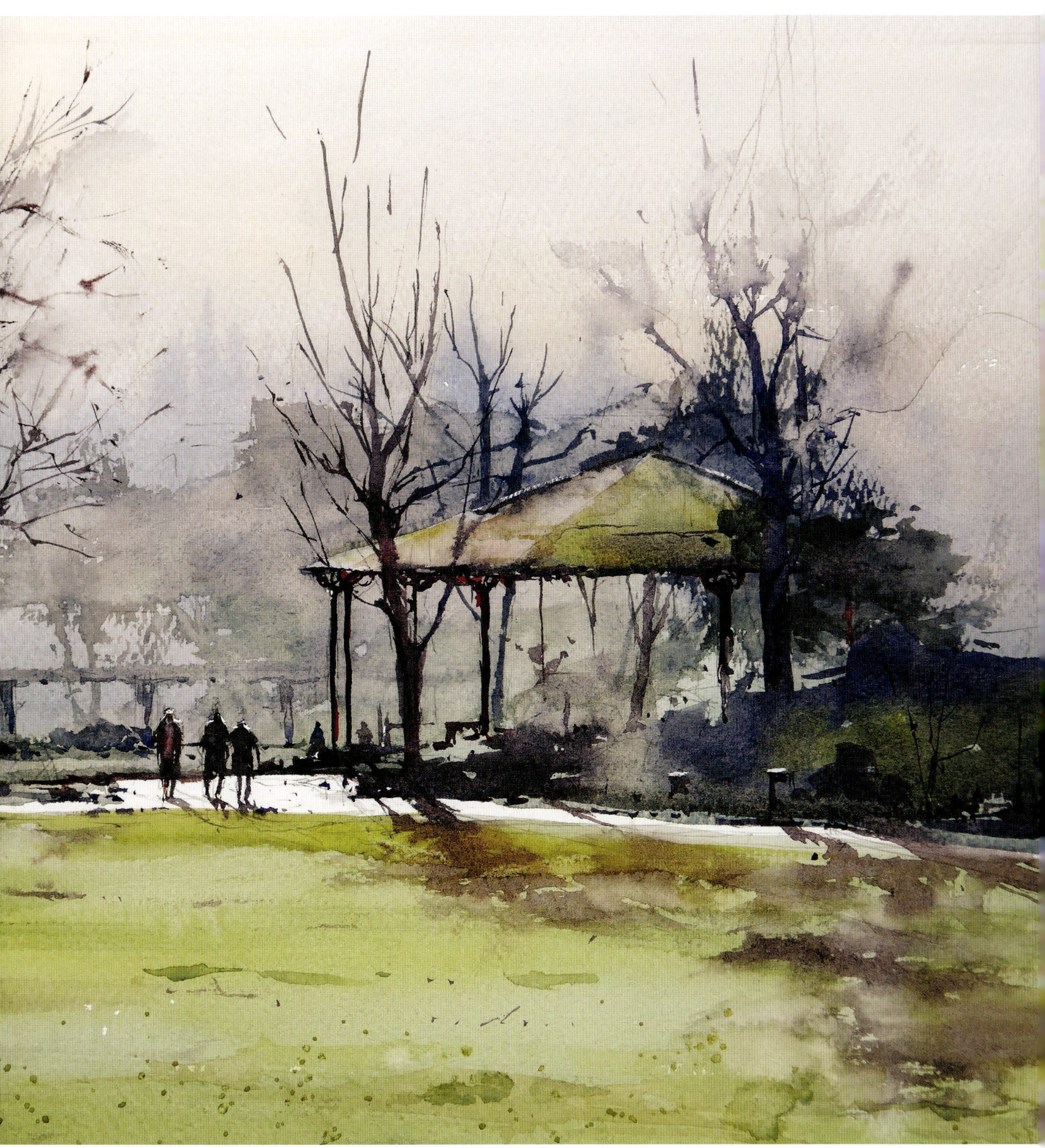

WINTER SUN
39 x 29cm (15¼ x 11½in), Millford CP 300gsm (140lb)

1. The initial sketch

I made a rough indication of trees and the bandstand was mostly hidden. I wasn't too sure about the large and frankly ugly building in the background, so I only sketched it very loosely.

If you refer to the photograph (1A), you can see which parts of the original scene I chose to omit, change or accentuate in the final sketch (1B).

» Note that I have completely omitted the central tree in full leaf – it would have been far too dominant and would have drawn the eye away from the bandstand.

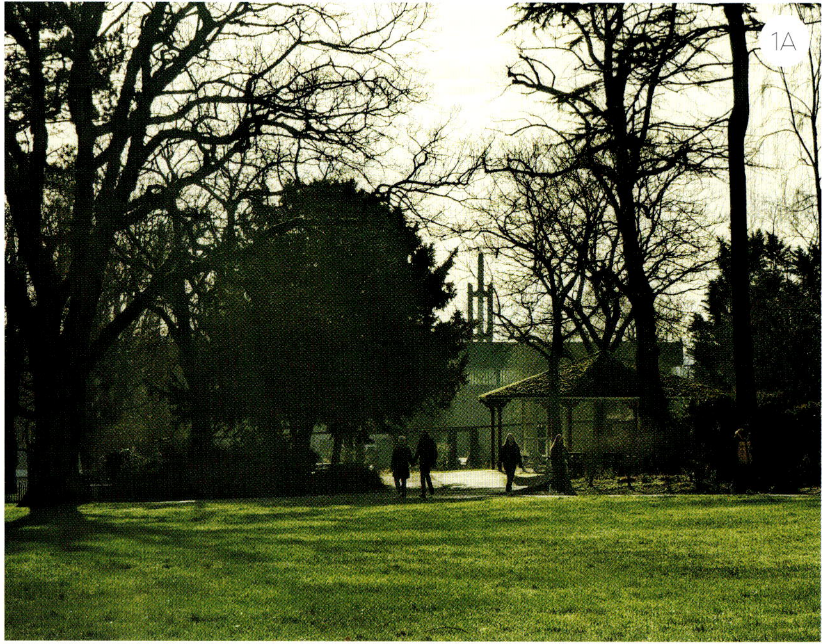

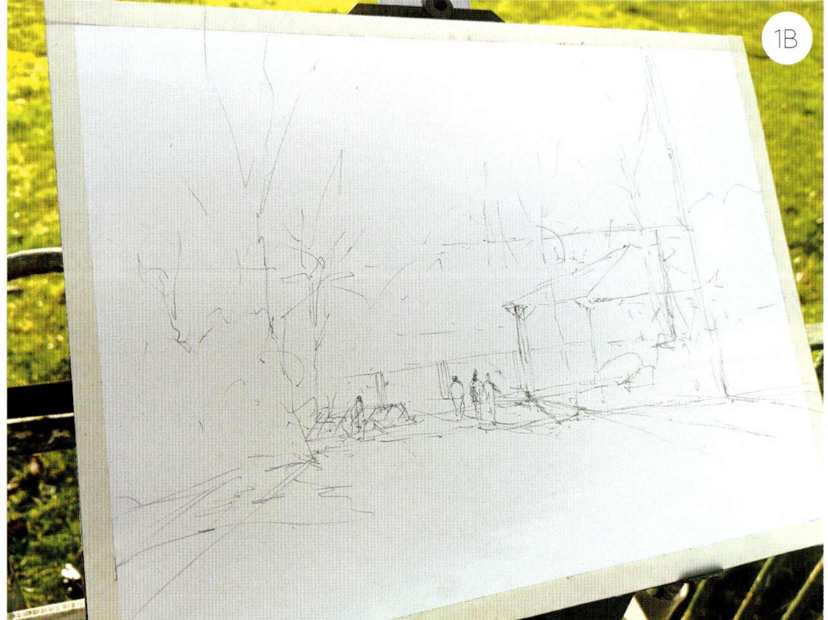

2. The first wash

With a soft mop, use a mix of burnt sienna, a touch of ultramarine and some white gouache for the sky area. As you work downwards, add a little more ultramarine and varied warm and cool yellow in the grassy area, leaving the little area of of light identified at the beginning unpainted. While the paint is still damp, use a mix of ultramarine with a touch of burnt sienna to roughly indicate a vague background (2A).

At this point I decided to forget about the ugly building and just to keep everything very soft (2B).

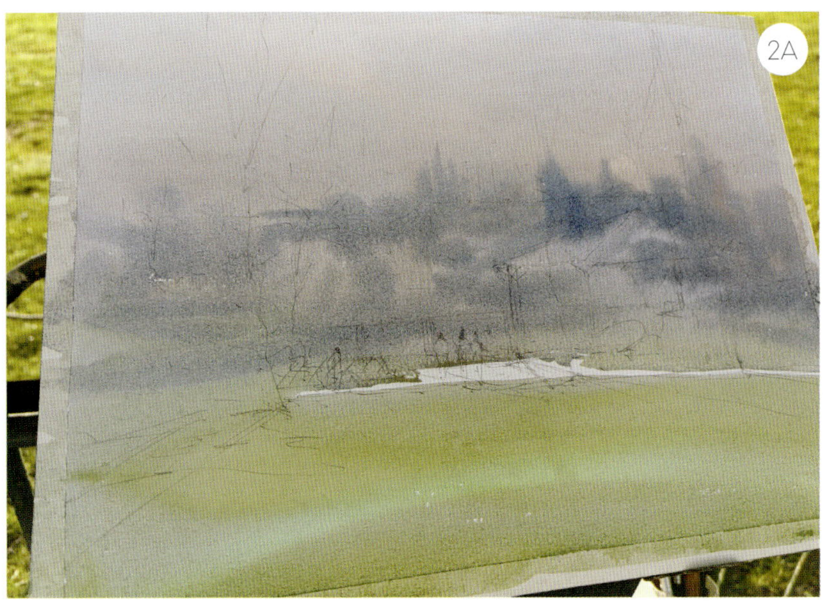

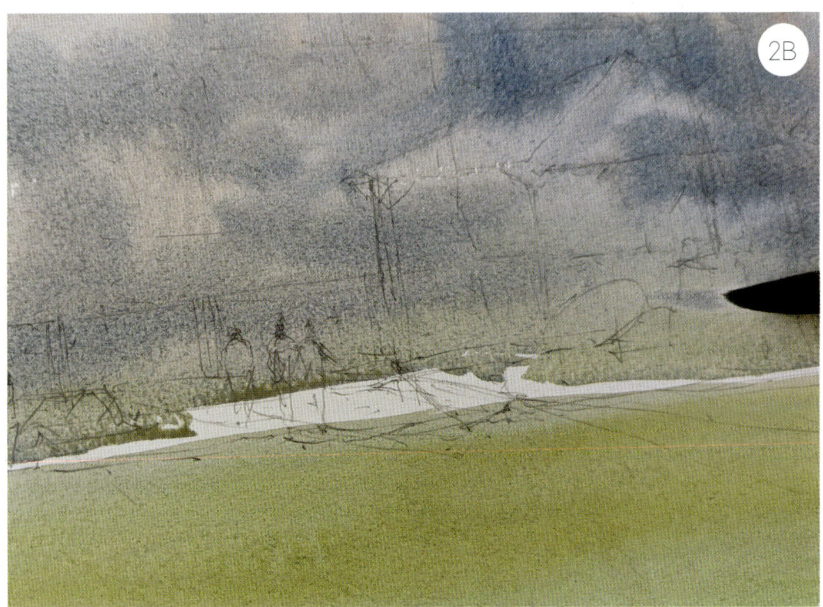

PLAYING WITH PAINT

I knew that the washes would be very slow to dry and that I would have plenty of time to play with the paint. Remember, the only time you should touch the paper is when it is either very dry or very wet.

3. The middle ground

Aiiow the background to dry a little (I used my little gas hot air torch), then add a darker, more neutral mix of ultramarine and burnt sienna to create a middle ground. Paint in distant trees, the pergola and around the sunlit roof of the bandstand using a size 12 brush, then add in the finer branches using a rigger. Leave to dry again.

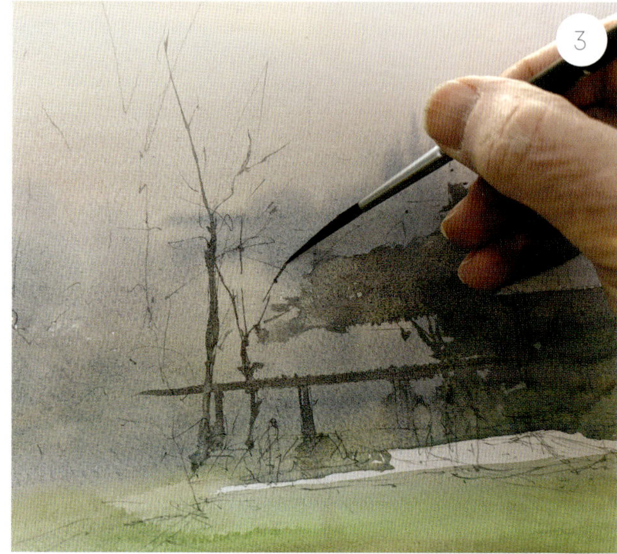

KEEPING IT SIMPLE

At this stage I really still kept everything fairly vague. I knew that if this painting was going to work it would be down to simple dark and light shapes. Now is the time to keep everything connected and not worry about over-defining individual objects.

4. Refining the middle ground

Use an even darker version of the same mix to create the next plane. Again, you don't want to add anything too fussy, but you do want to begin the process of creating darks. Add in darks around the pergola, to the bushes in front of the fence, and around the bandstand (4A).

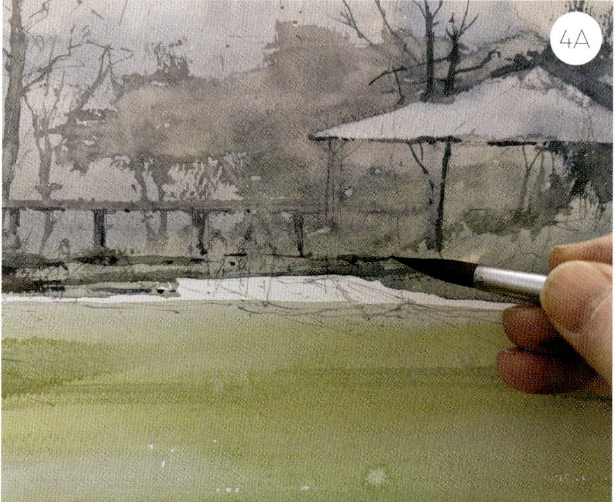

DODGING THE DRIPS (OR NOT!)

You would have thought I would have learned from the last demo, but no, a large drip of water from the tree overhead landed on my grass! What do I do? Nothing! (4B).

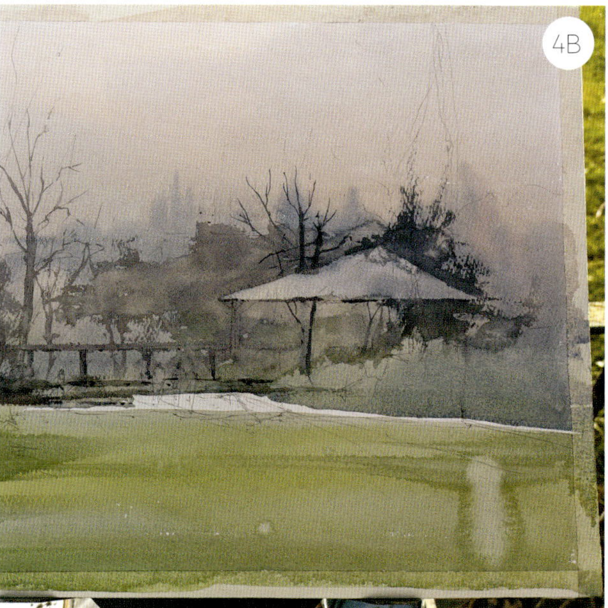

5. The bandstand

The roof of the bandstand was covered in moss. Use a warm mix of ultramarine and warm yellow to hint at the green – use a size 12 brush. Start introducing some brown madder to the mixes. Use this to suggest the red-coloured posts (albeit in deep shade), but also use it to introduce some warmth into the closest parts of the roof. Leave to dry.

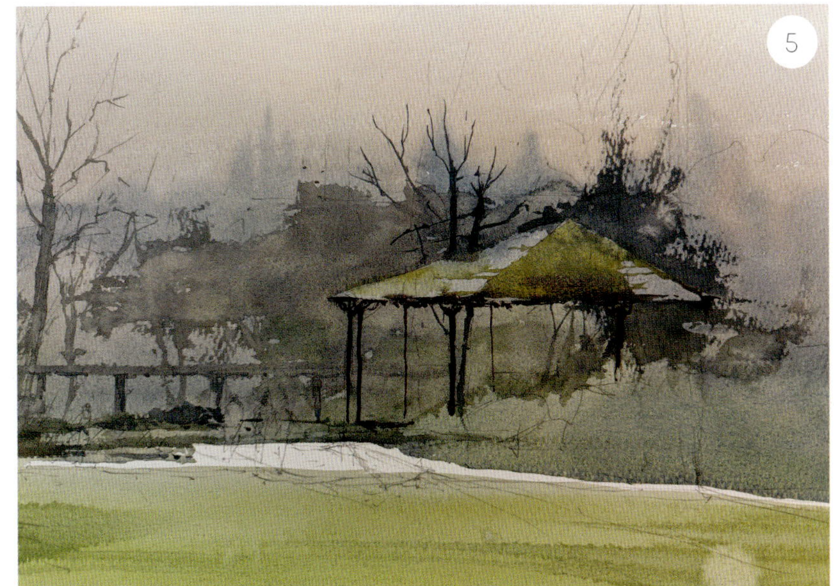

6. Surrounding the bandstand

Add in the trees that stand just in front of the bandstand. Use the same mix as in step 5 for the right-hand tree, and a darker mix with more brown madder for the left-hand tree; try to create elegant, simple shapes.

We still want to keep things connected in order to avoid single isolated shapes, so we just want to hint at the vegetation, and we want the trees we've just created to blend into it. Use a mix of ultramarine and brown madder to create the sweeping, shaded flowerbed in front of the bandstand, dabbing in touches of yellow to add highlights.

Use a softening brush to subdue some of the twigs on the left-hand tree if need be. I was concerned that everything would end up too sharp, unlike the softness of the winter day.

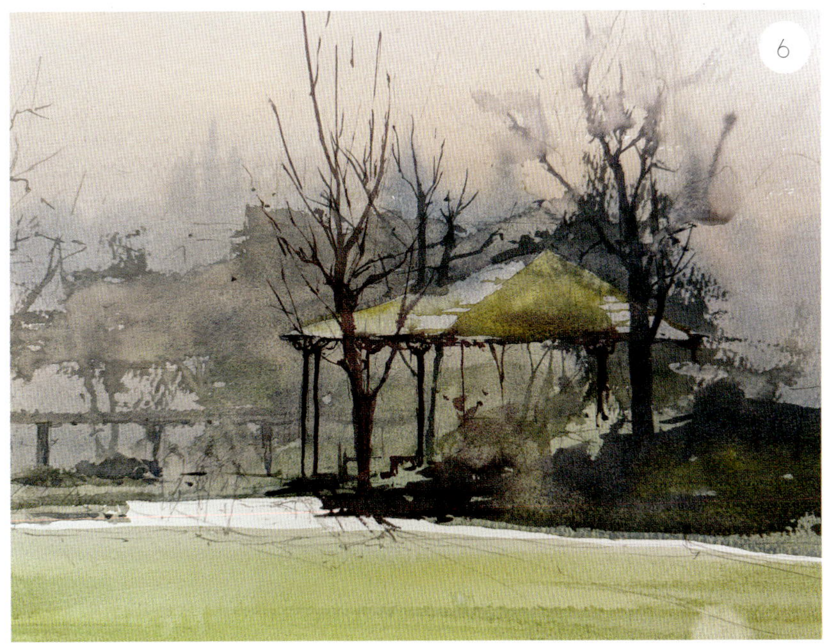

7. More branches

It is important not to overload the tree with branches and twigs as everything can become too fussy, but it is also important to do enough. Too little and the tree can take on an unhealthy appearance.

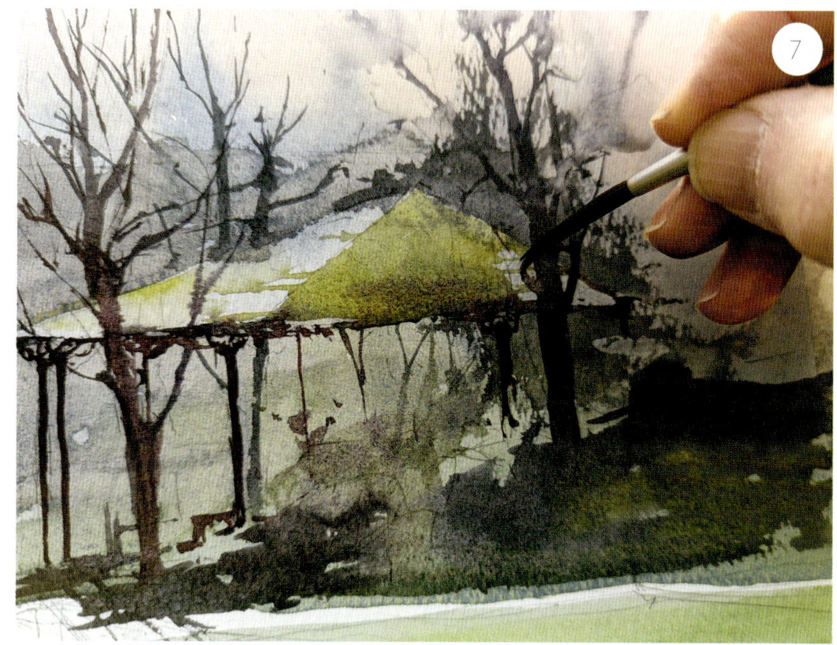

8. The figures

Figures will always add interest to a painting but you don't want them to seem isolated from each other. Allowing them to connect to each other and to other elements in that area literally makes them part of the broader picture. Using a size 8 brush and a mix of ultramarine and brown madder, loosely suggest the bodies and shadows – with the sun behind them, the figures are little more than silhouettes in this case. Concentrate on proportions: the legs are very roughly half the body height to the shoulders.

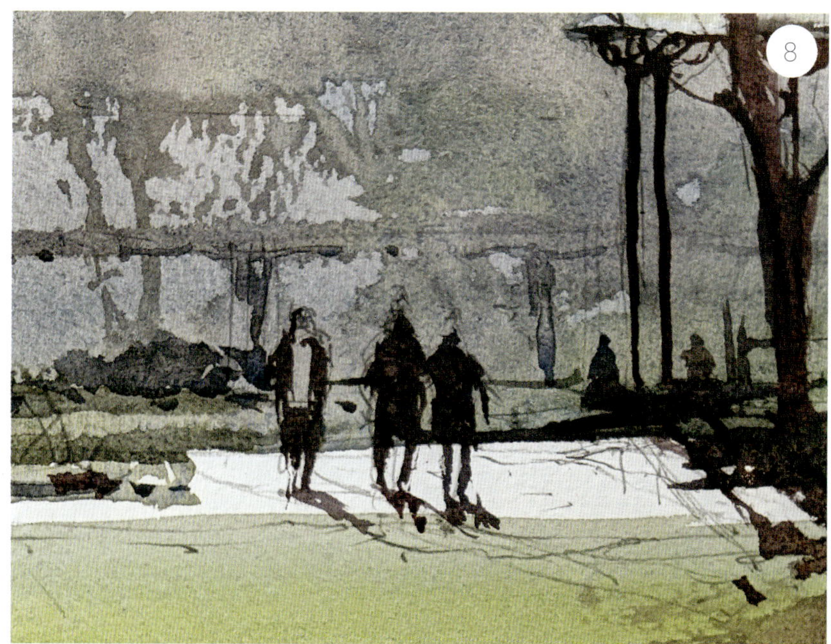

9. The left-hand tree

Balance is important in a painting. The number and sharpness of the twigs and branches must not dominate (9A). I softened more of the twigs to give a slight hazy effect, common on cold winter days (9B).

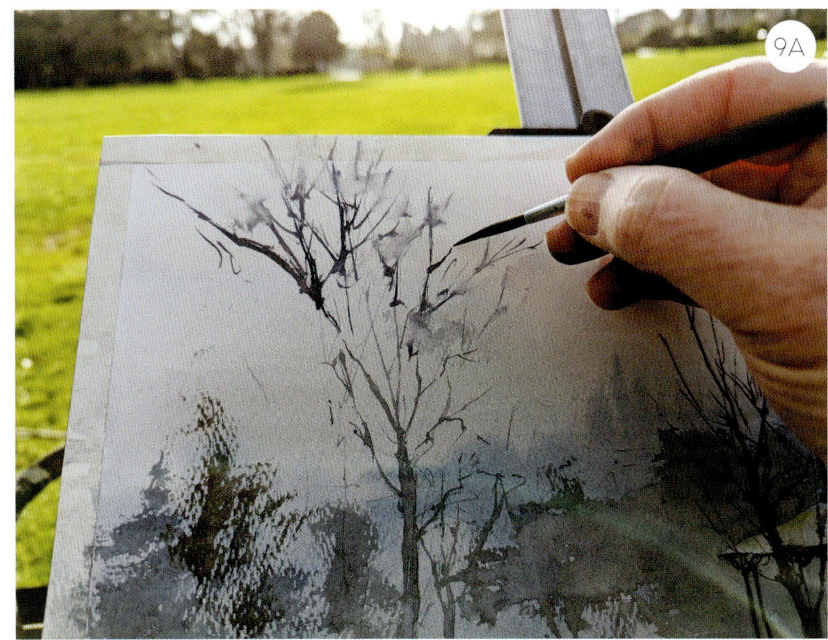

LOCATION INSIGHT: UNEXPECTED VISITORS

You wouldn't see this in your studio. Actually, that's probably just as well, but it is amazing how the animals and birds seem not to notice me standing there and come really quite close. As a plein air painter you really do start to feel part of your environment.

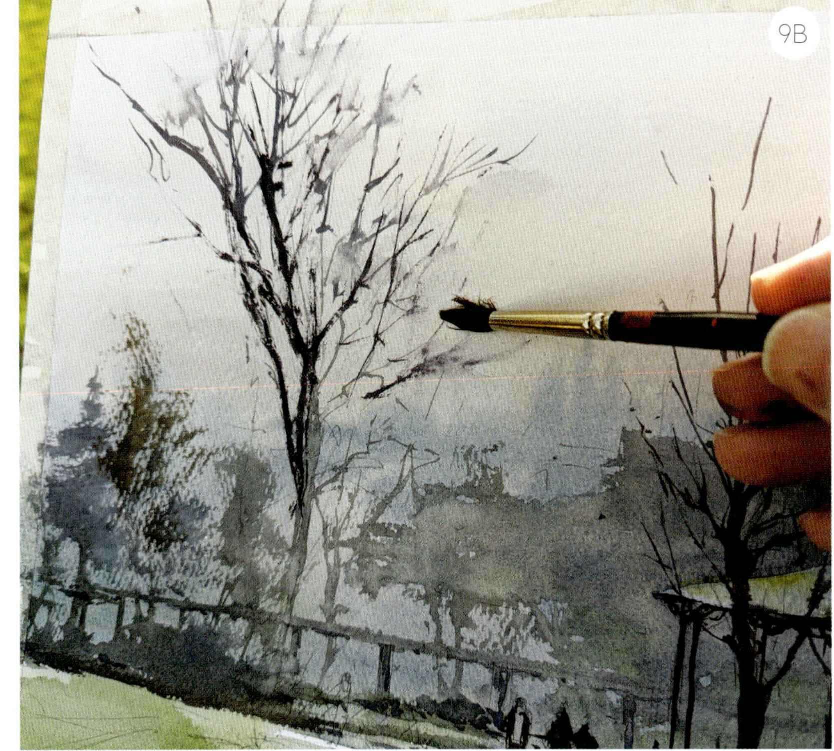

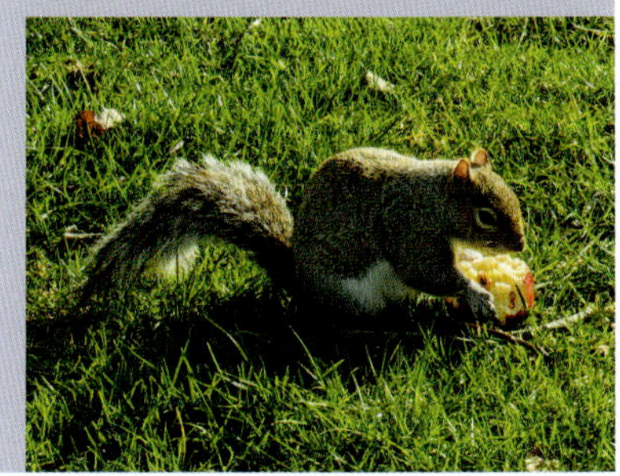

10. The shadows

Time for some shadows. Again, balance is so important at this point. The shadows need to look right compared with the rest of the painting. Not too dark or light and not too soft or hard.

Use ultramarine and brown madder for the shadows – make sure you mix plenty, as running out in the middle of a shadow wash is not ideal. Add the shadow of the largest tree, and to the area in front of the bandstand. Create irregular marks that indicate the undulation of the field (10A).

Use a softening brush to naturalize the shadows and blend them in a little. Add in a number of horizontal marks with your softening brush, as this helps to reinforce the flatness of the grass (10B).

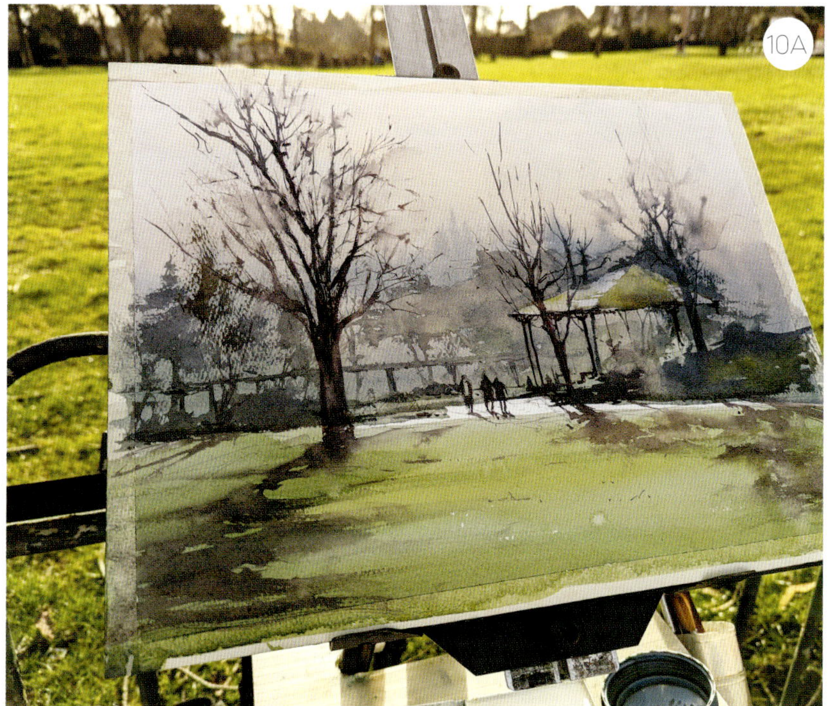

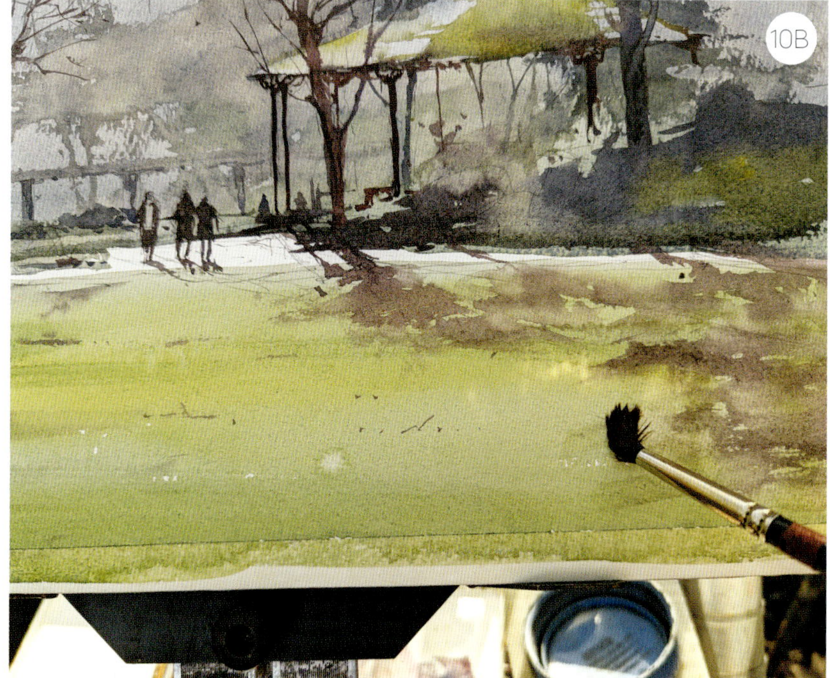

HIDING IN PLAIN SIGHT

Notice how I have completely covered up the large cauliflower on the right. It's technically incorrect, as the shadow didn't come forward this far, but it's better than having a very obvious fault.

11. Adjusting the figures

Add a few little white halos around the heads and shoulders of the figures to suggest the backlight. To keep the white gouache really white it is better to dip the brush straight into the tube. The brush is barely damp. Any water would reduce the opacity of the white.

Add a splash of red to the sweater of the left-hand figure in the group. Use this same red to add in a few tiny touches of red to the legs of the bandstand, to add more interest and to balance the use of red across the painting.

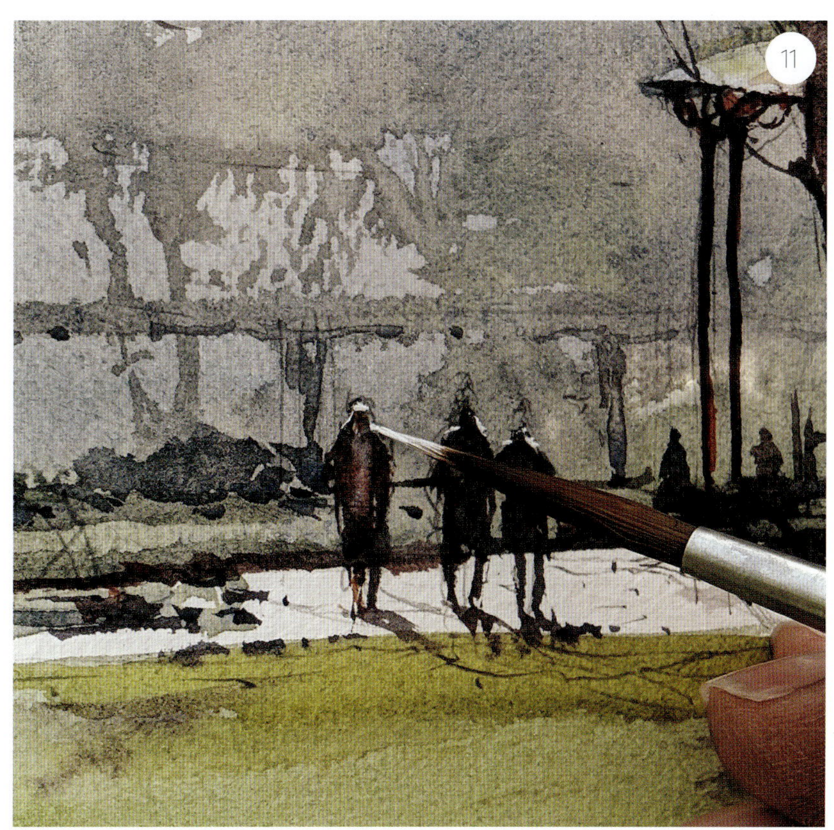

LOCATION INSIGHT: CHANGING LIGHT

Notice how much the light has changed in the couple of hours I have been here. That lovely splash of light that was there at the start has all but disappeared and the lovely shadows coming towards me have changed direction. It is important not to follow the light but to pick a time and stick with it. I have been painting for about 1½ hours and I'm beginning to feel quite cold. Time to call it a day, but I've really enjoyed the winter sunshine… which is more than I can say for some of the members of my plein air group. It is interesting that on cold days some of them manage to find lots of sketching subjects in the local coffee shop!

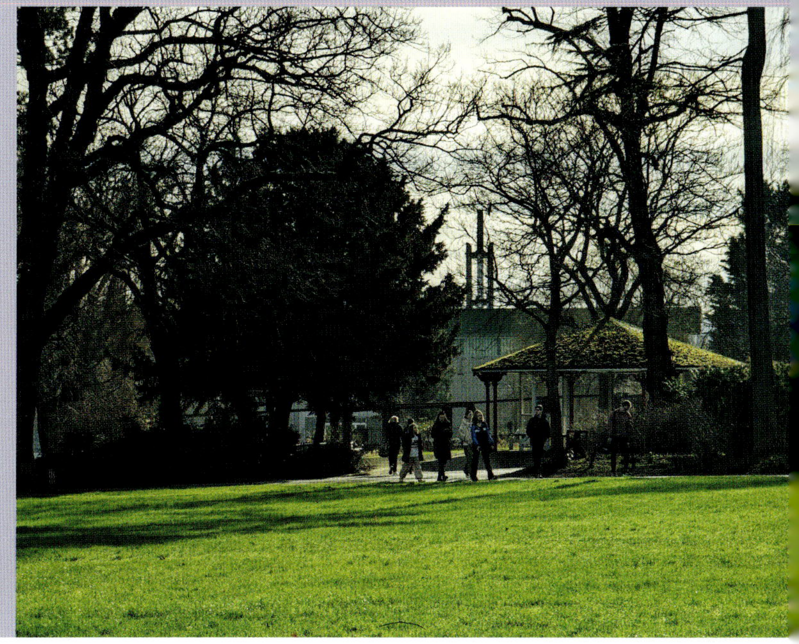

12. Final details

Add in some touches of green to the foreground using a varied mix of ultramarine and warm yellow to add a little visual interest. I also strengthened up the line of green underneath the burst of light, to give it more emphasis.

Indicate some fence posts in the right-hand flowerbed with some dark marks and a flash of white gouache on top.

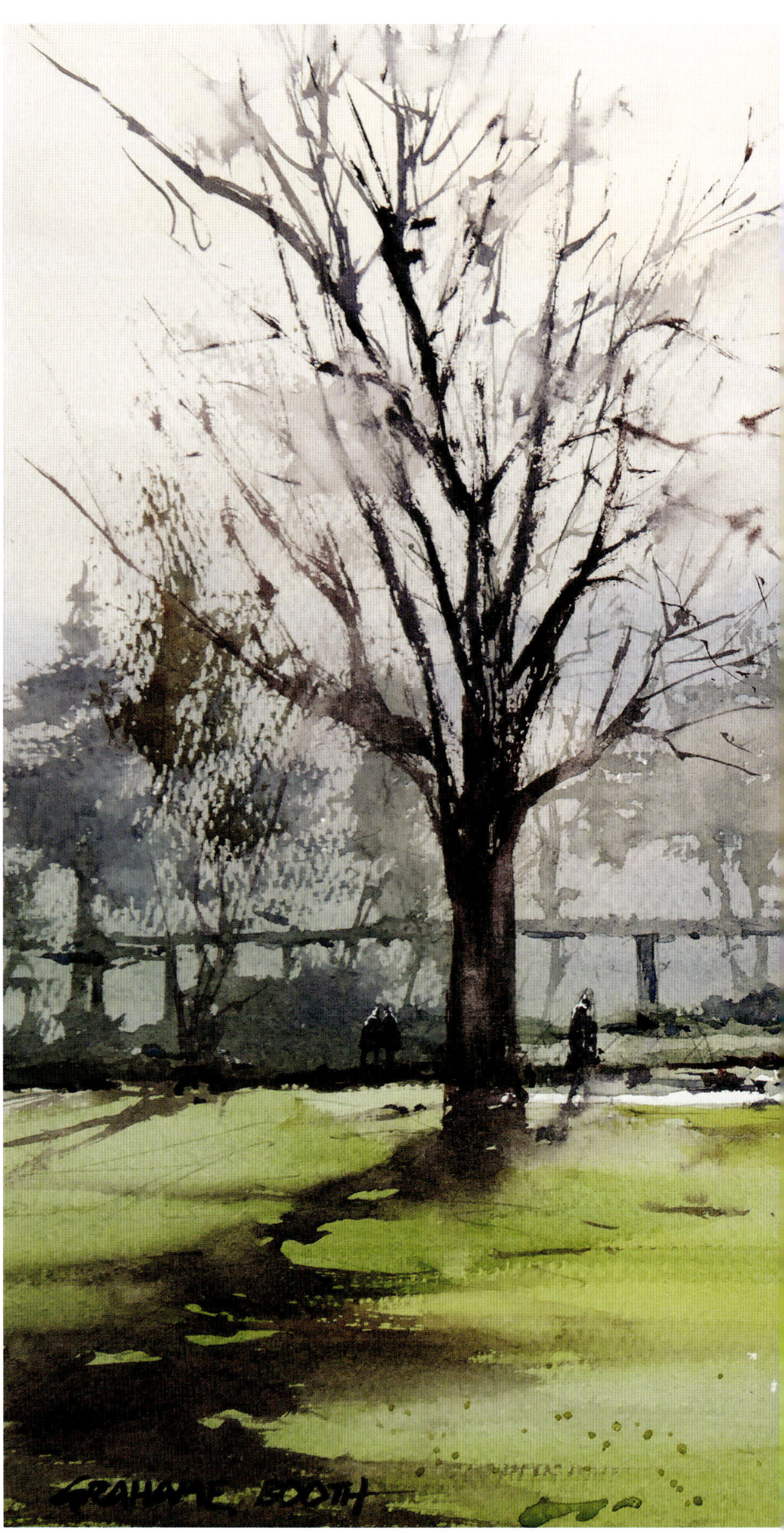

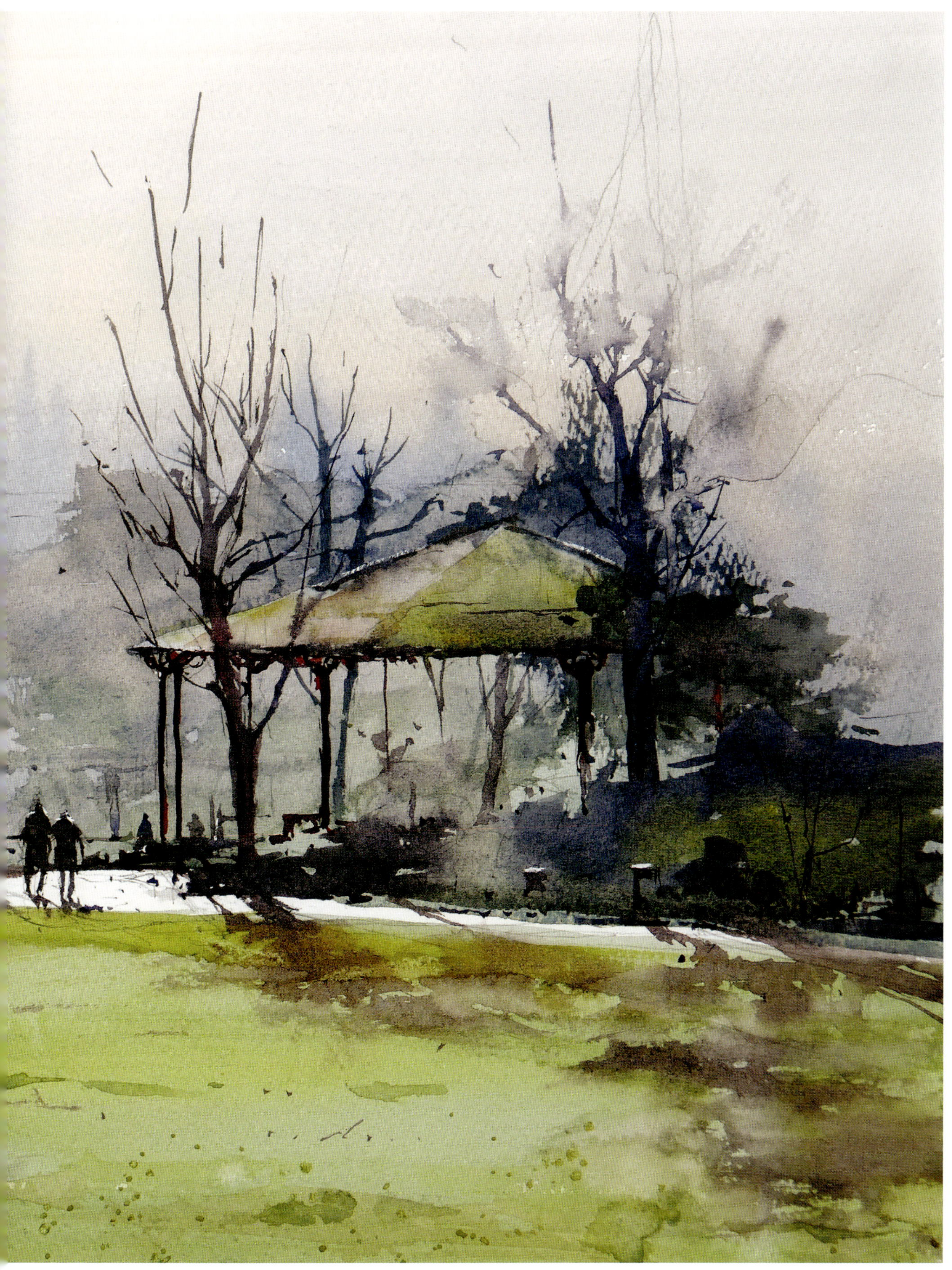

GLOSSARY

- **Aaargh (and variations)** – the noise made by a plein air watercolour painter when the rain starts.
- **Cauliflower** – an effect caused when weak paint or water is dropped into almost dry stronger paint. The resultant crinkly edge looks a little like a cauliflower. Also known (more correctly) as a runback.
- **Composition** – arranging the elements of your subject in a way that is pleasing to the eye.
- **CP** – cold pressed or NOT, the texture of paper between hot pressed and rough.
- **Dry brush** – using quick strokes of a brush containing very little paint. This results in a touch and go effect where only the high points of the paper texture are covered.
- **Ferrule** – the metal tube that contains the brush head and connects it to the shaft.
- **Fiddling** – the act of adding additional and entirely unnecessary details at the end of a painting. Sadly there is no treatment for this condition.
- **GSM** – grams per square metre. This indicates the 'heaviness' of the paper. Also expressed as the weight in pounds per ream of imperial sized paper. 300gsm = 140lb, 425gsm = 200lb.
- **HP** – Hot pressed, a smooth textured paper, created by pressing between hot rollers.

- **Impressionism** – creating a suggestion of the subject using shapes, colour and tone rather than expressed detail.
- **Lifting out** – removing small areas of paint to create highlights or to alter tone.
- **Loaded** – the term used for a brush full of paint mix.
- **Mahlstick** – a length of wood with an additional stub of wood at one end. Held by the other end, this allows a brush to be drawn against the side of the wood to create straight lines.
- **Masking fluid** – a rubber solution that can be applied to watercolour paper to act as a resist and create highlights when removed at the end of the painting.
- **Nocturne** – a painting of twilight, dusk or moonlight.
- **Pen and wash** – a medium that uses pen drawing enhanced with watercolour washes.
- **Perspective** – the way we create the illusion of depth in a painting. There are two types: linear and aerial.
- **Plein air** – painting outdoors.
- **Representational** – painting in a way that the subject is clearly recognizable.

- **Rule of thirds** – the simplest and most useful compositional aid. Divide your subject into thirds horizontally and vertically and your four crossing points are good places for your focal point.
- **Ruling pen** – a pen that can be used with watercolour to produce lines of constant width. Useful for cables and ropes.
- **Runback** – see *cauliflower*.
- **Sable** – one of the common hair types used to make watercolour brushes. True sable is very expensive. Springier than squirrel.
- **Scrubbing** – using a dry brush to gently scrub the wet edge of a wash in order to produce a dry-brush effect.
- **Softening** – a technique to allow an edge to blend with its surroundings and effectively disappear.
- **Softening brush** – a brush used to soften edges and to lift out colour. The techniques required will rapidly wear away any point so an old brush is ideal for this, ideally sable, as it will soak up any excess water or paint.
- **Squirrel** – squirrel hair is commonly used to make watercolour brushes. It is characterized by being very soft and holding large amounts of paint. Softer and less springy than sable.
- **Synthetic** – refers to brushes made with synthetic hair manufactured to mimic sable or squirrel. Synthetic hair has improved dramatically over the years and good synthetic brushes will perform as well as their natural hair counterparts.
- **Tone or value** – the lightness and darkness of the different areas of your painting. Tone will always create the structure of your painting.
- **Vignette** – a painting that stops short of the paper boundaries. Originally applied to photographs which had an oval shape with soft edges. In painting the edges are much more varied and the empty space left is almost as important as the shape of the painting itself.
- **Wash** – the basic building block of watercolour. A smooth transparent layer of paint.
- **Watercolour** – a painting medium in which pigment is mixed with a water-soluble binder. Refers mainly to painting with transparent washes.
- **Wet on dry** – the usual painting technique where wet paint is brushed onto a dry surface.
- **Wet-in-wet** – a technique where additional colour is added to an already wet area of the painting, creating blends and often unexpected but interesting results.

INDEX

CENTENARY STORES, WEXFORD
28 x 38cm (11 x 15in), Millford CP 300gsm (140lb)
This was painted during the Quick Draw competition at the Art in the Open plein air festival in Wexford, Ireland. Two hours are allotted and I think this was completed in about 90 minutes. The big advantage of speed is that it largely prevents too much fiddling.

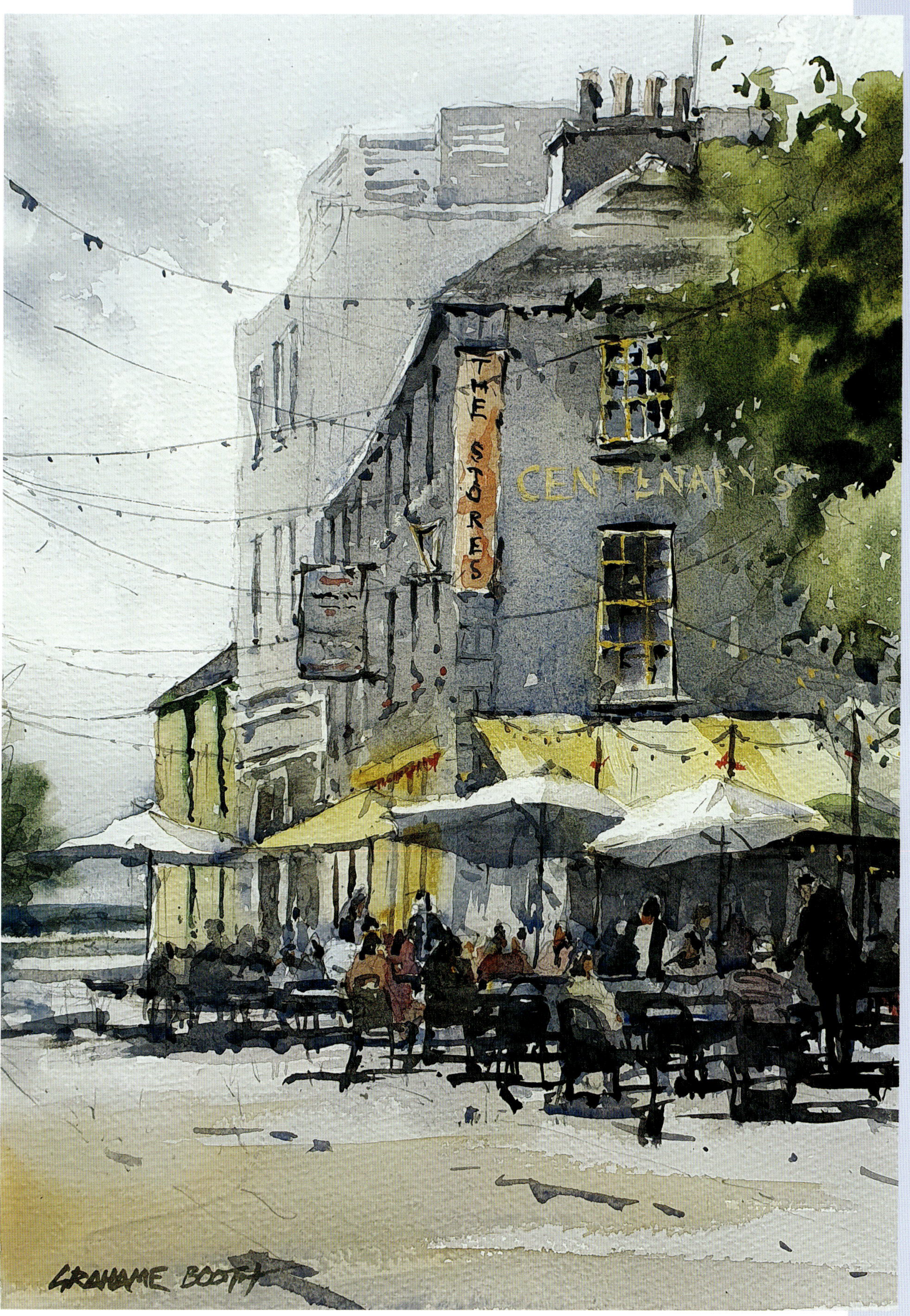
THE STORES
CENTENARY ST
GRAHAME BOOTH

COPYRIGHT

First published in 2025
Search Press Limited
Wellwood, North Farm Road,
Tunbridge Wells, Kent TN2 3DR

Text and photographs copyright © Grahame Booth, 2025
Design copyright © Search Press Ltd., 2025

All rights reserved. No part of this book, text or images may be reproduced or transmitted in any physical or electronic form known or as yet unknown, or used or reproduced in any manner for the purpose of training artificial intelligence technologies or systems, without written permission obtained beforehand from Search Press. Printed in China.

ISBN: 978-1-80092-232-7
ebook ISBN: 978-1-80093-212-8

The Publishers and author can accept no responsibility for any consequences arising from the information, advice or instructions given in this publication. GSPR information can be found at www.searchpress.com

Readers are permitted to reproduce any of the projects in this book for their personal use, or for the purpose of selling for charity, free of charge and without the prior permission of the Publishers. You are not permitted to use any of the projects or artworks for commercial purposes, or for the purpose of training artificial intelligence technologies or systems.

Suppliers
If you have difficulty in obtaining any of the materials and equipment mentioned in this book, then please visit the Search Press website for details of suppliers:
www.searchpress.com

Bookmarked Hub
For further ideas and inspiration, and to join our free online community,
visit www.bookmarkedhub.com

You are invited to visit the author's website: www.grahamebooth.com

Publishers' note
All the step-by-step photographs in this book feature the author, Grahame Booth.
No models have been used.

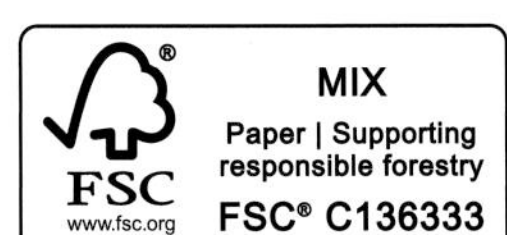